THE
Longman
Concise
Companion

CHRIS M. ANSON
North Carolina State University

ROBERT A. SCHWEGLER
University of Rhode Island

MARCIA F. MUTH
University of Colorado at Denver

PEARSON
Longman

New York   Boston   San Francisco
London   Toronto   Sydney   Tokyo   Singapore   Madrid
Mexico City   Munich   Paris   Cape Town   Hong Kong   Montreal

Acquisitions Editor: Lauren A. Finn
Director of Development: Mary Ellen Curley
Development Editor: Anne Brunell Ehrenworth
Executive Marketing Manager: Megan Galvin-Fak
Senior Supplements Editor: Donna Campion
Media Supplements Editor: Jenna Egan
Production Manager: Donna DeBenedictis
Project Coordination, Text Design, and Electronic Page Makeup:
   Nesbitt Graphics, Inc.
Cover Design Manager: John Callahan
Cover Designer: Kay Petronio
Manufacturing Buyer: Roy L. Pickering Jr.
Printer and Binder: RR Donnelley & Sons Company/Crawfordsville
Cover Printer: Coral Graphic Services

For permission to use copyrighted material, grateful acknowledgment is
made to the copyright holders on pp. 573–575, which are hereby made part
of this copyright page.

Library of Congress Cataloging-in-Publication Data

Anson, Christopher M., 1954–
   The Longman concise companion / Chris M. Anson, Robert A. Schwegler,
Marcia F. Muth.
      p. cm.
   Includes index.
   ISBN 0-321-43900-7
   1. English language--Rhetoric--Handbooks, manuals, etc. 2. English
language--Grammar--Handbooks, manuals, etc. 3. Reading comprehension--
Handbooks, manuals, etc. 4. Report writing--Handbooks, manuals, etc.
   I. Schwegler, Robert A. II. Muth, Marcia F. III. Title.
   PE1408A61842 2006
   808'.042--dc22

                                                                2006019927

Please visit us at www.ablongman.com

ISBN 0-321-43900-7

1 2 3 4 5 6 7 8 9 10—DOC—09 08 07 06

PREFACE FOR STUDENTS AND INSTRUCTORS

We've prepared this book for people who will be called on to write for different audiences and purposes—in short, for all writers. We know from experience and research that the demands of writing situations vary in important ways. We know, too, that writers need a range of concrete strategies in order to work successfully with the expectations and possibilities posed by each writing situation.

In response, we have produced an economy handbook filled with advice about writing and revising, creating correct and effective sentences, researching and reasoning, documenting and evaluating sources, representing yourself as a writer and speaker, and navigating the electronic world—all within three important communities: academic, public, and work. And we've made this advice easy to locate and use. We hope that you'll find this handbook to be just what its title promises—a true writer's companion.

How to Use This Book

- Use the **Detailed Contents** on the inside back cover to find specific topics.
- Use the **Index** to locate key concepts (beginning on page 525).
- Check **Ten Serious Errors to Recognize and Revise** to avoid the errors that are most likely to confuse your readers (page 579).
- See the **Guide to ESL Advice** for a complete index of ESL-related issues (page 577).
- See **Symbols for Revising and Editing** to decode editing notations (page 578).
- Use the **Glossary of Usage** to learn definitions of confusing words (beginning on page 493).
- Match up the marginal icons to specific content on the **Companion Website**, located at **www.ablongman.com/anson**.

Features

In preparing *The Longman Concise Companion*, we have incorporated innovative features while responding to the changing needs of student writers.

Emphasis on writing in three communities—academic, public, and work

Within different communities—academic, public, or work—the kinds of writing employed are likely to vary considerably. So, too, are expectations about style, reasoning, diction, correctness, and documentation. *The Longman Concise Companion* integrates and emphasizes three key communities in which students live and write.

ACADEMIC WRITERS AND READERS

WHO?   Students, instructors, researchers, and people interested in the results of research

WHAT?   Create and exchange knowledge through analysis, interpretation, and research

PUBLIC WRITERS AND READERS

WHO?   Residents, local leaders, activists, volunteers, members of civic organizations

WHAT?   Take a stand on an issue, support a cause, supply information, or participate in civic exchanges and activities

WORK WRITERS AND READERS

WHO?   Fellow workers, managers, clients, and customers

WHAT?   Exchange information; analyze and solve problems; and promote an organization, service, or product

Recognizing broad differences among communities is important for the many choices you need to make as you write. These differences are explained and highlighted throughout the text.

Community Boxes. These useful tools (in Chapters 1, 8, 12–14, 16–18, and 22) outline concrete strategies that help writers understand and respond to the needs of these communities.

Chapters geared toward writing for particular audiences. Part 3, "Writing for Specific Audiences," contains practical information on Academic Writing (Ch. 14), Public Writing (Ch. 16), and Workplace Writing (Ch. 17) and includes guidelines as well as multiple sample documents from different genres.

Strategies. Strategy sections appear throughout the handbook, placing special emphasis on concrete, practical strategies that writers can employ immediately in their work. See 1a and 1b for a few examples of this feature.

Importance of writing across the curriculum

Part 3 of this handbook, "Writing for Specific Audiences," covers writing in academic genres across the disciplines.

"Academic Writing" (Ch. 14) discusses the importance of analyzing your audience and provides samples from various types of academic writing, including essay exams, lab reports, and annotated bibliographies.

"Making Persuasive Arguments" (Ch. 13) discusses how to develop and formulate a coherent argument.

"Reading and Writing About Literature" (Ch. 15) discusses how to write a literary analysis and contains a complete sample student analysis paper.

Source documentation is covered thoroughly in all four major styles: MLA (Ch. 25), **APA** (Ch. 26), **CMS** (Ch. 27), and **CSE** (Ch. 28).

Unique approach to correcting errors—recognize and revise

It is hard to correct an error if you don't first recognize it as a problem. We have designed *The Longman Concise Companion* to help writers develop the ability to recognize problems in their work by viewing it as readers do. This unique approach to grammar and usage organizes the chapters in Parts 8–12, first helping writers identify problems and then suggesting how to revise or edit to repair them.

Reader's reactions. These comments, following examples of errors, convey possible responses to confusing or irritating sentences or passages, helping to explain errors or flaws in terms of their effects on readers.

Strategies. "Strategy" sections appear throughout the handbook, placing special emphasis on concrete, practical strategies that writers can employ immediately in their work.

Ten Serious Errors. We asked college instructors about the errors that are most likely to confuse readers and undermine their confidence in writers. Throughout Parts 8–12, sections discussing any of the "Ten Serious Errors" are highlighted with marginal icons. In addition, a table on page 579 at the back of this book summarizes these errors.

ESL Advice. This tool, designed for nonnative speakers, is interspersed throughout the text and strategically supplements discussions of both rhetoric and grammar. For a complete list of ESL advice in *The Longman Concise Companion*, see page 577 at the back of the book.

Discussion of reading, writing, and critical thinking

The Longman Concise Companion incorporates a distinct philosophy toward reading, writing, and thinking.

Writing for readers. Specific strategies help writers develop the ability to keep communities of readers and their likely responses in mind during planning, drafting, revising, and editing (Parts 1, 2, and 8–12).

Critical thinking and reading. Reading, thinking, and audience are intertwined in discussions of the roles and expectations of readers, analytical and critical reading, and critical thinking (Parts 1–4).

Collaboration and feedback. We offer practical advice about giving and receiving constructive criticism and about collaborating with other writers, whether in the classroom or in public and work settings (Parts 1–4).

Focus on technology

Because most students routinely use computers and the Internet, we offer realistic advice throughout the text on writing and conducting research in technologically enhanced environments.

> **"Writing in Online Communities"** (Ch. 10) includes information on writing emails and participating in online communities through blogs, newsgroups, and IMs.
>
> **"Web and Internet Resources"** (Ch. 20) and **"Library Resources and Research Databases"** (Ch. 19) include strategies for finding and evaluating electronic resources.
>
> **Comprehensive online and electronic source citations** model accurate Works Cited and References pages (see pages 222–228 and 252–255).

Application exercises

One of the many ways that students can apply their knowledge is by completing the **exercises that follow most chapters in this handbook**. These exercises employ chapter-specific concepts and aid students in their research and writing endeavors. Answers to selected exercises appear on pages 505–523 of *The Longman Concise Companion*. A complete **Answer Key** is also available for instructors.

Supplements

The Longman Concise Companion is accompanied by an extensive package of print and media supplements for both instructors and students. Please see your Longman representative for details on these and additional supplements.

For instructors and students

- **The Companion Website** for *The Longman Concise Companion*, located at **www.ablongman.com/anson**, includes writing and research project assignments, practice exercises, Web links to further resources, and more. Marginal Web icons appear throughout the book, directing students and teachers to resources on the Companion Website where relevant.
- **MyCompLab 2.0 Website (www.mycomplab.com)** provides the best available online solutions to a wide variety of grammar, writing, and research needs all in one easy-to-use place. *ExerciseZone* offers over 3,600 self-grading practice items in all major topics of grammar, style, and usage and now also includes sentence and paragraph editing exercises. The *ESL ExerciseZone* features over 650 self-grading practice tests for students whose first language is not English. *Exchange*, Pearson's online peer and instructor review program, is a flexible, easy-to-use program that makes both delivering peer review assignments and grading papers simpler and more effective. *Activities* provide 100 different writing activities in which

students respond to videos, images, websites, and writing prompts. *Model Documents Gallery* presents an extensive collection of sample papers, reports, and documents from across the curriculum. The complete research resource, *ResearchNavigator*™ offers access to credible, academic sources, including EBSCO's *ContentSelect* database and the *New York Times* Search-by-Subject archive. Students also have access to hundreds of pages on the research process itself, taken from JD Lester's best-selling *Writing Research Papers* as well as *AutoCite*, a bibliography-maker program. *Avoiding Plagiarism* tutorials teach students to recognize plagiarism and avoid its practice in both MLA and APA formats.

For instructors

- A full **Answer Key** (0-321-44771-9) is available for the exercises in *The Longman Concise Companion*.
- An extensive assessment package includes Competency Profile tests, sample CLAST and TASP exams, and *Diagnostic and Editing Tests and Exercises*, which aids in analyzing common errors and can supplement the handbook's exercises. (All these testing supplements are available in both print and electronic formats.)

For students

- **Real Visual CD-ROM** (0-321-42308-9) by Daniel Anderson, Patrick Cooper, Daniel Lupton, and Melissa Meeks groups 25 images around familiar themes (identity, place, commerce, culture, history) and teaches analysis using basic rhetorical concepts such as audience, message, and medium. A sequence of steps and relevant tutorials guide students in understanding different genres of visual and multimodal texts, developing their own visual and verbal texts, and revising their drafts.
- *80 Readings for Composition* (0-321-41991-X), edited by David Munger, is an engaging collection of professional and student essays arranged thematically with four alternate tables of contents: rhetorical, argument, literature, and writing about the disciplines.
- **ESL Worksheets**, by Jocelyn Steer and Dawn Schmid, provides nonnative speakers with practice in troublesome areas.
- **The Longman Writer's Journal**, by Mimi Markus, provides students with their own space for writing, interspersed with journal-writing strategies, sample journal entries by other students, and many writing prompts and topics.
- The Literacy Library Series—**Public Literacy**, by Elizabeth Ervin; **Workplace Literacy**, by Rachel Spilka; and **Academic Literacy**, by Stacia Neeley—offers instruction and models for writing in these three contexts.
- Additional Longman Resources for Students include **The Longman Researcher's Journal**, by Mimi Markus; **Analyzing Literature: A Guide for Students**, by Sharon James McGee; **A Guide for Peer Response**, by Tori Haring-Smith and Helon Raines; and **Ten Practices of Highly Successful Students**, by A. Murphy.

- *The Longman Concise Companion* may also be packaged with other books at a discount. Two dictionaries are available: *Merriam-Webster's Collegiate Dictionary*, a hardcover desk dictionary; and *The New American Webster Handy College Dictionary*, a briefer paperback. And, in conjunction with Penguin Putnam, Longman offers a variety of Penguin titles, such as Arthur Miller's *Death of a Salesman*, Julia Alvarez's *How the Garcia Girls Lost Their Accents*, and Mike Rose's *Lives on the Boundary*.

Acknowledgments

First we wish to thank the students who have generously allowed us to present their writing as an inspiration to others: David Aharonian, Summer Arrigo-Nelson, Pam Copass, Melanie Dedecker, Jennifer Figliozzi, Tammy Jo Helton, Jenny Latimer, Jennifer O'Berry, Ian Preston, Paul Pusateri, Sharon Salamone, Brian Schwegler, and Ted Wolfe. Marcia Muth also thanks the students in her writing workshops, which she offers through the School of Education at the University of Colorado at Denver.

We also thank the following instructors, who have provided invaluable feedback for the handbooks in our series: James Allen, College of DuPage; Sue Beebe, Southwest Texas State University; Steven Bellin, St. Norbert College; Laura J. Bird, Northern Illinois University; Stuart Brown, New Mexico State University; Lauren Sewell Ingraham, University of Tennessee at Chattanooga; Susan Jaye Dauer, Valencia Community College East; Erika Deiters, Moraine Valley Community College; James H. Donelan, UC Santa Barbara; Patricia Gordon, Central Carolina Technical College; Tim Gustafson, University of Minnesota; Mary Hocks, Georgia State University; Sandra Jamieson, Drew University; Winnie Kenney, Southwestern Illinois College; Lesley Lydell, University of Minnesota; Paul Kei Matsuda, University of New Hampshire; Marti L. Mundell, Washington State University; Michael Powell, Shawnee State University; Eric Pullin, Cardinal Stritch University; Elsa Rogers, International College; Lori Salem, Temple University; Myra Seaman, College of Charleston; George W. Semich, Robert Morris University; Matt Smith, University of Saint Francis; Jean Sorensen, Grayson County College; Roy T. Stamper, North Carolina State University; Mark Sutton, Kean University; Deborah Coxwell Teague, Florida State University; and Erin Webster-Garrett, Radford University.

Special thanks to Lee Torda, Bridgewater State College; Kathryn Riley, Illinois Institute of Technology; and Jenna Egan for their work on the revised and updated Companion Website. Thank you also to those who worked with us as consultants in the development and revision of selected chapters now incorporated in *The Longman Concise Companion*—Stevens Amidon, Indiana University–Purdue University Fort Wayne; Daniel Anderson, University of North Carolina, Chapel Hill; Ellen Bitterman, SUNY, New Paltz; Mick Doherty and Sandye Thompson; Jim Dubinsky, Virginia Tech; Elizabeth Ervin, University of North Carolina, Wilmington; Mary Finley, University

Library at California State University, Northridge; Christina Haas, Kent State University; Eric Pappas, James Madison University; Gladys Scott Vega, Arizona State University; Charlotte Smith, Adirondack Community College; and Victor Villanueva, Washington State University. We remain grateful for the advice, expertise, and creativity of all these writers and teachers.

We wish to thank Lauren Finn, our acquisitions editor, for overseeing this complicated project and attending to its many details with an innovative spirit. We are especially grateful to Anne Brunell Ehrenworth, our tenacious development editor, for guiding this project with clarity and for fitting together the many pieces, large and small, textual and visual, typographical and personal. On each page of the text, we can see the contributions of Susan McIntyre of Nesbitt Graphics, and we thank her for her patience and her keen eye. We acknowledge, too, the guidance and care of Donna DeBenedictis, who took us from manuscript to printed book.

Chris Anson thanks Geanie, Ian, and Graham for enduring yet another book project and for always being understanding (well, almost always) when long phone calls, hours at the computer, or thickets of manuscripts got in the way of backyard soccer, a leaking faucet, or something more than thirty minutes for dinner. Your patience has been my inspiration.

Bob Schwegler would like to acknowledge above all Nancy Newman Schwegler for sharing her understanding of readers, reading, and writers. "And I'll be sworn up 'y that he loves her; / For here's a paper written in his hand, / A halting sonnet . . ." He would also like to thank Brian and Tara Schwegler for their advice, Christopher for his smiles, Ashley Marie for her inspiration, and Lily for hope.

Marcia Muth thanks her family: Anderson and Liz, whose friends, crises, inspirations, and inventive papers continue to enlighten her about the rich and varied lives of student writers, and her husband, Rod, who remains the most patient, steadfast, and inspirational of friends, advisors, and companions.

CHRIS M. ANSON
ROBERT A. SCHWEGLER
MARCIA F. MUTH

PART 1

Writing and Reading

1 Communities of Writers and Readers

The Web page you browsed yesterday was not made by a computer. Someone wrote its text, planned its design, and anticipated readers' reactions. Someone else wrote the newsletter in your mailbox, the forms for your car loan, and the waiver you signed before the technician X-rayed your ankle. Writing and reading surround us, shaping our lives, choices, responsibilities, and values. This book looks at the roles of writers and readers in contemporary culture. It offers concrete strategies for writing, for critical reading and thinking, and for understanding your readers' expectations.

Whether you're drafting a psychology paper, an email message at work, or a neighborhood flyer, try to envision a **community of readers and writers**, people with shared—though not necessarily identical—goals, settings, preferences, and uses for verbal and visual texts. This book will help you develop your skill at recognizing different needs and expectations of writers, readers, and speakers in the academic, public, and work communities in which you may be active throughout your life.

1a Academic, public, and work communities

In a Denver suburb, pets have been disappearing. The culprits have been coyotes or other predators, crowded by new homes and industrial parks. Alarmed local residents wonder if a young child will be the next victim.

In such situations, problem solving often begins with written and oral presentations. City officials and citizens may turn to the **academic community** for studies of the habitat and feeding habits of coyotes and other predators. Their research documents may sound like this:

> This report summarizes and compares data from two studies of the habits of predators in areas with significant population growth and urbanization over the past ten years.

1.1

The scientific reports focus on one question: how do coyotes behave in a shrinking habitat? But parents, pet owners, and others in the **public community** are likely to ask a different question: how can we protect our children and pets without harming local wildlife? Tips created by the Colorado Division of Wildlife apply scientific knowledge to residents' concerns.

If you see a coyote:
- Leave it alone; do not approach it.

If a coyote approaches:
- Use an animal repellent such as pepper spray to ward off the coyote.
- Throw rocks or sticks at the coyote to scare it away.

- Use a loud, authoritative voice to frighten the animal away.

How to coexist with coyotes:
- Keep your pet on a leash.
- Do not let pets out between dusk and dawn, when most predators are active. . . .

(The Denver Post, 30 July 1998, 15A)

Neighborhood groups might distribute leaflets and organize meetings.

COYOTE ALERT!

Are your children safe in their own backyards? Coyotes attacked seven dogs and cats last summer. Find out what we can do. Join the Committee to Safeguard Our Children on Tuesday, October 2, at 7:00 p.m. in the high school gym.

Other reports might circulate in the **work community**, analyzing the frequency of complaints, summarizing business perspectives, or presenting policy options to help people, pets, and coyotes live in balance.

Participating in academic, public, and work communities means talking, listening, reading, and, especially, writing. Your immediate academic challenge—responding to assignments—helps prepare you to write more thoughtfully in other communities. In the same way, writing at work or in public situations can stimulate or enrich your writing for academic readers.

To communicate effectively within a community of readers and writers, pay attention to its roles, goals, forms, and writing characteristics. (See the chart on page 4.) These considerations can help you recognize both readers' expectations and your choices as a writer.

1b Electronic communities

The broad academic, public, and work communities all cohabit the intriguing world of the Internet. A click of a mouse connects you with large

Three Major Communities of Readers and Writers		
Academic	**Public**	**Work**
ROLES Students Teachers Researchers Committees gathering expert opinions Readers interested in specialized knowledge	Residents or group members Possible supporters Public officials or agencies Community activists Local groups Readers interested in an issue	Coworkers Supervisors Organizational work groups (management, accounting, public relations) Clients and customers Government agencies Public target groups
GOALS Creation or exchange of knowledge	Persuasion in support of a cause or issue Participation in democracy Provision of issue-oriented information	Provision of information Analysis of problems Proposal of solutions Promotion of organization
TYPICAL FORMS Analysis of text or phenomenon Interpretation of text, artwork, or event Research proposal Lab report Scholarly article Annotated bibliography Grant proposal Classroom presentation	Position paper Informative report Letter to group, supporters, officials, agency, organization, or publication Flyer, newsletter, pamphlet, or fact sheet Action or grant proposal Guidelines, charter, or principles Comments in public forum	Description of object, event, situation, or problem Proposal Report of findings Memos, letters, agendas, or minutes of meetings Guidelines or instructions Promotional materials Meeting presentation
WRITING CHARACTERISTICS Detailed reasoning Critical analysis Fresh insights or conclusions Extensive evidence Accurate detail that supports conclusions Balanced treatment Acknowledgment of other viewpoints Thoughtful, stimulating exploration of topic	Focus on shared values and goals Advocacy of cause Fair recognition of others' interests Relevant evidence that supports positions Concentration on own point of view or on need for information Orientation to actions or solutions	Concentration on task, problem, or goal Accurate and efficient presentation of problem or issue Concise, direct prose Promotion of product or service Attention to corporate image and design standards

and small electronic communities, each organized around a shared interest in a topic, point of view, or issue.

STRATEGY   Use TASALS to help you recognize electronic communities.

TOPIC. On what subject does the site focus? Do contributors belong to any organization or share any other affiliation?

ATTITUDE. Does the site have a clear point of view or set of values? Do contributors have similar perspectives or values?

STRATEGIES. Does the site use a particular written style or visual design?

AUTHORITY. Does the site support claims or information? Do contributors reason carefully, offering evidence rather than opinion?

LINKS. Do postings or links refer to related online resources?

SUMMARIZE. How can you sum up the qualities of the community, its expectations of participants, and its conventions?

Exercise 1

In groups of four or five, draft a "class charter," that is, a formal statement outlining the principles, purposes, or rules that you think should govern your class. Before you start drafting, discuss the roles, goals, forms, and characteristics of this situation. Which members of the class do you need to address? In what ways might their values or interests be similar or different? What do you hope to accomplish with the document you produce? What does a charter look like? How would you present it orally to the class?

Exercise 2

A. Find the official Web site of your school or city or of an organization to which you belong. Examine the Web site carefully using the TASALS strategy. How would you characterize the community that sponsors the site? What opportunities, if any, are there to participate in the site—to send comments, join a mailing list, or question an expert? What kinds of participation would be inappropriate for this site, and why?

B. Use a search engine to locate several Web sites maintained by or catering to professionals in your future field of work. Evaluate the Web site using TASALS.

2 Generating and Organizing Ideas

Imagine trying to build a house without drawing up any plans beforehand or going into the playoffs without a team strategy, just to "see what happens." Success would depend on luck, not design. The same is true for speaking and writing. For almost any formal project—in college, for a civic group, or on the job—you need to generate ideas and "rough out" a structure before you really get started. **Planning** before you write a full draft—often called **prewriting**—gives you a map of where you want to go in your writing.

2a Generating ideas

Whatever your writing task, you will want to ask, "What do I know about what I'm writing? What else do I need to know?" Gather ideas from your existing resources—your journal or notebook entries, readings annotated with your responses, class or meeting notes, your assignment sheet or job description, and any similar projects. (See also 3a.)

2.1

Freewrite. Write by hand or at the computer for five or ten minutes *without stopping*, even if you only repeat "I'm stuck." As such empty prose bores you, you'll almost magically slip into more engaging ideas. Or begin **focused freewriting** with an idea you already have—"I guess I support antigambling laws"—to start productively exploring the topic.

List. Lists can help you draw out your own knowledge, create ideas through association, and generalize from details. For her history paper on Soviet espionage during the Cold War, Annie Hanson listed her main points and, under her final point, key supporting details.

1. Cold War background from Yalta to Berlin Wall
2. Western vs. Soviet technology
3. Role of KGB training operatives and recruiting
4. Espionage examples (Fuchs, De Groot, Philby)

Write your topic at the top of a page, and then list ten thoughts, facts, impressions, ideas, or specifics about it. For example, begin with a general idea or a major part of your project, and list supporting details and new associations. Repeat the process with your other ideas or parts.

Ask strategic questions. Strategic questioning can pull information from your memory and direct you to other ideas to pursue. Begin with *what*, *why*, and *why not.* Ask *who, where, when,* and *how,* if they apply. Continue to ask questions as you develop ideas and probe more deeply. Brian Corby asked questions as he began his letter to the zoning board opposing a high-rise apartment next to a public park.

What?
- Proposed high-rise apt.—18 stories, 102 units
- East side of Piedmont Park by Sunrise Ave
- Planning by Feb., groundbreaking by June, done in a year

Why?
- Developers profit
- Provides medium-cost housing in growing area
- Develops ugly vacant lot by park

Why Not?
- "Citifies" one of the few green patches in town
- Traffic, crime rate, park use
- New zoning opens the door to other high-rises

ESL ADVICE: CLEAR AND FORCEFUL DETAILS

Most writing in English tends to be direct rather than abstract. Especially in the academic and work communities, a writer often makes a clear assertion about a topic, a problem, or an event and then supports that idea with facts, details, or research. In a sense, the writer must "prove" the point, and readers won't accept it on faith or by virtue of the writer's authority. If readers find your writing too broad, indirect, or poorly supported, compare their expectations with those of readers in your first language. American teachers and workplace supervisors generally want writers to ask questions about writing projects and are used to explaining what they expect.

2b Organizing ideas and information

Ideas and information alone will get you started, but most writing and speaking projects require **structure**—a pattern, outline, or plan to shape and organize. Use a structure readers expect in projects such as reports, or create a structure from the ideas you've generated.

Clusters. Draw a cluster by circling a concept, idea, or topic in the center of a page. Then jot down associations with this kernel topic, circling and connecting them with lines to the center, like the spokes of a wheel, or to each other to show interconnections. To create clusters in cycles, use each subsidiary idea as a new kernel topic. As she began her researched argument paper, Marianne Kidd used clustering to relate her ideas about censoring music lyrics. (See Figure 2.1 on p. 8.)

2b
org

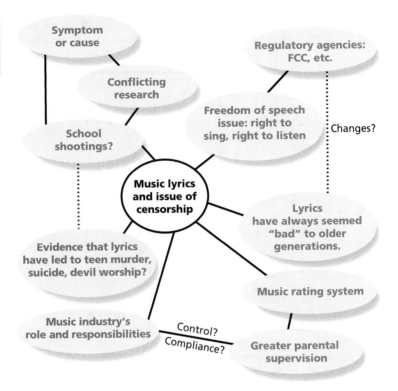

FIGURE 2.1   A simple conceptual cluster

Tree diagrams. A tree diagram resembles a cluster, but the branches tend to be more linear and hierarchical. Start with your topic as the trunk. Create main branches for central points and smaller branches for related ideas. Then "revise" your diagram into a working plan or outline for the paragraphs or sections of your project. Each main branch of Bill Chen's diagram became a "chunk" or section in his paper on possible uses of virtual reality. (See Figure 2.2.)

Time sequences. If your project involves chronology, use a time sequence. For example, in planning a self-guided tour of a museum exhibit, James Cole drew a time sequence detailing Andy Warhol's artistic life. When you build a time sequence, frame each event along a line, noting dates, ages, or other time markers. If you wish, add thick connecting lines to mark pivotal events that led to or caused other events and thin lines to show simple time links.

Problem-solution grids. Position papers, business reports, and other persuasive pieces often follow a problem-solution sequence, outlining a problem, offering workable solutions, or advocating one solution rather than another.

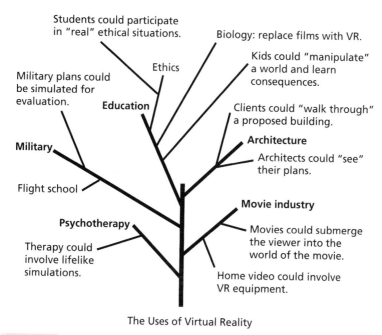

FIGURE 2.2   A simple tree diagram

Paula Masek used a problem-solution grid to plan her editorial exploring temporary solutions to the problem of feeding the homeless. Later she discussed each boxed item in a separate section of her draft. (See Figure 2.3 on p. 10.) To create a problem-solution grid, first state the problem. Underneath, in boxes or columns, identify possible solutions. Below these, identify problems each solution might create and then their solutions. Generate as many layers as you wish.

Outlines. The best-known planning technique is the trusty **outline**, complete with Roman numerals. The traditional outline may help you to label or arrange ideas but doesn't do much to help *generate* them. A **working outline**, however, can help you generate information or identify missing pieces. As you arrange ideas in an outline (or outline a draft to check its logic), consider whether your higher-level generalizations, interpretations, or conclusions are followed by enough supporting details and specifics to inform or persuade a reader. If you spot gaps or unbalanced coverage, consider breaking up a large topic, combining smaller points, expanding ideas, or adding more details or examples.

    With a simple topic as your main heading, commit yourself to three second-level headings by writing *A*, *B*, and *C* underneath. (Leave a lot of space in between.) Then fill in the subheadings. Now develop third-level headings by writing *1*, *2*, and *3* beneath *each* letter. Fill them in, too.

2.2

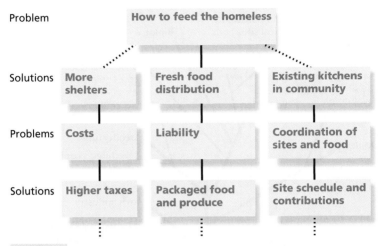

FIGURE 2.3 A problem-solution grid

Mitch Weber used a working outline to plan a brief history of the non-profit organization where he had a summer internship.

CREATION OF THE FAMILY HEALTH CENTER
A. Founding Work of Susan and Roger Ramstadt
   1. The "vision"
   2. Finding the money
   3. Support from the Crimp Foundation
B. The Early Years
   1. Building momentum
   2. The great financial disaster
   3. Rebirth
C. Toward Maturity
   1. Fund-raising after 2005
   2. State recognition and the big award
   3. The new vision: health and sustenance

STRATEGY Try electronic planning.
- Use your computer for planning so that you can easily reorganize and develop your ideas into a draft.
- Try interactive questions or prompts from your software, the Web, or the campus computer lab or tutoring center.
- Use a search engine to browse for Web sites on your topic.
- Skim links, gathering possible ideas from varied sites.

Exercise 1

Choose a topic, issue, or problem for a writing project. List ten things you know about your chosen topic. Then choose one item and generate a sublist beneath it. If you can, keep going to a third or fourth level.

Exercise 2

Choose a simple topic, issue, or problem whose details are familiar to you. Then try creating a cluster or a tree diagram. Does the result suggest a possible structure for a paper? What problems might arise in "translating" the cluster or diagram into an outline?

Exercise 3

Create a list of five topics, issues, or problems. Choose the one that most interests you. Then briefly try out three of the organizing techniques discussed in 2b–c. After experimenting with them, jot down some notes about which one(s) worked worst and best for you. Why do you think this was the case? What sort of topic did you choose, and how did the technique you used affect its development?

3 Purpose, Thesis, and Audience

Think about what writing (or speaking) actually *does*. It helps communicate ideas, develop policies, provide services, or make things work. It can sell, buy, or negotiate. It can be coolly informative or passionately persuasive. It can do public good or make private profit. And it can produce knowledge.

3a Identifying your focus and purpose

Given all that writing *can* do, one of your early steps is to decide just what a particular piece of writing *needs* to do.

1 Define the focus of your task

In many writing situations, someone hands you a task or assignment, and it's your job to produce effective writing. First think about the focus your assignment or task requires. Then concentrate on how to narrow your focus until you find the kernel or core that will lie at the center of your paper. Meg Satterfield began this process by underlining a key noun phrase in her assignment.

> Most of us have volunteered at some time—helping family or friends or joining a service-learning project. Tell your audience (our class) about <u>some unexpected outcome of your experience as a volunteer</u>.

Meg decided that her assignment left the topic open but valued something ("an unexpected outcome") that would surprise or engage readers.

> **STRATEGY**   **Target your topic.**
>
> On your assignment sheet or job description, underline any nouns or noun phrases; use them to invent and narrow possibilities (see 2a).

2 Define the purpose of your task

3.1

Focusing on a topic—a noun—gives you a clear sense of what your writing is *about*. But nouns don't act, and your writing needs to *do* something, too. Its **purpose** usually takes the form of an action statement—a verb or verb phrase like these two in Cory Meta's assignment.

> Find a magazine ad that catches your attention. <u>Analyze the ad for its hidden cultural assumptions</u>, being sure to <u>describe exactly what is happening in the ad</u>. Note techniques such as camera angle, coloration, and focus.

> **STRATEGY**   **Pinpoint what you need to *do*.**
>
> On your assignment sheet or job description, underline any verbs or verb phrases that tell you what to *do*. (See the chart on p. 15 for a list of verbs frequently used in academic writing situations.) Then use planning strategies to generate material related to these verbs (see 2a).

3 Rough out a purpose structure

State briefly the purpose of each section of your writing. A sequence such as "1-2-3-4" or "beginning-middle-ending" can help you decide what each part should do. Use verbs that clarify your purpose: *show, explain, claim, counter, build up to.* In planning a student housing guide, Carol Stotsky specified her purposes by developing a tentative order for her section on housing options.

BEGINNING   Show students why housing options are important for them.

MIDDLE   Explore advantages and disadvantages of each in detail.

ENDING   Recommend that traditional students move gradually from security (home or dorm) to independence (off campus).

3b Creating a thesis

Readers may expect you to clarify your point right away in a college paper, just as they may look for an executive summary with a report or an abstract before a professional article. For this reason, a thesis statement often ends the first paragraph in college writing. The **thesis**, generally expressed in a single sentence, is the controlling idea that you then explore, support, or illustrate using specific examples or arguments. You may draft a paper with a clear thesis in mind, discover your thesis later on and revise accordingly, or modify your thesis as you look for evidence or ideas to back up your assertions.

3.2

1 Develop a rough thesis

To begin developing a thesis, first narrow the topic to some specific angle or perspective. Then begin turning the topic from a noun (a "thing") into a statement that contains a verb (an "action"). Notice how Lynn Tarelli developed a thesis for her brochure for a parenting group.

VAGUE TOPIC   Ritalin

STILL A TOPIC   Ritalin for kids with attention-deficit disorder (ADD)

STILL A TOPIC   The problem of Ritalin use for kids with ADD

ROUGH THESIS   Parents should be careful about using medicines such as Ritalin for kids with ADD.

Lynn progressively sharpened the topic and brought the fourth version to life by expressing an assertion about it, seeing it from a specific perspective.

2 Complicate, develop, or modify your thesis

Lynn's thesis still didn't make a clear suggestion to parents about Ritalin: Should it not be used for kids with ADD? Should it be used judiciously?

FINAL THESIS   Although Ritalin is widely used to treat children with ADD, parents should not rely too heavily on such drugs until they have explored both their child's problem and all treatment options.

Lynn *complicated* her rough thesis by accepting Ritalin as a legitimate treatment for ADD; her cautions about overreliance and other options *developed* and *modified* it to create a clearer, more complex statement.

As your ideas evolve, be ready to modify or change your thesis. After outlining his contribution to a library publication on computer literacy, Joel Kitze modified his thesis to give readers more to consider.

THESIS	In spite of expanding technology, computers will never replace books as the chief medium of written literacy.
SUPPORTING IDEA 1	Books are more democratic, since not everyone can afford a personal computer.
SUPPORTING IDEA 2	Books can be enjoyed anywhere--on a bus or beach, in bed.
SUPPORTING IDEA 3	Children enjoy the physical comfort of reading with adults, a comfort harder to achieve with computers.
MODIFIED THESIS	Although computer technology allows masses of information to be stored and conveyed electronically, it will never replace the bound book as the most affordable, convenient, and magical medium for print.

STRATEGY   Develop and modify your thesis.

Help your reader anticipate and organize information in your writing, fitting separate chunks—paragraphs and sections—into your larger purpose. Use planning strategies (see Chapter 2) or research (see Part 4) to create a series of points that support, expand, or illustrate your thesis. Then develop and modify your thesis by asking *why*, *how*, and *for what reason*.

3 Choose an appropriate kind of thesis statement

Not all thesis statements take the same form. Choose the kind of thesis most appropriate for your purpose or readers. (See also 18d and 24c.)

Argumentative thesis. Readers will expect you to indicate your opinion on an issue and perhaps to acknowledge other views.

Although bioengineered crops may pose some dangers, their potential for combating worldwide hunger and disease justifies their careful use in farming.

General thesis. Readers will expect to learn your conclusions or special perspectives and perhaps understand their importance as well.

KEY VERBS USED TO SPECIFY WRITING PURPOSES

Analyze: Divide or break something into constituent parts so you can observe, describe, and study their relationships.

Analyze the relationships between form and color, light and shadow, and foreground and background in one of Titian's paintings.

Argue: Prove a point, or persuade a reader to accept or entertain a position. (See Chapters 9 and 13.)

In a letter to the College Senate, argue your position on a campuswide smoking ban.

Compare and contrast: Show similarities and differences for two or more things.

Compare and contrast costs at local hospitals for ten surgical procedures.

Describe: Show how something is experienced through sight, sound, taste, touch, or smell.

Describe obstacles in local historic homes met by visitors in wheelchairs.

Discuss: Provide an intelligent, focused commentary about a topic.

Discuss current transit needs in the metropolitan region.

Evaluate: Reach conclusions about something's value or worth, using substantiating evidence based on observation and analysis.

Evaluate the effectiveness of camera technique in Hitchcock's *The Birds*.

Extend: Apply an idea or concept more fully.

Extend last year's production figures to account for the April slowdown.

Inform: Present facts, views, phenomena, or events to enlighten your reader.

Inform homeowners about the hazards of lead paint.

Show: Demonstrate or provide evidence to explain something.

Show how Pip, in his later years, is influenced by Joe's working-class values in Dickens's *Great Expectations*.

Synthesize: Combine separate elements into a single or unified entity.

Synthesize this list of facts about energy consumption.

Trace: Map out a history, chronology, or explanation of origins.

Trace the development of Stalinism.

Use: Focus on the designated material, selecting specifics from it to explain and illustrate your broader points.

Use the three assigned poems to illustrate contemporary responses to death.

Sooner or later, teenagers stop listening to parents and turn to each other for advice, sometimes with disastrous results.

Academic thesis. Readers will expect to learn both your specific conclusion and your plan to support it, using terms appropriate to the field.

My survey of wedding announcements in local newspapers during the last three decades indicates that religious background and ethnicity have decreased in importance in mate selection but education and social background remain significant factors.

Informative thesis. Readers will expect to learn why information is interesting or useful and how you'll organize or synthesize it.

When you search for online advice about financial aid, you will find help on three very different kinds of Web sites.

3c Understanding your readers

As you write, you need to shape ideas and information to guide your readers' understanding and accomplish your purpose(s). To do this, you should identify your actual or potential readers as well as their likely perspectives, needs, and expectations.

1 Analyze your audience

Begin your audience analysis by asking *Who are my readers*? *How many readers can I anticipate*? and *How well do I know them*?

> **STRATEGY** Ask questions about your readers.
>
> - **Size and familiarity.** How large is your audience? How familiar or close to you? Are audience members known or unknown to you?.
> - **Community.** Which expectations of readers are typical of the community in which you are writing? Which are specialized or local? What roles in the community do your readers play or expect you to play?
> - **Knowledge.** What do readers already know about your topic? Are they novices or experts?
> - **Social context.** What characterizes your readers socially, culturally, and educationally? How do they spend their time?
> - **Intellectual disposition.** How do your readers think? Are they conservative? radical? apathetic?
> - **Conditions of reading.** Under what conditions will they read?
> - **Power.** What is your status relative to readers? Are they peers or superiors? Do you expect them, or do they expect you, to do something?

3.3

2 Respond to your audience

Determine your readers' needs and expectations by asking *What do my readers expect?* Take into account any particular community of readers—academic, public, or work—that you are addressing.

- **Select the genre readers expect.** The type of text you choose to write—the **genre**—depends on your purpose and likely readers. If you request funds for a volunteer project, readers will expect a grant proposal, not a poem.
- **Shape your content to the context.** If you're explaining how to remove mildew for a neighborhood newsletter, skip the history of mildew unless it's relevant to the remedies.
- **Adjust your structure to the situation.** In a letter to your investment firm's client whose stock has tumbled, you might lead up to this news with the circumstances of the loss. A lab report, however, should move directly to the conventional sections.
- **Anticipate possible responses of readers.** Will readers expect you to be clinical and detached, informal and chatty, or in between? How might they react if you're emotional, hostile, or legalistic?

Exercise 1

Below are two writing tasks, one a college writing assignment, the other a work assignment to an intern at a local nonprofit agency. Locate the noun(s) that indicate the *focus* of each task, and find the verb(s) that indicate its *purpose.* Restate the focus and purpose in your own words if necessary.

Sample Assignment: At some point, most people recognize in themselves a prejudice against another person or group. These prejudices often come from stereotypes—inaccurate generalizations based on limited experience, rumor, or what others tell us. Choose some past action in your life that came out of a prejudice. What caused the action? If the situation arose today, how would you behave?

Sample Task: Draft a proposal to the State Board on Aging for our planned ElderHelp Transport System. Refer to the current guidelines for contents of the proposal, length, and format. To include information on actual beneficiaries of our plan, conduct a few informal interviews with seniors—possibly ones who use our center. Rose has written successful proposals to the state board in the past, so get her input early, and also run your draft past Jim.

Exercise 2   *(Possible answers appear on p. 505.)*

Turn each of the following topics into two different thesis statements or main ideas. Be as inventive as you like.

EXAMPLE

TOPIC   Saw-blade sabotage in the timber industry

THESIS   Spiking trees to sabotage the saw blades of timber workers is both illegal and extremely dangerous, but it should be understood as a subversive act intended to stop further depletion of virgin forests.

THESIS   Protests that include the illegal spiking of trees to sabotage the saw blades of timber workers actually help the timber industry by suggesting to the public that conservationists are less concerned about human safety and human life than about trees.

Topic 1: Grandparents' visitation rights, which allow them to see grandchildren against the parents' will

Topic 2: Gay rights in the Boy Scouts

Topic 3: Metal detectors at public school entrances

Topic 4: Whose fault is air rage?

Topic 5: Laws declaring English the official language of the United States

Exercise 3

Imagine that your longtime next-door neighbors take a temporary position in another country and rent their house. Soon after the renters move in, they begin piling up the yard and driveway with junk cars, old refrigerators, tires, and other debris. The situation becomes so intolerable that you decide to write to the renters, calling attention to the problem. You also decide to write to the local city inspections office, which is responsible for enforcing various codes on yard debris. Write the two short letters, addressing the first to John and Susan Valentine, the renters, and the second to Betsy Lewis, City Inspections Office.

Exercise 4

Pick a specialized magazine with which you are very familiar (such as *Road & Track*, *Cooking Light*, or *Wired*). Glance through a recent copy, noting the topics, lengths, and formats of its articles; its advertisements; its layout; and its writing style. Then, following the advice in this chapter, select and use one method for analyzing the magazine's likely audience.

4 Drafting

If planning resembles storyboarding a movie, then drafting begins the filming, even though you may retake entire scenes and cut lots of footage. **Drafting** is the challenging process of stringing words together into sentences and paragraphs that make sense to a reader.

4a Moving from planning to drafting

Although all your planning (see Chapters 2 and 3) prepares you for drafting, you may not know how and where to begin writing. As Amy Burns reviewed a cluster she drew for her paper on superstition, she began jotting notes on "rabbit's foot," one of her "cases of superstition." Using these notes, she began drafting simply with a series of phrases.

> Rabbit's foot—common lucky charm. Omen of good fortune. Brasch says thumping noise from hind paws = communication. Thought to have magical powers. Newborns brushed to chase evil spirits.

Using a simple three-part scheme, Amy then developed a preliminary structure for grouping her ideas on superstition.

INTRODUCTION   Fear, people who believe, origins

BODY   Examples (black cat, #13, ladder, rabbit's foot, etc.)

CONCLUSION   Truth and falsity, mystery of superstitions

Amy used her plan as a way to start, writing an introduction about how superstitions originate in a fear of the unknown.

Group your ideas. Use your planning material to place ideas, topics, or terms into one of three categories: introduction, body, and conclusion. If your project has a required or expected structure, use it to define your groups. If you have made a rough outline of your paper, assign chunks of your outline to these parts. You might set up separate computer files so that you can work on these parts one section at a time. Later you can cut and paste the files into a single text.

4.1

As you draft, consider whether you're achieving your general purposes (persuading someone or explaining something) or your more specific purposes for different parts (enlivening a paragraph or illustrating a point). Given her specific purpose, to "grab my readers' attention and interest them in superstition," Amy moved some specific examples into her opening paragraph.

Do you knock on wood after making a prediction? Shiver when a black cat crosses your path? Consider 13 unlucky? If so, you have already been swept into the world of superstitions. Many people practice some of the bizarre rituals of superstition, but few know why.

What readers expect first, second, and third may help you determine how to organize to achieve your purpose. You'd probably arrange a local history of a ballpark chronologically but organize an argument for its preservation logically, using your paragraphs to support your assertions.

Write about your writing. Begin not by writing your paper but by writing *about* it. What concerns you most? What do you hope to do? How might you start?

As you jot notes, you'll be less anxious about starting—after all, you *have* started. As you continue, don't worry about choosing perfect words or crafting perfect sentences and paragraphs. Just write as much as you can quickly. When momentum develops, keep going.

Try semidrafting. Write full sentences until you're about to stall out. Then simply write *etc.* in place of the full text, and continue with your next point. Or add directions to yourself in brackets, noting what to do next. For documented projects or research papers, use semidrafting to note what you need to integrate from sources, as Kavita Kamal did when writing about "wild children" (supposedly raised by animals in the woods).

> The first case was that of Victor, the "Wild Boy of Aveyron." Victor first appeared in a village in southern France in January 1800. His age was estimated at eleven or twelve years. [Explain his adoption by Itard and Guerin and their subsequent studies.] People assumed that he was a mute because he did not speak. [Now go into the stuff from Shattuck about no malformation of the tongue, mouth, etc.]

ESL ADVICE: SEMIDRAFTING AND PHRASING

If you find composing in English difficult, type *XXX*, draw a circle, or make a note in your first language where you need to rework your phrasing. Continue semidrafting so that you get your main ideas down on paper, and fill in the small points later.

4b Drafting collaboratively

When you write with classmates, a civic group, or a work team, look for collaborative strategies that suit the group and the context.

4.2

- Organize **parallel drafting**, dividing up the project, perhaps by group members' specialties, so that each is responsible for drafting a particular section. You can exchange drafts as you revise and edit, but one person may need to act as editor, integrating the drafts.
- Try **team drafting** when writers share similar ideas and approaches, assigning two writers for each section. The first writer drafts until he or she gets stuck, and then the second begins where the first stopped. Recirculate the drafts when revising and editing.
- Consider **intensive drafting** when working with a close friend or colleague. Assemble materials in a space where you can work undistracted. Decide where each will begin drafting, and exchange sections at a certain time or as you finish segments. Continue exchanging drafts, or vary your pattern by having one person compose aloud as the other types.
- Use the "track changes" feature in most popular word-processing software to draft collaboratively in an electronic document file. This function allows changes to the original draft to appear in a different color onscreen. Every member's changes will appear in the draft for review.

4b
draft

Exercise 1

A. Thinking about your experiences as a writer, give some advice about drafting to an imaginary audience of high school students. Feel free to include personal experiences, tips, and specific techniques. When is the best time to write? What are some self-defeating habits? What's the best way to start writing a paper?

B. Share your "advice papers" in a small group. Are any behaviors typical? Is any advice consistent?

Exercise 2

Try one of the strategies for drafting described in this chapter. Jot down some notes about how well it worked to get you started drafting and keep you moving forward.

Exercise 3

A. Imagine you are part of a student organization that is raising funds for a community project in which volunteers read to children in school libraries. Your organization intends to submit a grant proposal to a local foundation or philanthropic group. Plan how the members might use the following equipment to draft the proposal collaboratively: telephones, email, computers, fax machines. What steps would your plan involve?

5a
revise

B. In a small group, compare the plans you developed in Exercise 3A. How comfortable are students in your group with the idea of drafting collaboratively? What are the pros and cons?

5 Revising, Editing, and Proofreading

Because so much of what we read is in final, published form, we forget the hours the author has spent **revising**—reconsidering content and structure in terms of community expectations, redrafting whole sections, and struggling to find just the right words. Revision is more than fine-tuning style, grammar, and sentence problems (**editing**) or searching for missing apostrophes and typographical errors (**proofreading**), important though these activities are. Instead, revision means *reading* your draft critically and *reworking* it to make effective changes. It means stepping outside the draft to assess its strengths and weaknesses and then deciding what to expand, clarify, reword, restructure—or just plain cut.

5a Making major revisions

5.1

Concentrate first on **major revisions**, large-scale changes that make your draft as a whole more effective. For example, if your report seems too informal for your work community, you may decide to redraft its introduction, delete an anecdote, or add more alternative solutions. Think critically about content, structure, tone, style, appeals to audience, and purpose.

1 Redraft workable material

Rework ineffective parts, as Jessica White did with her opening.

ORIGINAL DRAFT   I was a cheerleading captain and I loved basketball. I put a lot of work into my cheerleading season. We had great team spirit between the cheerleaders and the teammates. We led our crowd to great enthusiasm and spirit.

WRITER'S ASSESSMENT: I want people to feel what it was like after the state quarter-finals. This doesn't even say where I was or what was happening.

REVISED DRAFT   There we were, a bunch of cheerleaders packed into Rebecca's car. Everyone's spirits were soaring; we had won the quarter-final game of the state basketball championship. It was a bitterly cold night, but we laughed, joked, and endlessly replayed the highlights of the game.

STRATEGY   Use question marks.

Let your draft sit for a few hours or a day, and then read it (preferably aloud). Place a question mark next to any ineffective section. After you finish reading, go back to each question mark, and bracket the passage where the writing loses vitality or meaning. Ask yourself what you want to accomplish there, take out a new page (or open a new file), and say it again.

2 Reorganize paragraphs or sections

An early draft may reflect your process of discovery instead of the best order for your readers or subject. Keyshawn Williams drafted a memo from a committee looking for ways to cut company expenses. He originally opened with the committee's conclusions, but the group revised the memo to give readers more context—concise background on the committee's task, a clear statement of the problem, and then the recommendations.

STRATEGY   Summarize your paragraphs.

Number the paragraphs in your draft, and write a phrase or sentence to sum up the main point of each. Use this list to spot paragraphs that you could combine or reorganize to create a clearer flow of ideas. Consider whether points at the end belong at the beginning. (See 2b and 7f.)

3 Add new material

An addition can develop a paragraph (see 7f), enliven a dull passage, clarify or extend a point, or supply missing detail. When Gina Giacomo revised her Web page explaining the transfer to a new email system, she added the underlined material to clarify the transition for readers.

Your new email address is listed below. It should be easy to remember because it consists of the first six letters of your name. You may send your new address to people or groups that send you messages, but you don't need to. Our server will automatically forward any mail directed to your old address.

5b
revise

STRATEGY **Highlight paragraph openings and closings.**

Highlight the first and last sentence in each paragraph. Read through these highlighted sentences, identifying any gaps where a paragraph doesn't connect clearly to the one before or after it or where information or detail is missing within the paragraph. (See 7d.)

4 Delete unnecessary material

Don't be afraid to slash away large chunks if they're unnecessary, illogical, or redundant, as Brian Corby did in his letter to the zoning board.

> With eighteen stories, Regency Towers will cast a long, wide shadow over Piedmont Park. ~~The building will be quite tall and very wide.~~ For several hours a day, the toddler play area will be darkened. On summer afternoons, the shadow will cut across the baseball diamond. ~~This could be dangerous.~~

STRATEGY **Make 10 percent cuts.**

Imagine that your draft will be published if you trim at least 10 percent of the fat. Mark sentences where you can cut or paragraphs where you might merge the essentials. (See 44b.)

5b Making minor revisions

Minor revisions are fairly small changes, mostly refining and polishing passages for three reasons: *sense*, *style*, and *economy*.

1 Revise for sense

When you're immersed in your writing, you may forget what your reader *doesn't* know or think, leading to illogical or puzzling statements. Read your draft carefully to see whether each passage *makes sense* in the context of the whole project. Try to look at the text as your readers might, not in your own way. If possible, ask peer readers to place question marks next to any confusing text.

Paul Tichey asked his peer group to read his draft on Nevada's environmentally threatened wild mustangs. Paul revised the draft after his readers pointed out that they couldn't tell whether the Air Force was helping or harming the animals.

> The Air Force , which was partly responsible for the ∧reduction in the demise ~~reduction in the~~
> number ∧of ∧wild mustangs on the Tonopah missile range. , has now ∧ ~~The Air~~

joined forces with

~~Force is part of a team that also includes~~ the Bureau of Land
Management and a group of wild-horse preservationists. ~~All three~~
~~groups have banded together~~ to help *save* the wild mustangs *from dehydration and* ~~in this~~
~~death during the duration of the drought.~~
~~period of drought and dehydration.~~

2 Revise for style

Consider how your prose "sounds"—its rhythm and complexity. In any rough paragraph, place a +, ✓, −, or ? next to each sentence to indicate whether you feel positive, neutral, negative, or uncertain about it. Rewrite what you don't like; try to get readers' advice on questionable sentences. When in doubt, try an alternative. (See 43b and 45b.)

Paul placed a minus sign next to the sentence below. He decided that too many words began with *d*, and *during the duration* seemed redundant.

The Air Force, which was partly responsible for the demise of

the wild mustangs on the Tonopah missile range, has now joined

forces with the Bureau of Land Management and a group of wild-

horse preservationists to help save the mustangs from *fatal*

dehydration *while the drought persists.* ~~and death during the duration of the drought.~~

3 Revise for economy

Cut what you can without losing sense or coherence. Paul reduced seventy-eight words to thirty-six—a cut of over 50 percent!

SECOND DRAFT A serious problem confronting groups who want to manage wild mustangs on military sites in Nevada is the relative inaccessibility of the sites, since many require security passes or are fenced off, and environmentalists can't come and go as they please, as they can on public or even some private land. It's simply harder to study or help horses on restricted military installations. Open rangeland has easier access, and inspectors can simply move in and out at will.

THIRD DRAFT (REVISED FOR ECONOMY) Restricted access to Nevada military sites presents a serious obstacle to successful horse management. Unlike open rangeland, where inspectors can come and go as they please, military sites are often fenced off and require security clearance.

STRATEGY   **Count your words.**

Count the words in a passage that lacks economy. Then start cutting. See what percentage you can trim without changing meaning. (See 44b.)

5c Revising collaboratively

Honest feedback from a reader can give you a fresh perspective on your writing. When you act as a peer reader—or ask someone to read for you—begin by establishing the writer's purpose, audience, and concerns.

5.2

- What sort of project is it? What is the writer trying to do?
- For what community is it intended? What do readers expect?
- What does the writer want to learn from a reader?

STRATEGY   **Mix praise and criticism.**

Jot notes that balance praise with helpful criticism. Don't simply say, "It was really good," or give directions like "Move this to page 2." Instead, offer diplomatic advice: "What would happen if you moved this to page 2?"

Accept constructive comments from an honest reader gracefully. If you are defensive, your reader is unlikely to give you more feedback. But if a reader questions something you like, remember that you have the final say.

- Give your readers a list of your specific concerns about the draft.
- Minimize apologies. Everyone feels anxious about sharing a draft.
- If time is limited, consider taping reactions, meeting briefly to take notes on responses, emailing, or exchanging comments jotted on the drafts.

5d Writing correctly

Writing correctly means recognizing and using the **conventions**—the options for grammar, sentence structure and style, word choice, punctuation, and mechanics—that readers expect you to use. Some conventions don't vary much across communities, such as using complete sentences or standard spelling in formal prose. In these cases, most writers try to avoid challenging readers' strongly held expectations. After all, a reader irritated by errors isn't likely to give you a high grade, promote you, join your civic crusade, or view you as an attentive writer.

Other conventions, however, vary with the context. For example, newspaper readers wouldn't be surprised to find only one comma in this sentence: *The suspect jumped from the car, evaded the officers and ran into the motel.* But many academic readers would expect a second comma to follow *officers,* perhaps citing the well-known guides of the Modern Language Association (MLA) and the American Psychological Association (APA) as authorities on this comma issue (see Chapters 25–26). Likewise, a chemist would use numerals (such as *12* or *84*) in a lab report, while an art historian might spell out *twelve* and *eighty-four* in an interpretive paper. Effective writers learn how to recognize and edit for various conventions to meet readers' expectations.

5e Editing

Editing means adjusting sentences and words for clarity, style, economy, and correctness. You can improve your editing skills each time you prepare a college paper, a public communication, or a work project. Allow plenty of time to read carefully, and shift your attention from content (what's said) to form (how it's said). Noticing readers' reactions during class or meetings can alert you to their individual and community sensitivities. Check your writing for both the problems readers identify and the features they admire. As you edit, focus on one issue at a time—commas, perhaps, or wordiness—while you scour your text for specific cases. Then repeat the process for the next issue.

Many computer programs claim to offer shortcuts for editors. Some can identify features like passive voice verbs or calculate the average length of sentences. Nonetheless, they are no match for careful human readers and editors. They may skip errors or question correct sentences, and they can't help you adjust to different audiences or communities of readers and writers.

1 Edit for clarity, style, and economy

Most writing profits from final cosmetic surgery. If your grant proposal, oral presentation, letter to the editor, or other writing project has a length limit, edit ruthlessly to meet this expectation. Ask these questions as you edit:

5e
edit

5.3

- **Are my sentences clear and easy to read?** Try reading out loud. Whenever you stumble over the wording, rephrase or restructure.
- **Do I repeat some sentence structures too often?** If too many sentences begin with nouns or *I*, start some with prepositional phrases (see 30b-1) or subordinate clauses (see 30c and 42b–c).
- **Do any words seem odd or inappropriate?** If so, reword. Turn to a dictionary or thesaurus for help. (See 45b, 47b.)
- **If I had to cut ten words per page, which could I drop?** Cut, but avoid new problems (such as short, choppy sentences). (See 43b.)

DRAFT   The aligned pulleys are lined up so that they are located up above the center core of the machine.
READER'S REACTION: **This seems repetitive and boring.**

EDITED   The aligned pulleys are ~~lined up so that they are located~~ positioned ~~up~~ above ~~the center core of~~ the machine's core.

2 Edit for grammatical problems

SERIOUS
ERROR

Editing for grammatical problems challenges you first to *recognize* the problem and then to *edit* to repair or eliminate it. The chart inside the back cover lists ten errors identified by academic readers as likely to irritate readers and call into question a writer's skills. The sections that discuss these errors are marked by an icon as seen in the margin here. In addition, this handbook's editing advice uses the read-recognize-revise pattern to help you identify errors and select a useful editing strategy.

STRATEGY   Read for errors.

- Read your paper from start to finish, circling or marking any errors in grammar, punctuation, and sentence logic. If you can quickly correct an error, do so. Otherwise, finish identifying problems, and then look up the relevant advice in this handbook or other references.
- Read your paper again, this time marking all suspected problems in your text. Follow your instincts if you feel that a sentence is weak or flawed. Then look up the pertinent advice, and edit the errors or flaws. Stick to the possible errors unless you want to improve an awkward or wordy sentence. Ask a teacher, tutor, peer editor, colleague, or friend for advice as needed.

Paragraphs from Jim Tollefson's newsletter for his local nature conservancy show his circled errors and his edited version.

DRAFT WITH ERRORS MARKED Critics of the ⓔndangered ⓢpecies ⓐct think it is too brọ̈ad. Bec̣ause some ṣpecie's ṃay be less vital to environmental balance than others. (They) want to protect species selectiṿely, ḥowever, scientists do not know which species are more important.

caps
fragment
apostrophe
who?
comma splice

EDITED Critics of the Endangered Species Act think it is too broad because some species may be less vital to environmental balance than others. Our critics want to protect species selectively. However, scientists do not know which species are more important.

Look for patterns—repeated errors—that you recognize or that readers point out. Then you can make many corrections simply by identifying and repairing a specific type of error.

- Analyze your papers, keeping track of your repeated errors.
- Ask a teacher or expert writer to identify your *patterns* of error.
- Use the strategies in this book or create your own for *recognizing* and *editing* your errors. Collect them in a personal editing checklist.
- Use your checklist; replace items you master with new ones.

After editing her report on the effects of loud music, Carrie Brehe added this item to her editing checklist.

<u>A lot</u> sounds like one word but is actually two. Think of its opposite, <u>a little</u>. From the noise paper: "<u>Alot</u> of teenagers do not know how their hearing works." Strategy: Search for <u>alot</u>.

3 Edit collaboratively

When you edit collaboratively, you identify and talk about specific problems with "consulting readers," usually friends, peers, or colleagues who help you improve a particular writing project while you learn to identify and repair errors on your own. (See the guidelines on p. 30.)

5f Proofreading

After you've edited as thoughtfully as possible, it's time for **proofreading**, your last chance to make sure that errors in presentation don't annoy your reader or undermine your ideas and credibility as a writer. If mistakes accumulate in a college paper or project at work, these errors can lead to a poor assessment or hinder your advancement.

5f
proof

COLLABORATIVE EDITING GUIDELINES

GUIDELINES FOR WRITERS

- Revise content and organization first to prepare your draft for editing. (If necessary, ask your reader for feedback on larger revisions instead. See 5c.)
- Supply a clean draft; don't waste your reader's time on sloppiness.
- Share your requirements or writing concerns with your reader.

GUIDELINES FOR READERS

- Use familiar labels and symbols for comments. (The terms in this handbook are generally accepted in academic, public, and work communities. See the list of symbols on p. 578.)
- Just note possible errors. Let the writer use a dictionary, a style guide, or this handbook to identify and repair each problem.
- Be specific; *awkward* or *unclear* may not tell the writer exactly what's wrong. Briefly tell why something does or doesn't work.
- Identify outright errors, but don't "take over" the draft. Rewriting sentences and paragraphs is the writer's job.
- Look for patterns of error, noting repetition of the same mistakes.

STRATEGY   Focus your attention.

5.4

- Read out loud or even backwards from the last sentence to the first.
- Look for missing words, incorrect prepositions, missing punctuation marks (especially half of a pair of commas or parentheses), and accidental duplicates.
- Consciously fix your eyes on each word to be sure it doesn't contain transposed letters, typographical errors, and the like.

Your careful editing and proofreading will help ensure that your final version is clear, concise, and consistent.

Exercise 1   *(Answers appear on p. 506.)*

Compare the following first-draft and revised versions of Maureen Lagasse's paragraph on racism. Describe the nature of Lagasse's changes—did she redraft, reorganize, add, or cut? What do you think motivated her revisions?

FIRST DRAFT

In setting out to write this paper my concept to explain was racism, and in doing some reading and thinking, I realized that racism can't be defined or explained in one simple definition. In the dictionary the definition of racism is "the practice of racial discrimination or segregation, etc." Although this is what racism is, this definition doesn't fully explain racism. What exactly are races, and how do people actually develop these discriminations against people of different races?

REVISED DRAFT

Have you ever wondered why people view interracial relationships as unacceptable? Have you wondered whether there really is a difference between you and someone of another race? In the dictionary the definition of racism is "the practice of racial discrimination or segregation." Although this is a legitimate definition, it doesn't fully explain racism.

Exercise 2 *(Answers appear on p. 506.)*

Examine the following paragraphs from Anita Jackson's paper on Buddhism. What sorts of minor revisions did Jackson make? Did she revise for sense, style, or economy?

EARLY DRAFT

The man who became the first Buddha was named Siddhartha. Siddhartha was a prince in northern India who lived in a large palace. His father didn't allow him outside the palace because he wanted to spare Siddhartha from the miseries of the world.

Siddhartha became curious and one day he went riding outside the palace. What he saw would forever change his life and influence the lives of many thereafter. That which Siddhartha saw has since been named the Four Sights.

REVISED DRAFT

The man who became the first Buddha was Siddhartha, a pampered prince of northern India who lived in a lavish palace. Yet for all his riches his father would not allow him to venture beyond the castle walls because he wanted to spare Siddhartha the miseries of life. Siddhartha grew extremely curious about the outside world and one day went riding beyond the limits of the palace. What he saw that day would forever change his life and influence the lives of many thereafter.

What Siddhartha saw has since been named the Four Sights.

Exercise 3 *(A possible version appears on p. 507.)*

In a brochure-writing assignment, Kim Francis wrote the following draft paragraph for a pamphlet describing tourist attractions and accommodations near her Wisconsin home. Read the paragraph once for meaning and then a second time for editing. During the second reading, ask some of the questions listed in 5e-1. Then edit the paragraph to make it more effective.

> After spending a day exploring the countryside, rest and relax at a quaint country inn, relaxing by the fire and sipping on some mulled wine. After spending a quiet night in a room decorated with beautiful old antiques, wake up to a country breakfast. Then after your pleasant stay at the inn, explore the quaint towns and roads that have made Door County, Wisconsin, such an attractive vacation destination for people who like to escape and get away from it all.

Exercise 4

Working from a paper that your instructor has commented on (or that you have asked another teacher or expert writer to examine), begin creating your own editing checklist.

Exercise 5

Two versions of a paragraph follow—one in an unedited form, the other partly edited. Without looking at the edited version, read the unedited draft like an editor. Scrutinize the passage as ruthlessly as you can, making any corrections you wish and explaining them in a notebook. Then compare your editing with the changes made in the second paragraph. What differences do you find between your editing and the writer's editing?

UNEDITED DRAFT

At the start of her career, historian Barbara Smithey, felt forced to choose between a life of: public service vs. research. As curator of the Westville Museum of New England culture in Westville, Ct, she was passionately devoted to preserving or restoreing old houses in disrepair and seeing to it that they were entered if they qualified into the National Register of Historical Places. At the same time, she had a kean interest in research on the town of Westville which had been settled in the early 17th-Century. She manfully seized control of all public documents on the area, that were not already protected and got them housed in the local historical archives. These included, some early notes about the Indian savages that the White men encountered when they settled the land. Also some personal diaries lady settlers kept.

EDITED DRAFT

At the start of her career, ~~historian~~ the historian Barbara Smithey ~~felt~~ ~~y~~ felt forced to choose between a life of ~~public service~~ ~~vs.~~ public service and research. As curator of the Westville Museum of New England culture in Westville, C~~T~~ Connecticut, she was passionatl~~y~~ e devoted to preserving or restor~~g~~ing old houses in disrepair and seeing to it that they were entered (if they qualified) into the National Register of Historica~~l~~l Places. At the same time, she had a ke~~n~~e interest in research on the town of Westville , which had been settled in the early ~~17th-Century.~~ seventeenth century. She ~~manfully~~ seized control of all public documents on the area , that were not already protected and ~~got~~ had them ~~housed~~ placed in the local historical archives. These included , some early notes about ~~the Indian savages that the White men encountered~~ settlers' local Native Americans, as well as ~~when they settled the land. Also~~ some personal diaries , lady settlers of women settlers. ~~kept.~~

6 Reading Critically

When you read, you almost always respond, and responding can turn into critical understanding as well as writing of your own. **Critical reading**—interacting with a text and developing your own ideas, often in the form of notes—is a rich source for further writing. Whatever you read, including essays, articles, memos, reports, and Web pages, pay attention both to understanding the text and to developing your own critical perspective.

6a Reading for understanding

Like most people, you probably begin to read by going to the first page and plunging into the text. By starting "cold," however, you may have too much to do at once: understand the detailed information in the text, grasp the writer's conclusions, and develop your own critical responses. Instead, you may want to "warm up" by previewing a text and developing a reading plan.

1 Preread

Begin by figuring out the "big" features that shape a text's meaning, ideas, or relationship to readers before you jump right into the text.

Preview the form. Locate features that suggest the text's approach: long paragraphs or short, opening abstract, headings, sidebars, frames, glossary, references, links, visuals, one column or more.

Preview the organization. Skim a book's table of contents. Look for headings in articles, reports, or memos. Click on the site map.

Examine the context. Consider the author's background, the original readers and situation, the place and date of first publication, or a Web site's sponsor.

Sample and predict. Scan the text to activate your own knowledge and prepare for interpreting unfamiliar words and examples in context. Look up baffling words before you read. Recall similar texts; try to predict where the reading will go.

Learn some background. Talk to peers, coworkers, or others who know a difficult subject. Find an encyclopedia entry on key concepts.

Plan ahead. When you read Web pages or library articles, consider printing or duplicating the text so you can write on your own copy.

2 Follow a reading plan

As you read, look for the generalizations and conclusions that will help you make sense of unfamiliar material. Focus on beginnings—the thesis that guides the introduction, general statements that open sections, and topic sentences that begin paragraphs (see 3b, 7b, and 7g). Look also for paragraphs that supply an overview of the main ideas and the organizational plan. In addition, set aside extra time for reading sections devoted to new information and insights.

Find what's important. Read first—*without highlighting*—to capture the essentials. Go back again to note or highlight what's *really* important.

Read the visuals. Examine graphs, charts, diagrams, or other illustrations; analyze what they say and how they relate to the written text.

Pause and assess. Where are you? What have you learned so far? What confuses you? Jot down your answers; then skim what you've just read.

Summarize in chunks. Glance back over a section, and state the main point so far. Guess where the reading will go next.

Share insights. Meet with classmates or coworkers to discuss a text. Compare reactions, considering how the others reached their interpretations.

6b
read

3 Respond after reading

When you read carefully, you respond to the content and evaluate it according to your purposes and the standards of the community of readers and writers to which a text is addressed.

Record main ideas. Use a file card, journal, or computer file so you can review without leafing through copies, printouts, or books.

Add your own responses. Note what you already know as well as your own views about the topic. Don't simply accept what the author says.

Reread and review. Reread difficult material, first skimming more quickly and then studying the passages you've highlighted.

Write in your text. If a book or other text isn't yours, don't write in it. If it—or a photocopy or printout—is yours, annotate it.

STRATEGY   Annotate a text.

Write brief notes (perhaps in the margins of a text), responding in ways like these.

- **Interpretations:** What does the author or speaker mean?
- **Confusions:** At what points are you puzzled?
- **Questions:** What more do you need to know?
- **Objections or counterarguments:** Where do you disagree?
- **Restatements:** How can you say it in your own words?
- **Evaluations:** What do you like or dislike about the reading?
- **Applications:** What can you use for class, work, or activities?
- **Expectations:** How does this reading resemble or differ from others typical in your academic, public, or work community?

6b Reading analytically and critically

Your purposes and context shape your responses as a reader. If you are gathering details for an essay or oral presentation, your **analytical reading** will focus on *understanding* the content—the ideas, purposes, information, organization, perspective, and approaches. (See 18g.)

These activities can help guide your analytical reading of a text.

- **Summarize:** How can you sum up or restate its key ideas?
- **Paraphrase:** How can you state its main points in your own words?
- **Synthesize:** How can you connect its information with that in other texts?
- **Quote:** Which of the text's exact words make powerful statements?

Next, your **critical reading** will focus on *interacting* with the text, adding to it your knowledge and insight, analyzing what it does—and doesn't—address, relating it to other texts within the community, and assessing its strengths and limitations. Your critical reading will be active, engaged, and responsive as you ask questions, look for answers, and develop your own perspective.

6.1

- **Question:** What answers do you still want or need?
- **Synthesize perspectives:** How can you relate it to other views?
- **Interpret:** What do you conclude about its outlook and bias?
- **Assess:** How do you evaluate its value and accuracy?

The example below illustrates both analytical and critical comments.

ANALYTICAL COMMENTS		CRITICAL COMMENTS
Compares health care choices to grocery shopping	How is health care like going to the grocer? The more you put in the cart, the higher the bill. But unlike your grocery expedition, where all you pay for are the items in your own cart, with health care the other customer's cart is on your tab, too.	*Sounds good, but is it fair overall? Need to read more*
Admits benefits but claims costs will increase	Nor will the tab get any better with the patient protection legislation being considered in Washington. Sure, Americans will get guaranteed access to emergency rooms, medical clinical trials and specialists. Senate legislation even provides the right to sue your insurer and be awarded up to $5 million in punitive damages. . . .	*Lots of coverage problems—like my emergency room bill*
Supplies supporting evidence		
Projects costs and effects	The litigation costs, and the efforts by some employers to avoid liability, could lead to	*Does everyone agree on estimates?*

an additional 9 million
uninsured Americans by 2010.

—"Restrict Right to Sue or   *What's this*
We'll Pay in the End,"   *paper's usual*
Atlanta Journal-Constitution,   *viewpoint?*
July 19, 2001.

6c Using journals to turn reading into writing

A **journal** is a place to explore ideas, develop insights, experiment with your writing, and reflect on your reading. You may want to organize entries around a writing task, a reading assignment, a research question, or a regular schedule for recording observations. Unlike a diary, where you record daily activities, a journal encourages interpretation and speculation as you develop your voice as a writer. (See also 18e, 18f, and 47a.)

You can keep an informal journal in whatever form you prefer—an electronic file, a three-ring notebook, or a small binder—although you may appreciate being able to remove or reorganize pages. Stick to a regular schedule for writing because an abandoned journal soon withers away.

STRATEGY   **Make your thoughts visible in a journal.**

Nurture your own voice as a writer, and cultivate your creative insights as you turn reading, listening, and thinking into writing.

- Translate new ideas into your own words, clarifying and speculating about them for an imaginary reader or for yourself.
- Brainstorm, letting one thought lead to the next without immediate criticism or evaluation.
- Extend ideas, developing implications, applications, or solutions.
- Take issue with what you read or hear, flexing your critical thinking muscles as you challenge and critique other views. Then look for balance—areas where you respect or agree with others, too.

Exercise 1

Locate a short article, a short electronic document, or a portion of a longer text that has no overt structure—no headings, section divisions, or other organizational signals. Then skim (preread) the material and create headings or divisions for the main parts of the reading.

Exercise 2

The following journal entry was written by Kelly Odeen, a student in a course on literacy in America. Read Odeen's entry, and then identify specific functions for which she is using her journal. What characteristics of her entry suggest these functions?

> Reading on the Amish community left me with very mixed feelings--not sure what to make of them yet. I really admired the family support of Eli's literacy development. Sounded like the older family members did just what we've been encouraged to do as tutors. They gave him positive feedback, etc. Focused on accomplishments rather than failures. But the setting looked sort of ideal. Everyone in Eli's family reads and writes, even more than in my family. I don't think it's possible to make learning totally individualized in the public school system. Choices have to be made that are better for some children than others. I don't have a solution, but I think the author is being too idealistic to think there can be this match like the Amish have. I'd like to look into this more for my project, maybe. Because I do agree that there are many ways of perceiving literacy, each valid, and we have to be sensitive to where kids are coming from <u>compared</u> with the school system they're going into.

7 Paragraphs

Every time you indent to begin a new paragraph, you give readers a signal: watch for a shift in topic, another perspective, or a special emphasis. Whether you are writing a history paper, a letter to the editor, or a memo at work, readers will expect your paragraphs to guide them. Revising paragraphs to increase *focus, coherence,* and *development* helps readers figure out what's important, how ideas and details logically connect, and what's coming up.

7a Recognizing unfocused paragraphs

When you concentrate on a main idea throughout, you create a paragraph that is **focused** because it doesn't stray into unrelated details. A paragraph is **unified** when all its sentences directly relate to its point. Ask questions to help you recognize unfocused paragraphs.

STRATEGY   **Ask questions for paragraph focus.**

Use these questions to identify focused or unfocused paragraphs.

* What is the main point (or topic) in this paragraph?
* How many different topics does this paragraph cover?
* Is the focus announced to readers? Where? How?
* Does the paragraph elaborate on the main point? Do details fit the topic?

Jeanne Brown used questions to analyze a paragraph on color analysis.

UNFOCUSED

A color to look at is the color red. Red is often considered a very fast and sporty color for cars. Porsches that are red are likely to be chosen over blue ones. Red ties are often called "power ties." Red can also be a very daring color to wear. A woman who wears a long red dress and has painted fingernails to match is not a shy woman. She is going to be noticed and will revel in the attention.

WRITER'S REACTION: *My main point?* I want to talk about the strong effects red can have on people. I don't think that the focus on red's power is clear. *Focus announced to readers?* Not really. I need to say that I am discussing the effects red has, not simply that it is a color worth looking at. *Elaboration on the point?* No, not very much. I need to help readers understand how each example explains my view of red's effect on moods and attitudes.

REVISED

Red is a color that can affect how people feel and react. Red makes heads turn, and the person associated with the color often ends up feeling important and influential. A red Porsche draws more attention than a blue one. A red tie, or "power tie," can be bold and assertive. Worn with a blue or gray suit, the touch of red makes the wearer stand out in a crowd and builds self-confidence. A woman wearing a long red dress with nails painted to match is probably not shy. She is going to be noticed and will revel in the attention because it reinforces her positive self-image.

7b Revising for paragraph focus

Help your readers recognize a paragraph's focus by stating your topic and your main idea or perspective in a **topic sentence**. Begin with this sentence when you want readers to grasp the point right away.

When writing jokes, it's a good idea to avoid vague generalizations. Don't just talk about "fruit" when you can talk about "an apple." Strong writing creates a single image for everyone in the crowd, each person imagining a very similar thing. But when you say "fruit," people are either imagining several different kinds of fruit or they aren't really thinking of anything in particular, and both things can significantly reduce their emotional investment in the joke. But when you say "an apple," everyone has a *clear picture*, and thus a feeling.   —JAY SANKEY, *Zen and the Art of Stand-Up Comedy*

Experiment with other topic sentence options: placing it at the end of the paragraph, repeating it at the end from a different perspective, implying it if your point is unmistakably clear, or adding a limiting or clarifying sentence to narrow your point. Supplement your topic sentences with section headings if readers expect them in a report or proposal.

7.1

STRATEGY   **Highlight topic sentences.**

Skim your draft, using a highlighter (or bold type) to mark each topic sentence. When you note that one is missing or inadequate, read critically to decide whether to revise the topic sentence or refocus the paragraph. Skim your topic sentences again, tracing your explanation or argument through the draft as a whole.

7c Recognizing incoherent paragraphs

A paragraph is **coherent** if each sentence clearly leads a reader to the next or if the sentences form a recognizable, easy-to-understand arrangement. Paragraphs may lack coherence if sentences are out of logical order or change topic so abruptly that readers must struggle to follow the thought.

STRATEGY   **Questions for paragraph coherence.**

Use these questions to check paragraph coherence.

- What words name the topic and main points? Are they repeated?
- What transitions alert readers to relationships among sentences?
- What parallel words and structures highlight similar or related ideas?
- Does the arrangement of ideas and details clarify their relationships?

LACKS COHERENCE

Captain James Cook discovered the island of Hawaii in 1779. Mauna Kea, on Hawaii, is the tallest mountain in the Pacific. Cook might have noticed the many mountains on the island as he sailed into Kealakekua Bay. The island also has five major volcanoes. Mauna Loa, another mountain on the island, is a dormant volcano that last erupted in 1984. Kilauea is the most active volcano on earth. It continues to enlarge the land that makes up this largest island in the Hawaiian chain. The volcano sends forth lava continuously.

READER'S REACTION: **This paragraph provides lots of information, but it's hard to follow because the ideas don't seem connected.**

REVISED

In 1779, Captain James Cook sailed into Kealakekua Bay and discovered the island of Hawaii. As he entered the bay, did Cook **notice** the many **mountains** on the island? Perhaps he **noticed** Mauna Kea, the tallest **mountain** in the Pacific. Perhaps he **spotted** one or more of the five major **volcanoes**. **One of these**, Mauna Loa, is a dormant **volcano** that last erupted in 1984. **Another**, Kilauea, is the most active **volcano** on earth. It sends forth lava continuously. **In addition**, it keeps adding to the landmass of what is already the largest island in the Hawaiian chain.

7d Revising for paragraph coherence

By repeating key words, phrases, synonyms, and related words that refer to your topic and main point, you keep readers aware of your focus.

According to recent research, **people married for a long time** often develop similar **facial features**. The **faces** of **younger couples** show only chance resemblances. As **they** share emotions for many years, however, most **older couples** develop similar **expressions**.

Place key words prominently, beginning or ending sentences. Avoid burying them in the middle of sentences.

Transitional expressions like *in addition, therefore,* and *on the other hand* also alert readers to relationships among sentences. (See p. 42.)

Many people still consider your college choice your most important career decision. These days, **however**, graduate school is the most important choice **because** the competition for jobs has grown fiercer. **For example**, business positions at the entry level often go to people with MBAs and law degrees. **In addition**, many good jobs require advanced training and skills. **Moreover**, employers pay attention **not only** to the presence of an advanced degree on your résumé **but also** to the program of study **and** the quality of the school.

You can also link elements by using **parallelism**—repeating the same grammatical structures to highlight similar or related ideas (see 41b).

7.2

USEFUL TRANSITIONS FOR SHOWING RELATIONSHIPS

Time and Sequence	next, later, after, while, meanwhile, immediately, earlier, first, second, shortly, in the future, subsequently, as long as, soon, since, finally, last, at that time, as soon as
Comparison	likewise, similarly, also, too, again, in the same manner, in comparison, equally
Contrast	in contrast, on the one hand . . . on the other hand, however, although, even though, still, yet, but, nevertheless, conversely, at the same time, despite, regardless
Examples	for example, for instance, such as, specifically, thus, to illustrate, namely, in fact
Cause and Effect	as a result, consequently, accordingly, if . . . then, is due to this, for this reason, because, as a consequence of, thus
Place	next to, above, behind, beyond, near, here, across from, to the right, there, in front, in the background, in between, opposite
Addition	and, too, moreover, in addition, besides, furthermore, next, also, finally, again
Concession	of course, naturally, it may be the case that, granted, it is true that, certainly, though
Conclusion	in conclusion, in short, as a result, as the data show, finally, therefore
Repetition	to repeat, in other words, once again, as I said earlier
Summary	on the whole, to summarize, to sum up, in short, therefore, in brief

7e Recognizing poorly developed paragraphs

Paragraph development provides the examples, facts, concrete details, explanations, or supporting arguments that make a paragraph informative enough to support your ideas, opinions, and conclusions. Short paragraphs are not always underdeveloped, nor are long paragraphs always adequate—yet length can be an important cue. More than two sentences are generally necessary for a paragraph to explore a topic and support a generalization.

UNDERDEVELOPED

Recycling is always a good idea—or *almost* always. Recycling some products, even newsprint and other paper goods, may require more energy from fossil fuels and more valuable natural resources than making them over again.

READER'S REACTION: **I'd like to know more before I agree with this. What are these products? How much energy does it take to recycle them? What natural resources do they consume?**

7f
¶ dev

STRATEGY   Check paragraph development.

- Does the paragraph present enough material to *inform* readers?
- Does the paragraph adequately *support* any generalizations?

7f Revising for paragraph development

Examples, whether brief or extended, help clarify a concept, explain a generalization, or provide reasons to support your position. They help a reader see an idea in action and its consequences.

BRIEF EXAMPLES

All kinds of products have been included in the fast-track recalls. For example, a major manufacturer recently recalled tens of thousands of humidifiers that could potentially overheat or catch fire. A leading manufacturer of children's products recalled tens of thousands of baby monitors that could smoke and flame. A prominent clothing retailer recalled more than 100,000 children's jackets with zipper pulls containing unacceptable levels of lead. A well-known company recalled tens of thousands of gas grills because a defective hose could leak gas or cause fires.

—"Fast-Track Recalls," *Consumer Product Safety Review*

EXTENDED EXAMPLE

One day in 1957, the songwriter Johnny Mercer received a letter from Sadie Vimerstedt, a widowed grandmother who worked behind a cosmetics counter in Youngstown, Ohio. Mrs. Vimerstedt suggested Mercer write a song called "I Want to Be Around to Pick Up the Pieces When Somebody Breaks Your Heart." Five years later, Mercer got in touch to say he'd written the song and that Tony Bennett would record it. Today, if you look at the label on any recording of "I Wanna Be Around," you'll notice that the credits for words and music are shared by Johnny Mercer and Sadie Vimerstedt. The royalties were split fifty-fifty, too, thanks to which Mrs. Vimerstedt and her heirs have earned more than $100,000. In my opinion, Mercer's generosity was a class act.   —JOHN BERENDT, "Class Acts"

STRATEGY Add details and specifics to develop paragraph content.

- **Examples.** Use brief or extended illustrations.
- **Concrete detail.** Recreate sights, sounds, tastes, smells, movements, and sensations of touch.
- **Facts and statistics.** Offer precise data from your fieldwork or authoritative sources, perhaps in numerical form.
- **Supporting statements.** Explain your own interpretations, or quote people or sources that readers will trust.
- **Summaries.** Present other people's opinions, conclusions, or explanations in compressed form (see 23b), showing how your conclusions agree with, disagree with, or supplement theirs.

Patterns of development help you accomplish familiar tasks so that readers can readily recognize the purpose and arrangement of a paragraph or a cluster of paragraphs.

Narrating. Turn to **narration** to recount past or present events, recreate an experience, tell an anecdote, or envision the future.

Describing. You can create images of a place, an object, or a feeling or sketch a person's character through **description**, emphasizing emotional impact (**subjective description**) or physical details (**objective description**).

Comparing and contrasting. Paragraphs that **compare** and **contrast** can evaluate alternative policies or products, examine pros and cons, or compare qualities and explanations. A **point-by-point organization** examines each comparable feature for first one subject and then the next.

Topic sentence	But biology has a funny way of confounding expectations. Rather than disappear, the evidence for innate sexual
Feature 1	differences only began to mount. In medicine, researchers documented that heart disease strikes men at a younger age
Feature 2	than it does women and that women have a more moderate
Feature 3	physiological response to stress. Researchers found subtle neurological differences between the sexes both in the brain's
Feature 4	structure and in its functioning. In addition, another generation of parents discovered that, despite their best efforts to give baseballs to their daughters and sewing kits to their sons, girls still flocked to dollhouses while boys clambered into tree forts. Perhaps nature is more important than nurture after all.

—CHRISTINE GORMAN, "Sizing Up the Sexes"

A **subject-by-subject organization** considers each subject in its entirety, within a paragraph or a series of paragraphs.

Topic sentence
Subject 1

For everyone, home is a place to be offstage. But the comfort of home can have opposite and incompatible meanings for women and men. For many men, the comfort of home means freedom from having to prove themselves and impress through verbal display. At last, they are in a situation where talk is not required. They are free to remain silent. But

Subject 2

for women, home is a place where they are free to talk, and where they feel the greatest need for talk, with those they are closest to. For them, the comfort of home means the freedom to talk without worrying about how their talk will be judged.

— DEBORAH TANNEN, "Put Down That Paper and Talk to Me!"

Explaining a process. To give directions, show how a mechanism or procedure works, or explain other processes, label the steps or stages clearly. Arrange them logically, usually chronologically. Devote a paragraph to each part of the process if you wish to emphasize its stages.

Dividing and classifying. When you divide a subject, you split it into parts, explaining it and the relationships of its parts.

To classify, you sort several subjects into groups, exploring similarities *within* groups and differences and relationships *between* groups.

CLASSIFICATION

Men all have different styles of chopping wood, all of which are deemed by their practitioners as the only proper method. Often when I'm chopping wood in my own inept style, a neighbor will come over and "offer help." He'll bust up a few logs in his own manner, advising me as to the proper swing and means of analyzing the grain of the wood. There are "over the head" types and "swing from the shoulder" types, and guys who lay the logs down horizontally on the ground and still others who balance them on end, atop of stumps. I have one neighbor who uses what he calls "vector analysis." Using the right vectors, he says, the wood will practically *split itself*.

— JENNIFER FINNEY BOYLAN, "The Bean Curd Method"

Defining. When you introduce a term or concept to your readers, you may need to stipulate the meaning it will carry in your writing or want to contrast its definition with others.

You can eat lunch at a food court, as in any other restaurant, but a food court has some special traits. Go to a food court to see but not be heard. The open space jammed with tables will give you a chance to see and be seen; yet the clatter and bustle will make real conversation impossible. Food courts are world tours—Thai, Mexican, Chinese, and Italian with a side of sushi—where you can buy hot dogs, nuggets, and chocolate chip cookies. The quality beats a fast-food outlet but not a good restaurant. For two dollars more than a burger and fries and seven dollars less than a tablecloth and a waiter, food courts deliver a meal that comes somewhere in between.

—Bipin Roy, College Student

Analyzing causes and effects. You may explain why something has occurred (causes), explore consequences (effects), or combine both.

Television used to depress me with forecasts of stormy weather, losers on game shows, and dramas of failed love. Then I learned to control the future. What caused me to acquire this skill? One day, upset with my favorite team's losing ways, I turned the television off and sat on the couch imagining a great comeback. Now when people ask me why I turn off the set before the end of a show, I tell them that this way my imagination can reunite long-separated lovers, help contestants with prize-winning answers, and create an upcoming week of warm, sunny days without a drop of rain.

—Dazhane Robinson, College Student

7g Using special-purpose paragraphs

Introductory paragraphs build your relationship with readers, motivating them to continue reading. They can establish the tone, approach, and degree of formality expected by readers in an academic, public, or work community. They typically should answer questions like the following.

• What is the main idea or purpose of this writing project?
• What precise topic, problem, or issue will this text address?
• Why should readers be interested in this topic?

This anecdote, for example, introduces the environmental threat posed by Las Vegas.

It was advertised as the biggest non-nuclear explosion in Nevada history. On October 27, 1993, Steve Wynn, the State's official "god of hospitality," flashed his trademark smile and pushed the detonator button. As 200,000 Las Vegans cheered, the 18-story Dunes sign, once the tallest neon structure in the world, crumbled to the desert floor.

—Mike Davis, "House of Cards"

Concluding paragraphs may remind readers of key ideas and encourage them to think about information presented or actions proposed.

So if it's any consolation to those of us who just don't manage to fit enough sleep into our packed days, being chronically tired probably won't do us any permanent harm. And if things get desperate enough, we just might have to schedule a nap somewhere on our busy calendars.   —DANIEL GOLEMAN, "TOO LITTLE, TOO LATE"

Linking paragraphs work together to form a coherent whole. Add links to clarify their relationships within a cluster or section. Key words and transitional expressions (see 7d) identify connections between paragraphs just as they do between sentences. Specific sentences and paragraphs also can connect sections in a paper—supplying previews, bridges, and summaries.

STRATEGY   Link paragraphs to guide readers.

- Announce your purpose to help readers anticipate your reasoning.
- Provide a **boundary statement**—a sentence beginning one paragraph but acting as a bridge from the paragraph before. Remind the reader of material covered earlier as you present the topic sentence.
- Add a short **planning paragraph** to help readers anticipate the arrangement of the upcoming discussion.
- Create a **signal paragraph** to alert readers to a major change in direction or the beginning of a new section.
- Use a brief **summary paragraph** to mark the end of a discussion or to review main points for readers.

Exercise 1   *(A possible rewrite appears on p. 507.)*

A. In the following paragraph, increase coherence and readability by repeating words, adding transitions, using parallel structures, and making any other changes necessary.

Heart attacks have many causes. Some heart attacks occur because a blood clot closes a coronary artery. Sometimes a mass of fatty substances (plaque) has the same effect. Heart attacks with these causes are the most frequent. A spasm in an artery may also close it and prevent blood from reaching the heart. Smoking, hypertension, and diabetes can create conditions that keep blood from reaching the heart. The blood-starved tissue may die. This will cause permanent damage to the heart's ability to pump blood. A dead portion of the heart is called a myocardial infarction.

B. Copy a paragraph from one of your own essays, scrambling the order of the sentences, and then exchange scrambled paragraphs with a fellow student. Rewrite and strengthen your partner's paragraph by putting the sentences in the most effective order and revising to increase coherence among sentences.

7

Exercise 2

For each of the following topic sentences, explain which kinds of supporting information (examples, concrete details, facts and statistics, or supporting statements) you believe would create the most effective paragraph.

1. The fall promotional campaign increased sales of our October and November issues.
2. Upgrading our computer software would result in more efficient handling of our customer accounts.
3. Increased funding would enable us to extend our after-school basketball program for preteen boys and girls.
4. Should our budget surplus be used to fund additional hours at the senior center or to assist meal-delivery programs for the homebound?

Exercise 3

A. Choose one of the following pairs of topics. Drawing on your own knowledge, develop each topic into a paragraph, using the pattern of development indicated in brackets.

1. A paragraph about finding a part-time or summer job [process] and a paragraph on an unusual or memorable person [description or narration]
2. A paragraph exploring different outlooks on the relationships of parents and children [comparison-contrast] and a paragraph providing advice about dealing with a difficulty in parent-child relationships [question and answer]
3. A paragraph identifying the differences between educational requirements, expected income, and working conditions for two jobs (such as restaurant manager and doctor, or teacher and chemical engineer) [comparison-contrast] and a paragraph exploring a common work or college problem and offering possible solutions [problem-solution]
4. A paragraph identifying the reasons some students do well (or poorly) on tests [cause-effect] and a paragraph describing a good way to study for tests [process]
5. A paragraph exploring different views people hold about taking buses and driving cars [subject-by-subject comparison] and a paragraph identifying differences between educational requirements, expected income, and working conditions for two jobs [point-by-point comparison]

B. Identify the patterns of development in the following paragraph. There may be a single dominant pattern or more than one. Explain how each pattern or combination is used.

None of the foreign geologists had ever encountered anything quite like the disaster at Lake Nyos. Our earliest hypotheses seemed to be almost as numerous as the scientific teams present. Some workers, impressed by the accounts of survivors who reported smelling rotten eggs or gunpowder and hearing explosions, were convinced that a volcanic eruption beneath the lake had released sulfurous gases. Others, including me, suspected that the gas had come from within the sediments on the lake bed. Eventually, though, geological and chemical investigations made it obvious that the lake had released carbon dioxide from within its own waters—independent apparently of any other process. Like an enormous bottle of soda water, it belched and fizzed gas from its depths.   —SAMUEL J. FREETH, "Incident at Lake Nyos"

Exercise 4

Revise the following concluding paragraph to make it more effective.

I probably have left out some of the arguments for and against gun control, though I think I have covered the main ones. The point I really want to stress most is that gun control is a difficult question. Simple proposals such as banning all handguns or getting rid of all regulations won't work. We need new ideas that balance the rights of gun owners with the right to be free from violence and crime. Though I have not explained it in detail, we probably need a program like the national registration and education system that has been recently proposed. And we certainly need to do something about the many handguns readily available to teenagers.

PART 2

Reasoning and Presenting

8 Making Language Choices

Should you use *I* or *we* to describe yourself? Should you address readers as *you*? If you use technical terms, will readers find them pompous or appropriate?

DRAFT   I'm as thrilled as a grizzly in a trout pond to offer 20 percent off.
READER'S REACTION: What's with the bear and the trout? Isn't this a discount on an oil change?

REVISED   Mill Motors appreciates loyal customers like you. Please enjoy 20 percent off your next oil change.

Style often refers to choices reflecting individual preferences—your "voice" or personal style. Here, however, it refers to preferences taken for granted by communities of readers and writers and stemming from their values, goals, and typical relationships. These preferences should help guide—but not dictate—your choices as a writer or speaker.

8a Choosing a style

Academic, public, and workplace audiences have stylistic preferences you can identify with questions like the following.

8.1

Values. Are writers expected to address values, preferences, and emotions directly or leave them in the background?
Language. What **diction**—word choices—will readers expect?
Formality. Will readers expect writing that is formal, complicated, and somewhat technical or relaxed, direct, and everyday?
Writer's stance. What pronouns, if any, do writers use to identify themselves, readers, and subject matter: *I, we, you, he, she, it, they?*
Distance. Is a writer typically distant from or personally involved with the issue, problem, or topic?

Although specific written or spoken texts may have their own variations, each major community of writers and readers has a typical approach to style.

8b Recognizing home and community language varieties

How do you talk at school, at work, at home, or in your neighborhood? Do you use language to represent yourself differently with friends, teachers,

8.2

Style in Academic, Public, and Work Communities		
	Academic	Public	Work
APPROACH	Complex, formal, or detailed analysis	Emotional, value-laden, but reasoned argument	Clear, everyday, or informal explanation
VALUES	From the discipline's knowledge base or methods	From the cause, issue, or group's area of interest	From organizational goals such as service and efficiency
LANGUAGE	Technical terms and methods of the field	Lively and emotional with few technical terms and little slang	Plain or technical terms but little vivid, figurative wording
FORMALITY	Formality supports analytical approach and values of the field	Informality reveals personal involvement with serious issues	Informality reflects or builds sense of team-work or closeness
STANCE	Observer (*he, she, it*) or participant (*I, we*)	Involved individual (*I, you*) or representative (*we, you*)	Team member (*we*) with personal concern (*I, you*)
DISTANCE	Objective and dispassionate, not personal or emotional	Personal and passionate about cause, issue, or group	Supportive, committed closeness with mutual respect

8b
lang

or bosses? Every speaker of English uses a particular variety of the language shaped by region, culture, exposure to other languages, and home community. Where they're used, these varieties seem natural. In most academic, business, and broad public settings, however, variations aren't seen as acceptable but as "errors" or sloppiness.

HOME VARIETY   Unless **if** RayCorp ordered the resistors, the shipment was sent out **on** accident.

> READER'S REACTION: **Who made all these mistakes in a company memo?**

EDITED   Unless RayCorp ordered the resistors, the shipment was sent out **by** accident.

Except in casual, personal situations, writers substitute more general standards for their regional, cultural, and home language varieties. Readers, even in a local area, expect most writing to conform to general standards, partly because it can readily move to other settings. Becoming a flexible writer means developing awareness of differences between the habits of your own community and the expectations of more general communities of readers and writers.

8.3

1 Learn to see dialect variations as "rules"

Every major language is spoken in a variety of ways called **dialects**. English has dozens of dialects that vary between countries (like England and the United States) and between regions or specific places (like Tuscaloosa, Alabama, and Bar Harbor, Maine). Dialects can also vary by culture, ethnicity, and ancestry. Cuban and Puerto Rican Americans in New York City not only speak different dialects, but their dialects may vary between the Bronx and Brooklyn.

What counts for a "rule" in one dialect may break a rule in another. This is how all language works—the rules are simply structures and conventions that people within a group agree, unconsciously, to use in their speech. Pronouncing *pen* to rhyme with *hen* is a rule of Northern speech, but much of the South rhymes it with *tin*. Each group follows the *rules* of its own community. To break them is to be an outsider.

**8c
lang**

2 Understand "standard" English as a function of power and prestige

If every community has its own language rules, then who's to say why the so-called standard language should be "better"? Why *should* it be any more correct to say "There isn't anyone who can tell me anything" than to say "Ain't no body gon' tell me nuffin'"?

Around the world, languages have a prestige dialect considered more "correct" or "proper" than other dialects. How this dialect came to be preferred is almost always a matter of historical, political, and social forces. If your home dialect differs from this standard, you may be unfairly stereotyped or discriminated against by those in positions of power. Even unbiased people may not listen to you because they can't: they aren't part of your dialect group. Whether or not society ever accepts more language varieties, people without power will stay powerless if they can't communicate in the language of the powerful. But if they can gain positions of power, maybe they can help change public views of language.

3 Distinguish accents from written variations

While Americans don't usually mind differences in leaders' *accents*, people might balk at a president who said, "Them senators ain't ready for this-here veto." In writing, the most glaring (and least forgiven) variations are *grammatical*, followed by *lexical* differences (word choice, slang, jargon). Readers may unfairly see these as signs of ignorance or laziness.

8c Meeting language expectations

To avoid stereotypes and get others to listen to your ideas, you'll need to edit home or community language variations that are not widely shared.

1 Learn how to code-shift

One way speakers and writers adjust to differing expectations is by **code-shifting**. Many people use a home or community language with friends but shift into formal language in a college essay, letter to the mayor, or company report. There they adopt a variety that works across many communities, often called standard edited American English.

To learn to shift to more formal language, consult someone from your home language community who also has good facility with standard edited American English. Ask for advice about how to edit one of your papers for readers who expect this form of English. As you work together, try to figure out this person's techniques for using several language varieties successfully.

8c
lang

2 Focus on grammatical variations

Grammatical variations in your home dialect can be tricky to notice; after all, they may not look the least bit problematic—to you. But someone who isn't a member of your dialect community will see them right away.

HOME VARIETY   Miss Brill **know** that the lovers **making** fun of her, but she **act like** she **don't** care.

EDITED   Miss Brill **knows** that the lovers **are making** fun of her, but she **acts as if** she **doesn't** care.

STRATEGY   Look for the "rules" of your home language.

On the left side of a notebook page, record examples of patterns in your home language; on the right side, note corresponding examples in standard English. Explain the differences in your own terms.

Rule in KY: The lawn needs mowed.   *Rule elsewhere: The lawn needs to be mowed.*

3 Resist hypercorrection

Worrying about language habits that aren't seen as the norm can lead you to **hypercorrection**—unconsciously creating new errors by guessing that a construction is wrong and ironically substituting an error.

8.4

HYPERCORRECTED   Stuart gave the petitions to Mary and **I**.

EDITED   Stuart gave the petitions to Mary and **me**.

Similarly, if you try too hard to be formal and sophisticated, you may end up writing tangled prose that frustrates readers.

CONVOLUTED   That the girl walks away, and the showing of the parrot to the restaurant owner who, having closed shop, will not let her inside, is indicative of that which characterizes the novel, i.e., denial and deception.

EDITED   The central theme of denial and deception is illustrated when the girl tries to show the parrot to the restaurant owner and is turned away.

8c
lang

STRATEGY   Mark possible errors—then check.

When you feel unsure about your writing, circle the words or put a star in the margin. Then check the rule, or ask for advice. List any cases of hyper-correction you (or a reader) note; explain them in your own words.

Exercise 1

Briefly describe any features of your own home or community language that you're aware of in your speech or writing habits. What kinds of features are they: words? accent? grammar? What are their sources? Have you ever felt stereotyped or discriminated against because of your language or felt awkward in a situation in which your speech differed from that of others? Is there disagreement within your own community about what's correct? How do you feel about the issue of language authority? Do you want to hold on to your community language? Or do you want to get rid of all traces of that language? If you did, how do you think people in your home community would respond?

Exercise 2   *(An edited version appears on p. 507.)*

Consider the following excerpt from *Their Eyes Were Watching God*, a novel by the African American author Zora Neale Hurston. This conversation between two characters, Phoeby Watson and Janie Stark, represents the language variety used in the characters' home and community and is therefore the most expressive way for them to relate to each other.

[Phoeby] found [Janie] sitting on the steps of the back porch with the lamps all filled and the chimneys cleaned.
"Hello, Janie, how you comin'?"
"Aw, pretty good, Ah'm tryin' to soak some uh de tiredness and de dirt outa mah feet." She laughed a little.
"Ah see you is. Gal, you sho looks *good*. You looks like youse yo' own daughter." They both laughed. "Even wid dem overhalls on, you shows yo' womanhood."

"G'wan! G'wan! You must think Ah brought yuh somethin'.
When Ah ain't brought home a thing but mahself."
"Dat's a gracious plenty. Yo' friends wouldn't want nothin' better."
—Zora Neal Hurston, *Their Eyes Were Watching God*

Edit the passage to make it conform to standard written English. Now
reflect on the consequences of your changes. Has anything been lost
from the passage? Has anything been gained through editing? How appropriate are the changes?

9   Reasoning Critically

What convinces people to accept your conclusions, to share your view,
to follow your recommendations, or to trust your explanations? An important
factor is your **critical reasoning** or **critical thinking**: the careful, logical, in-
sightful thought your writing (or speaking) embodies.

WRITER 1   Foreign language classes are a waste of money. Anybody with a
brain knows that all our kids need is English.

> **READER'S REACTION: Don't children need language skills for business or
> travel—or for talking with family or others who don't speak English?
> And why attack people without giving any reasons or evidence?**

WRITER 2   Although foreign language requirements motivate some students,
others are discouraged by required courses. For example, a survey
of recent graduates showed . . .

> **READER'S REACTION: I'm not sure about this, but the writer notes several
> views and sounds reasonable. Let's see the evidence.**

Writer 1 opens with an opinion—and then simply restates it while at-
tacking others. In contrast, Writer 2 begins to reason—presenting a point of
view, recognizing other views, providing reasons and evidence. When you
write or speak, the quality of your thinking contributes to your **persona**, the
representation of yourself that you create for an audience. Do you present
yourself as thoughtful, informed, fair—hence persuasive? Or do you seem
illogical, careless, imprecise, or uninterested in other views?

9a Recognizing critical reasoning

Critical reasoning, a process of thinking through a problem, asking a question, or explaining, has four major characteristics.

- Reaches logical or reasonable conclusions supported by evidence
- Questions assumptions and tries to see differing outlooks
- Draws on precise information and clearly defined ideas
- Desires to go beyond the superficial to reach fresh insights

Good critical thinking means that you search for better evidence, consider alternatives, and check your logic to confirm, modify, or even reverse your conclusion. (See also Chapter 13.)

STRATEGY | **Use insights of others to improve your reasoning.**

- Use face-to-face or electronic discussions (see 10b–c) to identify issues, conclusions, evidence, and possible objections to your view.
- Put your tentative thoughts on paper, and then read what others say in order to identify gaps in your evidence or logic.
- Ask others to read your drafts critically and to identify reasonable objections so you can address them as you revise.
- Put your work aside for a while; then read it as your readers might. Note any gaps that undermine clarity, persuasiveness, or credibility.

9b Building a chain of reasoning

Critical thinking works toward a **chain of reasoning**, the path you take in linking observations, interpretations, conclusions, and evidence as you explore an academic topic, recommend a change at work, or urge people to take a stand. Some links in your chain may supply *information*: examples, facts, details, data. Others may offer *ideas*: reasons, comments by authorities, other views, analysis, logical argument. (See 13c.)

1 Reach conclusions

The important end point of a chain of reasoning—your **main conclusion**—is likely to be stated in an argumentative or academic thesis (see 3b-2). You may even offer multiple conclusions, such as adding workstations *and* upgrading software to track inventory.

Critical Reasoning in Academic, Public, and Work Communities

	Academic	Public	Work
GOAL	Analysis of text, phenomenon, or creative work to interpret, explain, or offer insights	Participation in democratic processes to contribute, inform, or persuade	Analysis of problems to supply information and propose solutions
REASONING PROCESS	Detailed reasoning, often explained at length, with tight logic leading to conclusions	Plausible reasoning, not ranting, focused on supporting own point of view	Accurate analysis of problem or need with clear explanation of solution
SPECIAL INTERESTS	Crucial citations of others as well as insights beyond common knowledge	Shared values and goals, often local, that support a cause or policy	Sharp focus on task, problem, or goal that promotes organization
EVIDENCE	Specific references to detailed evidence, gathered and presented to support conclusions	Relevant evidence, often local or interest-oriented, to support claims and substantiate probabilities	Sufficient evidence to show the importance of the problem and to justify an appropriate solution
VIEWPOINT	Balanced treatment recognizing and explaining other views	Fair recognition of other views, interests, and goals	Awareness of alternatives and likely results of actions

9b
reason

STRATEGY   Focus on your conclusions.

- List all your conclusions (interpretations, opinions, and so on). Use an outline, colored highlighters, a cluster or tree diagram, or two columns to identify and relate main and supporting conclusions.
- Review your conclusions. Do others come to mind? Are any important ones missing? Do you need to develop them?
- Think as readers might. Will they see any assertions as interpretations or judgments? Will they expect—and accept—your conclusions?

2 Provide supporting information

A chain of reasoning needs both information and inferences. **Information** includes facts of all kinds—examples, data, details, quotations—that you present as reliable, confirmable, or generally undisputed. Information turns into **evidence** when it's used to persuade a reader that an idea is reasonable. **Inferences** or **generalizations**, often stated in a thesis (see 3b), are your conclusions based on and supported by information.

Review your work to make sure you have distinguished between information and inference.

- List the key facts about your subject. Which will readers see as undisputed? Which can you confirm with observation or reliable sources? If facts are disputed, what reasons support your presentation?
- Next list your inferences. Which reflect your understanding? Which do the facts imply? Which *might* happen as a result of the facts?

3 Assess evidence and reasoning

Readers expect you to select evidence carefully and to link it reasonably with assertions—that is, to proceed logically. (See also 13c and 13e.) Ask yourself questions to evaluate evidence as you read and write.

- How *abundant* is the evidence? Is it *sufficient* to support your claim?
- Does it *directly* support the claim?
- How *relevant*, *accurate*, and *well documented* is the evidence?

Proceeding logically is complicated when evidence persuades one audience but not another. Consider, for example, how two citizen groups might respond to a proposed greenway between parks in two neighborhoods, one in economically depressed Coolidge and the other in wealthy Lake Stearns. Starting from the assumption that the generally law-abiding residents of Coolidge are deprived of shopping and services that have left the area because of a high crime rate, the Coolidge Consortium logically supports the greenway because it will give residents access to recreation and shopping in Lake Stearns. In contrast, starting from the assumption that the balance of a peaceful, low-crime neighborhood can easily be upset, a Lake Stearns group argues logically that, although most Coolidge residents are law-abiding, the greenway will draw habitual criminals who will undermine the quality of life in both neighborhoods. Each side reasons logically, but each starts with different assumptions and arrives at different conclusions. (See also 13e.)

STRATEGY   Evaluate your assumptions.

Ask questions like these in order to identify and evaluate your assumptions.

- How do I view the groups of people on each side of this issue?
- What will my readers want in a plan that addresses this problem?
- What do specialists in the field see as questions worth investigating?
- What might my peers suggest about my answers to these questions?

4 Review your assumptions

Some of your assumptions and values are easy to identify, but others are unspoken. After hearing the talk at work about efficiency, you might think your readers there want only to cut costs. But saving jobs and offering a quality product are also goals. The success of your reasoning may depend on how closely your assumptions match those of your audience.

- List your assertions that identify cause-effect links, classify, compare, connect generalizations and examples, or define (see 7f). Delete or rethink any that are weak or possibly illogical (see 13e).
- To spot weak reasoning, imagine a skeptical reader's reactions.

9c
reason

WEAK   Violence in schools is rising because of increased violence in movies and on TV.

READER'S REACTION: **Is this true? My kids watch TV, but they aren't more violent than I was as a kid when TV was far less violent.**

9c Representing your reasoning

How you present yourself and your reasoning to readers can do much to shape their willingness to accept your reasoning.

1 Be well informed

Issues, ideas, and insights are embedded in the social, occupational, historical, or disciplinary contexts around a topic. (See also 13b–c.) List what you know about your topic and its context. Note key areas, given your purpose. Then define what's unclear and strategize about how to fill the gaps.

2 Include readers' perspectives and likely reactions

If you fail to acknowledge other views, contrary arguments, conflicting evidence, or different solutions, your readers may find your presentation one-sided and question your credibility. By anticipating such reactions, even in a thesis (see 3b), you complete your chain of reasoning and build readers' confidence in your conclusions. (See 13c.)

3 Be balanced and reasonable

Emotional language may be just right for urging public action. The same language might irritate, even offend, coworkers or academic readers expecting critical analysis. As you pick the words and tone to represent your thinking, you create an image of yourself—a **persona**—whose qualities may make readers trust you, dislike you, or find your views rash. (See also 10a-3.)

4 Assess the appropriateness of strong bias

Writing effectively means knowing when to be cool and logical and when to show emotion. At work, bias is expected when you represent an organization but not when you write objective reports. In public, your devotion to a cause generally will be accepted as such, but your academic writing should favor unimpassioned reasoning. (See 8a.)

Exercise 1

Locate a document whose success or failure depends on the quality of its reasoning: a proposal, a position paper, an editorial, an academic article, or a memo on an important issue. Read it carefully, and identify its conclusions and the main kinds of evidence it presents. Next, try to identify any assumptions the writer makes that differ considerably from yours or those of another possible audience. Finally, use the questions posed in 9b-3 to assess the quality of the evidence.

Exercise 2

Locate an essay, article, or report on a controversial topic or issue, and analyze the ways in which the writer succeeds in or fails to convincingly represent his or her reasoning. Begin by deciding what community or communities of readers the author is addressing. Base your judgments on the presentation's appropriateness for particular readers, and on its purpose. Use the following questions to guide your analysis:

1. Does the writer appear well informed?
2. Does the writer acknowledge other perspectives?
3. Does the writer seem to respect his or her audience?
4. Is the presentation balanced and reasonable?
5. Does the writer anticipate readers' reactions?
6. Is the writer's bias appropriate for the occasion?

Exercise 3

A. Locate a Web site where two or more people discuss the same topic, preferably directly addressing each others' reasoning: an online discussion, a newspaper opinion page with contrasting editorials, a magazine article or interview, or records of a debate. Briefly summarize the position of each participant, and then discuss how each addresses or criticizes flaws or gaps in the reasoning of the other, either directly or by implication.

B. Working with a group in class or online, begin discussion by briefly stating your conclusions on an issue and giving the most important evidence for them. Pass this statement on, asking the next person to add other conclusions, evidence, objections, and counterarguments. Have the last person summarize conclusions, evidence, and objections and then circulate the original document and the summary to the rest of the group. Discuss how your group's reasoning was changed by the serial dialogue.

10 Writing in Online Communities

Technology has many sounds—hums, pings, whirs, and clicks. However, the most important sound is still that of your own personal or professional "voice" as you represent yourself in electronic communities.

TOO CASUAL   Hiya, Prof.! Sorry I slept late and missed your test. I really, really hope I can do the makeup this week. —Drake
READER'S REACTION: **Sounds like a goof-off to me.**

REVISED   Prof. Jones: Unfortunately, I missed the test today in Physics 130. Is it possible for me to do a makeup this week at your convenience? —Drake Long

Some online environments are like libraries: you visit to read and retrieve materials. But many others are interactive, involving exchanges among community members as you email, chat, read, and reply to messages from an electronic list, post a message in a forum, or respond to a blog—a "Web log." Each online community has accepted standards for group members, language and customs to help you represent yourself appropriately.

10a Online expectations

Expectations of participants may be as specific as the shared interest uniting an online community. A brief period of "lurking" (reading without participating) is a good way to discover who participates, what rules govern participation, and whether your expectations match those of the community.

1 Identify the type of online community

The **domain name** in an electronic address identifies an organization or other entity on the Internet, indicating the origin of material you access. For instance, the National Association for the Advancement of Colored People maintains the domain name *naacp.org*, which follows *www* in its Web site address and @ in its email addresses. Some suffixes also identify material from other countries (such as *.ca* for Canada, *.no* for Norway).

10b
email

COMMON DOMAIN SUFFIXES IN INTERNET ADDRESSES		
.com commercial sites	.edu	educational groups
.gov governmental sites	.net	network sites
.org nonprofit organizations		

2 Use netiquette as a guide to community standards

10.1

Netiquette defines the behavior and politeness expected online. It's your responsibility to observe the commonsense guidelines that apply across nearly all Internet communities and to learn the standards of the specific group that you want to address.

- **Think before you act.** Once sent or posted, a message is open to friends, relatives, instructors, or employers.
- **Learn the norms.** Read a site's FAQ (frequently asked questions) page, and lurk before you participate.
- **Respect a group's interests.** Avoid personal attacks ("flames"), off-topic messages, hoaxes, inappropriate jokes, spamming (sending unsolicited email to groups), irrelevant replies, and tedious copies of previous messages. When a topic is not of general interest, request or supply responses "off list," directing them to the recipient's email address rather than the list address.
- **Use conventional grammar and usage.** Avoid creating a sloppy persona with careless wording or a rude one with ALL CAPS.
- **Remember the Golden Rule of netiquette.** Real people receive your email or access your Web site. Be considerate of them.

10b Email conventions

Flexible and fast, email can create so much information that others may be irritated if you ignore conventions or lack purpose (see 3a).

1 Use the elements and functions of email

Online readers expect conventional elements in messages.

- **From.** State your identity in this line. Your email program may automatically show your address or your screen name.
- **Sent.** The date and time you send can help you track correspondence.
- **To.** Record the names of primary recipients. For copies sent to others, use the lines for **Cc:** (carbon copy) and **Bcc:** (blind carbon copy, sent without the knowledge of the main recipients).
- **Subject.** Use a short, clear subject line, like a news headline. If you're replying or forwarding from another message, keep this line current.
- **Message body.** Be concise. In a reply, clarify your topic, but follow the community's convention about including previous messages.
- **Signature or sig file.** Sign email for a reader's benefit. If you use a sig file to add your full name and contact details, consider your credibility and your readers before adding clever sayings, lyrics, or jokes.
- **Reply and reply-all.** Select "Reply" to answer the sender and "Reply-All" to include everyone who got the original. To avoid posting a personal note, check the "To:" and "Cc:" lines before hitting "Send."
- **Forward.** Use discretion if you send messages on to others.
- **Attach.** If you attach files, spreadsheets, or video clips, remember that not all recipients will be able to open these documents.

**10b
email**

2 Tailor your messages to the community

Individual email is like a letter; you specify who receives your message. List-based email, like contributions to printed newsletters, goes to all the list's subscribers. Individual mail isn't necessarily more "personal" or list mail more "professional." Recipients may expect different levels of formality, but most appreciate specificity, relevance, and brevity.

- Identify your *most essential* point. Present it early and briefly.
- Clarify what you want readers to do or think about as they respond.
- Break long blocks of text into short, readable paragraphs. Separate paragraphs with a blank line; consider adding headings.
- Replace detailed explanations with sources or an attached file.
- Reply economically, repeating only key material from prior messages. Consider how you're adding to what's come before.

Casual exchanges may use shortcuts inappropriate in professional or academic writing. Tilt your head to the left to see how **emoticons** (*emotion +* icon) add a jolt of feeling through faces drawn with keyboard characters.

:-) grin :-(frown ;-) wink 8-0 bug-eyed surprise

Abbreviations and **acronyms** (pronounceable abbreviations for common phrases) may also speed up casual communication. (See 58a-2.)

BTW by the way F2F face-to-face FYI for your information

10c Online communities

To join an **electronic mailing list** or **newsgroup**, email the host service. You'll then automatically receive all posted messages—individually or grouped in the day's "digest"—at your email address. Popular in the academic community, these lists allow private, focused discussion by a group of subscribers. In contrast, you access a **newsgroup** directly, and messages are immediately posted for anyone to read. These popular resources for public and civic groups generally welcome participants.

10d
Web

Web-based forums allow access to sites where users converse about shared interests. Some are moderated, many ask you to set up a user name and password, and a few charge fees. Forum readers may expect informal language, emoticons, acronyms, and citation of prior material for context. Interactive **blogs** (for "Web logs") are sites where owners post and encourage responses to information, reflections, and news. A **wiki** is an electronic information source that allows users to add or modify information.

Real-time discussion takes place instantly; words appear on each participant's screen as they are typed. The most popular real-time communities are **chat rooms**, informal conversations hosted by private Internet services or available via the Internet Relay Chat (IRC) network. The academic community often uses a **MUD**, or multi-user domain, which requires a series of commands for communication in a carefully described text environment. Users may adopt characters ("avatars") as they interact. Similarly, a **MOO**, a Multi-User Domain Object Oriented, allows participants to communicate in real time in a shared Internet space where they can also manipulate objects. More simply, **instant messaging** allows immediate, simultaneous electronic conversation—and, like other online exchanges, requires that you consider how to represent yourself and that you respect conventions expected by your readers.

10.2

10d Writing for the World Wide Web

Web pages offer many different types of writing.

TYPES OF WEB SITES

- **Personal home pages** sponsored by individuals to present personal, family, hobby, or special-interest news
- **Commercial sites** sponsored by corporations, businesses, or other enterprises to promote shopping or to explain products and services
- **Educational sites** sponsored by schools, colleges, libraries, scholarly journals, and other groups to supply access to resources or information
- **News or entertainment sites** sponsored by newspapers, magazines, and other media to supply breaking news or information archives
- **Search engines** dedicated to indexing Web pages for users

1 Design your Web page for readers

When building a Web page, first consider its format and purpose. Is it a class project on coral reef preservation, designed as a resource for those with similar interests? Is it an "online business card" limited to background and contact listings? Is it an autobiography for your friends and family?

Before you begin building, search for sites with similar purposes. Analyze how they work, listing what you like or dislike. Politely contact authors of notable pages for advice. Ask peers or colleagues for ideas, too.

Then consider how you want to present yourself. How will you establish your credibility? How will you react if an outsider comments on a site designed for your fellow students? Will you be comfortable if an employer or instructor visits your personal site? What might readers want to find? How are they likely to navigate? How will they expect its pages to relate? Finally, name your site carefully because search engines index words in the title and text. When your site is ready, visit the home pages of major search engines to register it so people can find your work.

10e
plag

2 Organize and manage your site

Maintain your site so that you engage readers and encourage visits.

- **Keep content key.** Web users want information, not "cool" graphics. Don't overcrowd pages; allow ample "white space." When appropriate, list information. Use visuals to reinforce your topic, not fill space.
- **Stay updated, not outdated.** Publish when ready; update as needed.
- **Check your links.** Regularly test any links to supporting documents, data, or related sites to make sure they still work.
- **Consider visitors.** Use multiple platforms and browsers to test user interfaces. Include contact details, preferably an automatic email link.

10e Avoiding plagiarism and behaving ethically online

The Internet gives you access to nearly limitless texts, images, music, streaming video, and other media, but you need to be careful to avoid plagiarism and to behave ethically online. Because you can easily download such material to your own computer—and then to CDs or disks—it's tempting to see all of it as yours, free for the asking. But it's not. In fact, it's not always clear whether online material is copyrighted and thus whether you're doing anything wrong when you copy or distribute it. Downloading songs, stories, cartoons, or other materials may violate federal copyright laws and result in fines (or worse) if you're caught. Avoid plagiarism and practices that are illegal or unethical or that can create suspicion or provoke investigation. (See also Chapter 22.)

10.3

Online communication also requires that you work ethically and professionally. When you use a school email account—even if you access it away from campus—you are responsible for abiding by the institution's policies and regulations. You are also obligated by the terms of a public Internet service provider's contract. If you use your employer's Internet account, your employer may monitor what sites you access, and you probably have no legal expectation of privacy for anything you write or post. You may also be accountable under local, state, federal, or international law.

Aside from possible institutional or legal restrictions and penalties, your own credibility as a writer rests on your careful use of online materials. Evaluate your sources to assure their credibility in your community, identify and credit what you use, and request permission when needed to copy images, quote from postings, or use similar materials. (See also Chapter 23.)

11a
design

11 Designing Documents

How can you prepare a report, a portfolio, or a visual aid that's clear and easy to read? How can you create a memorable document that engages readers and represents you as an effective writer or speaker? The answers often lie in document design—how you present your text on the page and integrate visual aids.

11a Goals of document design

Here's how document design can help you convey ideas, information, and conclusions effectively.

- Emphasize key points or ideas.
- Help readers readily locate and visualize information.
- Let readers know you've considered their needs.
- Signal readers about your knowledge and perspective.
- Create a positive, persuasive image of you (a persona).

For well-designed documents, consider both how the printed page (or computer screen) looks and how readers process information. If a document is crowded or hard to understand, a reader may not bother to read it. If it's easy to follow, with clear headings, graphics, and other design elements, readers will respond positively. Visual elements include layout, space, headings, type, and cues provided by letters or numbers on a page as well as any visual aid (such as a photo, chart, or graph).

11b Planning a design

Readers need different things from documents. The same reader approaches an essay about air pollution quite differently from a set of instructions concerning the operation of a chain saw. Equally true is the fact that two people might approach either document differently. An engineer for a chemical plant that is working to comply with EPA guidelines will read the essay about pollution very differently from a homeowner who lives downwind from the plant.

**11b
design**

1 Formulate the elements of your plan

Your design plan should answer these questions.

- What format or document type will I use?
- What medium will I use (print, electronic, Web, multimedia)?
- How will I divide the document into sections and make the organization visible to readers (table of contents, headings, color, paper choice, dividers, artwork)?
- What typeface and type size will I use?
- How will I highlight important information and ideas (type treatment, underlining, color, boxes, visual aids, marginal comments)?
- How will I use visual aids, and which kind will I employ (graphs, tables, charts, photographs, drawings, video)?

11.1

2 Prepare a design document

A design document is a statement of your plan for creating a report, Web site, article, or other document. If your project takes more than a few pages and includes a variety of design elements, take a few minutes to create a plan.

1. Begin your design document by writing down the purpose and audience for your text. State the purpose for each of the major design decisions you have made, including format, layout, sections, type, visuals, medium, and color. Indicate the main ideas, information, and insights you wish readers to take with them after reading your document.
2. Outline the content of your paper (informally), indicating where you will place major design elements such as headings, visuals, or columns.

Annotate your outline, indicating where you intend readers' attention to be focused and what reactions you want them to have. Your concern here should be with the **readability** (ease of reading) and **usability** (usefulness) of your document.

3. Conclude with a list of the resources you need to produce your document, such as software, paper, fresh cartridges for a printer, photographs, graphics, and clip art.

11c
design

11c Laying out your document

Layout is the arrangement of words, sentences, headings, lists, tables, graphs, and pictures on a page or computer screen.

11.2

1 Use visual cues

To increase readability, supply visual cues but avoid using too many elements. Typographic devices such as **boldface**, *italics*, shading, boxes, and divider lines signal distinctions; they emphasize items and parts. Use *italics*, **boldface**, CAPITALS, and exclamation marks (!!) sparingly to create emphasis. Limit underlines (especially online where links are underlined).

Connotations of colors may vary with the context and reader.

COLOR	ENGINEERING	MEDICINE	FINANCE
blue	cold/water	death/not oxygenated	reliable/corporate
red	danger	healthy/oxygenated	loss
green	safe/environmental	infection	profit

Use color to communicate rather than decorate.

- Accomplish specific goals (such as warning or caution).
- Prioritize and order; readers go to bright colors first.
- Symbolize, based on your knowledge of your readers.
- Identify a recurring theme, or connect a sequence.
- Show a pattern or relationship in a chart or graph.
- Code symbols or sections to simplify finding information.

2 Arrange information effectively

Use **white space**, open space not filled by other design elements, to organize text into chunks and guide the reader's eye. Consider the spaces around graphics and between letters, words, lines, or paragraphs. Note the margins (usually one inch to an inch and a half at the top, bottom, and sides). Try **lists** to break up dense text, emphasize points, itemize information, and group items, making it easy for readers to absorb ideas quickly. Consider highlighting items with bullets or numbers.

Headings, brief phrases that forecast or announce upcoming content, often are larger and darker than the rest of the text. Use them to move readers along so they see the organization and quickly find information.

* Use a consistent font and style for headings.
* Allow white space between headings and text.
* Position your headings consistently (for example, centering first-level headings and beginning second-level headings at the left margin).
* Focus headings for your specific content, task, or reader: *Deducting Student Loan Interest* rather than *Student Loans*.
* Make comparable headings parallel in structure (see 41a).
* Avoid clutter by using only the headings you need.

Depending on the audience you're addressing and the document you're writing, readers may expect specific features. Academic papers often use MLA or APA conventions (see Chapters 25–26). Newsletters, Web sites, letters, memos, and other documents all follow their own visual conventions (see pp. 75–76, 119, 125, and 127–29 for examples). Images prepared for presentations, often using software such as *PowerPoint*, require special attention to size, color, and clarity so that your listeners can easily see what's projected. (See 12c-3.)

11d design

11d Using type

Take judicious advantage of the fonts, typefaces, and type sizes available to highlight, organize, or connect text elements. A few—two or three fonts in a document—are generally better than too many.

Type size and weight. Select a readable typeface or font that enhances content. Type smaller than 8 points is hard to read; both 10- and 12-point type are easy to read. The latter is most common in academic texts. The larger the type, the more important the ideas will seem, but save sizes above 12 point for special purposes and documents, such as overhead transparencies.

8 point   10 point   12 point   16 point

Because some fonts have thicker or wider letters, you can use type weight to highlight without changing type style (**boldface**, *italics*, shadow).

Typefaces. Serif typefaces have little "feet" or small strokes at the end of each letterform. Sans serif typefaces lack them.

N serif   **N sans serif**

Readers tend to find serif typefaces easier to read in long documents but sans serif effective in titles, headings, labels, and onscreen material. Serif typefaces include Times New Roman, Courier, Garamond, and **Century Schoolbook**. Sans serif typefaces include Arial, **Impact**, and Futura.

Fonts. Use decorative fonts and symbols with discretion. *Mistral*, **Sixpack**, **Cooper Black**, or *Siglight* can add engaging or emotional touches to brochures, invitations, or posters. Symbol fonts (such as those in Zapf Dingbats, Monotype Sorts, or Wingdings) can direct a reader's attention, emphasize a point, identify comparable items, or add simple graphic flourishes. Your software may supply symbols and icons like these.

11e
design

11e Using visuals

Sometimes words aren't as efficient in making a point as tables, graphs, charts, photographs, maps, and drawings. Memorable visuals entice readers, are absorbed quickly, and communicate what words cannot.

1 Use tables, graphs, and charts to organize information

Tables concisely present information—usually text or numbers in columns and rows (see Table 1). **Graphs** rely on two labeled axes (vertical and horizontal) using **lines** (see Fig. 1) or **bars** (see Fig. 2) to compare items or

	Table 1 Web Site Services, 2005 (percentages, by sector)				
	PUBLIC UNIVERSITY	PRIVATE UNIVERSITY	PUBLIC 4-YR. COLLEGE	PRIVATE 4-YR. COLLEGE	COMMUNITY COLLEGE
Undergraduate Application	99	90	95	96	96
ePortfolio	32	27	37	28	10
Journals & Reference	92	96	92	94	84
Course Reserves	78	81	66	67	35
Course Registration	97	94	97	80	97
Online Course	95	67	88	54	94
E-Commerce Capacity	92	81	87	57	85

Source: "The Campus Computing Project," www.campuscomputing.net

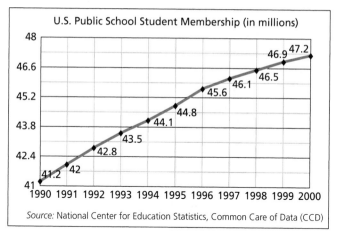

Fig. 1 Number of students enrolled in public schools.
Source: <http://nces.ed.gov>.

relate variables. **Pie charts** show percentages of a whole (see Fig. 3 on p. 74). Title, number, and label tables as such in your text; number and label all other graphics as figures, and supply a brief caption. In MLA style, abbreviate a label (Fig. 1); in APA style, spell it out (Figure 1).

2 Use other visual devices

Drawings and diagrams can show physical features, connect parts, and illustrate spatial relationships so readers *see* what to do or how something

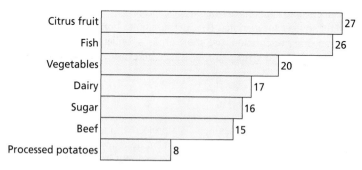

Fig. 2 US projected consumption growth, 2000–2020.
Source: <http://nationalatlas.gov/articles/agriculture/a_consumerAg.html/>.

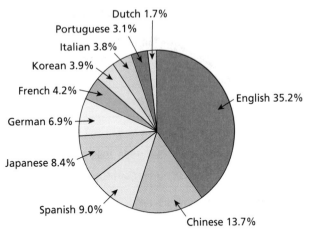

Online Language Populations
Total: 801.4 Million
(Sept. 2004)

Dutch 1.7%
Portuguese 3.1%
Italian 3.8%
Korean 3.9%
French 4.2%
German 6.9%
Japanese 8.4%
Spanish 9.0%
Chinese 13.7%
English 35.2%

Fig. 3 Online population by language group.
Source: GlobalReach, <http://global-reach.biz/globstats/index.php3>.

works. Photographs or illustrations record reality, as in newspapers and magazines. Simple drawings called "clip art," from software or the Web, are easy to paste into a document to enhance a point.

- Choose simple, appropriate visuals, not decorative filler.
- Use each visual to illustrate one main point that it clearly supports.
- Set off visuals with white space. Don't crowd them.
- Position graphics close to pertinent text. Supply verbal cues (labels, numbers, and captions) to link visuals and text.
- Credit sources for graphics. (Get permission to borrow, if needed.)
- For an oral presentation, use short phrases, bulleted points, and large type to keep your visuals simple, direct, and easy to read.

11f **Sample documents**

11.3

The following sample documents—a project with a varied layout and a Web site—show how the principles of document design work in different situations. Each document has been annotated to point out its features and layout.

Student project displaying variety in layout.

Thursday
July 8th, 2003

Volume XX
Issue 2

The Daily Moose

North America's Only Newspaper Devoted to Moose Lovers Everywhere. Twenty-Two Years and Growing.

Big Moose Comes From Small Dreams

Staff Reporter: Andrea White

Growing up, your favorite animal may have been a cat, dog, or turtle. Even as exotic as parrots, giraffes and elephants. But in areas north of Chicago and Boston, children wish for pets like deer, caribou and even moose. Moose usually occupy areas in the northern United States and Canada, finding them in southern California is quite unusual. However, traveling to Orange County, California you might see dozens, even hundreds of these winter-weather giants. Mainly Seconds, a craft/antique store in Orange County, has a display of numerous moose paraphernalia all collected by the "Moose" himself, Mike Bonk.

In 1982, Mike's first store opened and received a gift from his wife and former employees. It was a corduroy moose head with a plaque inscribed, "The Moose is Loose". This present hangs on the wall near the entrance next to painted words, *The Moose Museum*. The museum started when Mike put his personal items on display around the store. It seemed that as the store increased and prospered, his collection did also. Soon there was so much moose collectibles; it formed itself into a museum.

The Moose Museum Located at Mainly Seconds.

This museum is not like any other. Set in the back section of the store, it consists of about fifty cases and 10 aisles of various products either resembling or being moose associated. "If it's moose, it's in here" Mike said during a recent interview. And it's true (Cont. on page 2).

The Moose Museum
Cordially Invites You …

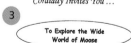

To Explore the Wide World of Moose

Come experience the Northern Wilderness in Sunny California.
New Exhibits! More Moose!

789 S. Tustin Avenue   555-9876

Warning: Moose X-ing

Travel columnist: Caroline Cesserta

My family and I always agonize about where to travel for our yearly summer vacation. This year, my daughter and I agreed on a nice mountain lodge in Colorado while my husband and other daughter sided on a tropical getaway to Mexico. To compromise, we decided to tour California starting from the Mexican border up to Oregon. One of my personal favorite spots is very unusual store I discovered when we were stopped at a rest stop and someone noticed my moose decal on the back window. (Cont. Pg. 2)

11f
design

① Uses varied typefaces and sizes for a system of headings

② Integrates photograph and text

③ Encloses highlighted text in oval-shaped "box"

④ Single-column format for lead story

⑤ Double-column format for additional text

Web site about mountain lions entices the reader with photo and buttons.

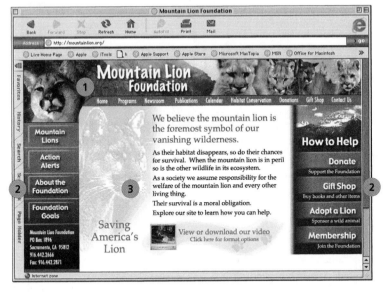

1 Picture highlights beauty of animal and calls attention to the site

2 Buttons provide site map and access to information categories and a video

3 White background makes text easy to read; ghosted profile of mountain lion emphasizes elusive nature of the animal

12 Speaking Effectively

Surveys show that people fear public speaking more than almost anything else, including losing a relative or being fired. Fear often comes from too little preparation—trying to "wing it" and hoping for the best.

SPEAKER   I can't get the computer to project the latest sales figures, but most of them are going up.

LISTENER'S REACTION: **What a disorganized waste of time—especially with our supervisor here.**

Good speakers use practice and experience to turn apprehension into energy, presenting themselves and their ideas enthusiastically and clearly. (See 14j on group, 16f on public, and 17h on committee presentations.)

12a Types of oral presentations

12c
speak

Oral presentations aren't limited to formal occasions when someone stands at a lectern on a stage to deliver a polished address. You might present your portfolio to your class or sum up a project's status at work. At a town meeting, you might express your views from the audience. In such settings, listeners expect speakers to follow accepted patterns. Ask yourself questions like these.

- How long do others speak?
- How formal is the usual style?
- What evidence and what persuasive strategies do others use?

12b Transferring skills from writing to speaking

Many strategies apply to both verbal and written texts. Before you begin to worry about making an oral presentation, assess your skills and strengths as a writer.

- Apply your planning and organizing skills (see 2a and b).
- Analyze your listeners and your purpose (see 3c).
- Draft your speaking notes (see 2b and 4a).
- Write out powerful opening and key sentences (see 43b).
- Practice and revise your oral presentation (see 4a and b).
- Add well-designed visuals (see 11a and e).

12c Preparing an effective oral presentation

12.1

You can greatly improve your performance—and your confidence—if you prepare in four stages: *planning, practice, delivery, reflection.*

1 Plan ahead when you speak formally

Keep a list of information about your presentation; let it shape your plans. For example, your time limit will help you decide what details, points, and materials (such as handouts) to include. (See 3a and c.)

Speaking in Academic, Public, and Work Communities		
	Academic	Public	Work
AUDIENCE EXPECTATIONS	Explore, advance, or exchange knowledge	Support position, policy, or proposal	Advance product, service, or mission
	Develop clear topic with solid, logical evidence	Present position with compelling reasons and evidence	Present clear information on problem, task, or situation
GOALS OF ORAL EXCHANGES	Develop and exchange information or interpretations	Publicize issue, promote views or position, or reach compromise	Make decisions or solve problems to improve product or service
	Reflect on and respond to shared interests	Explore issues and options	Inform about products and services
TYPES OF INFORMAL ORAL EXCHANGES	Class, peer, or collaborative discussion	Civic exchange, board discussion, or committee discussion	Work group, client, or committee discussion
GOALS OF ORAL PRESENTATIONS	Present creative, applied, or theoretical work	Advocate position, policy, or proposal	Analyze problems and recommend solutions
	Analyze, synthesize, or interpret sources or findings	Inform group, officials, or community about issue or proposal	Promote product development, assembly, marketing, or delivery
	Engage intellectual interest of group	Motivate others to care or act	Inspire employees or customers
TYPES OF FORMAL ORAL PRESENTATIONS	Description, explanation, interpretation, or demonstration	Public statement or appeal on issue, action, or proposal	Progress report, analysis, proposal, or recommendation
	Conference panel, poster session, lecture, or address	Interviews or press statements on issue	Telephone, video, Web, and in-person presentations

12c
speak

Analyze your speaking situation. Consider where, when, and how you'll speak.

- What's the occasion? How many people will be there?
- How long is the event? How long will you speak?
- What place or space will you speak in? Where will you be?

- How will you know when to speak?
- What do you hope your presentation will accomplish?
- What will your audience expect to find out or experience?
- What do you know—or need to find out—about your topic?

Begin organizing your remarks. Group your remarks or create an informal outline.

1. *Introductory remarks*: introduce yourself and give your audience a preview of what you'll say, show, or cover.
2. *Content or substance of the presentation*: present your main ideas, illustrations, and supporting material (see 7f).
3. *Conclusion*: sum up, restate your purpose, and remind your audience of what you have shown or offered.

12c
speak

Develop your talking points. Write out your **talking points**—key phrases, words, visual cues, or other reminders to guide you as you speak.

- Jot down both your main points and signals to help you coordinate your talk: "Check time," "Show overhead."
- Use transitions (*next* or *to sum up*; see 7d) to link the parts and guide your audience: "As we've seen, the Valdez oil spill initially devastated the Alaskan shoreline. I want to turn now to its long-term impact."
- Match your style to your situation, audience, and topic.
- Estimate the time for each group of talking points. If necessary, consolidate, trim, or use a handout.
- Transfer your final talking points—content and cues—to 3" × 5" cards. Write out your first and last sentences to begin and end confidently.
- Number your cards so you always know where you are. At the top of every fifth card, estimate the time used by that point.

To involve your listeners, have them read a handout, view a slide, talk in pairs, or tackle an activity—but allow the *time* for participation.

2 Rehearse your presentation

Try to anticipate the physical conditions of your talk—body position, foot placement, breathing, eye movements. Rehearse alone first; then invite a few trusted listeners. Ask for advice on pacing, volume, body movements, transitions, and the like. Videotape or record a rehearsal to spot problems, distracting habits, or unclear points. Keep rehearsing until you know every transition, dramatic pause, and reminder to look around.

3 Deliver your presentation

Although reading a printed paper aloud is common in some fields, most audiences prefer speakers to *present* their ideas instead of *read* them. This type of **extemporaneous** or **conversational speaking** emphasizes greater interaction among the speaker, audience, and ideas.

- Use your talking points to recall what to say, not to read out loud.
- Speak loudly and clearly, projecting your voice over the audience.
- Vary pitch and cadence for emphasis; don't exaggerate emotions.
- Avoid distracting verbal habits—"um," "like," or "you know."
- Move around if you wish, but don't pace, drum on the podium, or jingle your keys.

12d
speak

Vary your eye contact so you don't favor the same person, group, or part of the room. Look directly at listeners (for only a few seconds unless you're answering a question). Glance at your visuals, but focus on your audience. Don't make them wait while you write out a transparency.

STRATEGY   Use visuals to enhance your speech.

- Prepare your visuals ahead, whether you use a chalkboard, flip chart, overhead transparency, or audiovisual projection.
- Try to rehearse with any equipment to figure out how to run it, where to stand, and how to coordinate your visuals with your remarks.
- Use a large readable font, or pass out copies of your visuals to simplify taking notes.
- If you use software such as *PowerPoint*, practice with the technology, avoid too much glitz, and always bring backup overheads.
- Let listeners read visuals for themselves. Paraphrase, note, or sum up in bulleted points what you present in detail.

4 Assess your results

Look for feedback on what you did well and what you can improve. If possible, ask someone to attend and honestly appraise your presentation. Your instructor may provide a scoring guide, evaluation sheet, or advice. Write out a self-assessment to strategize about future problems.

12d Managing speech anxiety

12.2

Like pilots with thousands of flight hours, experienced speakers have learned to control their apprehension. Giving oral presentations in college provides you with experience and confidence. These techniques can help reduce and control your anxiety.

- Write down your fears; look for strategies to overcome them.
- Before presentations, rest and eat well despite your anxiety.
- Sweaty palms and butterflies don't predict the quality of your talk.

- Take long, deep breaths to slow your heart rate, calm your nerves, and provide oxygen to your brain. Deliberately relax any tense spots.
- Focus on your ideas, not your looks or your worries.
- Move confidently to your speaking position. Face your audience before you begin; take a few seconds to organize your materials or adjust a microphone.
- Don't panic if you get lost or distracted: pause, breathe, cope.

12e Fielding questions

Presentations often end with questions—a dialogue with listeners. Anticipate what your audience might ask, plan brief answers, and remain flexible. Ask for clarification if you don't understand a question. Respond directly, not evasively. If you don't know an answer, say so, and don't make one up. Answer any hostile questions diplomatically, with "Yes," "No," or "I'm not sure," and move on.

Exercise 1

Choose a subject that you know something about and that would make a good informative presentation. First describe a purpose for conveying this information and an audience that might find it useful. Create an outline for a ten-minute oral presentation on this subject to this audience; then sketch out a series of talking points, following the advice in 12c-1, including transitions between points and an estimate of the time for each part of the presentation.

Exercise 2

A. Write down what you consider your two primary delivery difficulties (nervous gestures, filler words, or voice projection). For each, describe (1) when the difficulty usually happens (for example, during transitions or when you look at notes) and (2) something you can do to resolve this difficulty (such as pausing instead of using filler words or placing your hands on the table instead of in your pockets).

B. In a small group, compare your difficulties. Note any similar difficulties and add to your list of possible solutions for each.

PART 3

Writing for Specific Audiences

13 Persuasive Arguments

Argument can persuade a foundation to support an academic research grant, encourage a production team to alter a process at work, or convince a county airport to curtail expansion in the public community. Because value judgments, policy questions, and proposed actions seldom lend themselves to proof or absolute certainty, readers are aware of other opinions and evidence. They'll expect you to argue with good reasons, logic, evidence, and attention to other opinions before they decide to agree with you. You'll need to encourage them to share your perspective or values, convincing them that your line of reasoning—your argument—is fair and justifiable. (See also Chapter 9.)

13.1

13a Recognizing occasions for argument

Argumentative writing begins with an *issue*—a subject or situation about which opinions clearly differ. Such disagreements are common in public settings, where people with different values, cultures, and perspectives meet to address problems. Serious differences about policies, interpretations, and solutions are frequent in academic and work settings, too. Your argument develops around *your* opinion, that is, the value judgment, action, or interpretation you propose and wish your readers to endorse. Your aim initially is to answer two questions: What issue am I arguing about? What, precisely, is my opinion? To find (or more sharply focus) an issue that interests you, look for significant problems, judgments, and disagreements.

1 Identify an existing issue

Many arguments you construct will address existing issues. Some, such as gun control or global warming, will have broad relevance. Others will concern a specific audience, for example, proposals for a new campus drinking policy or limitations on business and residential development. Issues of this sort come to you partly formed; other people have already identified the dimensions of disagreement, gathered supporting ideas and information, and taken stances, pro and con. You need to focus more sharply, looking for significant problems, judgments, and disagreements.

13a
arg

STRATEGY List issues and get involved.

- **List current issues.** Make a list of disagreements you encounter in various settings—academic, public, and work—to help you focus your own response to the issues.
- **Read.** Turn to news and opinion magazines (such as *The Nation* or *National Review*); editorials in local and national newspapers (available in libraries or online); or periodical databases indexing a wide range of articles on civic, professional, academic, and business controversies.
- **Interview.** Talk with people about issues that inspire strong opinions.
- **Write.** For each possible issue, write a one- or two-sentence summary of at least two different opinions. Look for a focused subject, even a limited or local issue such as parking policies or garbage problems.

2 Recognize a potential issue

When you focus on a problem others have not identified, offer an opinion or evaluation likely to be controversial, or propose a change in a long-agreed-upon policy, you address a potential issue.

STRATEGY Question and evaluate.

Use these techniques to recognize potential issues.

- **Review the consequences.** Question and evaluate the consequences of policies or actions.
- **Question the "taken-for-granted."** Challenge commonly held beliefs or routine policies; explore contrasting perspectives or alternative approaches.
- **Offer an evaluation.** When you state a judgment about the quality of a performance, policy, work of art, or product, you create an issue, at least to the extent that you are trying to convince others to share your opinion and are not simply making a personal statement about your preferences.

3 Assess the issue

A problem is not automatically an issue, nor is every opinion worth arguing about. Drunk driving, for example, is certainly a problem but is not in itself an issue. Anyone advocating drunk driving would seem foolish, but reasonable people do disagree about how to discourage it.

Sometimes you'll identify an intriguing topic but need to investigate it to decide whether it's an arguable issue. For example, when Paul Pusateri heard about fast food restaurants being sued for causing obesity, he thought

Issues in Academic, Public, and Work Communities		
	Academic	**Public**	**Work**
GENERAL	Standardized testing Affirmative action in college admissions	Genetically altered foods Violence and sex on television	Child care at work Ethnically targeted marketing
LOCAL	Housing regulations at Nontanko River State University	A local crusade against a television series	Discipline policies at Abtech's Child-Care Center

that the complainants had no case. After doing a bit of research, however, he discovered a debatable issue: Are fast food restaurants at least partly responsible for growing rates of obesity? Some people argue that consumers are responsible when they choose to eat fattening foods. Others argue that the practices of fast food chains encourage unhealthy diets, thus affecting the lives of millions of people.

13b
arg

STRATEGY   Evaluate the issue.

Ask yourself these questions to evaluate the issue.

- Is the issue clearly debatable? Are there two or more reasonable contrasting opinions? Is there evidence to back opinion?
- Is the issue more than individual preference or personal taste? Reasoning generally can't change likes and dislikes.
- Does the issue avoid deeply held assumptions that cannot be argued? Social and political issues are arguable unless they rest on systems of belief such as religion.

13b Developing your stance

A good argument is positive: you try to persuade people to accept your opinion, but you don't attack them for having another point of view. To do this, you need a clear idea of your own opinion and the reasons why you hold it, and you need to anticipate readers' arguments. (See 9b.)

STRATEGY   Explore your stance.

- **Write informally** about an issue. Do you feel scornful, fearful, indignant, or outraged? Why?
- **List** key elements of your issue, summarizing your responses.
- **Add** facts, examples, and ideas that support your reactions.
- **Think about** other perspectives. Read, talk, and listen. Make a preliminary research plan, or test your views on friends or online.

1 Focus on your purpose

Opinions can take three different forms. Each commits you to a different purpose for argument.

Value judgment. Do you want to argue that some activity, policy, belief, performance, book, or situation is good or bad, healthful or harmful, effective or ineffective, desirable or undesirable?

> College students who eat regularly at fast food restaurants may invite a lifetime of health problems.

Policy. Do you want readers to accept or follow a course of action?

> The Caraway College Health Services Center should initiate an extensive campaign to educate students about the possible long-term consequences of eating unhealthy fast food.

Interpretation. Do you want readers to agree that one point of view about a subject is better or weaker than alternatives?

13b
arg

> Although customers are responsible for placing their fast food orders, their unhealthy choices are often heavily influenced by advertising strategies, unclear information, and other practices of fast food chains.

2 Create your thesis

To organize your writing and help readers focus on your outlook and your evidence, state a **proposition** or **claim**—a **thesis** (see 3b) specifying the issue and your opinion. As you refine your rough thesis, look for blurred or illogical propositions, especially in a complex thesis.

BLURRED AND ILLOGICAL	Police should stop conducting unconstitutional roadblocks to identify drunk drivers and substitute more frequent visual checks of erratic driving.
	READER'S REACTION: **This proposition seems to assume that roadblocks are unconstitutional. Is the writer supporting this value judgment or proposing a policy?**

Make sure your thesis either focuses on one proposition or identifies related propositions you will argue in an appropriate order.

SINGLE PROPOSITIONS	Roadblocks to identify drunk drivers are unconstitutional. Police should make more frequent visual checks of erratic driving.
RELATED PROPOSITIONS	The current practice of using roadblocks to identify drunk drivers is unconstitutional; therefore, police should use another procedure such as visual checks for erratic driving.

13c Developing reasons and evidence

As you consider your issue or research it, develop reasons supported by varied, sound evidence that your particular audience will find persuasive (see 9b). For example, your field study of recycling attitudes might well enlighten academic readers, but readers at work might want evidence of recycling's cost-effectiveness. In a public forum, detailing conditions at the local landfill might help influence a policy change.

Details. Look for statistics, technical information, surveys, interviews, and background or historical information for text or visuals (see 11e–f). Be prepared to justify the validity and authority of your sources, especially if they come from the Web. (See 20d.)

Comparisons. You can compare a particular issue, problem, policy, or situation about which you are uncertain to one about which you (and your readers) are more certain, but avoid far-fetched or unreasonable comparisons.

Quotations and ideas from authorities. The words of experts can lend support, but readers will expect them to be fair and authoritative.

Examples. Events, people, ideas, objects, feelings, stories, images, and texts drawn from your own or others' experience all can be used as brief or extended examples to support a thesis. Supply both *explanation* to make your point and *concrete detail* to give it power.

Logical links. To use your evidence effectively, you'll need to link it logically to a series of reasons that support your viewpoint. Try using a word such as *because, therefore,* or *consequently* in your rough thesis to establish this connection.

> **Claim or Opinion Stated in a Rough Thesis:** New classroom teachers should be required to continue coursework because it will improve the quality of their teaching, support their motivation to succeed as teachers, and help to address teacher shortages.
>
> **Reason 1:** People master a skill or activity best by doing it.
> **Evidence:** Comparisons with medical internships, examples and data from research on innovative teacher preparation programs
> **Reason 2:** Practicing teachers are often more motivated than preservice teachers.
> **Evidence:** Information from scholarly article comparing outcomes of preservice and inservice courses
> **Reason 3:** Reducing the time required for preservice preparation would help increase the number of new teachers available in a time of teacher shortages.

Evidence: Interviews with teacher interns, federal employment statistics, postings from a teacher preparation discussion group

Reason 4 (Possible Counterargument): New teachers will still be effective in the classroom, especially if they are supervised and mentored by administrators in the schools that hire them.

Evidence: Newspaper profiles and reports on new teachers, interview with principal and associate superintendent

13d Acknowledging other perspectives

Traditional argument resembles debate: you imagine an adversary and try to undermine that person's points or **counterarguments**. Most contemporary approaches to argument, however, expect you to acknowledge other people's perspectives yet still try to convince them of your views. Especially within a workplace or in public where your opponents on one issue may be your allies on another, treat others respectfully. (See 9b–c.)

> **STRATEGY** Anticipate counterarguments.
>
> Divide a sheet of paper into three columns. On the left, list the main points supporting your opinion. Write opposing points in the middle. On the right, counter the opposing points.

13e
arg

13e Arguing logically

Strategies of argument are ways to organize and check the logic of your opinions and supporting evidence (see 9b).

1 Use data-warrant-claim (Toulmin) reasoning

In *The Uses of Argument* (1964), Stephen Toulmin proposes **data-warrant-claim reasoning**, which draws on several kinds of statements reasonable people usually make when they argue: statements of data, claim, and warrant. A statement of **data** corresponds to your evidence and **claim** to your conclusion or proposition. **Warrant**, however, refers to the mental process by which a reader connects the data to the claim, answering "How?"

13.2

In constructing a line of reasoning, you present the data or indisputable facts that lead to your claim, but you also present the warrants, the probable facts and assertions that will encourage readers to accept your claim. This approach does not assume that an argument can provide absolute proof of a proposition. It aims instead at showing readers that an opinion or proposed action is plausible, grounded on good evidence and reasons, and worth their endorsement.

Suppose you are examining the relative safety of cars. As data, you have a study on the odds of injury in different models of cars. To argue effectively, you need to show readers *how* the data and your claim are connected, what patterns (probable facts—warrants) link the data to your claim.

DATA	WARRANT	CLAIM
Ratings of each car model by likelihood of injury (scale: 1 to 10)	• The cars in the ratings fall into three easily recognized groups: small, medium, large. (probable fact) • The large cars as a group have a lower average likelihood of injury to passengers than either of the other groups. (probable fact) • Although some other cars have low likelihood of injury, almost all the large cars seem safe. (assertion + probable fact) • Few consumers will go over the crash ratings to see which models get good or poor scores. (assertion)	For the average consumer, buying a large car is a good way to reduce the likelihood of being injured in an accident.

2 Use Rogerian argument

Effective argument requires a relationship between you and your reader, an issue that **Rogerian argument** considers, based on the theories of psychologist Carl Rogers. Rogers argues that people are more easily persuaded when an opponent seems an ally, not an enemy. To practice Rogerian strategies, imagine the views of someone opposed to your opinion. What is that person's frame of reference? What assumptions are behind those views?

Once you understand the other person's ideas, you may wish to work a **concession** into your argument, acknowledging an opposing view. A concession doesn't have to be so strong that it undermines your argument. But placed strategically, it can show your effort to be fair and help persuade a reader to listen. Highlight brief concessions with *although* or *of course*.

3 Use deductive and inductive reasoning

A **deductive argument** states and then supports an explicit premise (assertion or claim) using syllogistic reasoning as its basic logical format. A **syllogism** includes a major premise, a minor premise, and a conclusion.

MAJOR PREMISE   All landowners in Clarksville must pay taxes.

MINOR PREMISE   Gary Hayes owns land in Clarksville.

CONCLUSION   Therefore, Gary Hayes must pay taxes.

A flawed syllogism can often pinpoint faulty reasoning.

MAJOR PREMISE   All Ferraris are fast.

MINOR PREMISE   That car is fast.

CONCLUSION   Therefore, that car is a Ferrari.

MISLEADING AND ILLOGICAL REASONING: LOGICAL FALLACIES

Faulty Cause-Effect Relationship (*post hoc, ergo propter hoc* reasoning—"after this, therefore because of this"): attempts to persuade you that because one event follows another, the first causes the second.

The increase in violence on television is making the crime rate soar.

READER'S REACTION: **This *may* be true, but no evidence here links the two situations.**

False Analogy: compares two things that seem, but aren't, comparable.

Raising the speed limit is like offering free cocktails at a meeting of recovering alcoholics.

READER'S REACTION: **I don't see the connection. Most drivers aren't recovering from an addiction to high-speed driving.**

Red Herring: distracts readers from the real argument.

Gun control laws need to be passed as soon as possible to decrease domestic violence and accidents. The people who think guns should not be controlled are probably criminals themselves.

READER'S REACTION: **The second sentence doesn't follow logically or add support. It's just a distracting attack on people who disagree.**

Ad Hominem: attacks the person, not the issue.

Of course Walt Smith would support a bill to aid farmers—he owns several farms in the Midwest.

READER'S REACTION: **I'd like to hear reactions to his ideas, please.**

Begging the Question: presents assumptions as facts.

Most people try to be physically fit; obviously, they fear getting old.

READER'S REACTION: **I don't see any evidence that people fear aging—or that they are working on their physical fitness, either.**

Circular Reasoning: supports an assertion with the assertion itself.

The university should increase funding of intramural sports because it has a responsibility to back its sports programs financially.

READER'S REACTION: **So the university should fund sports because it should fund sports?**

13.3

13e
arg

In a complex argument your reasoning will be more elaborate, but the syllogistic pattern can frame and test your reasoning.

An **inductive argument** does not explicitly state the premise; rather, it leads readers through accumulated evidence to a conclusion. It usually begins with a **hypothesis**, more tentative than an assertion, and the ideas the writer wants to consider. The writer has, but withholds, a conclusion until readers are convinced by the supporting points.

4 Use logical and emotional appeals

Adapt your strategies for argument to your readers, arranging reasons and evidence in ways that most people will accept as reasonable and convincing and that will enhance your credibility as a writer. Emotional strategies focus on the values, beliefs, and emotions that can engage readers and motivate them to care about an issue. However, such appeals are generally best accepted when they are also supported by logical strategies—reasoning based on likely good or bad consequences, relevant comparisons, authoritative experts, trustworthy testimony, pertinent illustrations, and statistics. Watch for **logical fallacies** or flaws in reasoning as you evaluate your evidence and shape your argument.

13f | **Writing a position paper**

A short **position paper** or documented argument defines an issue, considers its audience, and uses evidence and reasoning to advance the writer's thesis.

Paul Pusateri

Dr. Drept

WRT 101

5 Nov. 2003

Running Uphill

Introduces issue Who is at fault? Is it the fast-food chains for putting such fattening items in front of consumers with endless promotions and marketing schemes? Or is it the consumer's fault for eating the unhealthy meals, knowing full well the negative consequences? Suing a fast-food chain for causing your own obesity, as some people have done (Cohen), may be extreme. As one report puts it, "Fast-food litigation has been greeted coolly so far because it appears to run up against a core American value: personal responsibility" (Cohen). At the same time, this does not mean that the fast-food chains are free from significant blame for the rise of obesity and similar health problems that affect many people today (Surgeon General). The truth is that most people know fast food may not be good for them; they simply don't realize just how unhealthy it is. For example, how many of us know that a "quick lunch" at McDonald's including a Big Mac, fries, and a Coke, has 62 grams of fat and 1,500 calories (Barrett 74)? Even though the chains are starting to make their menus healthier, they are still to blame. Their pricing policies, overall menus, and marketing techniques lead people to eat fast food no matter how much fat it contains or how many calories it provides.

> Cites authorities

> Presents position

13f
arg

2

> Establishes criteria for evaluation

How are we to know what is good for us and not so good in the food we eat? What standard can we use to judge the meals offered by fast-food restaurants? To maintain a desirable, healthy weight, men need about 2,700 calories per day and women need about 2,000. The American Heart Association recommends less than three hundred milligrams of cholesterol and fifty to eighty grams of fat per day, while the National Academy of Sciences recommends 1,100 to 3,300 milligrams of salt per day (Minnesota Attorney General). In each case, the national average intake for these is higher (Minnesota Attorney General), driven in part, perhaps, by the amount of fast food we eat.

3

> Develops explanation of problem

Not all fast food contains excessive salt, cholesterol, and calories, of course, but the items that dominate the menus at a Wendy's, Burger King, McDonald's, and other fast-food restaurants and that appear frequently in advertising generally do. For example, a report by the Minnesota Attorney General gives these nutrition facts for two staples of fast-food menus, a cheeseburger dinner and a pizza dinner.

Provides
supporting
examples
and detail

1. Quarter-pound cheeseburger, large fries, 16 oz. soda (McDonald's)

This meal:	*Recommended daily intake:*
1,166 calories	2,000-2,700 calories
51 g fat	No more than 50-80 g
95 mg cholesterol	No more than 300 mg
1,450 mg sodium	No more than 1,100-3,300 mg

2. 4 slices sausage and mushroom pizza, 16 oz. soda (Domino's)

This meal:	*Recommended daily intake:*
1,000 calories	2,000-2,700 calories
28 g fat	No more than 50-80 g
62 mg cholesterol	No more than 300 mg
2,302 mg sodium	No more than 1,100-3,300 mg

13f
arg

Discusses
convenience
and price

4   The information in these charts is probably astonishing to most of us. Even though restaurants make nutrition facts available to customers and publish them online--for example, at a McDonald's Web site (McDonald's USA)--the "need for speed" and convenience that makes us turn to fast-food restaurants in the first place means that most of us do not consult the lists of nutritional facts. Instead, we order foods prominently displayed on menus or we order by price, from a value menu or a promotional special, both of which in my experience feature familiar and relatively unhealthful choices. In so doing, we often pass by the better choices, the small fries rather than the large, for example. At McDonald's, instead of a quarter-pound cheeseburger and large fries, we might choose a hamburger and small fries with 481 calories and 19 grams of fat, a healthier solution (Minnesota Attorney General).

Makes
concession

5   Admittedly, fast-food chains have been adding healthier options to their menus. Arby's Light Roast Chicken has 276 calories and only 7 grams of fat; Wendy's has a healthy chili with 210 calories and 7 grams of fat. Burger King and McDonald's

have a vanilla shake with 5 grams of fat and a chicken salad wth only 4 grams of fat, respectively (Minnesota Attorney General).

These items often do not receive adequate emphasis in advertising or menu placement, however. In addition, the lack of adequate emphasis frequently means that customers end up thinking that some kinds of food are healthy when they are not. As Kelly Frey points out in "Salad Not Always Healthiest Fast-Food Choice," a Crispy Chicken Salad with ranch dressing at McDonald's has 8 more calories and 19 more grams of fat than a Big Mac. Salads from Wendy's and Burger King may also have fat and calories than the burgers. Even a Cobb salad with low-fat dressing at McDonald's would take a 150-pound person sixty minutes to walk off all the 320 calories it contains (Barrett 74).

 Discusses menu placement

Even television ads that pass certain tests for truthfulness can be misleading. The ads for Subway, for example, leave the impression that the chain's sandwiches are healthful. Some are, yet many are not. Subway's advertising is factually true. The specific sandwiches advertised as healthful actually are; it is the others that are not, but they tend to fall within the general impression of healthfulness created by the advertising. At Subway, a 6-inch BMT Italian sandwich has 39 grams of fat, the same as a Big Mac from McDonald's and a Bacon Double Cheeseburger from Burger King (Diet Riot). A Quarter Pounder or a Whopper Jr. would be a better choice for me than the Cold Cut Trio I commonly eat at Subway.

 13f arg

 Discusses marketing techniques

The blame may lie with the fast-food chains, but the responsibility for making healthier choices is ours as well. There are ways we can do this, but even the available healthy choices are outside the range of those usually marketed by the chains. Nonetheless, an article like Jo Licten's "Healthiest Fast Food for Busy Travelers" can be a guide. From it I learned that Burger King's Mustard Whopper Jr., which replaces mayonnaise with mustard,

8 Refines position

Advocates course of action

decreases calories by 80. I thought that Mexican fast food could not taste good and be healthy, but I found that a Bean Burrito from Taco Bell can be a complete meal with only 370 calories and 12 grams of fat (Licten). It's like running uphill, but it is possible to begin reversing the unhealthy practices for which fast-food chains are still to blame.

[New page]

Works Cited

Barrett, Jennifer. "Fast Food Need Not Be Fat Food." Newsweek
　　13 Oct. 2003: 73-74. Academic First Search. EBSCO. U of
　　Rhode Island Lib. 21 Oct. 2003 <http://search.epnet.com>.

Cohen, Adam. "The McNugget of Truth in the Fast-Food Lawsuits."
　　New York Times 3 Feb. 2003: A24.

"Diet Riot." DietRiot.com 14 Oct. 2003. 19 Oct. 2003 <http://
　　www.dietriot.com/fff/rest.html>.

Frey, Kelly. "Salad Not Always Healthiest Fast-Food Choice." The
　　Pittsburgh Channel.com 15 May 2003. 19 Oct. 2003 <http://
　　www.thepittsburghchannel.com/ health/2206321/
　　detail.html>.

Licten, Jo. "Healthiest Fast Food for Busy Travelers."
　　American Woman Road and Travel. 2003. 5 Oct. 2003
　　<http://www.roadandtravel.com/health/
　　healthiestfastfood.htm>.

McDonald's USA. "McDonald's USA Nutrition Information." 21 Oct.
　　2003. 31 Oct. 2003 <http://www.mcdonalds.com/countries/
　　usa/food/nutrition/categories/nutrition/>.

Minnesota Attorney General. Fast Food Facts 19 Oct. 2003
　　<http://www.olen.com/food/book.html>.

Surgeon General of the United States. The Surgeon General's
　　Call to Action: Prevent and Decrease Overweight and Obesity.
　　Washington: GPO, 2003.

13f
arg

Exercise 1

Using strategies in 13a for involving yourself in the flow of opinions and ideas, prepare a list of issues or controversies that interest you. Choose one, summarize the issue or controversy in a sentence or two, and then summarize the main conflicting opinions (pro and con), each in a sentence.

Exercise 2

Use two of the strategies described in 13a-2 for identifying potential issues. Identify at least five potential issues, making sure you employ both techniques at least twice. Then summarize each issue in a sentence or two, and summarize any potentially conflicting opinions about it in a sentence each.

Exercise 3 *(Answers appear on p. 507.)*

Examine the following propositions as possible thesis statements for argumentative essays. Decide whether each example provides an adequate thesis, and explain your judgments.

1. The United States should deregulate all mail service in order to increase competition and improve the quality of service.
2. Rap music, which is violent, vulgar, and sexist, should be banned from public consumption, and fines should be imposed on anyone listening to it in public places.
3. Arson is not a crime; it is a mental disease and should be treated as such.
4. If children read when they are growing up, they will become literate.
5. Orange juice tastes better than cranberry juice.
6. Humanity's woes began when Eve tasted the forbidden fruit in the Garden of Eden.
7. The telephone resulted in a society less prone to writing, but email will likely lead us right back into the written word as a primary form of communication.

Exercise 4

Develop a workable thesis statement for a paper you are planning to write. List at least three pieces of supporting evidence or arguments for your assertion. Next, create a list of counterarguments you might wish to address.

13
arg

14 Academic Writing

Academic settings are places for both learning and teaching—for taking in knowledge and for communicating it. The forms and techniques for doing so become increasingly specialized as you move from your initial general education courses to the more specialized, advanced courses in your major. As you become immersed in the customs and habits of that discipline, you'll learn its methods and conventions, its ways of creating and presenting knowledge.

14a Goals of academic writing

Academic writers are often apprentices—students writing to learn in history, biology, or nursing. At the other end of a continuum are professionals (and some students) presenting new, specialized knowledge.

←——————————————————————————→

Apprentice with teachers and mentors	**ROLE**	Professional with colleagues
Practice and learn	**GOAL**	Contribute to knowledge
General, introductory	**LEVEL**	Highly specialized

General education courses (often called surveys or introductions) usually require writing that helps you learn the subject matter, practice the field's ways of thinking, and show a teacher what you've learned. As you specialize within a major, you move toward professional conversations in your field.

STRATEGY Analyze your academic writing situation.

- Where would you place yourself on the continuum?
- Why are you writing? to learn something new? to show what you've learned? to inform others about new knowledge?
- What expertise or knowledge is expected at your level?

14b Analyzing academic audiences

Like the goals of academic writing, academic readers vary from experts with considerable knowledge in a field to general readers with little or none.

98

General ———→ Greater knowledge and expertise ———→ Expert

Nevertheless, academic writing often addresses multiple audiences.

- Your instructor is an expert, and you've done specialized research, but your assignment is to explain key concepts to novices.
- You know your topic well, but you need to address general readers (your classmates) and to offer new ideas to experts (your instructor).
- Your course journal is intended to help you learn, yet it is read by your instructor, who may be influenced by your reactions and insights.

STRATEGY   **Ask what your academic readers expect.**
- What does your main reader want—the person whose assessment counts the most? What do your secondary readers expect?
- How will your main reader evaluate your writing: in terms of his or her own expertise or in terms of a specified secondary audience?

14c acad

14c Understanding academic writing tasks

Academic writing tasks come as handouts, directions on a board, on-line postings, textbook assignments, or explanations during class. "Unpack" an assignment. If its parts are unclear, ask for clarification.

- Examine its main verbs (such as *analyze* or *show*) and main nouns (the *causes* of the *stock market crash*).
- Figure out its goals: the primary goal, secondary goals, and any assumed or "hidden" goals that appear as additions or explanations.

Instead of fearing evaluation or resigning yourself to guesswork and hope, use the course standards to guide your writing process. Ask your instructor to discuss the goals of an assignment, explicit and implicit.

STRATEGY   **Set goals for your writing.**
- How will your writing be judged? What explicit criteria do you have (such as a description of strong and weak papers)?
- Are there any implicit criteria (such as precision rather than elegance)?
- List the criteria you have identified. Turn the evaluative statements ("Your paper should begin with a clear point or thesis") into questions ("Does my paper begin with a clear point or thesis?").
- Use your questions as a drafting guide and a revision checklist.

14d Types of academic writing

Most forms of academic writing fall into one of five categories, although assignments may have mixed goals or require several forms of writing. When academic writing *reflects*, it draws on personal experience and insight in response to events, readings, and ideas. In contrast, writing that *draws on sources* goes outside personal experience to integrate information and ideas from articles, reports, books, or Web sites. Academic writing may also *interpret* meaning or significance—of a historical event, a text, a painting, a cultural pattern, or a social phenomenon—or grow from *observing and experimenting*, examining human behavior or the natural world. The final activity, *testing*, often demonstrates a student's mastery of a subject although experts, too, are routinely evaluated by colleagues as they present conference papers, publish articles, or submit grant proposals.

Types of Academic Writing		
Type	**Characteristic Activities**	**Common Forms**
DRAWING ON SOURCES	Summarizing, paraphrasing, synthesizing, analyzing, comparing, compiling, evaluating	Summaries and abstracts, reviews and syntheses (research, ideas, or information), book reviews and reports, annotated bibliographies, informative research papers, poster presentations, analyses of issues or controversies
REFLECTING	Responding, reacting, speculating, exploring, inquiring	Reading journals, logs (data observations and insights), personal essays, reaction papers, autobiographies, reflexive writing (self-observing and self-critical)
INTERPRETING	Analyzing, defining key ideas and meanings, identifying causes and effects, describing patterns, applying a theory, drawing a conclusion, taking a stand on an issue	Interpretations of a text or work of art (documented or not), analyses of phenomena (historical, social, or cultural), "thesis" papers taking a stand on scholarly issues, documented arguments drawing on research
OBSERVING/ EXPERIMENTING	Making observations; designing surveys and experiments; collecting, synthesizing, and analyzing data; recognizing patterns	Scientific reports and articles, logs of observations and experiments, lab reports, field research reports, project evaluations
TESTING	Explaining, supporting, defining, presenting information and ideas, offering conclusions	Essay tests, take-home exams, tests requiring sentence- or paragraph-length answers, written responses to readings

14e Short documented paper

In many courses, you may write a short paper that draws on a few sources and argues, interprets, or simply presents information.

ELEMENTS OF A SHORT DOCUMENTED PAPER
- It summarizes or synthesizes others' views, results, or positions.
- It presents information fairly in your own words.
- It may provide reasoned conclusions or interpretations based on cited sources but may allow readers to apply these to their actions or beliefs.
- It is well organized and easy to read.

Following are excerpts from a short documented paper. Although the paper cites facts and statistics from four articles, it also has its own thesis.

Desperate Times for Teachers

by David Aharonian

There is a major controversy regarding teacher salaries presently in this country. Many people feel that teachers are overpaid because they have summers off from work. They feel that teachers do not truly work year-round and therefore are either getting a fair rate of pay or getting too much. Many teachers, however, disagree with this assessment. They feel that they are underpaid for the work that they do. Most teachers find it very difficult just to make ends meet on a teacher's salary, and often they resort to moonlighting.

Moonlighting means that a person holds another job in addition to his or her career. . . .

[Four additional paragraphs supply information and data from two sources on moonlighting teachers.]

But there really are no easy solutions to the problem. One obvious answer would be to increase teacher salaries (Alley 21). This would lead to less moonlighting and allow teachers to concentrate more on their primary occupation. But there are still plenty of people who oppose raising teacher salaries. Many times teachers may go two or three

1 · **14e acad**
Synthesizes opposing positions

States thesis

2–6 Defines key term

7 Presents alternatives, leaving reader to decide

Supplies detail

years without any raise in their pay. Then when the
teachers do get a raise, it may only be 2 or 4 percent.
This certainly lowers the morale of the teachers and can
cause teachers to become frustrated (Henderson 12). As

Concludes with pertinent quotation

one teacher in Oklahoma put it, "It's hard to look
across the hall and see a teacher who's taught 14 years,
making only $4,000 more than you are" (Wisniewski and
Kleine 1).

[The paper ends with a list of works cited.]

14f Lab report

14f
lab

In fields like biology, chemistry, or engineering, you are likely to write
lab reports on experiments. Lab reports need to be clear and concise, describing exactly what you did and what happened as a result.

Lab reports vary in style and format, depending on the field. Check with
each instructor about requirements, such as section numbers and headings. A
typical structure begins with an overview or abstract of the focus or goal (why it
was done), introduces the problem or principles (what it shows), describes the
methods (how it was done), explains the results (what happened), discusses the
outcomes (what the results mean), and states a conclusion (what it shows).

ELEMENTS OF A LAB REPORT

- It strictly follows the format required by the instructor or field.
- It does not digress into unnecessary commentary on the experiment.
- It uses specific terminology and unambiguous language.
- It presents data and results accurately, without distortion.

Typical sections of a lab report include the Abstract, Introduction, Experiment (Materials and Procedure), Results, Discussion, and Conclusion. Here is
a selection from the closing section of a chemistry lab report.

Butane: Determining Molecular Weight from Vapor

by Melanie Dedecker

[The report follows the brief assigned format, beginning with Materials,
Procedure, and Calculations.]

Includes required section headings

Conclusion. The purpose of this experiment was to determine the
molecular weight of butane gas through the use of the ideal gas

law and to learn how to write an accurate procedure. In order to determine the molecular weight of butane gas, a lighter was weighed and then lighted underneath a graduated cylinder full of water. The gas that was emitted from the lighter displaced the water in the graduated cylinder. From this data and the mass of used butane gas, the density of the gas was determined. This value was used in an altered form of the ideal gas law to ascertain the molecular weight of butane gas. Although the actual molar mass of butane gas is 58 g/mol, this experiment determined the molar mass of butane to be 61.4 g/mol, resulting in a 5.86% error.

Uses specific terms

Supplies detailed results

[The report ends with possible reasons for this result.]

14g Essay exam

14g essay

14.2

When you work on an essay exam, even a take-home exam, you have only a short time to write. Read the question carefully, and jot down a working thesis and specific evidence. State your points clearly, especially beginning each paragraph. Watch your time.

ELEMENTS OF AN ESSAY EXAM ANSWER
- It addresses all parts of the exam question directly.
- It follows directions about the approach (such as comparison or explanation) and covers the number of points or examples expected.
- It uses references—quotations, facts, and other information—efficiently, illustrating the point without overloading the essay.
- It connects references and synthesizes material to show significance.
- It interprets, supporting a point, not merely listing details.

Here are selections from an open-book essay exam that asked students to identify a common theme running through a survey of American literature and to discuss this theme in two stories.

Moral Perfection in "Young Goodman Brown"

and "The Birthmark"

by Ted Wolfe

Hawthorne's "Young Goodman Brown" explores the conflict between good and evil. Young Goodman Brown has his religious faith tested during a journey into the woods. In

1

States theme selected

what may or may not be a dream, he is shown by the devil that everyone he believed to be good is evil. . . . When the devil is about to baptize him, Brown calls out for Faith, his wife, telling her to resist the temptation. He is really calling out for faith, as in faith in God. When he does this, the hellish vision passes, and he is alone in the woods. From this, I think we can conclude that Hawthorne believes that people should try to resist temptation and live moral lives.

But Goodman Brown is never the same after the experience, be it dream or reality. He becomes "a stern, a sad, a darkly meditative, if not a desperate man." In his heart he doubts the goodness of Faith/faith, Deacon Gookin, Goody Cloyse, and everyone else. . . . Symbolically, the experience in the woods causes him to give up his faith. The overriding message that Hawthorne is trying to convey is that one should try to keep one's faith, to believe in others' inherent goodness, and to live morally. If one doesn't, life becomes as barren and miserable as it became for Goodman Brown.

Hawthorne's "The Birthmark" also addresses . . .

[Continues with second short story.]

. . . Hawthorne's point is that one should not get so caught up in trying to be morally perfect that it ruins one's life. People must learn to "find the perfect future in the present."

Margin annotations:

Refers to events in story

Interprets events and character's name

Draws conclusion about story

② Uses short supporting quotation

14h biblio

Develops conclusion further

③ Follows directions to discuss two stories

④ Concludes essay

14h Annotated bibliography

An annotated bibliography is just like a regular bibliography (see Chapters 25–28) except that each entry includes a description or summary of the work's aim, purpose, or contents. Annotated bibliographies are commonly assigned in college courses to help students survey and report on a body of scholarship or prepare for a longer research paper.

ELEMENTS OF AN ANNOTATED BIBLIOGRAPHY

- Its brief introduction orients readers to the topic being covered.
- It lists references to the literature cited, each followed by a clear description or summary that briefly but accurately represents the work.
- It supplies accurate references and follows the expected documentation style so that readers can easily locate the works listed. (See Chapters 25–28.)
- It arranges entries alphabetically, sometimes grouped in sections by date or by general topic or focus.

An annotated bibliography typically introduces the topic briefly, perhaps highlighting the kinds of works it covers. Then each work is cited and followed with an annotation, usually a short paragraph or two. Annotations sometimes use an abbreviated sentence structure like this: Summarizes research on the development of the Cherokee syllabary.

Following is a sample entry from an annotated bibliography that consisted of an introduction to the topic followed by twelve entries.

14i
review

Annotated Bibliography on Bilingualism

by Ian Preston

Glazer, Nathan. "Where Is Multiculturalism Leading Us?" <u>Phi</u>   **Cites source**

    <u>Delta Kappan</u> 75 (1993): 319-24. This article describes

    the Center for the Study of Books in Spanish for

    Children and Adolescents, an organization that

    promotes the positive aspects of bilingualism. Unlike

    other organizations that portray their ethnic groups   **Sums up viewpoint**

    as victims, the Center, Glazer argues, ought to be

    followed as a model of a bilingual program.

14i Literature review

The literature review, sometimes called a survey paper or a review of the literature, is usually one section of a longer paper but may be assigned as a paper in itself. In a psychology paper reporting the results of an experiment, for instance, the literature review is typically the first section after the introduction. Its purpose is to synthesize the existing research on your topic and thus establish a context for your own research. Most literature reviews present the findings of others in a fair and balanced manner, summarizing the literature instead of critiquing it.

ELEMENTS OF A LITERATURE REVIEW

- It accurately and concisely summarizes other researchers' work.
- It synthesizes these other studies, combining results where they overlap, while giving credit to each researcher.
- It includes major points of agreement or disagreement among the other studies.
- It establishes a context for your own study.

Following is part of a sample literature review originally prepared as part of a longer APA-style paper studying the ways cat owners' human perspectives affect their pets' health and longevity. This section provides scientific background for the study. In the original paper, the writer also included a list of references. Note how the writer connects her sources to each other. In the opening of the review, she also gives readers an idea of the problem the paper addresses and the general conclusion it reaches.

14i
review

A Healthier Diet for Cats

by Sarah Andrea

Literature Review

1
Focuses on problem

Provides glimpse of overall conclusion

In the wild, animals innately know to avoid excessive consumption, eating only to maintain themselves. At the same time, 25% of this country's domesticated cats are morbidly obese or diabetic. Studies suggest that the diet of most domesticated cats is to blame. With a digestive tract much simpler than a human's, a feline is not able to catabolize vegetable protein and does not have a dietary requirement for carbohydrates. Cats have thus evolved with an ability to digest food high in protein and low in carbohydrates. The diet of a wild cat is dependent on mainly one element, animal protein, such as a mouse, made up of 3%

Summarizes important information

carbohydrates, 40% protein, and 50% fat (Riond, 2003; Russell, 2002).

2

Dry cat foods, often purchased because of their lower cost, contain high percentages of carbohydrates from cereal grains.

Groups related studies

According to studies conducted by Appleton (2001) and Mazzabero (2003), a cat's inability to adapt to the drastic change in the dietary ingredients of dry food causes high blood glucose and an overall exhausting of beta cells, leading to diabetes mellitus. Studies by Rand (2002, 2003) of dry, wet, and raw meat feline diets demonstrate the contribution of dry foods to feline diabetes and obesity.

14j Speaking in the academic community

Planning a presentation with a partner or team takes time but provides valuable experience for work and public communities. (See 16h and 17f.)

STRATEGY Work together as a speaking team.

- Split up research responsibilities; collaborate as you create and exchange talking points; rehearse as a group (see 12c).
- Unify around your purpose, theme, and organization.
- Coordinate all contributions, and divide the time evenly; plan how to monitor and cue each other on time limits.
- Have the first presenter introduce the team; then have each speaker create a transition to the next. Create a single presentation that reveals differences in the subject, not oppositions in the team.

14j
speak

Exercise 1

Choose an academic writing task from another course you are taking, or get one from a friend or roommate. Using the strategies in 14c, analyze the task, paying attention to any cues about its purpose, audience, form, and appropriate language.

Exercise 2

Interview a student about his or her academic writing experiences. First ask the student to name a *kind* of paper he or she was asked to write. (Try to get a name for the genre, such as "character sketch" or "interview paper.") Then ask the student to describe what he or she knows about this type of paper, based on the categories of information presented in this chapter, such as audience, purpose, and characteristic activities. Identify gaps or uncertainties in the student's account.

15 Reading and Writing About Literature

Imagine a world without imagination. Literature—works of fiction, poetry, and drama—gives us a doorway into imaginary worlds, where we can suffer with characters or share their triumphs, feel their misery or their elation. Reading literature critically, however, goes beyond unconsidered experience to new understandings. These insights are the basis for most writing about literature, whether that takes the form of a review for your neighborhood book club or an interpretive paper in an English course.

15a Reading literary texts

When you read a novel, short story, or poem or view a drama or film, pay attention to meaning and to artistic technique.

1 Read through "lenses"

15.1

Your perspective as a reader may determine your strategies for reading and interpreting. From a psychological view, you might note how a character tries to overcome feelings of childhood abandonment. Or, through a feminist lens, you might examine the portrayal of women in a novel. How particular groups or communities see the world may be reflected in the lenses of academic fields such as psychology or feminist theory or those of other groups bound by occupation, race, culture, or social status.

> **STRATEGY** Shift your reading lens.
>
> After reading a literary work, recall the key events, characters, and settings through a series of lenses appropriate to the work. What happens when you use the lens of economics or, more specifically, capitalism or socialism? What happens if you shift to the lens of technology? or religion? or biology? Test as many lenses as you can to see what insights you gain.

2 Read for theme

For many critics and students of literature, to read for meaning is to read for theme. You can view **theme** as an idea, perspective, insight, or cluster of feelings that a work conveys or that permeates a work, organizing the relationships among its parts. Or you can view theme as the insights readers are likely to derive from their reading experience.

108

As you read, write down your ideas, responses, or clusters of feelings. Note the techniques writers use to convey meaning (see 15a-3). Look especially for repeated words and ideas, contrasting characters or events, and patterns of images, which can signal possible themes.

In reading a short poem, Sevon Randall notes repetitions and contrasts that reveal a cluster of feelings and ideas (a theme).

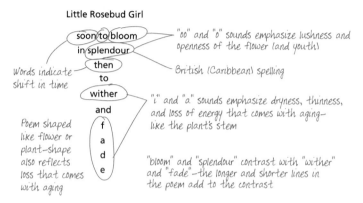

Little Rosebud Girl

soon to bloom — "oo" and "o" sounds emphasize lushness and openness of the flower (and youth)

in splendour

Words indicate shift in time — then — British (Caribbean) spelling

to

wither — "i" and "a" sounds emphasize dryness, thinness, and loss of energy that comes with aging— like the plant's stem

and

Poem shaped like flower or plant-shape also reflects loss that comes with aging
f
a
d
e

"bloom" and "splendour" contrast with "wither" and "fade"—the longer and shorter lines in the poem add to the contrast

—Anson Gonzalez, "Little Rosebud Girl" (1968)

15a
lit

3 Read for technique

When you read for meaning, you inevitably read for technique. A writer can't create events, portray characters, represent scenes, or elicit a reader's reactions without using techniques of characterization, plot, setting, or imaginative language.

Examine the following key elements as you read.

Character. Who are the major and minor characters? What are their traits? Are the characters complex or one-dimensional? How do they change—or fail to change—in response to events? How self-aware are they? Which ones are presented positively, which negatively?

Plot. Are events presented in chronological order, or have they been rearranged? What is the role of conflict in the plot? Do events spring from the characters' personalities or serve mainly to reveal character traits? Is there a main conflict, a chain of conflicts, or a climax?

Setting. Where and when do events occur? Does the setting help explain characters' actions or convey a mood that shapes readers' reactions?

Point of view. Who tells the story? Is the narrator a character or a persona, a voice adopted by the writer or poet? Is the story narrated in the first person (*I*) or in the third person by a narrator who is not identified as *I* but speaks of the characters as *he* or *she*? Is the narrator *omniscient* (all-knowing)? limited in knowledge? reliable?

Language. How does the work use imaginative language—simile, metaphor, understatement, paradox, or irony? Does it use vivid description, unusual wording, rhythms, rhymes, or other sound patterns?

Genre. What's its form: novel, short story, poem, drama, or film? Is it a specific *type* of one of these, such as a novella or allegory? Do its characteristics define a specific genre (such as cinema verité for film)?

15.2

15b lit

15b Writing about literary texts

When you write about a literary text, you interpret and analyze an author's words and techniques. You reach reasonable conclusions—judgments and observations—supported by evidence from the text or secondary sources. Recall the academic conventions for verb tense (see 31b): use present tense to summarize a text ("Falstaff acts . . .") or to discuss what an author does ("Toni Morrison gives her characters . . ."); use past tense for historical context ("During the Vietnam War, Levertov's poetry *took on* a political tone").

1 Write about meaning

You may explain and support your conclusions about a work's theme or focus on insights you develop by applying a particular perspective to a work (historical, feminist, and so forth).

Develop a thesis. Make sure readers can easily identify your statement of the theme. Try stating your conclusion about it early in a thesis. (See 3b.)

Select evidence. For supporting evidence, you can turn to passages in the text, not just quoting but analyzing them to show readers why they support your interpretation. You can also show how elements such as events, characters, and symbols support your interpretation. If you use outside sources, you can cite the work of critics and scholars.

Organize. Consider two common ways to present an interpretation effectively. You can separate your thesis into parts or subtopics and take up each of these in its own section. Or you can divide your paper to correspond to different segments of the work (beginning, middle, end) or different elements (characters, language, symbols). Then, in each section of your paper, show how the particular segment or element supports your thesis.

2 Write about technique

Try to highlight the author's use of language, setting, or characterization, drawing conclusions about how the techniques shape the work's meaning and the likely responses of readers.

Develop a thesis. Your thesis should reflect your dual purpose of describing and analyzing one or more techniques and then relating technique to meaning. In writing about "Young Goodman Brown," for example, you might say, "Hawthorne uses ambiguity in setting, symbolism, and characterization to suggest how excessive concern with the self can alter one's perception of everyday events."

Select evidence. Your main evidence about technique is detail from the text itself, presented through quotation, paraphrase, or summary and then connected to the work's meaning. (See 18f–g.)

Organize. If you examine one technique, try dividing your essay into parts corresponding to sections of the work, showing how and why the technique is used in each section. If you treat more than one technique, try devoting a part of the paper to each technique.

15c
lit

15c Sample literary analysis

Images of Self in "The Yellow Wallpaper"

by Jennifer O'Berry

During the 1800s the idea of the "new woman" was appearing. Women began to realize that they were seen only as their husbands' and society's "property." They began to pursue their independence and create their own identities. In Charlotte Perkins Gilman's short story "The Yellow Wallpaper," a nameless woman is searching for her personal identity and freedom from the oppressive childlike treatment inflicted on her by her doctor/husband. Gilman presents an elaborate metaphor about the images seen by the woman within the wallpaper found in her nursery/bedroom. This metaphor and the images the woman finds in the wallpaper play a significant role in the woman's achievement of finding her true self. Her state of insanity at the end of the story serves as a safe mask for her newly found freedom from alienation and oppression.

1

Identifies
context and
literary
work

States
thesis
about
theme

2

Interprets
characters
using
quotations
and
summaries
for support

Gilman presents the woman in her story as a somewhat unstable character who believes that she is sick, although John, her doctor/husband, believes that she is only suffering from a "slight hysterical tendency" (416). This characterization seems intentional on the part of Gilman because it makes the reader see clearly that the woman's ideas are oppressed, even from the beginning, by her husband. John thinks that all his wife needs is a strict rest schedule in which she is "absolutely forbidden to 'work'" (416) until she is "well" again. Gilman seems to suggest, by putting work in quotes, that the duties of the woman, and all women at that time, were not truly

15c
lit

considered work. She was forbidden to write and to have visitors. Early in the story, when the "rules" for her recovery are stated, the woman begins to comment on her disagreement with her husband, but she stops abruptly, as if she does not dare to have such thoughts. She believes that she would recover more quickly if, instead of being quarantined and forbidden from such pleasures as her writing, she "had less opposition and more society and stimulus" (416).

3

Deepens
interpretation
of woman's
condition in
terms of
theme

The woman tells the reader that "Mary is so good with the baby" (417), implying that she herself does not want to spend time with the baby. The child is also never mentioned by the woman as being with her or spending time with her. This seems to suggest that she may actually be experiencing a type of postpartum depression, causing her to want to abandon her child. The thoughts that lead her to feel that she may be ill may actually be due to her desire to abandon her role of wife and mother which was so rigidly demanded by society at that time. She gets "unreasonably angry"

(416) about the condition of things sometimes, but she blames this anger on her "nervous condition" (416). She tries to dismiss these thoughts because she feels that they are not proper. Therefore, she feels that she must be ill.

Gilman uses many images to enlighten the reader about the childlike treatment of the woman by her husband. The woman is directed by her husband to rest in a bedroom that used to serve as a nursery. Gilman chooses this room to show how John thinks of his wife. When referring to his wife, John commonly chooses names such as "blessed little goose" (418), "blessed child" (420), and "little girl" (421). This shows that he does not see his wife as an equal but rather as a helpless child who is solely dependent on him. As the woman begins to realize that she has been a subject of this type of oppression, she begins to be "a little afraid of John" (422) and to "wish he would take another room" (424), which exhibits her awareness of this treatment and the desire to be free from it, and from him.

Because of her rigid rest schedule, the woman is forced to spend most of her time in her nursery/bedroom, where she begins to explore the "worst [wall]paper" (417) she has ever seen in her life. Since she is not allowed to do much else, she commits herself to "follow that pointless pattern to some sort of conclusion" (419). She finds many images in the pattern, all of which aid in her "improvement" (423) "because of the wallpaper" (423) out of her mother/wife roles. She describes the pattern as images that will "plunge off at outrageous angles, [and] destroy themselves in unheard-of contradiction" (417). These "contradictions" seem to be referring to the contradictory treatment of her by her husband and society's contradictory expectations of her to be the perfect wife and

4

Identifies imagery related to theme

15c
lit

5

Focuses on imagery in wallpaper

mother. She becomes entranced by the wallpaper and "follows the pattern about by the hour" (419). With each second, the images become more numerous and complex. She begins to see "a broken neck and two bulbous eyes" (418), a woman behind the pattern in wallpaper. This woman "is all the time trying to climb through . . . but nobody could climb through . . . it strangles so" (424). She begins to identify with the woman and decides that she will stop at nothing until the woman is released from her entrapment.

6

15c
lit

Interprets
climax of
plot

At the end of the story, the woman is simultaneously on the brink of self–identity and insanity. On the last night she is to stay in the house, she is left alone in the room where she finally frees the woman in the wallpaper. When the woman in the wallpaper begins to "crawl and shake the pattern" (425), the main character "[runs] to help her" (425). Through the night, the two women pull and shake the bars and are able to "peel off yards of that paper" (425). She breaks down some of these cultural bars with the help from the woman in the wallpaper. When morning arrives, there is only one woman––the two have merged, and the woman's true identity has been found. In the remaining wallpaper are "many of those creeping women" (426). This symbolically represents the great number of women who also desire to be freed from the bars put up by society. She wonders if those women will ever "come out of the wallpaper as [she] did" (426). This shows her symbolic escape and her desire for other women to experience this personal freedom.

7

Contrasts
main
characters
at story's
conclusion

John returns at the end of the story to discover his wife in a state of insanity. When he sees her as the woman in the wallpaper, creeping around the room, he faints. She "had to creep over him" (426) because he was blocking her path. This strongly symbolizes the conquering of her husband because of her dominant position over him. She tells him that he cannot "put [her] back" (426) because she is finally free. Her creeping, which is like that of an infant, seems to represent a birth of her new self. At the same time, she has become completely insane. It is rather ironic that she must move into this state in order to be free from oppression. This seems to represent society's view of a liberated and self-identified woman. John believes that his wife is not ill before she begins her pursuit of self-discovery. When this discovery is complete, he sees her as insane. The opposite is true for the woman herself. She sees herself as ill before her process of identification and fully healthy afterward.

Points out irony

The woman in Gilman's short story uses the yellow wallpaper as a tool to find her true self. The color of the wallpaper itself seems to represent the brightness and hope of a new horizon, yet at the same time, it is a reminder of the "old, foul, bad yellow things" (423), like a fungus that grows and decays. This is representative of the woman's life. She can never truly be free because society's views and ideas will never acknowledge that a liberated woman can achieve her own identity.

⑧

Returns to thesis and restates theme

Exercise 1

Choose a short text or part of a text you are planning to write about. Read it, making notes on the meaning and technique in the margins or in a journal.

Exercise 2

Choose a work you plan to write about. Read it, and write out a tentative thesis statement presenting your conclusions about the work's meaning and technique. Then prepare a list of particular passages or sections of the work you plan to use as evidence in your paper. Finally, create a rough outline or some other kind of plan for this paper.

16 Public Writing

In every public and civic context, people write to convey information, express their views, organize collective efforts, and challenge injustice. Such writing not only improves your skills and flexibility but also helps you to become a better-informed citizen.

16a Goals of public writing

When you address a public audience, you're likely to think of yourself as a volunteer, an activist, or a committee member, not as a writer. Your first concern will be to organize a beach cleanup or elect a mayor. You'll write to achieve your civic goals: to motivate others to support your cause, to influence policy decisions, and to promote democratic processes.

16b Analyzing public audiences

When you prepare a meeting reminder for your book club or a newsletter for your neighbors, you will know your readers personally. They expect clear information and may appreciate motivation, but they often already agree about issues or activities. But when you begin to draft publicity for the tennis club's pasta dinner—its big fund-raiser—you'll need to address a wider circle, readers you don't know personally and who won't support the dinner unless you can persuade them that your cause is worthwhile.

Connect readers and goals. Use questions like the following to frame your writing in a strong relationship to your audiences' values and expectations.

- Why are you writing? What do you hope to accomplish?
- Who are your readers? What do they value? How much do they know or care about your project or issue?
- Do you primarily want to inform or to motivate them? Do you want readers to agree with you or to take action—go to a meeting, contribute time or money, vote "yes" or "no," call an official, or join your group?

- What appeals to your readers' passion, anger, or fear might persuade them to do what you want—your sincerity, testimonials from others, information, or connections to their own interests or community values?
- How might you approach these readers? Will they respond best to impassioned appeals, logical analyses, or combined strategies? Will they expect a neighborly letter, a flyer, or a polished brochure?
- How can you contact prospective readers—through flyers at a meeting, appeals by mail or email, or letters in the newspaper?

STRATEGY Focus your public writing.

Work with others to answer these questions and make appropriate decisions.

- What is your task? Who will do what as you work on it?
- What's your deadline? How soon will recipients need information? How much time should you allow for printing, mailing, or other steps?
- What type of material should you prepare? What is the usual format? Do you have models or samples of past materials?
- Does your material require approval from anyone?
- Do you need to reserve a meeting room, coordinate with another group, or make other arrangements before you can finish your text?
- How will you distribute your material? Do you need to arrange duplication, mailing, or volunteers to deliver or post materials?

16d
public

16c Types of public writing

Many types of public writing—letters, flyers, pamphlets, newsletters—are flexible documents. They can be directed to different readers, such as group members, newspaper readers, officials, or local residents. They can address different—or multiple—goals by providing information, building support, motivating to action, or supporting participatory democracy.

16d Public flyer

A common form of public writing is the flyer informing people about a meeting, activity, or event. Flyers also supply directions, advice, and information to residents, citizens, and other groups. (See also Chapter 11.)

Types of Public Writing		
Type	**Characteristic Activities**	**Common Forms**
PROVIDING INFORMATION	Gathering information, exploring issues, examining other views and alternative solutions, comparing, summarizing, synthesizing, and presenting material	Flyer, newsletter, fact sheet, informative report or article, letter (to group supporters, interested parties, officials, residents, or community in general), pamphlet, poster
BUILDING SUPPORT	Reaching consensus within a group, articulating a stance, defining a problem, proposing a solution, appealing to others with similar or different values, presenting evidence, finding shared values, advocating, persuading	Position paper, letter (to prospective supporters, officials, newspaper, or others concerned or involved), policy guidelines, statement of principles
MOTIVATING TO ACTION	Defining action, orchestrating participation, supplying information about involvement, motivating participants	Action proposal, grant proposal, flyer, letter, call to action in newsletter or other publication
PARTICIPATING IN DEMOCRATIC PROCESSES	Attending public meetings, meeting with officials, understanding legislative processes and timing, advocating civic involvement, distributing information on public or civic actions	Meeting minutes, committee report, legislative update, letter to officials, letter to group members, call to participate in newsletters or other publications, summary or analysis of public actions, petitions

16d
public

Sometimes they are prepared as companions to posters—which may supply similar information as they promote events.

ELEMENTS OF A PUBLIC FLYER

- It may open with its topic ("Hostetler Annual Reunion"), a general appeal ("Light a candle for peace!"), or a greeting ("Dear Choir Members").
- It clearly presents the essentials needed to attend or participate: date, time, place, directions, plans, equipment or supplies, contact and emergency telephone numbers, rain date, and so forth.
- It sticks to essentials and omits long explanations or background.
- It uses visual features, headings, graphics, and white space to highlight the most crucial information. (See 11c–d.)
- It may be informal or formal, depending on the group and the topic.

The following flyer announces a group's special event—a meeting to collect signed petitions for presentation to the school board.

Uses white space for readability

Identifies group

Provides address and directions

Expresses appreciation of volunteer effort

HAND IN YOUR PETITION TONIGHT!

Save Our Schools

Tuesday, March 4   7:30 to 9 p.m.

132 West Sloan

(Go north on Main, past the main library, and turn left at the third street.)

Meet our other volunteers!
Be the first to hear the latest signature counts!

And thank you again for getting
your petition signed!

Opens with purpose of event and appeal to recipients

Supplies date and time

Varies type sizes for emphasis and contrast

Encourages attendance

**16e
public**

16e Letter to the editor

Both partisans and interested citizens submit letters to the editor in order to comment on current issues or engage in topical debate. Check the opinion section of your local or campus paper, either in print or online, to read the current letters selected for publication and to locate directions for submitting your own letter.

ELEMENTS OF A LETTER TO THE EDITOR

- It respects the length limit established by the newspaper or publication.
- It clearly identifies its topic and its point of view or proposal.
- It briefly supplies reasons and evidence that may persuade readers to consider or agree with its point of view. (See Chapter 13.)
- It treats other views and writers respectfully, even if it disagrees with their opinions.

16.1

Following are two letters to the editor (see pp. 120 and 121), the first primarily informative, the second defending a group criticized by the writer of an earlier letter.

Letter to the Editor
April 16, 2006
Greeks Wrong in Punishing Critics

I am writing in response to the recent letter from Jillian Soares (April 14, 2006). As president of the Pan-Hellenic Council, she claims that the Council has the right to fine a fraternity or sorority if any of its members "speak publicly in ways that undermine the integrity or reputation of the Greek societies at Central Range State University." She uses this passage from the Pan-Hellenic Council's bylaws to justify fining Nina Campbell's sorority for statements she made in a recent Snowcap Advocate column. In it, Campbell criticized lack of fraternity and sorority support for the University's "All Campus Diversity Initiative."

As a sorority member myself, I think Campbell's criticisms were inaccurate and overstated. Certainly the Greeks can do a better job of promoting diversity—but then everybody can. After all, would a "Diversity Initiative" be necessary if everyone were doing a good job? But I think the Greeks have done more than most others on campus and that Campbell simply ignores all sorts of positive evidence. Campbell's opinions aren't the real problem, however. The proposed punishment is, along with the policy that makes it possible.

In her letter, Soares claims that the issue isn't a question of free speech because no one is trying to prevent Campbell from stating her opinion. She says that Campbell can avoid the fine for her sorority by resigning from the organization. She also states that the Council is not trying to prevent any Pan-Hellenic members from criticizing fraternity or sororitiy activities—the policy is only for statements that "distort the facts" or that are "needlessly insulting." But who is to determine the "facts"? When people don't like what they are hearing, they often claim that critics have "got the facts wrong."

The biggest problem with the policy is that it might discourage people from speaking out about actions that are truly discriminatory, unjust, or illegal. Soares says that anyone who wishes to speak out without violating the policy can resign from the fraternity or sorority. The policy might not prevent people from making reasonable criticisms, but it would certainly discourage them. Even when a person knows she is right to criticize, she might not want to cause trouble or expense for her "sisters."

Do we really want to force people to resign when they are speaking from the heart about things they believe are wrong—even if we disagree with them or even if they see the "facts" differently? Isn't this discriminatory?

Rebecca Fala

Sorority Circle

16f
speak

16f   Speaking in public settings

People gather daily to exchange opinions about local concerns. Citizens lobby officials for actions. Campus forums draw students, faculty, and administrators to discuss policies. Interest groups engage members and visitors. (See Chapter 12, 14j, and 17h.)

Letter to the Editor
February 18, 2006
"Balanced Education" Limits Diversity in Ideas

Last week at the South Valley School Board meeting, Concerned Citizens for a Balanced Education made a proposal that ought to be voted down at the next meeting. Concerned Citizens is critical of student government at South Valley High for sponsoring a talk by Malcom Zindt, who disapproves of the current president and many of his policies. They want to ban any speakers who "do not offer students a balanced perspective on issues or current events" in order to guarantee that "a South Valley education is a balanced education."

I believe that there are three important reasons for voting against this proposal.

(1) The proposal requires that any speakers present a "balanced" view. Speakers worth listening to generally present their own views, however. We want to listen to them because they offer special insights or because they are strong representatives of a point of view. Speakers who offer balanced perspectives are often less interesting—even boring. As a result, fewer students will attend their presentations and fewer will have a chance to encounter challenging ideas.

(2) By requiring that each speaker provide a balance of ideas, the proposal will eliminate the possibility of a set of lectures that create balance by presenting speakers with very different points of view. The student government has already set up a talk by Rose Azavone, a well-known critic of Zindt's and a supporter of current government policies. Concerned Citizens opposes this proposal because it would "require spending extra money for a job that one speaker could do." I believe Concerned Citizens is less interested in balance than in making sure students do not get to hear ideas the Citizens don't like!

(3) Concerned Citizens makes it clear that its idea of "balance" is pro versus con, left versus right. They seem to think that each issue has only two sides. This view is too simple. As a college student, I have come to realize that there are usually more than two ways of looking at an issue.

I hope the Concerned Citizens proposal will be defeated. I would like students at my former high school to get a chance to hear many voices and then make their own conclusions.

Ken Park, S.V.H.S., Class of 2003

16f
speak

STRATEGY Prepare to speak in a public forum.

- Attend meetings, listen, and read to get informed about issues.
- Plan and rehearse (see 12c), even to speak for a minute or two.
- Be reasonable; don't alienate those who are undecided or disagree.
- Use facts, details, and other evidence—not emotion—for support.
- Stay calm at a tense meeting so that fear and nervousness don't lead you to speak angrily, make accusations, or even cry.

Exercise 1

Find a flyer intended to be seen and read by a public audience (look on bulletin boards or in public places). If there are multiple copies of the flyer, take one; if not, make a photocopy of it or, if that is not possible, examine the flyer and take careful notes on it, even sketching its layout if necessary. Using the information in this chapter, analyze and critique the flyer, paying special attention to its use of language.

Exercise 2

Follow an issue in your local newspaper, and read any editorials or letters to the editor about the issue in that section of the newspaper. Then write your own letter to the editor, expressing your views on the topic or responding to the views of others who have written about it in the newspaper.

17 Workplace Writing

Whether you work for a major corporation, run your own small business, join a government agency, or serve in a nonprofit organization, much of your work life will be spent communicating with others. As technology increases the pace and quantity of written exchanges, your ability to write is likely to become even more critical to your success.

17a Goals of workplace writing

Although workplaces vary greatly, their goals tend to be similar—to meet the needs and expectations of readers by providing and promoting the organization's products or services. Use questions like the following to help analyze workplace writing situations.

- What is my purpose? What do I want to accomplish?
- What type of document am I writing?
- What do readers expect me to do: provide information? identify a problem? analyze alternatives? propose a solution?
- What level of information do I have? what level of responsibility?
- How does my organization handle writing processes, file exchanges, document templates, or technical specifications?

- How are collaborative writing teams organized?
- How do the editing and text approval processes work?

17b Analyzing workplace audiences

Your writing may address very different readers, from your colleague at the next desk to the government official who processes your forms. Because your busy readers value clear, accessible documents, try to meet different needs simultaneously—providing a summary for your overloaded supervisor along with detailed charts in the appendix for the sales team. These questions can help you assess what your readers expect and need.

- How large is my audience? Who does it include? a coworker? a supervisor? a committee? a customer or client? an outside agency?
- Do readers expect a draft or a finished product? Will they implement my recommendations? Will they rely on my technical data?
- How much time do my readers have? Do they need detailed analysis or focused summary? Will they read carefully or skim the headings?
- What do my readers need to do with my writing? Will they revise it? approve it? implement it? incorporate it in their own writing?

17d
work

17c Understanding workplace writing tasks

You'll want your clarity, tone, and language to represent you and your organization well. Many writing tasks will be similarly structured because you'll supply standard comparable information about comparable situations. For example, using the standard form for a status report or evaluation simplifies your task and aligns your writing with readers' expectations.

When your project is complex or no form is specified, ask others how similar materials have been prepared. Keep samples of well-regarded documents that might be useful models. Notice what characteristics and structures your readers favor in other written materials.

17d Types of workplace writing

Reports, memos, and letters can serve many different purposes. For example, an engineer writes technical reports, while a teacher writes progress reports (or, indeed, report cards). Proposals are adapted to internal and external purposes; memos, however, tend to be used internally and letters externally. Ask advice, and observe existing communication patterns to determine preferred forms. (See also 10b, 11b–f.)

Types of Workplace Writing		
Type	**Characteristic Activities**	**Common Forms**
PROVIDING INFORMATION	Gathering information; exploring issues; comparing competing products or services; tracing background information; summarizing, synthesizing, compiling, and presenting information	Report, study, agenda, minutes, instructions, employee manual, procedural manual, policy guidelines, memo, email message, summary, technical description, organizational chart, brochure, letter (of transmittal, response, adjustment, acknowledgment, good news, bad news, or application), position description, résumé, visuals
REQUESTING INFORMATION OR ACTION	Identifying an issue or a problem, identifying objectives or operational goals, identifying gaps in data or other information, identifying and evaluating potential sources and resources	Memo, email message, directive, letter (of request, inquiry, commitment, or complaint), sales letter, marketing material, advertisements, order form, other forms, letter of application, contract
IDENTIFYING ALTERNATIVES OR RECOMMENDING SOLUTIONS	Analyzing, evaluating, or selecting alternatives; comparing and contrasting; organizing supporting evidence; clarifying implications; advocating	Proposal, report, study, analysis, letter, email message, memo, summary, abstract, projection, evaluation, recommendation

17e
work

17e Business letter

17.1

The business letter serves many ends but generally follows the practices and format expected by readers. The first sample letter included here is a sales contact (see p. 125); the second focuses on a job applicant's accomplishments and abilities (see p. 128).

- **Stationery.** The best is 25 or 50 percent white cotton bond, usually twenty-pound weight. Avoid colors and fancy paper.
- **Print quality.** Use a laser printer or a letter-quality impact printer. Your credibility will be damaged by fuzzy print or nonstandard fonts.
- **Format.** In **modified block format**, often used for longer letters, the return address and the closing and signature are centered on the page, but the paragraphs are not indented from the left margin (see p. 128). In **block format**, often used for short letters, all paragraphs (including the greeting and signature) are flush at the left margin (see p. 125).
- **Salutations.** Use the recipient's first name only if you are already on a first-name basis. Use the full name if you don't know the person's

Acme Technical Products

3515 Lansing Road/Jackson, Michigan 49203
(517) 555-6651
www.acme.com

Uses
letterhead
paper

February 15, 2006

Ms. Janet Anderson
Purchasing Agent
Everett Batteries
15 Johnstown Boulevard
Westerly, RI 02891

Supplies
full address
of recipient

Dear Ms. Anderson,

Identifies
recipient in
salutation

Thank you for using Acme products in your lithium-ion battery research and
development program. Acme is ready to support you with your future needs as
you transition from this developmental battery into a manufacturable consumer
product. We are ready to provide you with volume discounts and to work with
you to develop a "just-in-time" inventory control, which will save you
inventory and storage costs.

We also would like to provide you with information on our new separator
materials designed specifically for lithium-ion battery development. The
enclosed catalog provides you with pricing and technical data on a number of
different separator products designed for a variety of battery needs.

17e
work

I look forward to working with you in the future.

Sincerely,

Steve Adams

Steve Adams
Sales Associate

Supplies
writer's
name and
position

Enclosure (1)

Notes
enclosure,
typist, and
copies

SA: rd
cc: Sales Manager

gender. Avoid male-specific salutations such as *Dear Sir*. If you don't
know which person to address, use salutations such as *Dear Credit
Manager*.

- **Notations following the signature.** Place any notations flush left, including initials for writer and typist: *RL: gw*, *Enc.* or *Enclosure*, *cc: Nancy
  Harris* (naming a person who is sent a copy).
- **Longer letters.** Use letterhead stationery only for the first page. For
  subsequent pages, use plain paper of the same weight.

- **Envelope.** Match the letter in color, weight, and type.
- **Electronic transmittal.** If you are expected to email or fax your letter, adapt its features for easy scanning or conversion to a company's word processor. Avoid multiple typefaces and type sizes, underlining, bullets, boxes, columns, or other features that might scramble.

ELEMENTS OF A BUSINESS LETTER

- It follows conventional form, identifying sender and recipient.
- It is prepared carefully, using appropriate visual features (see 11c–d).
- It has a few well-written paragraphs, each clarifying a specific point.
- It summarizes and synthesizes, respecting the reader's time.
- It specifies what the writer wants, whether information, service, agreement, or employment.

17f Memo

Most companies use a corporate memo template or a standard word-processing template. The organization's name and logo or letterhead may appear at the top. Unlike letters, which circulate externally, memos circulate internally and need no address.

ELEMENTS OF A MEMO

- It precedes the message with the words *To*, *From*, *Date*, and *Subject*, efficiently identifying the readers, writer, topic, and date.
- It typically distills its message into a few concise paragraphs, briefly outlining the situation or topic.
- It generally identifies any action or response required, including deadlines for replies.
- It follows the same conventions for spacing, enclosure notations, attachments, and copies as letters do.

17g Résumé and application letter

Your résumé and cover letter sell your most important "product," you and your accomplishments. Develop your résumé around categories: your career objective, education, work or volunteer experience, activities or skills, awards, and references. Arrange information by time order or major skills. Use your cover letter to discuss, highlight, or add to your résumé; to connect the job requirements to your skills; and to express your spirit and interest. (See pp. 128–29.)

17.2

Edit, proofread, and design your final documents carefully (see 11b–d). Prepare both for print or electronic submission (plain text without formatting but with searchable keywords). Turn to your campus career center, job-hunting Web sites, or books for advice and samples.

Everett Batteries: Internal Memo

TO: Bob Rogers, Director of Battery Research and Development

FROM: Janet Anderson, Purchasing Agent

Supplies
conventional
four lines

DATE: March 11, 2006

SUBJECT: Evaluation of Future Separator Needs

Outlines
situation

I recently received correspondence from Acme Technical Products with pricing information on their battery separator, as well as a catalog of new separator products. I am in the process of developing a purchasing plan detailing our separator needs for the next twelve months. Could you please provide me with a forecast of your department's projected use of Acme separator material on a month-by-month basis? I need this information by April 12 in order to meet MRP system deadlines.

Requests
follow-up

I have enclosed a copy of the new catalog which contains technical specifications and pricing information for your use.

Identifies
purpose of
enclosure

17g
work

jck
Attachment

ELEMENTS OF A RÉSUMÉ

- It complements your letter of application by concisely presenting your background, education, experience, skills, and achievements to a prospective employer.
- It uses headings to identify the sections or categories that organize your information.
- It generally arranges the specifics in each section in reverse chronological order, placing the most current information first.
- It is carefully designed and printed for clarity and easy reading.

½" margin at top above
writer's complete address

550 Sundown Ct.
Dayton, OH 45420
June 12, 2006

1" margin
on each
side

Jennifer Low, Director of Personnel
Marshall School
232 Willow Way
Huber Heights, OH 45424

Recipient's
complete
address

Salutation
with colon

Dear Ms. Low:

Identifies
job
sought

I am seeking employment in elementary education, grades one through eight, and Jan Blake informed me of your junior high opening. During the past year as a student teacher, I have met many people at Marshall School, and I would love the opportunity to work with such a wonderful teaching staff.

Highlights
recent
training

My recent schooling at Wright State University has equipped me with many strategies that I am excited about implementing into my teaching. One strategy I am ready to try is the use of procedures. If students know what is expected of them, I believe that they can and will live up to those expectations.

Single-
spaced
text with
double-
spaced ¶s

Identifies
special
skills that
supplement
résumé

My greatest strengths as a teacher are my creativity and time management skills. Both are assets when planning my lessons and keeping students interested while using class time wisely. During one past teaching experience, my task seemed impossible until I designed learning centers to combat time constraints.

Explains
benefits of
experience

I firmly believe in inquiry teaching, a technique that always worked well during my student teaching. One of the joys of working with children has been seeing their eyes light up when they begin to understand new information.

Supplies
contact
information

I feel that I would be an asset to Marshall School and hope to start my career in your district next fall. I can be reached at 453-555-5555 and look forward to an interview with you.

Sincerely,

Tammy Helton

Tammy Helton

Notes
enclosure
(résumé)

Enclosure

Tammy Jo Helton
550 Sundown Ct., Dayton, OH 45420
453-555-5555   TJ@mailnow.com

CERTIFICATION
Elementary Education (grades 1-8)
Bachelor of Arts, August 2006, Wright State University,
Dayton, OH

EDUCATION
Wright State University, 2003-2006, College of Education
Sinclair Community College, 2002-2003, general education
Wayne High School, 2002 graduate, college preparatory

AWARDS
Phi Kappa Phi National Honor Society 2005, 2006
Dean's list 2004, 2005, 2006

TEACHING EXPERIENCE
Student Teaching
Seventh grade physical science, L. T. Ball Junior High, Tipp City, OH
Planned and implemented lessons while maintaining classroom control.

Observation
Shilohview, Trotwood, OH
Implemented preplanned lessons.

Teaching
Sixth-grade religious education class, Dayton, OH
Currently responsible for planning and implementing lessons.

WORK EXPERIENCE
Goal Line Sports Grill, 2003-present: Server, cash register, supervisor
Frisch's Big Boy, 2001-2003: Server, inventory, preparation
Shilohview Park, 2000-2002: Park counselor, activity planner

INTERESTS AND ACTIVITIES
Took dance lessons for ten years; played drums in the school band.

References available on request.

Centers name, address, phone, and email address

Begins with required teaching credential

Summarizes education and awards

Uses capitals for main headings

17g
work

Organizes experience to show skills

Uses reverse chronological order

Adds optional information

ELEMENTS OF A LETTER OF APPLICATION

- It follows a traditional business letter format.
- It begins by identifying the job and conveying your enthusiasm about it.
- It complements your résumé by adding details and examples that show the pertinence of your experience.
- It ends by looking forward to an interview, supplying contact and availability information.

17h Speaking in the workplace

Committees and boards have their own conventions for communication, which, if violated, can weaken a member's standing. Observe carefully to figure out whether a group interacts formally (using parliamentary procedure), informally (allowing spontaneous comments), or even ineffectively (needing guidelines). (See Chapter 12, 14j, and 16f.) Plan your participation.

- Study the agenda ahead; read documents, or gather background.
- Plan, rehearse, and prepare any visuals or materials (see 13c).
- Focus in order to time comments well, advance discussion, offer new ideas, and link your remarks to those of others. Don't dominate.
- Adjust to the group's formality and any shifts to social talk.
- Consider how others may react to assumptions you imply. Control your emotions to avoid rash or potentially offensive remarks.

Exercise 1

Interview a supervisor or a writer at a local company. Ask the person to describe how the editing and revision process is controlled in the company. Also ask which type of errors are most troubling. Prepare a short presentation to share what you learned about this local business community with the class or your collaborative group.

Exercise 2

Think of a problem you experienced recently as a customer or consumer—for example, poor service in a restaurant or store, the ineffective handling of one of your concerns, or a design flaw or malfunction in a product that you could not return. Decide who could best address your problem and locate the appropriate contact information. Formulate a *purpose* for writing; then, using the strategies in this chapter, write a business letter explaining your concern.

PART 4

Researching and Writing

18 Getting Started: Researching and Writing

Research can take many forms, and it can play many roles in your writing. Put simply, **research** means systematic inquiry into a subject. Your research may lead you to written sources (print or electronic), to fieldwork (interviews, surveys, ethnographic observations), or even to a systematic examination of your own experience. Along the way, you are likely to encounter **research conversations**, exchanges among writers, readers, and speakers investigating certain aspects of a subject. Their shared focus on these aspects or elements of the subject makes it a particular matter of interest—a **research topic**.

You can use the depth of information, ideas, and insights you develop through research for a number of purposes. You might create an **informative** essay, report, or brochure.

"Everybody's Wheezin': My Generation's Collective Journey with Asthma"
(informative essay on rising incidence of the affliction)

"Unions versus Tobacco Growers in Mid-Twentieth Century America"
(academic paper)

You might create an **argumentative** paper taking a stand on an issue or a **proposal** supporting a particular course of action.

"Bring the Gray Wolf Back"
(essay or editorial)

Or you might explain and support an **interpretation** or **analysis**.

"Rebuilding America: Images of National Identity in Contemporary Popular Song"
(interpretation of contemporary song lyrics and music videos)

18a Beginning your research

Research is a careful, sustained inquiry into a question, phenomenon, or topic—guided by **research questions** that set goals for gathering and examining information. Managing the process of identifying resources, evaluating them, and integrating them with your own ideas and insights requires considerable attention and detailed recordkeeping. The process usually begins simply enough, however, either with your own experiences and reading or in an assignment in class or at work.

1 Choosing a topic

18.1

Your research can grow from a personal interest, an assignment, a strong feeling or point of view, a pressing issue or problem, or the interests and needs of potential readers.

| **STRATEGY** | **Respond to your assignment.** |

Begin by reading your assignment carefully, underlining key terms. Then respond to the assignment in these ways.

- If a word or phrase immediately suggests a topic, write it down, followed by a list of synonyms or alternate terms.
- If you can't identify a topic right away, take key words and phrases, write them down, and brainstorm related words and phrases, along with the topics they suggest.
- Consider asking the person or people who gave the assignment what they think of a potential topic—and for further topic suggestions. Consider asking potential readers for their reactions.

In an intermediate composition course, Jennifer Figliozzi and Summer Arrigo-Nelson underlined important words in their assignment to "investigate the psychological or social dimensions of a local or campus problem." They then listed some campus problems.

canceled classes	student fees	date rape	parking
library hours	role of sports	student alcohol use	crime

They chose "student alcohol use" because the topic sounded interesting with sources readily available and the field research manageable.

Try to balance your interests with readers' expectations. For example, Jennifer and Summer knew that their audience wanted an academic report using print and electronic sources with field research on a problem. They also considered likely questions and expectations of their audience—the local campus community—as they planned.

AUDIENCE QUESTIONS   What discoveries or information about student alcohol use might benefit the campus community?

RESPONSE   Our conclusion about local student drinking behavior could help the campus program to reduce student alcohol use.

Recognize your interests. Perhaps you have an interest, a passion, a job you like (or hate), a sport or recreation activity, a curiosity, or some other involvement that is part of your life and might be intriguing to readers. You don't need to start with a precise opinion or conclusion—a strong feeling or interest will do. It will help you identify a specific issue or subject worth further

18a
resrch

study. Here is how two students turned their interests and feelings into research projects.

INTEREST	TITLE OF FINAL PAPER
Curiosity: Why do so many workers in fast-food restaurants seem to be recent immigrants?	Easy to Hire, Easy to Fire: Recent Immigrants and the Fast-Food Industry
Job: I have been working as an EMT, but I'll bet most people don't know anything about the job.	You Won't Meet Us Until You Need Us: What EMTs Do

Read for an issue or problem. So much has been written about topics such as global warming, political bias in the media, or the influence of television violence on behavior that these topics easily exceed the scope of even the most ambitious research paper. A quick bit of browsing, however, can lead you to more focused issues, problems, and topics. Where can you do this browsing? Glance quickly through one or two issues of a magazine or newspaper, scan the entries in a database, or consult informational Web sites. Look for words, phrases, and titles that suggest possible topics, especially questions that are unanswered and issues that (for most people at least) remain unresolved.

STRATEGY | Consult academic databases.

18a
resrch

Turn to academic databases such as *PsychLIT*, *First Search*, *ScienceDirect*, and *MEDLINE*, choosing a database that covers a field that interests you. Then type in a subject (such as *breast cancer*) and terms that researchers often use to identify questions worth investigating (e.g., *recent issues*, *controversies*, *discoveries*, *risks*, *new developments*, or *alternatives*).

Draw on your experience. Research can begin with your personal or professional interest in a subject, a question or problem, a puzzling phenomenon, or a community's need for information. For example, if you begin sneezing every time you walk past the perfume area in a department store, you might try informal experiments, perhaps seeing how close you can get without sneezing. You might also seek advice from a Web site such as the *Health and Environmental Resource Center* at <http://www.herc.org>. Once you begin searching for an explanation, you're asking a research question: What is the relationship between perfume and sneezing?

Even a few words can spark an interest, as Jenny Latimer describes.

> After I had stuffed a couple of red licorice sticks into my mouth in front of my coworker Julie, she picked up the wrapper and said, "I didn't realize they had hydrogenated oils in them. I'll never eat them again!" I started wondering

about hydrogenated oils. What are they, and why do they seem to be in everything we eat? When did this start? What do they do to you? Do we need to worry or do something about them?

Your own emotions and attitudes can suggest topics as well.

EMOTION	POSSIBLE TOPIC	TITLE OF FINAL PAPER
Fear	I've never seen a tornado, but I've always feared them. I'd like to explore the dangers (real or exaggerated) that they pose.	Seven Good Reasons for Fearing Tornados
Sadness	Other students often say, "I'm depressed." I'd like to know whether depression is really a serious problem for college students.	Depression and College Students: How Often and How Serious?
Anger	I lose my temper easily. Friends say I'm just hot-tempered, but I worry I'm out of control. What causes anger to boil up so easily?	Two Views of Anger: Letting Off Steam or Losing Control?

Pay attention to your audience. The interests and expectations of your audience can help guide your choice of a topic. The chart on page 136 can help you identify your potential readers' likely concerns and perspectives.

18a
resrch

2 Narrowing a topic

Think of a **subject** as a broad field, filled with clusters of information, ideas, and written interchanges—clusters that are often only loosely related to each other even though they fall within the same subject area. A **topic** is a single cluster of ideas and information within a broader subject. Writers interested in questions surrounding the cluster of ideas and information often "speak" to each other through their writing, creating an ongoing **conversation** you can enter through your own writing.

By limiting your attention to a particular topic, you take an important step toward making your research project manageable. But how can you identify potential topics (or subtopics) that are limited enough to provide a real focus for your writing yet are the subject of enough discussion to provide adequate resources for your work? Pay attention to issues, disagreements, points of discussion, new discoveries, and intriguing ideas or interpretations as you do preliminary research on a subject. These focal points in what others have to say about the subject can suggest ways to narrow your topic choice.

Audience Expectations for Research Writing		
	Academic	Public	Work
GOALS	Explain or show, offer well-supported interpretations or conclusions, analyze or synthesize information for use in other settings	Support arguments for policy or course of action, inform or advise for the public good	Document problems, propose a project or course of action, compare information, improve performance
TYPICAL QUESTIONS	What does it mean? What happened? How does it occur? How might it be modified?	How can this policy be made better? What do people need or want to know?	What is the problem? How can we solve it? What course of action will help us achieve our goals?
TYPICAL FORMS	Interpretive (thesis) paper, informative paper, research report, grant report	Position paper, editorial, proposal, informative article, pamphlet, guidelines	Proposal, report, feasibility study, memorandum
AUDIENCE EXPECTATIONS	Detailed evidence from varied sources including quotations, paraphrases, and summaries; documented sources that acknowledge scholarship	Accessible, fair, and persuasive information with evidence; informal documentation	Clear, direct, and precise information; appropriate detail; less formal documentation

As you browse print and online sources, review your assignment, or talk with an authority on the subject, take note of key words and phrases they use to identify topics of discussion. Pay attention, as well, to questions they raise to identify directions for inquiry and argument. Then respond with statements or questions of your own that focus and narrow potential topics to reasonable limits.

Here are some notes Tou Yang made from articles on the topic *athletic dietary supplements* that he located in the database *Academic Search Premier*.

NOTES

"Eat Powder? Build Muscle! Burn Calories!"—creatine monohydrate; lots of
  athletes swear by it and claim it has only good effects
"Creatine Monohydrate Supplementation Enhances High-Intensity Exercise
  Performance in Males and Females"—controversy over whether creatine
  works or not; they claim it does

"From Ephedra to Creatine: Using Theory to Respond to Dietary Supplement Use in Young Athletes"—understanding why athletes use dietary supplements even though they are probably not effective

RESPONSES

Some disagreement over whether creatine works or at least over how well it works—take a position on this?

Or explain how it works and what it seems to add to sports performance?

3 Identifying keywords

Keywords—words or phrases identifying important ideas and clusters of information—are often used in library catalogs and by Web or database search engines (19d, 19f, 20b) to link discussions of a subject. As you examine print or electronic sources, make a list of all the keywords, names, or phrases that might refer to your topic. Note synonyms, such as *maturation* for *growth*. Initially, your keywords can help you define your topic. Later, they can help you develop research questions (18c) and guide your research (19a-3).

18b Types of research writing

No matter what subject you investigate, the specific steps you take will be heavily influenced by your answer to this question: Will I use my research to *inform* or to *persuade*?

An **informative** research paper, report, or Web site focuses on your subject: the phenomenon, discovery, process, controversy, question, person, or performance you are exploring. Your research and writing will focus on discovering information and ideas and sharing them with readers. Your efforts will be subject-driven.

Taking this approach does not mean that your writing will be a dull recitation of facts. On the contrary, you'll use your understanding, insights, and conclusions to organize information from sources to help readers understand, answer potential questions, and reach substantiated conclusions about the topic.

A **persuasive** research project focuses on your **thesis** (see 3b) or conclusion. You'll concentrate on evidence and explanatory details that logically support your point of view, persuade readers, and explain issues or problems (see 19c and 13c). You'll need to do more than just support your conclusions, however. To convince readers, an argument needs to offer detailed information about the issue or problem and the viewpoints involved. It needs to develop, refine, and support your thesis, your proposal, or your interpretation.

Research Writing: Informative and Persuasive			
Purpose for Writing	**Possible Form**	**Possible Title**	**Possible Focus**
Informative	Documented essay	"Everybody's Wheezin': My Generation's Collective Journey with Asthma"	Exploration of rising incidence of the affliction
Informative	Report	"'Buy U.S. Bonds': How Posters Helped Shape Public Opinion During World War II"	Historical examination of the ways the government employed posters
Informative	Brochure or pamphlet	"What Linux Can (and Can't) Do for Your Computers"	Investigation of both strengths and limitations
Informative	Academic research paper	"Unions versus Tobacco Growers in Mid-Twentieth Century America"	Analysis of conflicts during a specific time period
Persuasive	Documented essay or editorial	"Bring the Gray Wolf Back"	Presentation and support of stand with reasons and evidence
Persuasive	Position paper or *PowerPoint* presentation	"Meeting Objections to Gray Wolf Reintroduction in the Adirondack Region of New York"	Advocacy of position with recognition of alternate views
Persuasive	Proposal	"A Three-Step Process for Reintroducing Gray Wolves to Adirondack State Park"	Presentation and support of proposed actions
Persuasive (interpretation)	Academic essay	"Dream Interpretation: Three Current Approaches"	Explanation and application of three interpretive approaches to one of the writer's dreams
Persuasive (interpretation)	Report on field research	"Diversity on Campus: What Do Western College Students *Really* Think?"	Analysis and interpretation of data gathered on student views
Persuasive (interpretation)	Thesis-and-support essay	"Rebuilding America: Images of National Identity in Contemporary Popular Song"	Interpretation of contemporary song lyrics and music videos

18c Developing a research question

Research writing, especially informative writing, aims to answer questions, both those raised by specialized research and those likely to interest readers. By developing one or more **research questions**—simple questions about your subject—and by doing this early in the research process, you can set goals for gathering and examining possible sources.

> **STRATEGY**   **State your research questions.**
>
> Work toward one or two questions early in your research process. Relate your questions to your general and specific goals for writing. Design questions to enlighten both yourself and your readers.

For example, Summer Arrigo-Nelson and Jennifer Figliozzi developed the following questions for their academic research project on the relationship of parental behaviors to college student drinking.

- Will students with permission to drink at home show different drinking behaviors at college than those without permission to drink at home?
- Do the students feel that a correlation exists between drinking behaviors at home and at college?

Research questions can take several forms, depending on your individual preferences and your purposes for writing. Some writers prefer questions that focus on factual or informational matters: *who, what, where, when, why,* and *how.* Other writers prefer questions suggesting both a purpose and an organizational pattern for writing. Jennifer Latimer, for example, arrived at her research questions this way:

> I looked at the red licorice sticks package, the fruit-flavored candy package, the wheat crackers box, even the pudding pack—all contained hydrogenated oils. I did some preliminary research and developed two questions for my research and my readers:
>
> What effects do hydrogenated oils have on us?
>
> Should I (and we) ever again eat delicious treats containing them?

18d Developing a preliminary thesis

Research essays, reports, and even Web sites generally use a **thesis statement** (see 3b) to guide readers' attention and state the writer's key idea or theme. Your thesis should grow from and reflect your research questions, of course (see 18c). Creating a preliminary thesis early on helps you focus and shape your search strategy (see 19a). Later, complicating, developing, and

18d
resrch

18.3

qualifying your thesis in response to your research will help you review or revise the direction of your work.

Thesis statements in research writing help indicate your purpose for writing (inform or persuade, see 18c). They often follow one of these patterns.

- **Issue.** What is the issue, and what is my stand on it?
- **Problem.** What is the problem, and what solution am I proposing?
- **Public question.** What is the situation we are facing, and how should we respond?
- **Academic question.** What is the phenomenon, and what is my analysis and interpretation of it?

18e Creating a research file and a timeline

In a **research file**, you can record and systematically store your activities throughout the research and writing process. It is a good place to accumulate materials and keep them ready for later use. You can build a portable research file in a notebook, in a folder, on note cards, or in a word-processing file in your desktop, laptop, or handheld computer.

1 Building your research file

- Identify your topic, research questions, or rough thesis (see 3b).
- Create a research plan, listing possible resources and assembling a working bibliography (see 19a).
- Divide your file into sections for your main research and writing stages, and keep it with you as you work.
- Take notes, recording relevant ideas and information from sources (see 18f), including summaries, paraphrases, and quotations (see 18f–g).
- Copy or record passages or images with their sources, ready for possible inclusion.
- Document sources (see Chapters 25–28) of all materials in your file.
- Add reactions, chunks, drafts, and revisions integrating your insights with ideas and information from your sources (see 23a).

Besides creating a research file for material, you need to stick to a schedule so that you finish on time. Because college research projects require sustained effort over several weeks or months, by planning carefully and using your time efficiently, you can avoid the stress of a looming deadline and the fear of turning in an incomplete or substandard paper.

2 Constructing a timeline

- Use a printed calendar or your computer to record your plans.
- Divide up the work, noting likely activities and due dates.

- Allow several days or a week for activities such as choosing your topic, stating your research questions and rough thesis, beginning your working bibliography, reviewing your notes and revising your plans, finishing your research, planning or outlining your paper, drafting the paper and source list, getting feedback from peer readers, revising, editing, and proofreading.
- Work backward from the final deadline, scheduling each stage.
- Keep your timeline in your research file, and check it regularly.

18f Reading and note taking

A research project calls for two types of reading—analytical and critical. When you read *analytically*, you try to understand the ideas and information presented in a source. When you read *critically*, you interact with the source, assessing its strengths, limitations, and biases; analyzing its relationships to other texts produced by a research community; and identifying questions or issues it leaves unaddressed. (See also Chapter 6.)

Analytical reading leads to the summaries, paraphrases, syntheses, quotations, and details you develop into much of the content of a research report or paper. Critical reading leads to many of the insights you contribute to an understanding of the topic.

ANALYTICAL READING	CRITICAL READING
What does it say?	What does it mean or imply?
(literal)	(interpretive)
—summary	—interpretation
—paraphrase	—position of author
—synthesis	—nature of publication
—quotations	—use in one's own ideas
—details	—reception of audience

18f
resrch

1 Taking notes

Because analytical reading concentrates on understanding information, **analytical notes** record facts, details, concepts, and quotations from your sources, focusing on what's relevant to your research questions. **Critical notes** often accompany them, adding your comments, interpretations, or assessments of a source in relation to your research questions.

2 Recording notes

Here are three formats for note taking. (See also 19a-4.)

Note cards. Some writers prefer portable, convenient index cards, generally 4" × 6" or 5" × 7". If you identify the card's topic clearly at the top and restrict each card to one kind of note (quotation, summary, paraphrase, synthesis), you can group, add, or rearrange cards as you plan or write.

Research journal. A research journal (usually a notebook) provides space to record information, reflect on new knowledge, and begin assembling your project. Add headings or marginal comments to identify the topics of the notes. Store photocopies or printouts in any pockets or in a folder.

Electronic notes. You can use software designed for note taking or set up word-processing files like a research journal or set of note cards (one page = one card). If you specify a subtopic or research question for each entry, you can use these labels to sort, reorganize, or retrieve material.

> **STRATEGY**   **Link your notes.**
>
> • **Link notes to your keywords or research questions.** At the top of each card, page, or entry, use your keywords, research questions, or subtopics to identify how material relates to your topic.
> • **Link notes to sources.** Clearly note the source on each card, page, or entry. Use the author's last name or a short version of the title to connect each note to its corresponding working bibliography entry (see 19a-4).
> • **Link notes to exact locations.** Include the page numbers of the source, especially for any material quoted or paraphrased. If an electronic source uses paragraph numbers instead of page numbers, note them.

3 Recording quotations

When you're using actual books and journals, not photocopies or downloads, be *absolutely certain* that you copy quotations word for word and record the exact page number where each quotation appears. If a quotation runs on to a second page in the source, note both numbers and the place where the page changes. (After all, you don't know what you might finally quote.)

18.4

18g Summarizing, paraphrasing, and synthesizing

Analytical reading and note taking require careful, critical thinking as you draw information and ideas from a source and put them into forms useful in your own writing: quotations, summaries, paraphrases, and syntheses. In a **summary**, you present the essential information in a text without interpreting it. In a **paraphrase**, you restate an author's ideas in your own words, retaining the content and sense of the original but providing your own expression.

A **synthesis** brings together summaries of several sources and points out the relationships among the ideas and information.

1 Summarizing

A summary helps you understand the key ideas and content in an article, part of a book, a Web site, or a cluster of paragraphs. You can also create summaries as a concise way of presenting ideas and information from a source in your own writing. In an **objective summary**, you focus on presenting the content of the source in compressed form and avoid speculating on the source's line of reasoning. In an **evaluative summary**, you add your opinions, evaluating or commenting on the original passage.

STRATEGY   Prepare a summary.

To prepare a summary of information relating to your topic, follow this process.

- **Read** the selection, looking for the most important ideas, evidence, and information. Underline, highlight, or make note of key points and information that you think should be mentioned in your summary.
- **Scan** (reread quickly) the selection to decide which of the ideas and bits of information you noted during your first reading are the *most* important. Try also to decide on the writer's main purpose in the selection and to identify the major sections of the discussion.
- **Summarize** *each section* of the source (each step in the argument, each stage in the explanation) in a *single sentence* that mentions the key ideas and information.
- **Encapsulate** the *entire passage* in a *single sentence* that captures its main point or conclusion.
- **Combine** your section summaries with your overall summary to produce a draft summary of the main point, other important points, and the most important information.
- **Revise** to make sure your summary is logical and easy to read. Check against the source for accuracy.
- **Document** clearly the source of your summary using a standard style of documentation (see Chapters 25–28).

18g
resrch

In a summary, you can present the key ideas from a source without including unnecessary detail that might distract readers. Summer Arrigo-Nelson and Jennifer Figliozzi used two one-sentence summaries of research to help introduce one of the questions for their academic research paper.

> First, research has shown that adolescents who have open and close relationships with their parents use alcohol less often than do those with conflictual relationships (Sieving). For example, a survey given to

students in seventh through twelfth grades reported that approximately 35 percent of adolescent drinkers were under parental supervision while drinking (Department of Education). Based on this research, we are interested in determining if students who were given permission to drink while living with their parents would possess different drinking patterns, upon reaching college, than those who did not previously have permission to drink.

2 Paraphrasing

A good paraphrase doesn't add to or detract from the original but often helps you understand a difficult work. When you want to incorporate the detailed ideas and information from a passage into your own writing but don't want to quote your source because the wording is too dense or confusing, then a paraphrase can be the answer.

To paraphrase part of a source, put the information in your own words, retaining the content and ideas of the original as well as the sequence of presentation. (Many paraphrases contain sentences that correspond with the original except for changes in wording and sentence structure.)

STRATEGY   **Paraphrase a source.**

Use these steps in preparing a paraphrase.

- **Read** the selection carefully so that you understand the wording as well as the content.
- **Write** a draft of your paraphrase, using your own words and phrases in place of the original. Rely on synonyms and equivalent expressions. You can retain names, proper nouns, and the like from the original, of course.
- **Revise** for smooth reading and clarity. Change sentence structures and phrasing to make sure your version is easier to understand than your source.
- **Document** clearly the source of your paraphrase using a standard style of documentation (see Chapters 25–28).

As part of her research about alcohol abuse on her campus, Jennifer Figliozzi encountered the following passage in Leo Reisberg's article "Colleges Step Up Efforts to Combat Alcohol Abuse" in the June 12, 1998, *Chronicle of Higher Education.*

The university also now notifies parents when their sons or daughters violate the alcohol policy or any other aspect of the student code of conduct. "We were hoping that the support of parents would help change students' behavior, and we believe it has," says Timothy F. Brooks, an assistant vice-president and the dean of students at the University of Delaware.

Because she wanted to avoid long quotations and instead integrate the information smoothly into her discussion, Jennifer paraphrased part of the passage.

> Officials at the University of Delaware thought that letting parents know when students violate regulations on alcohol use would change students' drinking habits, and one administrator now says, "We believe it has" (Reisberg A42).

3 Synthesizing

By bringing together summaries of several sources and pointing out their relationships in a synthesis, you can use your sources in some special ways: to provide background information, to explore causes and effects, to look at contrasting explanations or arguments, or to bring together ideas and information in support of a thesis.

STRATEGY   Synthesize sources.

To create a synthesis of your source materials, follow this process.

- **Identify** the role a synthesis will play in your explanation or argument as well as the kind of information and ideas you wish to share with readers.
- **Gather** the sources you plan to synthesize.
- **Read** your sources, and summarize each of them (see 18g-1).
- **Focus** on the purpose of your synthesis, and draft a sentence summing up your conclusion about the relationships of the sources.
- **Arrange** your summaries in the order in which you will present your sources in the synthesis.
- **Write** a draft of your synthesis, presenting summaries of your sources and offering your conclusion about the relationship(s).
- **Revise** so that your synthesis is easy to read. Make sure readers can easily identify the sources of the ideas and information.
- **Document** clearly the sources for your synthesis using a standard style of documentation (see Chapters 25–28).

18g
resrch

Many academic papers begin with a summary of prior research designed to identify a need for further research and to provide justification for the research questions. The opening section of Summer Arrigo-Nelson and Jennifer Figliozzi's academic research paper uses synthesis for this purpose.

> Research dealing with student alcohol use most often focuses on children's perceptions of their parents' actions and on the relationship between child and parent. Studies conducted with high school students have supported the hypothesis that positive family relationships are more likely to be associated with less frequent alcohol use among adolescents than are

negative relationships. Adolescents model the limited substance use of their parents where there is a good or moderate parent-adolescent relationship (Andrews, Hops, and Duncan). Other factors the studies found to be associated with positive family relationships, along with substance use, were academic achievement, family structure, place of residence, self-esteem, and emotional tone (Martsh and Miller; Weschler, Dowdall, Davenport, and Castillo).

Work and public writing often use synthesis in a similar fashion to identify a problem that needs to be addressed or a policy that needs to be examined or reconsidered.

Exercise 1

Start your research project in one of four ways.

1. Create a journal entry in which you explore your experience, looking for incidents, interests, or questions that suggest a subject for research and writing.
2. Look through magazines, newspapers, or Web sites for discussions and topics that interest you as a subject for research; take notes on the areas of interest you encounter.
3. Underline key words in your assignment, then create a paragraph explaining your understanding of the assignment and naming one or more subjects you consider appropriate to it.
4. Identify an audience for your research paper or report and then write out an explanation of what your potential readers might look for in a choice of subject and goals for the writing. (Draw on the chart in 18a-2.)

18g
resrch

Exercise 2

Choose a format for a research file: folder, electronic file, notebook, word-processing document, or whatever form you find comfortable and useful. Make sure it can be divided into parts for your various research and writing activities. Create some initial entries to see if the format you have chosen is accessible and useful. Then, take the file with you wherever you plan to do research—at the library, online, or in the field—and add information to the entries you have already created. If the format you have chosen seems cumbersome, revise it before you move further into the research process.

Exercise 3

While browsing a print or online source for possible topics, write down those you discover in your research file. As you make notes, try turning the topics into paper titles; in this way, you begin to envision the kinds of research you will need to do and the kind of paper you will write.

Exercise 4

Create an entry for your research file in which you record the steps you have taken to narrow your topic. List different options you have for narrowing your topic and the advantages or disadvantages of each. Then create a statement identifying the focused topic you have chosen and your reasons for choosing it.

Exercise 5

Create a preliminary thesis statement to narrow your focus to a specific issue or problem. You might use several sentences at this point in the process, one stating the issue, problem, question, or phenomenon you are addressing, the other offering your (tentative) opinion or conclusion.

Exercise 6

Develop a timeline for your research and writing project. Put it in the form of a calendar, a project graph, or a chart of activities. Work backward from your due date and estimate the amount of time you will need to allot to each activity.

Exercise 7

Choose an article that interests you in a magazine such as *Natural History* or *Scientific American*. Paraphrase the first paragraph or two or any passage of a few lines or more. Then try to integrate the passage into an imaginary research report, putting much or most of the passage into your own words.

19 Library Resources and Research Databases

A good **search strategy** is a plan for locating the resources you need to answer your research question or support your thesis. It will help you to consult a variety of sources addressing various aspects of your topic and offering varied opinions.

19a Developing a search strategy and working bibliography

A search strategy has five elements: resources, search tools, keywords, working bibliography, and timeline.

19.1

1 List resources

Your search strategy should include a list of the kinds of resources you plan to use—printed books, scholarly journals, newspapers, Web sites, interviews, and surveys, for example. Draw on your preliminary research (18a–d) to create your initial resource list, and update it as you discover other potential resources. If you have specific titles, Web sites, or people in mind as sources, list them here, too, and update your list periodically.

2 Identify search tools

The most obvious search tools come readily to mind when you begin researching: your library's online catalog and Web search engines such as *Google*. However, more specialized research tools can often lead you to fresh information and ideas worth sharing with your readers.

STRATEGY   Try specialized research tools.

- Indexes of magazine and periodical articles: *Readers' Guide to Periodical Literature, New York Times Index, Wall Street Journal Index*
- Indexes of articles in scholarly journals in professional publications in fields such as business, public health, law, or engineering: *Social Sciences Index, Applied Science and Technology Index, MLA International Bibliography, Humanities Index, Education Index*
- Academic and professional databases with built-in search engines: *PSYCHLIT, MEDLINE, OCLC First Search;* specialized Web search engines and indexed databases, *Search Questia, AltaVista, Cata List, Metacrawler, Dogpile*

19a
library

---

3 Use keywords

Many people begin searching for sources using general terms to identify their topic, only to discover that these are not the terms used in an index or search engine. Indexes, databases, library catalogs (19d–f, 20b), and many other reference sources are arranged (or searched) by keywords (see also 18a). Sometimes it helps to have two or three alternative keywords or phrases so that, if a particular database or other resource yields little under one, you can try the others before moving to another resource.

4 Compile references for a working bibliography

Your search strategy should make provision for recording information that will help you or your readers locate a source. A list of sources you have examined and may decide to draw on as you write is called a **working bibliography**.

19.2

INFORMATION FOR A WORKING BIBLIOGRAPHY

When you examine a source, record the following kinds of information to include in your working bibliography and to use, eventually, in compiling the list of sources for your final paper.

PRINTED BOOKS

- Author(s) or editor(s)
- Title
- Publication information: place of publication, name of publisher, date of publication
- Volume or edition numbers, if any
- Call number (to help locate the book in library stacks)

PRINTED ARTICLES

- Author(s) or editor(s)
- Title
- Name of journal, magazine, newspaper, or collection of articles
- Publication information
  - Article in a periodical: volume number, issue number, month or day of publication, page numbers of article (inclusive)
  - Article in a collection: title of collection and editor's name, place of publication, name of publisher, date of publication, page numbers of article (inclusive)

ELECTRONIC OR ONLINE WORKS

- Author(s), editor(s), or group(s) responsible for the document
- Title or name of the Web site and the document
- Information about any corresponding print publication (as above)
- Electronic publication information: date of electronic publication or latest update, date you accessed the document, and complete URL; (for online journal) volume and issue number, publication date; (for databases or CD-ROM) document access number or version number; (for email or post to a discussion list) name of sender, subject line, date of posting, name of list, and date of access

19a
library

In a working bibliography, you record information you will need to provide in your final paper in a list of works cited, references list, list of works consulted, or footnotes (see Chapters 25–28).

When you are doing research, keep a copy of your working bibliography close at hand so you can make notes about entries to add or delete. (If it is in electronic form, you may be able to make changes right away.)

> **STRATEGY** **Organize your working bibliography·**
>
> Choose one of these strategies to organize your working bibliography.
>
> - **Alphabetically**, the way entries will eventually appear in a list of works cited or references page. This strategy can save time and effort when you are preparing your final text.
> - In **categories** reflecting the parts of your subject or the kinds of evidence they provide for your argument. This strategy can help you identify at a glance areas covered well and those needing further investigation.
> - According to the **plan for your paper**. This strategy can help you gather your resources efficiently as you write.

5 Revise and update timeline

Your timeline should be part of your search plan (see 18e). Revise and update it to reflect changes in direction or emphasis that arise from discoveries or new ideas that emerge from your research.

19b Searching library resources and databases

Your specific search strategy for library resources and research databases should reflect both the advantages and disadvantages of these forms of research, especially in comparison to the readily available resources on Web sites.

Advantages. Many important resources are available *at* a library (printed books and articles, microforms, CD-ROM databases, for example) or *through* a library (online databases available only through a library's Web site or on library terminals). Scholarly publications, technical and specialized reports, and government publications are more likely to be available at libraries than on Web sites.

Reference librarians can provide considerable help and advice—and are glad to do so. Libraries often provide Internet and Web access so you can follow a strand of research at *one* location, whether it takes you to printed sources, databases, the Web—or back and forth among them.

Disadvantages. Library research may require a substantial time commitment; library schedules may not correspond with your schedule. Library resources can also be difficult to navigate, especially if you are not familiar with the organization of research libraries.

1 Examine different kinds of library resources

In general, library resources fall into three categories, each with its own system for locating specific sources.

- Books, **pamphlets**, and miscellaneous resources including photographs, films, and recordings: Use **online catalogs**.
- **Articles** in magazines, scholarly journals, and other periodicals: Use **electronic and print indexes**, some of which may be accessed through a library's Web site.
- **Databases** of articles and information: Use **search engines** embedded in the databases; these also may be available on a library's Web site.

2 Move from general to specific resources

Your research will often move from general, less-detailed sources to more specific and detailed ones as you narrow your topic and begin adding depth of detail and specific evidence to your writing. The distinction between general and specific treatment of a topic holds true for online and field resources also, but it is especially sharp for library resources.

Another important distinction to bear in mind is that between **primary sources**, consisting of information and ideas in original or close-to-original form (such as historical records, literary works, raw statistics, and actual documents), and **secondary sources**, consisting of works that analyze, summarize, interpret, or explain primary sources.

19c General resources

You can use general resources to gain a broad overview of a topic, including background information and a sense of relationships to other subjects. General references can also provide names, keywords, and phrases useful for tracing a topic, as well as bibliographies of potential resources. (Many are available both in print and online.)

19c
library

General encyclopedias, ready references, maps, and dictionaries. These provide basic information on a wide range of topics and are good places to begin research for an overview of your topic.

New Encyclopaedia Britannica, Columbia Encyclopedia, Microsoft Encarta, World Almanac and Book of Facts, Canadian Almanac and Directory, Statistical Abstract of the United States, National Geographic Atlas of the World, The American Heritage Dictionary of the English Language, Oxford English Dictionary

Specialized encyclopedias and dictionaries. These provide in-depth coverage of a specific topic or area. The range of resources is wide.

Dictionary of the Social Sciences, Current Biography, Who's Who in America, McGraw-Hill Encyclopedia of Science and Technology, International Encyclopedia of Business and Management, Encyclopedia of Advertising,

> *International Encyclopedia of Film, International Television Almanac, Encyclopedia of Computer Science, Encyclopedia of Educational Research, Dictionary of Anthropology, Encyclopedia of Psychology, Encyclopedia of the Environment, New Grove Dictionary of Music and Musicians, Encyclopedia of Religion, Women's Studies Encyclopedia*

Bibliographies. These provide organized lists of books and articles on specific topics within a field of study or interest.

> *Bibliographic Index: A Cumulative Bibliography of Bibliographies, MLA Bibliography of Books and Articles on the Modern Languages and Literatures, International Bibliography of the Social Sciences, Foreign Affairs Bibliography, Film Research: A Critical Bibliography with Annotations and Essays*

19d Books and online catalogs

Library catalogs give you access to books and to many other resources, including periodicals, recordings, government documents, films, historical archives, and collections of photographs. Your library's catalog is most likely an **online catalog**, although **card catalogs** are still occasionally in use in small libraries. You can search under the *author's name*, the *title of a work*, the *subject area*, the title of a *series or periodical containing the work*, and, in some libraries, *words in the title or in a work's description*. Some catalogs list works not only in their home library but also in other libraries in a region or in a consortium, such as a group of college libraries.

Rachel Torres discovered that her library belonged to just such a group when she began her search for resources, especially printed books, on her topic, Afro-Cuban music. She began by typing her topic into the search screen for "words in title or description," and the catalog returned a number of possible sources (see Figure 19.1).

Rachel chose the tenth item on the list, and moved to the next catalog screen, which provided detailed information about the book along with a list of copies available in the cooperating libraries (see Figure 19.2 on p. 154).

19e Periodicals, print or electronic indexes, and government documents

Periodicals are publications that appear at intervals and contain articles by different authors. **General-interest magazines** appear once a month or weekly, with each issue paginated separately. **Scholarly journals** generally appear less frequently than magazines, perhaps four times a year, with the page numbering running continuously throughout the separate issues that make up an annual volume. **Newspapers** generally appear daily or weekly and frequently consist of separately numbered sections. Most schol-

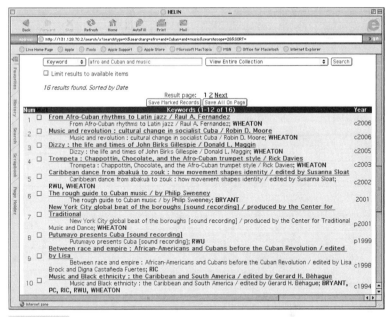

FIGURE 19.1   Sample search results for keywords *Afro-Cuban music*

arly journals are still available primarily in printed form, although recently many colleges and universities have begun subscribing to journals in electronic form, with current and back issues available online, either through terminals in the library or through the library's Web site. Many general-interest magazines and newspapers are now also available in electronic as well as printed form.

1 Indexes

You can locate articles in print (and in electronic form) by consulting some of the many print and online **indexes**.

General and newspaper indexes. These give you a way to search for topics in the news and in magazines and other periodicals intended for the general public as well as some intended for more specialized audiences. They include *Academic Index, Readers' Guide to Periodical Literature, Wall Street Journal Index, Washington Post Index, Expanded Academic, Editorials on File*, and *OCLC/World Catalog*.

Specialized indexes. These provide ways to search for publications offering more specialized, technical, or academic resources. Among these are *Anthropological Literature, Humanities Index, Music Index, BIZZ (Business Index),*

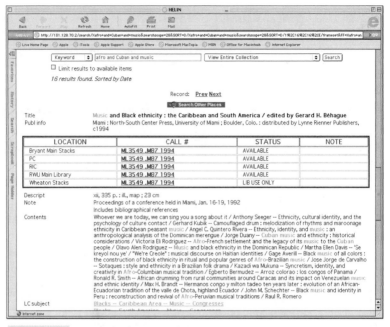

FIGURE 19.2   Detailed information for one entry

EconLit, Education Index, ERIC Current Index to Journals in Education, Index to Legal Periodicals, Social Sciences Index, Applied Science and Technology Index, and *MEDLINE.*

Abstracts. Collections of abstracts provide brief summaries of articles in specialized fields. They include *Abstracts of English Studies, Biological Abstracts, Dissertation Abstracts International, Historical Abstracts, Newspaper Abstracts, Psychological Abstracts,* and *Sociological Abstracts.*

2 Government documents

Government documents include reports of information and research, records of hearings, pamphlets, public information publications, and regulations issued by Congress, federal agencies, and state and local governments. These rich sources of information, both general and technical, are sometimes housed in separate collections in a library.

To access government documents published after 1976, search the *Catalog of U.S. Government Publications* at <http://www.access.gpo.gov/su_docs/locators/cgp/index.html>. Many government documents are available electronically. For government documents published before 1976, consult the printed *Monthly Catalog of United States Government Publications.*

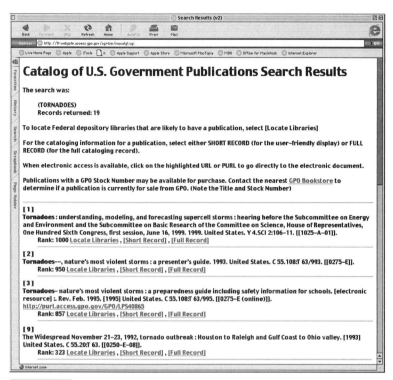

19f
library

FIGURE 19.3   Search results in *Catalog of U.S. Government Publications* for keyword *tornadoes*

After reading several magazine and newspaper articles about tornadoes, Michael Micchie noticed that some of the writers cited government documents and government-sponsored research. He decided to see if any government publications addressed the subject. His search of the *Catalog of U.S. Government Publications* using the keyword *tornadoes* returned sixteen citations, each with a link to a full description of the document and a link to a list of libraries likely to have a copy of it. Figure 19.3 shows part of the response he received.

19f   Online databases

In recent years, researchers (both student and professional) have come to rely on electronic databases for all kinds of information, especially for texts of scholarly and technical articles and for general-interest periodical articles. College, university, and public libraries offer a wide range of databases.

Online databases are simply files of information available only through the Internet or Web, or, occasionally, on CD-ROMs. Most databases focus on specialized or technical fields and are expensive to construct and maintain. Consequently, most databases restrict access to paying customers, including students and faculty whose fees are paid by their institutions.

Most databases are quite specialized, but also useful and interesting. Here, for example, is a description of one such reference database, the *Family Index*, which covers a range of topics most people would consider well worth learning about.

> *Family Index.* Indexes articles on the family from approximately 1,500 interdisciplinary journals. Family-related articles include family history and trends; education; economics, public policy and the law; health care; gerontology; religion; diverse families; marriage; parenthood and child development; sexuality; abuse and neglect; and other family problems.

This typical database provides information about articles from a large number of journals, more than would be indexed by a Web search engine (20b). It is updated on a regular basis and its focus is contemporary, containing references to documents only from 1995 on. If you wish to know about the latest work in the field, this may be the best choice for you.

Databases vary according to the kinds of information they provide: *full-text databases*, *abstracts databases*, and *indexing or bibliographic databases*. They also differ according to field of interest and number or range of resources they contain.

Databases are generally searchable by author, title, and keyword, or by special categories reflecting the scope and emphasis of the collection.

19f
library

1 Full-text databases

Full-text databases list articles or documents and provide brief summaries of each. In addition, they provide complete texts of most of the items. As a result, they can save you time and effort locating potential sources. Full-text databases range from extensive collections of scholarly or general-interest articles like *Academic Search Premier* or *Academic Universe* to highly focused collections like *Health Reference Center Academic*. Some of the most useful full-text databases are listed below.

- **General**
  Academic Search Premier (EBSCO)
  Provides full texts of more than 3,180 scholarly publications in social sciences, humanities, education, computer sciences, engineering, language and linguistics, arts and literature, medical sciences, and ethnic studies and similar academic fields.

Academic Universe (LexisNexis)
Provides news, law, and business information drawing from national and international newspapers and periodicals. Full texts of the articles.

National Newspapers
Offers indexing, abstracts, and full text of the *New York Times*, the *Wall Street Journal*, the *Washington Post*, and the *Christian Science Monitor*.

InfoTrac OneFile (InfoTrac)
Contains news and periodical articles. Subjects covered include business, computers, current events, economics, education, environmental issues, health care, humanities, law, politics, science, social science, and sports.

* **Specialized**
  CQ Researcher
  Collection of weekly reports, each exploring a single, controversial issue. Each report discusses pros and cons, offers comments from experts, includes charts and graphs, offers a timeline of events, and provides lengthy bibliographies.

  National Environmental Publications Internet Site
  Database of over 6,000 full-text EPA documents.

  Health Reference Center Academic (InfoTrac)
  Contains articles on fitness, pregnancy, medicine, nutrition, diseases, public health, occupational health and safety, alcohol and drug abuse, HMOs, prescription drugs, and similar subjects.

19f
library

Jenny Latimer was looking for detailed information to use for her paper about the presence of hydrogenated oils in snack foods, especially candy. She knew her research would involve technical information but didn't know which fields of study would provide information she needed: food science and nutrition, health sciences, chemistry, or biology. In addition, she was worried about finding herself limited to sources that were too technical for her to understand or explain to readers. As a result, she decided to consult a database covering general-interest as well as academic publications and to use one that provided both abstracts and full texts so she could sample the available sources online.

Here are some of the steps she followed. First she entered her search terms into the query screen of the database using the terms *hydrogenated oils* and *candy,* but the search engine was unable to identify sources using these terms. She then broadened the search using the terms *hydrogenated oils* and *food* connected by AND to search for documents with both (see 20b-2). This search identified sixteen sources, some of which seemed promising (see Figure 19.4 on p. 158).

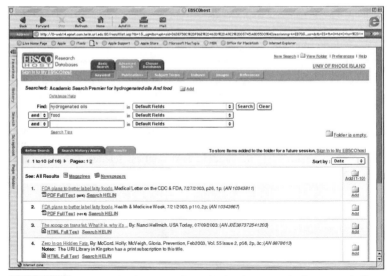

FIGURE 19.4 Sample database search results for the terms *hydrogenated oils* and *food.*

Jenny looked at all the articles in abstract and full-text form and took notes on several, including one that provided specific examples she felt might be important for her paper (see Figure 19.5).

After reading and taking notes, Jenny decided that the areas of study most likely to provide her with the kinds of information and insights she needed for her paper were nutrition studies and health sciences.

2 Databases containing abstracts

A large number of databases, especially those focusing on academic or technical fields, provide abstracts (brief summaries of a document's content) and sometimes full texts of selected items. Some databases link to a library's online subscription to academic and technical journals. Some useful databases containing abstracts are listed below.

PsycINFO
Indexing and abstracts of journal articles and books in psychology.

CINAHL (OVID)
Indexing and abstracts of journal articles and other materials in nursing and allied health.

Sociological Abstracts (CSA)
Abstracts and indexing in sociology and related disciplines.

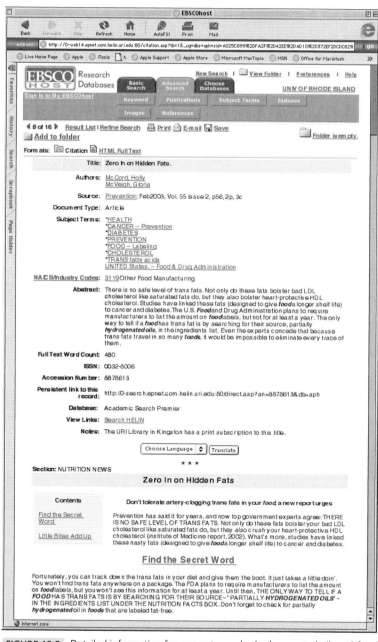

FIGURE 19.5 Detailed information for one entry under *hydrogenated oils* and *food*

Biological Abstracts
Indexing and abstracts of journals in the life sciences.

America: History and Life (ABC-CLIO)
Indexing and abstracts of journal articles and materials on U.S. and Canadian history.

MLA Bibliography (FirstSearch)
Indexing and abstracts of journals, books, and other materials in language and literature.

ComAbstracts
Abstracts of articles published in the field of communication.

MEDLINE (FirstSearch)
Indexing and abstracts of journals in medicine.

ERIC (FirstSearch)
Indexing and abstracts of journals and other materials in education.

Jenny Latimer's search for information on the presence and effects of hydrogenated oils in foods, especially snack foods and candy, led her to research in nutrition and health sciences and to the database *Health Reference Center—Academic*, which provides abstracts of scholarly articles and conference presentations. In this database she found two abstracts that added breadth and complexity to her research because they suggested that the dangers of hydrogenated oils are not as clear as many people claim (see Figure 19.6).

19f
library

3 Indexing or bibliographic databases

Many databases provide titles and publication (or access) information for articles and documents in a specialized field. They can be quite useful for identifying and locating potential sources. You will generally need to locate the texts of these sources through some other means, although some databases may provide a link to a library's online subscription to a scholarly journal.

Art Index (FirstSearch)
Indexes over 400 publications in the arts.

GEOBASE (FirstSearch)
Indexes articles on geology, geography, and ecology.

4 Resource databases

Resource databases provide access to information, images, and documents arranged in the form of an electronic reference work, or they offer tools for researchers. Here are several useful resource databases.

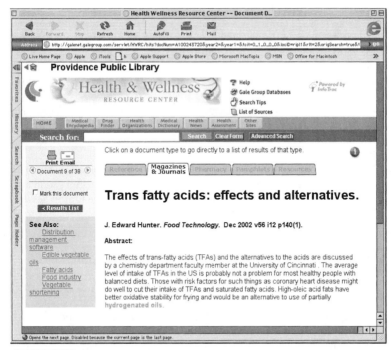

FIGURE 19.6 Sample of an abstract from the database *Health Reference Center—Academic*

19f
library

Web of Science (ISI)
Web access to databases (*Science Citation Index*, *Social Sciences Citation Index*, and *Arts & Humanities Citation Index*) of citations in research journals. Citation indexes allow you to identify the sources used by researchers in their work and to track the strands of a research "conversation."

RefWorks (CSA)
Web-based, bibliographic management service you can use to create a list of sources by drawing bibliographical information from online databases and automatically creating entries in a variety of documentation styles.

WorldCat (FirstSearch)
Catalog of library holdings and Internet resources worldwide.

STRATEGY **Consult online databases.**

1. Use the descriptions of databases in this section only as a *starting point*. Be alert for databases that are even better suited to your needs.

2. Most libraries prepare handouts describing the online databases to which they subscribe. These handouts will provide you with up-to-date information on the availability and features of the library's databases.
3. Move from general databases to more specialized ones.
4. Keep detailed records of the databases you have consulted as well as possible sources, and abstracts or full texts you have located. Download or print out copies.
5. Pay attention to links and alternative search paths suggested by a database.
6. If the full text of an article is not available online, check your library's catalog to see if it is available. (Many libraries provide links to their catalogs as part of their database programs.)
7. If a database provides only an abstract or a bibliographical reference to an article, check to see if the database will email you the full text of articles you find potentially useful. Some databases charge for this service; others will provide texts for free.

19g Evaluating library sources

19.3

Library sources—books from reputable publishers, articles from scholarly or well-known periodicals, government documents—often have been reviewed by experts and produced with editorial checks. Even so, once you locate these sources, you'll need to decide whether they are appropriate for your research community and your questions and whether they support or deepen your thesis.

19g
eval

> **STRATEGY** Use questions to evaluate your sources.
>
> • Does the publisher, journal, or sponsoring organization have a reputation for balance and accuracy? Is it an advocate whose views require caution?
> • Is the author's reputation clear? What do other sources think of the author's trustworthiness, fairness, and importance?
> • How accurate is your source, especially if it presents facts as truth? Can you spot obvious errors? Which points are well documented?
> • How does the writer support generalizations? Do they go beyond the facts? Are they consistent with your knowledge?
> • Are the ideas generally consistent with those in your other sources? If different, do they seem insightful or misleading and eccentric?
> • Does the source meet the expectations of your research community?
> • Does the source appropriately document information, quotations, and ideas or clearly attribute them to the author?
> • Has the source appeared without an editorial or review process? Does it apply only to a specific setting? Is its information outdated? Does it cite experts who have political or financial interests? Does it try to obscure its own bias? If so, consider it questionable; use it with caution.

Exercise 1

As part of your developing search strategy, make a list of possible sources you have discovered and a list of keywords and phrases that may help guide your research.

Exercise 2

Assemble the notes you have taken for your working bibliography. Use them to create a working bibliography as part of your research file. Organize the entries in a manner appropriate to your purposes for researching and writing. If possible, link the entries electronically to notes you have taken on the sources.

Exercise 3

Make a list of the resources named in 19e–f that you are not familiar with but that might be appropriate for your research. Choose two and examine them briefly. List the potential sources about which they provide information.

Exercise 4

Spend some time searching electronic databases (general and specialized) for possible sources, and take notes on one or more full-text documents appropriate for your project. Then list briefly what you consider the advantages and disadvantages of databases as a resource.

20 Web and Internet Resources

Many writers begin their research on the World Wide Web or the Internet. They do so because of accessibility and the wide range of current resources available. Email, discussion groups, and, above all, Web sites provide varied interpretations, opinions, and information, ranging from text to data to visuals and audio. To access a Web site, you simply need a **browser**, such as *Internet Explorer* or *Netscape*, and an electronic address, known as a **URL** (uniform resource locator). Or you can follow links embedded in an online document (usually marked by an icon or highlighted line).

Web and Internet resources are rich and varied, but they have limitations, too. The texts are often shorter, less detailed, and provide less developed explanations or arguments than print texts do. The electronic texts have not necessarily been reviewed and edited carefully in the ways many print texts have. And the absence of systematic cataloging and indexing on the Web and Internet makes search tools and an efficient search strategy very important.

20a Developing a Web and Internet search strategy

In creating your Web and Internet search strategy, emphasize diversity. Go beyond Web sites to electronic versions of printed texts (books, magazines, scholarly and professional journals, and newspapers); electronic databases and collections of documents (including government publications); discussion groups and newsgroups; visual and audio resources; synchronous devices including Webcams; and the links embedded in Web texts.

> **STRATEGY** Make a checklist.
>
> Turn your plan for Web and Internet research into a checklist you have at hand while you are working online. Include in your checklist reminders to examine a variety of resources, including the following.

Web sites and Web pages	Online versions of printed texts	Online databases (see 19f)
Synchronous devices	Discussion groups and newsgroups	Visual and audio documents
Embedded links	Collections of documents	Online periodicals

20b
Web

20b Search engines

To locate Web and Internet resources, use a **search engine**, an electronic tool that identifies and gathers data about Web pages and Internet sites such as discussion groups. The sites a search engine identifies, the information it gathers, and the way it selects and organizes information depend on two things: (1) the principles on which it operates and (2) the questions you ask of it.

1 General search engines

General search engines typically search for resources according to keywords or phrases you type into a search box. Results from different search engines may both overlap and differ because each search engine indexes only a selection of the sites on the Web or Internet. Each also uses its own principles of selection and arrangement, identifying different sites and providing different

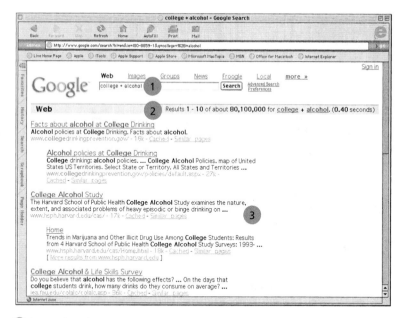

① Keywords used in search
② Results of search
③ One source with annotation

FIGURE 20.1 Results of a *Google* search using the keywords *alcohol* and *college*

20b
Web

information about them (see Figure 20.1). Using several search engines is worthwhile, although each search may turn up many irrelevant, dated, or untrustworthy sites for every one that is relevant.

Sometimes a search returns disappointing or confusing results. Perhaps the keywords or phrases in your query are not the ones used by some sites, so the search engine passes them by. Your query may be fine, but the results may be disappointing because the search engine finds the parts of a phrase or name rather than the whole.

Rashelle Jackson was working on a project guided by this research question: "What techniques used in hip hop performance make it different from other kinds of music?" She typed the words *hip hop techniques* into several search engines, and each responded with lists of resources including a site with the title "The Phonograph Turntable and Performance Practice in Hip Hop." The descriptions she encountered using the first three search engines were uninformative, incomplete, and even misleading. Only the fourth gave her a good idea of the site's contents and its relevance to her search (see Figure 20.2 on p. 166).

The Phonograph Turntable and Performance Practice in **Hip Hop** ...
... This transformation has been concurrent with the invention by the
Hip Hop DJ of a ... sliding lever which allows the performer to effect
certain **techniques** on a ...

The **Phonograph Turntable** and Performance Practice in **Hip Hop** Music
The **Phonograph Turntable** and Performance Practice in **Hip Hop** Music
Miles White ... globalization of **Hip Hop** music and culture ... invention by
the **Hip Hop** DJ of a new technical ... capabilities of...

The **Phonograph Turntable** and Performance Practice in **Hip Hop** Music
White. Introduction...

The **Phonograph Turntable** and Performance Practice in **Hip Hop** Music
The **Phonograph Turntable** and Performance Practice in **Hip Hop** Music
Miles White ... globalization of **Hip Hop** music and culture ... invention by
the **Hip Hop** DJ of a new technical ... capabilities of the **phonograph**, a
process which ... Description: The popularization and globalization of **Hip
Hop** music and culture over the past twenty or so years has provided new
and refreshing areas of inquiry and research across a number of academic
disciplines and critical approaches. The scholarly work...

20b
Web

FIGURE 20.2 Search engine results for the keywords *hip hop techniques*

2 Advanced searches

If your results for a search seem uneven or unhelpful—too many items,
too few items, or mostly irrelevant items—click on the advanced search advice available on most search engines. Find out how to search most productively, using specific words, math signs (+, -), symbols (* to look for all variations using part of a word), or automatic default combinations.

Word your query to combine, rule out, or treat terms as alternatives.
Use the principles of Boolean logic to focus on what you actually want to
know.

OR (expands)   Search for either term (documents referring to
                    either X OR Y)

AND (restricts)   Search for both terms (documents referring to
                       both X AND Y, but not to either alone)
NOT (excludes)   Search for X unless X includes the term Y (docu-
                       ments referring to X, but not those referring also to
                       Y; X NOT Y)

3 Metasearch sites

A **metasearch** site enables you to conduct your search using several
search engines simultaneously—and then to compare the results. Conducted
early in your research, a metasearch can help you identify which search engines are most likely to be useful for your task. Metasearches can also suggest
interesting new directions for your inquiry.

Dogpile	<http://dogpile.com>
Mamma	<http://www.mamma.com>
MetaCrawler	<http://metacrawler.com>
Profusion	<http://www.profusion.com>

4 Focused and question-oriented sites

Some search sites focus on specific disciplines, fields of inquiry, or content
areas. As you narrow your search or look for more complex information or the
results of academic studies, these focused search sites will become more useful.

Other search tools allow you to ask questions rather than use keywords,
for example, *Ask.com* at <http://ask.com>. Or they may link keyword queries
to what (sometimes) are related, relevant resources as does *WebReference* at
<http://www.webreference.com>.

20c
Web

20c Web sites and Internet resources

To identify and use appropriate resources on the World Wide Web and the
Internet, you should recognize some important kinds of Web sites and Internet
sites, their content and purposes, and the uses you can make of them.

1 Individual Web sites

Individual Web sites are not necessarily *about* individuals, although they
may be, as is the case with *home pages* created by individuals to share events in
their lives or to broadcast their opinions. Individuals may share accounts of
experiences: white water rafting, service on a United Nations peacekeeping
force, or work on an oil rig in Northern Alaska. Home pages maintained by researchers often contain links to their research articles, both those that have
appeared in print and those in progress.

Blogs are Web sites offering daily or weekly accounts of a person's activity and thoughts. They can be fascinating sources of information from people in war zones, in dangerous parts of the world, or in important jobs. Others can be just plain boring. The search engine *Lycos* at <http://lycos.com> maintains a focus area on blogs under the title *Tripod Blog Builder* that includes these topics: "Create and Edit Your Blog," "What Is a Blog?" "Recently Updated Blogs" (examples of ongoing Blogs), and a "Blog Directory."

2 Sponsored Web sites

All kinds of organizations—public, private, corporate, academic, government, religious, and social—sponsor Web sites. The suffixes on the electronic addresses often indicate what kind of organization the sponsor is.

edu	educational institution
gov	government agency
org	nonprofit or service organization
com	business organization (commercial)
net	network organization

A sponsored Web site may be little more than a billboard or marketing device, yet sponsored Web sites can also be excellent sources of up-to-date information and articulate, fair advocates for a cause. The usefulness and the integrity of a sponsored Web site generally depend on the character of the sponsoring organization and the resources devoted to creating and maintaining it.

20c
Web

3 Advocacy Web sites

Advocacy Web sites explain or defend an organization's actions and beliefs and argue for specific policies. Although they are biased in favor of the organization's position—after all, they *advocate* for the point of view—many are of high quality: explaining positions, answering critics, and providing detailed supporting evidence and documentation along with lists of readings on the topic or issue. Some even provide links to Web sites with opposing points of view as a way of stimulating open discussion.

4 Informational Web sites

Carefully organized informational Web sites provide tables of data, historical background, reports of research, answers to frequently asked questions (FAQs), links, and lists of references. Large Web sites may also provide site maps and allow for keyword searches.

Be aware, however, that many informational Web sites are poorly organized, unevenly developed, and even untrustworthy. Look on the Web site for information about the sponsoring organization, the way the information for the Web site is gathered and maintained, and the date of the last update.

Informational Web sites may focus on a particular subject such as sleep research, horror movies, or poetry from the Beat Generation of the 1950s, or an activity such as an environmental project or steps to developing a healthy lifestyle. Or they may focus on the sponsoring institution itself, providing information about its activities, ongoing research projects, and research results.

5 Research-oriented Web sites

Research-oriented Web sites are informational in a broad sense, but they are more narrowly focused than most informational Web sites and are arranged in different ways. Research-oriented Web sites typically contain one or more of the following.

1. Full texts of research reports (sometimes twenty-five or more pages)
2. Summaries of completed or ongoing research projects
3. Electronic texts of research articles that appeared in print journals or book-length collections
4. Extensive data frequently presented in the form of downloadable tables, graphs, and charts or available as texts of field notes and discussions of statistics
5. Reviews of current research
6. Texts of unpublished conference papers and other presentations
7. Announcements of grants, conferences, and forthcoming publications
8. Addresses or phone numbers for researchers
9. Bibliographies of books and articles; links to related Web sites
10. Artistic performances and creations

Universities, research institutes, and professional organizations (such as the American Psychological Association) often maintain research-oriented Web sites.

20c
Web

6 Online periodicals and books; electronic versions of print publications

Online magazines, newspapers, and scholarly journals are similar to print publications in many ways. Indeed, many appear in both online and print versions.

Los Angeles Times	<http://www.latimes.com>
Newsweek	<http://www.newsweek.com>
Business Week	<http://www.businessweek.com>
Weekly Standard	<http://www.weeklystandard.com>

The Nation	\<http://www.thenation.com\>
Dallas Star-Telegram	\<http://www.dfw.com\>

Many online sites go one step further and make back issues or selected articles available, as is the case with publications like the following.

Scientific American (general-interest magazine of science and technology)	\<http://www.sciam.com\>
Salon (general-interest magazine of social and cultural commentary)	\<http://www.salon.com\>
Journal of Mundane Behavior (academic articles on popular culture)	\<http://www.mundanebehavior.org\>

7 Electronic lists and discussion groups

The Internet and the Web play host to many discussion groups, some focusing on highly specialized topics like beekeeping, small countries in Eastern Europe or Africa, and poetry slams. The postings to such lists vary in quality, from inquiries by novices to discussions and responses from nationally recognized experts. It can be difficult to judge the quality of contributions because the writers may identify themselves only by screen names.

An **electronic list** posts messages from members of a mailing list to all other members and gives them a chance to respond. **Newsgroups** or **bulletin boards** are open sites where you can post messages or questions of your own and read postings from other people. Both kinds of sites are good places to gather opinions, possible sources, and an understanding of readers' expectations about a topic. Many search engines will help you locate postings, as shown in Figure 20.3.

8 Government publications sites

Government publications on an astonishing range of topics are available in print form in most college and university libraries. In addition, many government agencies have spent considerable effort developing Web sites for access to their reports and documents. Use the following sites to identify government publications relevant to your research.

FirstGov	\<http://www.firstgov.gov\>
Catalog of U.S. Government Publications	\<http://catalogs.gpo.gov/\>

20c
Web

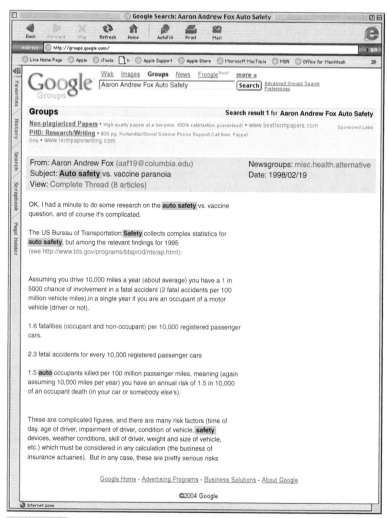

FIGURE 20.3   Newsgroup message from *Google* requesting research help

FedStats   <http://www.search.fedstats.gov/>
FedWorld   <http://www.fedworld.gov>

20d Evaluating Web and Internet sources

Web and Internet sources often have not been edited or reviewed by outside readers, so you can't assume that they are credible or reliable.

20.1

1 Examine Web materials

Examine Web sources carefully and ask questions appropriate to the kinds of information and ideas being presented.

- Is the material documentary (films, sounds, images, surveys)? If so, consider authenticity, biases, and relevance to your research questions.
- Is the resource textual (essays, narratives, studies, articles)? If so, consider its authorship, construction, level of detail, support for reasoning, complexity, fairness, sources, and documentation.
- Is the resource peculiar to the Web (personal, educational, corporate, organizational sites)? If so, consider its genre, affiliation, reputation, possible motivation, construction, design, and value in terms of content.
- Is the resource conversational? If so, analyze it as primary material (see 20d-3).

2 Ask critical questions about Web materials

To evaluate the strengths, weaknesses, and credibility of Web resources such as personal pages and organizational sites, ask the following questions developed by Paula Mathieu and Ken McAllister at the University of Illinois at Chicago as part of the *Critical Resources in Teaching with Technology* (CRITT) project.

Who benefits? What difference does that make? On many Web sites, the information presented seems designed primarily for the reader's benefit. Advice about a healthy diet, information about the best product, information about lodging and travel, or tips about the best ways to get a car loan—sites devoted to topics like these may seem unbiased and helpful. Yet no site can offer all the available information, and the selection is likely to benefit someone: producers of a specific kind of food, product manufacturers, or loan companies, for example. Before you decide to use the information from a site, consider who benefits from it.

Who's talking? What difference does that make? If the identity of the group or persons responsible for the site is clear from the pages, you can find out more about them and judge their likely credibility or bias. Remember, though, a group whose name makes it sound like it is dedicated purely to the general public interest may actually have a strong bias. Having a set of values and conveying them to readers is perfectly appropriate, of course, but readers need to be aware of these values so that they do not treat information as purely objective. If the source of the information on a site is not made plain, you may have to search the site for it, looking at the end of the text, the information presented in the URL, or in any linked files, such as a privacy statement or a page for further information.

20d
eval

What's missing? What difference does that make? Every resource has a point of view that guides its selection and presentation of information. A site promoting milk drinking might mention lactose intolerance only briefly (or not at all). A site devoted to understanding lactose intolerance would probably not spend much time (if any) discussing the benefits of milk drinking. When you are aware that most sites are likely to limit some information and focus on other information, you are likely to look to other sources to fill in the missing pieces.

3 Evaluate conversational resources

Electronic mailing lists, newsgroups, or Web-based forums can provide you with instant access to firsthand information. However, you need extra vigilance to distinguish authoritative comments, backed by genuine expertise, from unsupported opinions (see 9a–b and 13c–e). One strategy is to treat conversational materials as primary resources, data which you need to analyze and interpret for your readers. Ask critical questions: What do you know about the author's expertise, credibility, fairness, logical reasoning, or supporting evidence? Do other resources substantiate the author's claims? How does the author's view relate to your research thread? How would your research community react to the material?

Exercise 1

Create a Web and Internet *search strategy* for a project you are working on, using the information in 20a. Create a list of all possible electronic resources.

20d
eval

Exercise 2

Using a variety of relevant search engines, look for resources on your chosen topic. Rank the resources in order of their usefulness to your project.

Exercise 3

After locating two Web-based resources on your topic, analyze them thoroughly, using the strategies in 20d; look especially for bias (based on an analysis of the materials' source) and comprehensiveness (what's included and what's missing).

21 Fieldwork

Field research is firsthand research, gathering material directly from people you interview or survey or from events and places you observe. Your fieldwork addresses your research questions with original, even surprising, findings that are the product of your own investigation, not somebody else's research. Because you may find that your results vary or are more complex than you expected, it's important to plan your field research with an open mind or a "neutral" perspective on what you're investigating. This perspective will help you to avoid leading questionnaires, biased notes during an observation, or data-gathering methods that skew your results, such as interviewing only one social group about food in the student union.

Good field research also involves interpretation. Give the data you collect the same critical "reading" and analysis you give to all other sources. Secondary sources from your research may suggest how to present your findings and what to conclude from your data. Of course, your fieldwork goals and methods depend on your task and research community.

Academic. Field research in sociology, psychology, business, education, or urban planning often means studying people's behaviors or outlooks to find patterns, causes, or effects. In chemistry, engineering, or pharmacy, it inquires into how substances, organisms, objects, or machines work. When you plan your fieldwork, find out about any institutional approval needed for research involving other people (see 21d).

Public. Field research in public settings often gathers (and measures) people's opinions on issues or policies. Government research in the public interest can profoundly affect laws and regulations. Researchers for the Environmental Protection Agency, for instance, sample soil, water, and air across the country to test levels of pollutants or contaminants.

Work. Field research in businesses and organizations often looks at how customers (or staff) act and interact, how problems might be solved, or how quality or efficiency might be improved. Market researchers gauge interest in a product or recruit consumers for taste tests or "focus groups" that respond to products or marketing strategies.

STRATEGY **Prepare for your fieldwork.**

Do background research, and plan your fieldwork carefully. To identify worthwhile questions or problems, look over research already conducted. Use the methods of others as models for your own.

21a Interviewing

Talk with experts or people with pertinent experiences or opinions to test or supplement your other sources. An interview can be structured or open-ended. As you plan, think about your goals, and shape the interview questions accordingly.

STRATEGY Organize a productive interview.

- List potential interviewees and possible questions. Consider whether you will need a lengthy conversation or just a few short answers.
- Write out your questions, arranging them logically. Avoid any that could be answered by *yes* or *no* or that are unclear or leading.
- Use your questions, but don't be shackled by them. In the interview, follow up on new information and ideas that serve your purpose.
- If you wish to tape-record instead of taking notes, always ask permission. Bring extra tapes and batteries as well as backup paper and pen.
- After an interview, send a thank-you note—both to be polite and in case you need a follow-up interview.

21b Surveying, polling, or using questionnaires

Surveys, polls, and questionnaires gather opinions or information about specific behaviors and possible future actions. They can be administered orally (asking questions in a mall or on the phone), on paper (filling out a survey in a restaurant), or, increasingly, in electronic form (responding in a file on the Web). In any case, you'll need to think through your questions carefully and test your instrument before you administer it for your study.

21b
field

1 Use surveys or polls

Surveys and **polls** collect short answers, often in *yes/no* form, providing statistics for charts, comparisons, or support. All can provide basic information, but what they supply in simplicity and speed, they lack in depth and complexity.

STRATEGY Plan and test a survey or poll.

- Decide which people you want to survey or poll. How many do you need to contact? Of what gender, age, or occupation?
- Always draft, test, and revise your questions in advance.
- Consider your location; it may determine who answers your questions.

Shane Hand marked answers to his recycling questions on a tally sheet.

Do you . . .

Use coffee mugs instead of polystyrene cups?	Yes	No
Reuse plastic wrap, foil, and plastic bags?	Yes	No
Recycle newspapers and/or magazines?	Yes	No

Are you willing to . . .

Take your own bags to the store?	Yes	No

2 Use questionnaires

Usually mailed, **questionnaires** can gather in-depth information from many people but need careful preparation for clarity. (See the sample questionnaire at the end of the research paper in 26c.)

STRATEGY | **Design and test a questionnaire.**

- Decide on your purpose (what you want to find out and why), the selection of your participants (the characteristics of the people you will question), and your expectations (possible problems).
- Choose whether to group questions in sections. Decide whether to ask multiple-choice or yes-no questions that supply numerical data; open-ended questions that supply narrative detail; or a combination of these.
- Figure out what respondents might be willing to do (writing, checking, circling, or marking answers) and how you will analyze answers.
- Draft your questions, and test them on several people. Ask your testers to identify where they were confused or lacked information.
- Revise the questionnaire, and prepare it for distribution. Try to fit your questions on one page (front and back), but leave room for comments.

21c
field

21c Conducting an ethnographic study

You can use **ethnographic research** to interpret practices, behaviors, language, and attitudes of groups connected by interests or ways of understanding and acting. Because an **ethnography**—the written report of this cultural analysis—aims for in-depth understanding, you may use several methods to gather detailed information about your subject, including observations of people, events, and settings; conversations or interviews with **informants** (people who provide information about the group to which they belong); and collection of **artifacts** (characteristic material objects).

Focus your fieldwork on a specific setting, activity, person, or group. Conduct **structured observations** in which you objectively watch a situation, behavior, or relationship in order to understand its elements and processes. For instance, to study how preschoolers use language during play, you might conduct a series of structured observations at a day-care center.

STRATEGY   **Plan a structured observation.**

- Choose the site; if necessary, get permission to observe.
- Decide how to situate yourself (in one spot or moving) and how to explain your presence to those observed.
- Decide what information or artifacts you want to gather and why. Try to anticipate how you will use this material in your report.
- Consider what equipment you will use to record information: tape recorder, camera, notepad, or video camera.
- Anticipate problems, and plan strategies for dealing with them.

The following notes were transcribed from an audiotape for an anthropology study of a person with an unusual occupation.

Dave Glovsky—Palace Playland: Dave's Guessing Stand
(Sound of game, the Striker: hammer swings in background)
[First interchange between Brian Schwegler and Dave Glovsky is inaudible because of background noise.]
BS: So, Dave, can you tell me a little something about how you guess? Can you tell me how you guess?
DG: Ages? I read the lower lids. I read the lower lid. It deteriorates as we get older. The more it gets darker, they get older. Even children of sixteen can fool me with the deterioration under the eyes. They can have beautiful skin, but I don't check the skin. I check the lower lid of their eyes.
[The interview continues until a customer arrives.]
DG: Hey, come on in, have fun. What do you want me to guess?
Female cust: My age.
DG: All right, that's a dollar. (Holds up one dollar bill.) A hundred dollar bill. Step into the office here. (Points to a patch of pavement.)

21c
field

When you report ethnographic data, be precise. Offer interpretations that go beyond simply presenting details.

First Draft: Dave the Guesser
by Brian Schwegler
"Come on in, have some fun with the famous guesser of Old Orchard," says Dave "The Guesser" Glovsky. Relying on his voice and personality to attract customers, he seems out of place in this mechanized wonderland. Hand-painted signs covered with cramped writing are his advertisement. . . .

As I stand in front of his stand and read his signs, a young woman approaches Dave.

"Hey, come on in, have fun. What do you want me to guess?" Dave asks.

"My age," says the young woman.

"All right, that's a dollar." Holding up the dollar bill that the woman gives him, Dave examines it the way a jeweler examines a precious stone. "A hundred dollar bill." Pointing to a space on the pavement, Dave says, "Step into the office here." Dave checks her out from all angles, looking for the clue that will let him know her age within two years, his margin of error. . . .

21d Obtaining consent and approval for research on human subjects

Whenever you conduct research on human subjects, even when administering a short questionnaire, you need to abide by certain ethical and legal principles to avoid injuring your subjects. (This is also true of animal research.) "Injury" doesn't just mean physical harm, such as testing a product known to cause cancer. It also refers to possible psychological injury, such as might occur when interviewing children about traumatic events in their lives. Furthermore, participants are protected by privacy laws; although most people know when they become uncomfortable answering questions, they may not always be aware of how the law protects them. Consult with a teacher or a human subjects board member on your campus to ensure that your research meets the proper standards.

Most campuses have a committee, board, or administrative unit that provides information about using human subjects in research. Such groups are responsible for approving research plans after considering their legal and ethical implications as well as the kinds of information that the researcher proposes to gather. The group can approve, disapprove, or return a proposal for revision.

Gaining approval to conduct human subject research is required on most campuses—and has the benefit of protecting the researcher as well as the people who participate. However, whether you need approval for field research involving people will depend on various factors. In some cases, an entire class can receive general approval to conduct surveys, polls, or questionnaires; in other cases, no approval may be necessary. Be sure that you and your instructor know the practices on your campus, and follow the requirements accordingly.

Follow conventions for informed consent.

Besides meeting institutional guidelines and regulations, ethical field research involves some commonsense principles.

- Explain your research to participants. You may need to keep the explanation general so that you don't influence their responses, but you should not conceal the purpose and nature of your study.
- Make clear to participants what will happen with the data you gather. Who will see it? How long will it be kept? (Human subject committees have requirements for the collection, use, storage, and disposal of data, and you should follow those requirements.)
- Explain whether you will preserve anonymity or offer an option of anonymity. If you need to use names, will you use pseudonyms?
- Give your subjects the option of seeing the results of your research.

Exercise 1

If you need to do fieldwork for a project you are working on, decide what kind of information you will need to gather. Then consider the pros and cons of gathering that information using the following methods: interview, survey, poll, questionnaire, or ethnographic study. Which method is best suited to the research question(s) you are asking? Why?

Exercise 2

Using your school's Web site or phone book, find out who is in charge of your Institutional Review Board. Find out as much as you can about the processes you need to go through in obtaining human subject consent for your study, if relevant. Obtain any forms you need to fill out or instructions you need to follow, as well as samples if possible.

21d
field

22 Avoiding Plagiarism

Consider the following cases. (1) After procrastinating for weeks, Kim can't imagine finishing her research paper on time. Following a friend's advice, she uses her credit card to buy a paper for $50 from an Internet paper mill, puts her name on it, and hands it in. (2) Paul realizes that a research paper he wrote the previous semester also fits the assignment in his spring class. He makes some minor changes and hands it in without mentioning that he originally wrote it for another course. (3) In her research paper, Tisha quotes a paragraph from an excellent source, dutifully citing it in her text and her references. A paragraph later, she adds more from the source, but forgets to put quotation marks around the text or include an in-text citation.

Which of these cases is plagiarism? Which falls under "academic dishonesty"? Are they of equal severity? If someone like Tisha just makes an honest mistake while writing a paper, should she be guilty of plagiarism and suffer the (increasingly harsh) consequences?

22a Recognizing plagiarism

Plagiarism, which comes from a Latin word for "kidnapping," generally refers to the theft of another person's ideas or words. However, plagiarism is part of a system of beliefs and regulations that govern the ways we write and the ways we use people's words. The standards for acknowledging and citing sources vary with the context. In college, you are in a setting where the rules about plagiarism are strict and apply to almost any kind of work you do for a course. Not learning and following those rules can lead to a failing grade for either a paper or an entire course, a special plagiarism notation on your transcript, or expulsion from your college or university. Very serious plagiarism, especially at higher levels of research and scholarship, can result in lawsuits and can ruin a career.

22.1

According to the Council of Writing Program Administrators (WPA), plagiarism in an academic setting "occurs when a writer deliberately uses someone else's language, ideas, or original (not common-knowledge) material without acknowledging its source" (<www.wpacouncil.org>). Thus, turning in someone else's paper as your own, taking someone's original idea from a book as your own, and copying passages or even sentences into your paper without noting their source all represent plagiarism.

General Attitudes About Plagiarism in Three Communities		
Academic	**Public**	**Work**
BELIEFS ABOUT PLAGIARISM Strongly believes in individual ownership of ideas, texts, inventions, and other products of research and scholarship	Remains relatively unconcerned about the ownership of words produced for wide public or civic circulation, not for profit	Vigorously protects slogans, icons, language, and organizational representations from general use or appropriation by competitors
BELIEFS ABOUT WRITTEN MATERIALS Views writing as intellectual property of writer (but sometimes owned by institution)	May view materials as part of group identity or mission, but sees public benefit or advocacy, not ownership, as goal	Views written materials as part of mission, products, or services, often owned by organization (not writer)
ATTITUDES ABOUT TEAMWORK Generally accepts teamwork and team credits (with disciplinary differences)	May expect collaboration to facilitate consensus and efficiency within and among groups	Relies on internal work teams, all expected to defend organization's territory
EXPECTATIONS OF WRITERS Expects writers to credit original author of almost any written source and to distinguish the writer's words and ideas from the source's	Expects writers to share generously, freely adapting and circulating materials, but to credit local or national authorities who substantiate values, claims, and advocacy	Expects careful protection of organizational materials, but accepts unattributed use of "boilerplate" language of unclear origin or value
REGULATORY MECHANISMS Codifies and enforces strict plagiarism rules that can lead to paper, course, or status penalties	Generally accepts shared materials such as flyers, bylaws, and brochures, but could resort to legal protection of group identity or integrity	Turns to lawsuits to challenge theft of corporate identity, products, services, or intellectual property

22b
plag

22b The problem of intention

Some cases of plagiarism are conscious and deliberate. In other cases, the writers are trying to work honestly but haven't learned appropriate documentation practices or they have come from a culture with different norms. Even so, for many readers and teachers, your naiveté makes no difference at

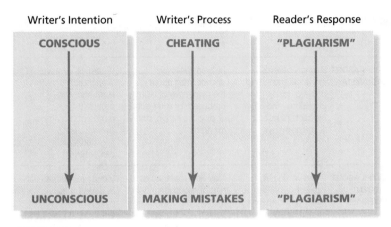

Writer's Intention	Writer's Process	Reader's Response
CONSCIOUS	**CHEATING**	**"PLAGIARISM"**
↓	↓	↓
UNCONSCIOUS	**MAKING MISTAKES**	**"PLAGIARISM"**

FIGURE 22.1 Representation of plagiarism from the perspective of the writer and of a reader or teacher

all. If the result *looks* like plagiarism, you may still be found guilty of academic misconduct.

Figure 22.1 represents plagiarism from the perspective of both the writer and a reader or teacher. At the top of the figure are cases of deliberate and conscious plagiarism. For most honest writers, the problem of plagiarism begins somewhere at the bottom of the figure, as they try to acknowledge sources but do so clumsily or incorrectly. But the reader's response is the same.

If you choose to plagiarize consciously and deceptively (placing yourself at the top of Figure 22.1), remember that plagiarism hurts everyone—including you: it cheats you out of your own learning opportunity, it robs others (parents, taxpayers) who may be funding your education; it subverts and complicates the work of teachers who are trying to help you learn; it slows social progress by undermining the achievement of higher standards of education and work; and it damages those who put time and energy into producing the work you're now stealing. By using this book to learn how to cite sources carefully and responsibly, you can avoid the situations represented by the bottom part of Figure 22.1.

22c Recognizing when to document sources

In general, you need to document the words, ideas, and information you draw from another person's work. Keep in mind the three most important reasons for documenting sources:

1. To add support to your conclusions and credibility to your explanations by showing that they are based on careful research
2. To give credit to others for their original work
3. To show your readers where they can obtain the materials you cite (and from there, perhaps others)

Decisions on what needs documenting may vary from audience to audience. If you're writing to a general audience, readers may expect you to cite sources for your discussion of subatomic particles. If you're writing for a physics professor or an audience of physicists, you might assume that such matters are common knowledge. However, in some college classrooms, your teacher may want to know all the works you have consulted in order to see the evidence of your explorations.

YOU MUST DOCUMENT

- Word-for-word (direct) quotations taken from someone else's work
- Paraphrases or summaries of someone else's work, whether published or presented more informally in an interview or email message
- Ideas, opinions, and interpretations that others have developed and presented, even if they are based on common knowledge
- Facts or data that someone else has gathered or identified if the information is not widely enough known to be considered common knowledge
- Information that is not widely accepted or that is disputed
- Illustrations, charts, graphs, photographs, recordings, original software, performances, interviews, and the like
- Anything from the Internet that you can reasonably cite, including emails from mailing lists, text from blogs and chatrooms, and so on

22.2

BUT DO NOT DOCUMENT

- Ideas, opinions, and interpretations that are your own
- Widely known ideas and information—the sort you can locate in common reference works or that people writing or speaking on a topic usually present as common knowledge
- Commonly used quotations ("To be, or not to be")

22d plag

22d Working with common knowledge

In every field, researchers share certain kinds of knowledge. Everyone in biological fields, for example, knows what a "double helix" is and would not need to cite a source for such information, which is called **common knowledge**. When your topic or discipline is unfamiliar to you, however, you may not know what counts as common knowledge.

> **STRATEGY** | **Test whether information is common knowledge.**
>
> - Consider whether information seems to be widely accepted and frequently repeated in sources or generally shared by educated readers. If it's not, *cite the source.*
> - Consider your composition teacher—who wants to know that you have learned from your sources—as your primary reader. To show your learning, cite what might be regarded as common knowledge in a specialized field.
> - Ask several people whether they know a particular fact that might be considered common knowledge. Or ask yourself. If the answer is "no," cite it.
> - When in doubt, *cite.* It's easier to cut an unnecessary reference when you revise than to have to find it again in your research file.

22e Citing sources responsibly

When you include quotations, paraphrases, and summaries in your writing, you *must* acknowledge their sources. If you don't, you're treating someone else's work as your own.

- Be sure you enclose someone else's exact words in quotation marks.
- Make sure that paraphrases and summaries are in your own words.
- Be sure to cite the source of any ideas or information that you quote, paraphrase, or summarize.

The following paraphrase is too close to the original to be presented without quotation marks and would be considered plagiarized, even if you had done so without knowing better.

**22e
plag**

ORIGINAL PASSAGE

Malnutrition was a widespread and increasingly severe problem throughout the least developed parts of the world in the 1970s, and would continue to be serious, occasionally reaching famine conditions, as the millennium approached. Among the cells of the human body most dependent upon a steady source of nutrients are those of the immune system, most of which live, even under ideal conditions, for only days at a time. (From Laurie Garrett, *The Coming Plague*, New York: Penguin, 1994, p. 199)

POORLY PARAPHRASED VERSION

Garrett points out that malnutrition can give microbes an advantage as they spread through the population. Malnutrition continues to be a severe problem throughout the least developed parts of the world. The human immune system contains cells that are dependent upon a steady source of nutrients. These cells may live, even under ideal conditions, for only days at a time.

The writer of the poorly paraphrased version made only minor changes in some phrases and "lifted" others verbatim. It's difficult, therefore, to tell which words or ideas are Garrett's and which are the writer's.

APPROPRIATE PARAPHRASE

Garrett points out that malnutrition can give microbes an advantage as they spread through the population. The human body contains immune cells that help to fight off various diseases. When the body is deprived of nutrients, these immune cells will weaken (Garrett 199).

Because this writer's paper focused on the general threat of global disease, he also could have simply summarized the passage. (See 18g-1, 23b-3.)

APPROPRIATE SUMMARY

It has been suggested that malnutrition can weaken the immune system and make people more susceptible to diseases they would otherwise fight off (Garrett 199).

Inadvertent plagiarism—really a kind of sloppiness in your writing process—often happens when you are working between your source material and your developing paper. You *think* you're using your own words, but the words of your source are so fresh in your mind that they creep in and "become" yours.

STRATEGY Watch out for inadvertent plagiarism.

Keep your distance whenever you paraphrase or summarize a source.

- Be sure to look back at the source and compare your words with those of the source.
- If any phrases or sentences are too close to the original, either quote the material directly and exactly (using quotation marks), or revise your summary or paraphrase so that you're not using the author's words as your own.

22f
plag

22f Citing sources in context

Academic research usually acknowledges and draws on the work of previous scholars and researchers. Most academic writers indicate where they fit in the tradition of research on a topic and explain any agreements and disagreements with earlier work. As they present their explanations, arguments, and evidence, they also supply precise, formal documentation in the style favored by their academic field. For four common styles used to cite sources as they are mentioned in the text and then listed at the end of the paper, see Chapters 25–28 on MLA, APA, CMS, and CSE documentation. If your instructor does not specify a documentation style, ask what is expected, and follow directions carefully.

The following excerpt from Summer Arrigo-Nelson and Jennifer Figliozzi's research report shows their careful integration (and critique) of a research study, cited in MLA style.

> First, although both questions 1 and 4 looked to determine student alcohol use within the home, a discrepancy appeared between the percentage of people who replied that they were offered alcohol at home and those who said that their parents believed alcohol was only for those over twenty-one years of age. This discrepancy could have arisen if the students in the sample were not thorough in their evaluation of their parents' views, in which case, correlations drawn from this data should not be relied upon (Aas, Jakobsen, and Anderssen).

Material from nonacademic settings, however, may follow somewhat different conventions. Work audiences will expect concise treatment of things they already know and extended summaries, tables, graphs, and illustrations—all carefully documented with a recognizable citation system (see Chapters 25–28). Material designed for general public consumption may cite sources in a somewhat informal fashion; texts with many footnotes or academic-sounding references can confuse or put off some public audiences.

The following paragraph is excerpted from a publication of the "Exxon Valdez Oil Spill Trustee Council" (<http://www.evostc.state.ak.us>) which contains documents of public interest with special focus on the Exxon Valdez cleanup effort and that spill's impact on the Alaskan shoreline environment. The excerpt comes from a report of research investigating the recovery of the harlequin duck from the effects of the oil spill. Notice how the writer condenses several important and scientifically complex studies into a research synthesis that is readily understandable by a reasonably educated public audience but does not overwhelm the reader with complex references.

> Winter surveys from 1995–1998 found that adult female survival was lower in oiled versus unoiled areas, and a similar survival scenario is suggested from data collected in 2000 to 2002. Oil remained in the subsurface of the intertidal zone through 2001, including under some mussel beds where harlequin ducks could be feeding. Biopsies from harlequin and Barrow's goldeneye ducks continue to show differences in an enzyme indicative of exposure to hydrocarbons between birds from oiled versus unoiled parts of the sound. These differences are consistent with the possibility of continued exposure to spill-derived hydrocarbons in the western sound. The biological effect of this possible exposure has not been established, but the declining trend of female survivability in the oiled areas may be continuing. Although this result cannot be attributed unequivocally to oil exposure, there is reason for concern about

possible oil exposure and reduced survival for harlequin ducks in the western sound.

If you cite such work in your own papers or projects, you may wish to "unpack" the general references into specific citations. In more informal and less research-oriented public writing, be sure that you check any quotations or material that appear to be from a source other than the public document itself. If you encounter an unreferenced quotation, try contacting the organization or author of the document to get the full citation for the source.

In contrast, consider an excerpt from a document at the same oil spill site that is clearly intended for other researchers and scholars with technical backgrounds (<http://www.evostc.state.ak.us>). Notice especially how careful the authors are to cite the sources of their information. Notice, too, how specialized their language and terminology are and how they rely on established studies (dating back two decades) to provide their background information.

> The composition, distribution, abundance, and productivity of plant and animal plankton communities in the GOA have been reviewed by Sambrotto and Lorenzen (1986); Cooney (1986); Miller (1993); and Mackas and Frost (1993). In general, dramatic differences are observed between pelagic communities over the deep ocean, and those found in shelf, coastal, and protected inside waters (sounds, fjords, and estuaries). Specifically, the euphotic zone seaward of the shelf edge is dominated year round by very small phytoplankters—tiny diatoms, naked flagellates, and cyanobacteria (Booth 1988). Most are smaller than 10 microns in size, and their combined standing stocks (measured as chlorophyll concentration) occur at very low and seasonally stable levels. It was originally hypothesized that a small group of large oceanic copepods (*Neocalanus spp.* and *Eucalanus bungii*) limited plant numbers and open ocean production by efficiently controlling the plant stocks through grazing (Heinrich 1962). More recent evidence, however, indicates the predominant grazers on the oceanic flora are not the large calanoids (Dagg 1993), but instead abundant populations of ciliate protozoans and heterotrophic microflagellates (Miller et al. 1991a, 1991b; Frost 1993).

22f
plag

Exercise 1

Choose a passage from one of your secondary sources and write a summary and paraphrase of it. Then embed a quotation from the source into a sentence of your own.

Exercise 2

With a group or partner, discuss your writing for Exercise 1. How carefully does the summarized and paraphrased material avoid using the exact words of the original source? Suggest ways to rewrite the passages to make them more effective. How can you make them read more smoothly? How can you make them more concise?

23 Integrating Sources

No doubt you've had the experience of being surrounded by photo-copied pages from books and articles, note cards or slips of paper with quotations on them, and ideas scribbled on a notepad along with references to various sources. Now you're facing the daunting task of weaving all this information into your own words as you create a research paper.

23a Choosing purposes for your sources

23.1

Your research paper is an original contribution to a subject area—something *you* create through your thorough sleuthing for information and your way of pulling all that information together and presenting it for others. Yet it's also about *other people's* work. It's your way of representing what a community of scholars and researchers and commentators has said about a topic or how this community has tried to answer a question. Weaving other people's words and ideas into your own paper can accomplish many specific purposes. The way you integrate outside material into your writing often depends on what you're trying to *do* with the source.

23a
integr

STRATEGY   **Consider your paper's goal.**

- As you gather and read your source material, take notes about the possible purposes it might serve in your paper.
- As you write the paper (see Chapter 24), refer to your notes to make strategic decisions about what to incorporate at different points in the paper.
- Avoid trying to "force" a quotation to fit a purpose it doesn't serve; for example, if an author has objectively cited a controversial position, it would misrepresent that author to imply that he or she holds that position as well.
- Be willing to scrap a source or citation if it serves no purpose in your paper.
- Avoid the "display for teacher" syndrome—putting in quotations and referencing sources just to show your instructor that you have collected some information.

1 Introducing a topic and providing background

Especially at the beginning of your paper, you may want to use some of your sources to explain a context, introduce your topic, or provide a history or background.

In his paper on conspiracy theories, Sam Roles decided to use his sources to provide background on why conspiracy theories are hard to refute. Material from Sam's paper shows that he has followed the MLA style in documenting his sources (see Chapter 25).

> Conspiracy theories arise, according to scholars, for a number of reasons: political fragmentation and suspicion of difference (Pipes); something to occupy the imagination of a bored subculture (Fenster); and fear of more powerful groups (Johnson). For example, in the 1950s and 1960s, communism provided a . . .

2 Summarizing prior research

In some cases, your research paper may be exploring a topic or relationship many others have written about. Instead of trying to provide lots of references, you can use some of your sources selectively to give a brief summary of others' work.

To introduce his paper about conspiracy theories, for example, Sam Roles summarized the different categories of research on the topic, selecting representative references in each category.

> Conspiracy theories are studied within several disciplines. Psychologists, for example, consider the relationship between conspiracy theories and disorders such as paranoia (Edmunds). Sociologists examine the formation and spread of conspiracy theories within a culture or group, and its underlying causes (Haskins). Political scientists focus on the way that political ideologies can lead to the creation of beliefs about leaders' motives (Argyle). And experts in anthropology consider the cultural bases of myth creation, fear of persecution, or the construction of alternative realities (Lizaro). In my . . .

23a
integr

3 Providing examples and cases

If you begin with generalizations about your topic or question, you will want to provide specific examples to illustrate your points. In the following paragraph, Sam Roles's generalization (in green) is illustrated by three examples. Notice how each example comes from a different source.

> Many conspiracy theories surround political figures or political events.
>
> The Apollo moon missions, for example, are now questioned by conspiracy theorists as having been staged by the government in a studio (Adams). For

decades, it has been thought that Jack the Ripper was actually Prince Albert Victor Christian Edward ("Prince Eddy"), the Duke of Clarence (Evans and Skinner). And theories of who assassinated President John F. Kennedy abound (Posner).

4 Showing evidence or support

When you make a point or state part of your argument, the words of experts can help you support your ideas. To present both sides of the debate over whether a UFO was found in New Mexico in the 1940s and the discovery covered up by the government, Sam Roles incorporated a quotation from a book taking one side of the issue.

> But were these sightings really UFOs? As Berlitz and Moore have pointed out, New Mexico in the late 1940s was "the site of the major portion of America's postwar defense efforts in atomic research, rocketry, aircraft and missile development, and radar-electronics experimentation" (18). Such activity, such as flashes of light in the sky, could have been mistaken for the presence of UFOs.

In his notes on his sources, Sam had written the following, indicating a specific purpose for the quotation, related to the broader plan for his paper.

Use to begin showing disagreement with UFO claim.

5 Expanding an idea

As you develop ideas, use your sources to help extend, refine, or elaborate on them. This approach is especially useful when you make a transition from one part of your paper to the next. Short quotations, summaries, and paraphrases can serve this purpose when woven together with your words and ideas. Occasionally, a block quotation may be effective, as in the following example. Note that there is no page reference following the block quote because the source is an unpaged Web site.

> Joltes (1995) points out how difficult it is to change the views of conspiracy theorists even when there is overwhelming evidence and rational explanation to account for a phenomenon:
>
> > Likewise, when the US Air Force discloses the existence of a weather balloon experiment that offers a rational explanation for the "Roswell incident," a conspiracy buff will claim that records were faked, witnesses bought off

or silenced, or whatever else was necessary to conceal evidence of alien contact. The aliens really do exist, but all the evidence has been suppressed, destroyed, or altered; therefore, the conspiracy theorist has had to work diligently to reconstruct what really happened, often producing "evidence" that is obviously contrived and illogical. But this matters not as long as it fits the theory.

6 Taking issue with a claim

You may want to argue against what someone else has said or what some group (of scholars or others) believes. After clearly explaining and citing sources for the opinion or belief, you can refute or "answer" the claim by drawing on other sources. Your artful use of sources can show weaknesses in a line of reasoning, or it can advance your own point of view on a topic, as in the following example.

In summarizing his report of a carefully coordinated 1994 investigation of the Roswell incident, Col. Richard M. Weaver says that "the Air Force research did not locate or develop any information that the 'Roswell Incident' was a UFO event" (1). Records did indicate, however, that the government was engaged in a "top secret balloon project, designed to attempt to monitor Soviet nuclear tests, known as Project Mogul" (1). Tests of these balloons are the only plausible explanation of numerous UFO sightings and of the desert debris assumed to be an alien spacecraft.

23b
integr

23b Summarizing, paraphrasing, and synthesizing

You can integrate sources into your paper in several ways: as quotations, paraphrases, or summaries. Furthermore, not all sources will appear in words; for example, you might want to include charts of facts, details, and statistics, or other visuals such as pictures, graphs, and screen shots.

23.2

1 Integrating quotations

Quoting someone's words means putting them into your paper or oral presentation in the *exact* way that they appeared in the original text (an obvious reason why it's so important for you to be accurate when taking notes during the research stage of your project). Avoid stringing quotations together or using many long quotations set off in blocks (which may look like padding). Instead, use direct quotations for these purposes.

- To show that you're accurately representing ideas that you want to challenge, modify, or extend
- To preserve an especially stylish, persuasive, or concise way of saying something
- To show vividly and dramatically what other people think
- To provide a jumping-off point for your thoughts or a change of pace

You can set off the exact words of a source with quotation marks as you blend them into your discussion. For example, you can quote entire sentences, interpreting them or linking them to your point.

> Yet alcohol awareness campaigns have seen only moderate success. "Although heavy drinking and monthly and daily alcohol use among high school seniors have declined since the 1980s, the decline is less among college-bound seniors, and binge drinking is a widespread problem on college campuses" (Bradley and Miller 1).

Or you can use an **embedded quotation**, weaving in key wording if it is less than a line or two.

EFFECTIVE   Yet a 1994 government investigation of the Roswell incident "located no records at existing Air Force offices that indicated any 'cover-up' by the USAF or any indication of such a recovery" of alien debris (Weaver 1).

23b
integr

GENERAL GUIDELINES FOR INTEGRATING SHORT QUOTATIONS

- Follow your introductory line with a colon only if that line is a complete sentence. Use commas to set off a tag such as "X says" that introduces or interrupts a quotation; vary *says* with other verbs (*claims*, *explains*, *shows*).
- When you work a quotation into your own sentence, use the context to decide whether it should be separated with a comma.
- If you leave out words or add to a quotation, use ellipses (see 53d) or brackets (see 53b) to identify your changes.
- Position these punctuation marks *inside* concluding single or double quotation marks: commas, periods, and question or exclamation marks that apply to the quoted material.
- Position these punctuation marks *outside* concluding single or double quotation marks: semicolons, colons, and question or exclamation marks that apply to the whole sentence.

2 Using block quotations

A **block quotation** is a longer passage from a source, set off from your own prose because of length. Remember that readers expect you to *do* something with block quotations, not just insert them.

If you quote a passage longer than four lines typed (MLA style) or forty words or more (APA style), set it off from your prose. Begin on the line after your introduction. Indent one inch or ten spaces (MLA style) or 1/2" or five spaces (APA style). Double-space the quotation; do not use quotation marks (unless they appear in the source).

MLA STYLE

Some psychologists believe that conspiracy theories have their
origins in the public's trust in authority. If that "authority" is not
fully credentialed but appears to be, the public may formulate
beliefs that are not supported by evidence, a point made by Robyn
M. Dawes in an analysis of why people believe in epidemic cases of
child sexual abuse and the presence of satanic cults:

> Asking people to doubt the conclusions concerning
> widespread childhood sexual abuse and satanic cults is
> asking them not only to reject the usual bases of authority
> and consensus for establishing reality, but in addition to
> accept principles that violate foundations of everyday
> functioning. Now in point of fact we do ask people to
> accept such principles, and they do. Few people, for
> example, believe that the world is flat, even though it
> appears to be, or believe that cigarettes and alcohol are
> good for them, even though both may have very pleasant
> effects. We return once more to the efficacy of authority.
> People who have no direct experience of the curvature of
> the earth believe that it is not flat, and even the greatest
> devotees of tobacco and alcohol believe that these drugs
> are harming them. We accept what we have been told by
> "reputable authorities." (We even accept what has been
> communicated by very minor authority figures, such as

23b
integr

the person who draws a map that shows the Suez Canal to be longer than the Panama Canal.) (Dawes 3)

Perez (1998) anticipates profound shifts in staff training.

> The greatest challenge for most school districts is to earmark sufficient funds for training personnel, not for purchasing or upgrading hardware and software. The technological revolution in the average classroom will depend to a large degree on innovation in professional development. (p. 64)

Begin the first line without further indentation if you are quoting from one paragraph. Otherwise, indent all paragraphs 1/4" or three spaces (MLA style) or any additional paragraphs 1/2" or five spaces (APA style).

Also present four or more lines of poetry in a double-spaced block quotation. On the line after your introduction, indent ten spaces or an inch from the left margin (MLA style). Do not use any quotation marks unless the verse contains them.

Donald Hall also varies line length and rhythm, as "The Black-Faced Sheep" illustrates.

> My grandfather spent all day searching the valley
>
> and edges of Ragged Mountain,
>
> calling "Ke-<u>day</u>!" as if he brought you salt,
>
> "Ke-<u>day</u>! Ke-<u>day</u>!" (lines 9-12)

3 Paraphrasing and summarizing

To make your writing smoother and more sophisticated, be selective in using quotations. Usually you can summarize, even combining several sources, or paraphrase rather than quoting sources directly.

> Yet at first, government officials denied they had any tests underway in New Mexico. Many officials were as baffled as the general public, including Captain Tom Brown, AAF information officer, who told reporters that he and his colleagues were as mystified as everyone else about the phenomena (Rotondo A1).

4 Integrating facts, details, and statistics

You can build entire paragraphs around facts, details, and statistics drawn from your sources as long as you indicate clearly the sources of your information. You may retain some of the emphasis of your source in using these materials; more likely, you'll end up integrating these details into prose that reflects your own purposes.

5 Using visuals

Visuals (drawings, photos, graphs, and the like) can sometimes present or emphasize data better than words. If you copy a visual from print or download it from an electronic resource, you'll need to cite the source, and you may need permission to use it. Whether you create a visual yourself or draw it from your research, make sure it adds to the written text and doesn't simply substitute for it. Visuals that add to a written explanation or extend it imaginatively can increase the credibility and effectiveness of your writing (see Chapter 11).

STRATEGY   Use visuals for emphasis or for an imaginative approach.

- Put the visual as near to the relevant written text as you can without disrupting the flow of the text or distorting the visual.
- Don't interrupt the writing in ways that make it hard to read.
- Make sure your visuals are of good quality and of appropriate size for the page.
- Ask one or more readers whether your visuals are easy to understand and whether they add to the text's ideas and effect.
- Label each visual (*Figure 1, Figure 2* . . . ; *Table 1, Table 2* . . .) in a form appropriate to the documentation style you are using (see Chapters 25–28).

Exercise 1

Make a list of the sources you have collected for your research paper, leaving several lines after each source. For each source, think of one or more purposes it might serve in your paper. Consider the purposes discussed in 23a. What could you use the source to *do*? (In some cases, you may not be ready to answer this question completely until your paper is further developed; yet even tentative notes at this point will help you to think about the potential role of your sources and help you to know their contexts more clearly.)

Exercise 2

Below is a paragraph from Sam Roles's research on the Roswell Incident; it comes from a Web site that shows problems with the Air Force's conclusion that the Roswell Incident was not the crash of an alien spacecraft. Consider Sam's lead-in to this information; then incorporate the material into the text by (1) quoting it directly, (2) paraphrasing it, and (3) summarizing it.

SAM'S LEAD-IN

In keeping with the processes of building a conspiracy theory, detractors of the Air Force report about the incident try to poke holes in specific versions of the historical record. For example, the Air Force report indicates that the testimony of Frank Kaufman, who was stationed in Roswell, was ignored. Seizing on this omission, Mark Rodeghier, writing for the J. Allen Hynek Center for UFO Studies, argues that

PASSAGE TO INCORPORATE (EXACT WORDS FROM THE SOURCE)
Kaufman claims to have been involved with the recovery of the alien bodies, and he was in the military stationed at Roswell. His claims have never been convincingly refuted. His testimony should have been included in the report. It was, most likely, not included because it is impossible to suggest that Kaufman could be confused about events in which he participated and for which he took written notes. (<http://www.cufos.org/airforce.htm>)

24 Writing, Revising, and Presenting Your Research

How do you know when to begin *writing* your research paper? Actually, there's no set time. If you've been recording your responses as a critical reader and assembling material as answers to your research questions, you've already begun drafting. Think strategically about your task as you move toward a more complete text.

24a Reviewing your research questions

You began with a clear research question (see 18c) or rough thesis (see 18d) and developed it as you consulted sources, took notes, and built your research file. Do you still want to *explain* and present detailed information, or is your goal now to *persuade* readers to share the strong opinions you have developed? Are your original research questions still worthwhile, or have you arrived at a new set to answer for readers? Has your research changed your outlook and your thesis, too?

> **STRATEGY** Let your research questions guide your draft.
>
> Arrange your research questions in a logical sequence, adding any others that you now think you ought to address. Answer the questions, and use them to determine the tentative order of material in your draft.

24b Reviewing your purpose

Review your readers' expectations, values, questions, and likely reactions to your project (see 3c and see the chart on p. 136). Try to respond with clear explanations, arguments, and supporting evidence. Also consider the goals that your research questions reflect (see 18c).

I'm going to tell readers about the three kinds of depression that may afflict college students—"the blues," common depression, and clinical depression.
(informative paper)

I want readers to agree with me that hunting is an acceptable activity when not excessive.
(persuasive paper)

I have a three-step solution to the problem of people downloading music without paying for it.
(persuasive problem-solution paper)

You also began with a plan, perhaps a formal outline, a set of notes, or a **purpose structure**, a series of statements briefly describing what you intend to do in each section of your paper, like this one for a paper on the problem of sleep deficits among high school students.

Beginning: Explain what sleep deficits are and how studies show that most high school students' schoolwork suffers because of them. Argue that the solution to the problem is to begin the school day later.

First Middle: Explain the problem that high school students need more sleep than most people think; the early beginning of the high school day robs them of sleep they need.

Second Middle: Explain that the high school day begins early because the buses have to be used by elementary, middle, and high school students; most districts can't afford more buses. Show that most school administrators believe it's OK for high school students to get up early.

Third Middle: Argue that changing starting times is important despite the difficulties. Tell how high schools that have changed their start times show improved student performance linked to overcoming sleep deficits. Explain that they claim the change has been worth the cost.

Fourth Middle: Outline the cost-effective strategies used by districts with later start times. Argue that these strategies should be adopted by almost all districts to help solve the problem.

End: Summarize solution; urge readers to take action in their districts.

24c Building from a thesis to a draft

24.1

Begin with a thesis statement (see 3b) based on your research questions. Modify it as you draft, perhaps breaking it into several sentences, or organize around its parts, repeated at key points. Instead of a detailed traditional outline, try a working outline, blocking out the general sequence and relating the segments (see 2b). Pull together the materials that belong in each part using whatever method of grouping suits your resources and notes.

STRATEGY Group your materials in sequence.

- Arrange your cards or notes in relation to one another. As patterns emerge, you may see how other material fits.
- Prepare pieces of paper describing available information—major points from sources, paraphrases, summaries, or ideas to include. Arrange these in relation to each other until you find a workable grouping (see Chapter 23 on integrating sources).
- Photocopy your research journal if you've written on both sides of the pages or don't want to cut it up. Then cut out the separate entries, arrange them in a sequence, and draft transitions to connect them.
- Use your word-processing program to cut and paste relevant electronic notes into a new file wherever they seem to fit.

Once you have chunks of related materials, move from the largest units to the smaller sections, interweaving notes, source materials, and additions. Write transitions between the chunks, explaining how they fit together. Use your research questions to focus your introduction and conclusion, but direct these key parts to your readers as you draft.

STRATEGY Design an introduction and a conclusion for readers.

For the introduction, ask, "How can I make readers want to read on?" For the conclusion, ask, "How can I keep readers thinking about my topic?" Try several versions of each, experimenting with style and content.

24c
write

1 Organize an informative research paper

It's true that an informative research paper follows the shape of its subject. But it also needs to take into account your readers' expectations, knowledge, and values in addition to your desire to make sure that readers understand your insights and conclusions. If you don't have an overall plan in mind, however, consider building your writing around one or more of these familiar informative plans.

* Describe a surprising or puzzling phenomenon, then explain it.
* Outline a challenging task or goal and the ways to accomplish it.
* Explain a common view; then suggest a new perspective.
* Focus on relationships, events, or objects that people consider unimportant. Explain why, to the contrary, they are very important.
* Compare the customs, values, or beliefs of one social or cultural group to those of another. Or explain them to people unfamiliar or (initially, at least) unsympathetic to these customs or beliefs.
* Start with a phenomenon that people have explained differently and generally unsatisfactorily. Then offer your detailed explanation, indicating why you think it is more satisfactory.
* Concentrate on your own insights, explanations, and conclusions. Organize around *your* selection and arrangement of information.

2 Organize a persuasive research paper

A persuasive research essay advances, supports, and defends a thesis. The thesis may be a stand on an issue (an argumentative proposition), a proposed policy or solution to a problem, or an interpretation of a subject. What sets persuasive research writing apart is the acknowledgment of alternative opinions, policies, or interpretations. Thus, your plan needs to account not only for reasons and evidence to support your thesis but also for grounds for preferring it to the alternatives.

24c
write

* Explain the issue, problem, or object of interpretation—the focal point of differing opinions or interpretations.
* State your thesis, and add other indications of your opinion, proposition, solution, or interpretation.
* Acknowledge and summarize other points of view, and demonstrate why yours is preferable.

Organize logically, perhaps following one of these arrangements.

* *Present alternatives.* Begin by discussing the issue or problem. Then discuss the alternatives in detail, indicating why each is lacking in whole or part. End with the presentation of your own perspective, which may incorporate parts of the alternatives. This strategy is useful when your

research has identified extensive arguments in favor of other opinions or solutions.

- *Summarize the scholarship.* Begin with a detailed analysis of other interpretations, solutions, or policies. Indicate why this prior work is limited, flawed, or inadequate. Then offer your own solution or interpretation that addresses the weaknesses.
- *Find a middle ground.* Begin by outlining other views, interpretations, or solutions that take unsatisfactory, even extreme, positions. Then present your own reasonable middle perspective.

24d Revising and editing

Allow time to revise what you've written based on your audience's needs, the community for which you're writing, your research questions, and your purposes (see 5a–b). Ask others to respond to your draft (see 5c). Carefully edit (see 5e), proofread (see 5f), and design your document (see 11b–e). Make sure that any quotations are accurate and that page numbers and authors are cited correctly (see 23b). Double-check your documentation form (see Chapters 25–28).

24e Presenting your research

24e
present

Be certain, especially for academic readers, that you supply your paper in exactly the print form or electronic format expected. For a print paper following an academic style such as MLA or APA, be sure to lay out the paper precisely as that style requires. For examples, see the sample MLA (Chapter 25) and APA (Chapter 26) papers. If your document can be submitted electronically, use any required software, and submit the file on a disk or as an attachment. If approved by your instructor or expected by your workplace or public audience, you may want to use a presentation program like *PowerPoint* that encourages the combination of text and graphics.

If you are expected to prepare a Web document in HTML or a similar language, be sure that readers will be able to move around at will and follow links to related documents or sources. A multimedia presentation using a program such as Macromedia *Dreamweaver* enables you to incorporate text, audio, still visuals, and action video. The result can be similar to a television documentary with the option of combining extensive text with detailed information, references, and documentation. Check with your instructor, supervisor, civic colleagues, or others involved to be certain that a particular electronic format will meet their expectations.

Exercise 1

To help bring your readers and your research together, write down five reasons why readers *might* or *ought to be* interested in your topic. Then try a bit harder and write down five more reasons. Next, identify those aspects of your topic you think are most likely to interest readers or to be of use to them. The aim of this activity is to help you see your topic from a reader's perspective as well as your own.

Draw on all three lists as you plan your paper and prepare an introduction designed to lead readers into your paper. Create an informal outline of the information and ideas you plan to discuss, arranging them in an order that reflects both your interests and those of your readers.

24

PART 5

Documenting Sources: MLA Style

25 MLA Documentation Style

The MLA (Modern Language Association) documentation style offers a convenient system for acknowledging and directing readers to your sources for ideas, information, and quotations. It consists of an in-text citation (generally in parentheses) that leads a reader to the corresponding entry in a list of works cited (at the end of the text).

25.1

STRATEGY Decide when to use MLA style.

ACADEMIC SETTINGS

When readers expect MLA style or simple parenthetical documentation, especially for writing in the humanities

WORK AND PUBLIC SETTINGS

When your subject and readers would be well served by a simple documentation style that seldom uses footnotes or endnotes

When you need an easy way to identify exact sources of quotations, paraphrases, or summaries

When other writers or publications in your setting use MLA, modified MLA, or a similar informal style

For more on MLA style, see the *MLA Handbook for Writers of Research Papers* (6th ed., New York: MLA, 2003), the *MLA Style Manual and Guide to Scholarly Publishing* (2nd ed., New York: MLA, 1998), or updates posted on the MLA Web site at <http://www.mla.org/style/style_main.htm>.

IN-TEXT CITATION

We think of the 1800s as the time when large corporations appeared, but at the beginning of the century, "business enterprises were generally small, family affairs" (Yates xv).

—Kevin Park, College Student

ENTRY IN THE LIST OF WORKS CITED

Yates, JoAnne. <u>Control Through Communication: The Rise of System in American Management</u>. Baltimore: Johns Hopkins UP, 1989.

25a MLA in-text (parenthetical) citations

The MLA documentation style uses a citation in the text (usually an author's name) to identify a source. Readers can easily locate this source, described in full, in the list of works cited that ends the paper. In-text citations follow standard patterns, and many note the exact page in the source where readers can find the particular information mentioned.

DRAFT   Even costumes convey the film's theme (Dell, p. 134).

EDITED   Even costumes convey the film's theme (Dell 134).

Guide to MLA Formats for In-Text (Parenthetical) Citations

---

1. Author's Name in Parentheses

You can provide the author's name in parentheses. For a quotation, paraphrase, or specific detail, give the page number in the source.

IN PARENTHESES   When people marry now "there is an important sense in which they don't know what they are doing" (Giddens 46).

2. Author's Name in Discussion

You can include the author's name (or other information) in your discussion, clarifying which observations are your source's.

IN DISCUSSION   Giddens claims that when people marry now "there is an important sense in which they don't know what they are doing" (46).

3. General Reference

A **general reference** refers to a source as a whole, to its main ideas, or to information throughout; it needs no page number.

25a
MLA

<table>
<tr><td>IN PARENTHESES</td><td>Many species of animals have complex systems of communication (Bright).</td></tr>
<tr><td>IN DISCUSSION</td><td>As Michael Bright observes, many species of animals have complex systems of communication.</td></tr>
</table>

4. Specific Reference

A **specific reference** documents words, ideas, or facts from a particular place in a source, such as the page for a quotation or paraphrase.

<table>
<tr><td>QUOTATION</td><td>Dolphins can perceive clicking sounds "made up of 700 units of sound per second" (Bright 52).</td></tr>
<tr><td>PARAPHRASE
+ FACTS</td><td>Bright reports that dolphins recognize patterns consisting of seven hundred clicks each second (52).</td></tr>
</table>

5. One Author

Provide the author's last name in parentheses, or integrate either the full name or last name alone into the discussion.

According to Maureen Honey, government posters during World War II often portrayed homemakers "as vital defenders of the nation's homes" (135).

6. Two or Three Authors

Name all the authors in parentheses or in the discussion.

The item is noted in a partial list of Francis Bacon's debts from 1603 on (Jardine and Stewart 275).

For three authors, do the same: (Norman, Fraser, and Jenko 209).

7. More Than Three Authors

Within parentheses, name the first author and add *et al.* ("and others"). Within your discussion, use a phrase like "Chen and his colleagues point out . . ." or something similar. If you name all the authors in the works cited list rather than using *et al.*, do the same in the text citation (see Entry 3 on p. 212).

More funding would encourage creative research on complementary medicine (Chen et al. 82).

8. Corporate or Group Author

When an organization is the author, name it in the text or the citation, but shorten or abbreviate a cumbersome name.

The consortium gathers journalists at "a critical moment" (Committee of Concerned Journalists 187).

9. No Author Given

When no author is named, use the title instead. Shorten a long title as in this version of *Baedeker's Czech/Slovak Republics*.

In 1993, Czechoslovakia split into the Czech Republic and the Slovak Republic (<u>Baedeker's</u> 67).

10. More Than One Work by the Same Author

When the list of works cited includes more than one work by an author, add a shortened form of the title to your citation.

One writer claims that "quaintness glorifies the unassuming industriousness" in these social classes (Harris, <u>Cute</u> 46).

11. Authors with the Same Name

When authors have the same last name, identify each by first initial (or entire first name, if necessary for clarity).

Despite improved health information systems (J. Adams 308), medical errors continue to increase (D. Adams 1).

12. Indirect Source

Use *qtd. in* ("quoted in") to indicate when your source provides you with a quotation (or paraphrase) taken from yet another source. Here, Feuch is the source of the quotation from Vitz.

For Vitz, "art, especially great art, must engage all or almost all of the major capacities of the nervous system" (qtd. in Feuch 65).

13. Multivolume Work

To cite a whole volume, add a comma after the author's name and *vol.* before the number (Cao, vol. 4). To specify one of several volumes that you cite, add volume and page numbers (Cao 4: 177).

In 1888, Lewis Carroll let two students call their school paper <u>Jabberwock</u>, a made-up word from <u>Alice's Adventures in Wonderland</u> (Cohen 2: 695).

14. Literary Work

After the page number in your edition, add the chapter (*ch.*), part (*pt.*), or section (*sec.*) number to help readers find the passage in any edition.

> In Huckleberry Finn, Mark Twain ridicules an actor who "would squeeze his hand on his forehead and stagger back and kind of moan" (178; ch. 21).

Identify a part as in (386; pt. 3, ch. 2) or, for a play, the act, scene, and line numbers, as in (Ham. 1.2.76). For poems, give line numbers (lines 55–57) or (55–57) after the first case; if needed, give both part and line numbers (4.220–23).

15. Bible

Place a period between the chapter and verse numbers (Mark 2.3–4). In parenthetical citations, abbreviate names with five or more letters, as in the case of Deuteronomy (Deut. 16.21–22).

16. Two or More Sources in a Citation

Separate sources within a citation with a semicolon.

> Differences in the ways men and women use language can often be traced to who has power (Tanner 83-86; Tavris 297-301).

17. Selection in Anthology

For an essay, story, poem, or other work in an anthology, cite the work's author (not the anthology's editor), but give page numbers in the anthology.

> According to Corry, the battle for Internet censorship has crossed party lines (112).

18. Electronic or Other Nonprint Source

After identifying the author or title, add numbers for the page, paragraph (*par.*, *pars.*), section (*sec.*), or screen (*screen*) if given. Otherwise, no number is needed.

> Offspringmag.com summarizes current research on adolescent behavior (Boynton, screen 2).

> The heroine's mother in the film Clueless died as the result of an accident during liposuction.

PLACEMENT AND PUNCTUATION OF PARENTHETICAL CITATIONS

Put parenthetical citations close to the quotation, information, paraphrase, or summary you are documenting.

* At the end of a sentence before the final punctuation

Wayland Hand reports on a folk belief that going to sleep on a rug made of bearskin can relieve backache (183).

* After the part of the sentence to which the citation applies, at a natural pause in the sentence so that you do not disrupt it, or after the last of several quotations in a paragraph, all from one page of the same source

The folk belief that "sleeping on a bear rug will cure backache" (Hand 183) illustrates the magic of external objects producing results inside the body.

* At the end of a long quotation set off as a block (see 23b), after the end punctuation with a space before the parentheses

Many baseball players are superstitious, especially pitchers.

> Some pitchers refuse to walk anywhere on the day of the game in the belief that every little exertion subtracts from their playing strength. One pitcher would never put on his cap until the game started and would not wear it at all on the days he did not pitch. (Gmelch 280)

19. Informative Footnote or Endnote

Use a note when you wish to comment on a source, provide background details, or supply lengthy information of use to only a few readers. Place a superscript number (raised slightly above the line of text) at a suitable point in your paper. Label the note itself with a corresponding number, and provide it as a footnote at the bottom of the page or as an endnote at the end of the paper, before the list of works cited, on a page titled "Notes."

[1]Before changing your eating habits or beginning an exercise program, check with your doctor.

25b MLA list of works cited

Provide readers with full detail about your sources in an alphabetical list following the last page of your text.

- **Page format.** Use the heading "Works Cited" (or "Works Consulted," for all sources used) centered one inch below the top edge of a new page. Continue the page numbering from the body of the paper.
- **Indentation.** Do not indent the first line of each entry. Indent additional lines one-half inch or five spaces.
- **Spacing.** Double-space all lines within and between the entries. Leave a single space (or two spaces, if you wish) after a period within an entry. Use consistent spacing throughout all entries.
- **Alphabetizing.** Alphabetize by last names of authors (or first names for authors with the same last name); then alphabetize by title multiple works by the same author. For sources without an author, use the first word in the title (other than *A*, *An*, or *The*).

DRAFT   Fem. and Polit. Theory, by C. Sunstein. UCP, 1990.

EDITED   Sunstein, Cass R. Feminism and Political Theory. Chicago: U of

Chicago P, 1990.

STRATEGY   **Find and match the MLA models.**

- Take bibliographic notes as you use a source (see 19a-4).
- Figure out what type of source you've used—book, article, online document, or other form. Use the Guide on page 211 to find the sample entry for that type. Prepare your entry following this pattern.
- Identify how many authors or other features your source has. Find the patterns for these, and rework your entry as needed.
- Check the details in each entry for the sequence of information, capitalization, punctuation, and abbreviations.

25b
MLA

Books and Works Treated as Books

MODEL FORMAT FOR BOOKS AND WORKS TREATED AS BOOKS

period + space   period + space   colon + space
↓   ↓   ↓
Author(s). Title of Work. Place of Publication:

Publisher, Year Published.
↑   ↑   ↑
indent ½"   comma + space   period
or five spaces

Guide to MLA Formats for List of Works Cited

25b
MLA

- **Author.** Give the last name first, followed by a comma, and then the first name and any middle name or initial. End with a period.
- **Title.** Underline the title (and any subtitle), and capitalize the main words (see 54b). End with a period (unless the title concludes with a question or exclamation mark).
- **Publication information.** Begin with city of publication, a colon, and a space. Give the publisher's name in shortened form (*U of Chicago P* for *University of Chicago Press* or *McGraw* for *McGraw-Hill, Inc.*) followed by a comma, the year of publication, and a period.

1. One Author

Hockney, David. <u>Secret Knowledge: Recovering the Lost Techniques of the Old Masters</u>. New York: Viking Studio, 2001.

2. Two or Three Authors

Begin with the first author's last name. Add other names in regular order, separated by commas with *and* before the final name.

Kress, Gunther, and Theo van Leeuwen. <u>Reading Images: The Grammar of Graphic Design</u>. London: Routledge, 1996.

3. Four or More Authors

After the first name, add *et al.* ("and others"). You may give all the names; if so, list them in the text citations too (see Entry 7 on p. 206).

Bellah, Robert N., et al. <u>Habits of the Heart: Individualism and Commitment in American Life</u>. Berkeley: U of California P, 1985.

Bellah, Robert N., Richard Madsen, William M. Sullivan, Ann Swidler, and Steven M. Tipton. <u>Habits of the Heart: Individualism and Commitment in American Life</u>. Berkeley: U of California P, 1985.

25b
MLA

4. Corporate or Group Author

Alphabetize by the first main word of the group's name. If this body is also the publisher, repeat its name, abbreviated if appropriate.

Nemours Children's Clinic. <u>Diabetes and Me</u>. Wilmington, DE: Nemours, 2001.

5. No Author Given

Alphabetize by the first main word of the title.

<u>Guide for Authors</u>. Oxford: Blackwell, 1985.

6. More Than One Work by the Same Author

List multiple works by an author alphabetically by the first main word of each title. For the first entry, include the name of the author. For additional entries, use three hyphens instead of the name, ending with a period. If the author or authors are not *exactly* the same for each work, include the names in full.

> Tannen, Deborah. <u>The Argument Culture: Moving from Debate to Dialogue</u>.
>
> > New York: Random, 1998.
>
> ---. <u>You Just Don't Understand: Women and Men in Conversation</u>.
>
> > New York: Ballantine, 1991.

7. One or More Editors

Begin with the editor's name followed by *ed.* (or *eds.*).

> Achebe, Chinua, and C. L. Innes, eds. <u>African Short Stories</u>. London:
>
> > Heinemann, 1985.

8. Author and Editor

Begin with either the author's or the editor's name depending on whether you are using the text itself or the editor's contributions.

> Wardlow, Gayle Dean. <u>Chasin' That Devil Music: Searching for the Blues</u>.
>
> > Ed. Edward Komara. San Francisco: Miller, 1998.

9. Translator

Begin with the author unless you emphasize the translator's work.

> Baudrillard, Jean. <u>Cool Memories II: 1978-1990</u>. Trans. Chris Turner.
>
> > Durham: Duke UP, 1996.

10. Edition Following the First

Note the edition (*Rev. ed.*, *1998 ed.*, *2nd ed.*) after the title.

> Coe, Michael D. <u>The Maya</u>. 6th ed. New York: Thames, 1999.

11. Reprint

Supply the original publication date after the title; follow with the publication information from the version you are using.

> Ishiguro, Kazuo. <u>A Pale View of Hills</u>. 1982. New York: Vintage Intl., 1990.

25b
MLA

12. Multivolume Work

Indicate the total number of volumes after the title (or after the editor's or translator's name).

> Tsao, Hsueh-chin. <u>The Story of the Stone</u>. Trans. David Hawkes.
>
> 5 vols. Harmondsworth, Eng.: Penguin, 1983-86.

If you cite only a specific volume, supply that volume number and publication information. End with the total number or the full range of dates, if you wish.

> Tsao, Hsueh-chin. <u>The Story of the Stone</u>. Trans. David Hawkes. Vol. 1.
>
> Harmondsworth, Eng.: Penguin, 1983. 5 vols.

13. Work in a Series

Add the series (*Ser.*) name and any item number after the title.

> Hess, Gary R. <u>Vietnam and the United States: Origins and Legacy of War</u>.
>
> Intl. Hist. Ser. 7. Boston: Twayne, 1990.

14. Book Pre-1900

The publisher's name is optional; when omitted, add a comma after place of publication.

> Darwin, Charles. <u>Descent of Man and Selection in Relation to Sex</u>.
>
> New York, 1896.

15. Book with Publisher's Imprint

Give the imprint name, a hyphen, and the publisher's name.

> Sikes, Gini. <u>8 Ball Chicks: A Year in the Violent World of Girl Gangs</u>.
>
> New York: Anchor-Doubleday, 1997.

16. Anthology or Collection of Articles

Supply the editor's name, with *ed.*, and then the title of the collection. (To cite a selection, see Entry 34 on p. 218.)

> Wu, Duncan, ed. <u>Romantic Women Poets: An Anthology</u>. Oxford:
>
> Blackwell, 1997.

17. Conference Proceedings

Begin with the title unless an editor is named. Follow with details about the conference, including name and date.

Childhood Obesity: Causes and Prevention. Symposium Proc., 27 Oct.

1998. Washington: Center for Nutrition Policy and Promotion, 1999.

18. Title Within a Title

Within a book title, don't underline another book's title, but underline a title normally in quotation marks.

Weick, Carl F. Refiguring Huckleberry Finn. Athens: U of Georgia P, 2000.

Golden, Catherine, ed. The Captive Imagination: A Casebook on "The

Yellow Wallpaper." New York: Feminist, 1992.

19. Pamphlet

Use the same form for a pamphlet as for a book.

Vareika, William. John La Farge: An American Master (1835-1910).

Newport: Gallery of American Art, 1989.

20. Dissertation (Published)

When published, a doctoral dissertation is treated as a book. Add *Diss.*, the school, and the date of the degree.

Said, Edward W. Joseph Conrad and the Fiction of Autobiography.

Diss. Harvard U, 1964. Cambridge: Harvard UP, 1966.

21. Dissertation (Unpublished)

Use quotation marks for the title; add *Diss.*, the school, and the date.

Swope, Catherine Theodora. "Redesigning Downtown: The Fabrication of

German-Themed Villages in Small-Town America." Diss. U of

Washington, 2003.

22. Government Document

Begin with the name of the government agency, the independent agency, or the author, if any. Start with *United States* for a report from a federal agency or for congressional documents, adding *Cong.* (*Congress*), the branch (*Senate* or *House*), and the number and session (*101st Cong.*, *1st sess.*). Include the titles of both the document and any book in which it is printed. Use *GPO* for the federal Government Printing Office.

25b
MLA

Sheppard, David I., and Shay Bilchick, comps. Promising Strategies to

Reduce Gun Violence Report. US Dept. of Justice. Office of Juvenile

Justice and Delinquency Prevention. Washington: GPO, 1999.

> United States. Cong. House. <u>Anti-Spamming Act of 2001</u>. 107th Cong., 1st
>
> sess. Washington: GPO, 2001.

Articles from Periodicals and Selections from Books

MODEL FORMAT FOR ARTICLES AND SELECTIONS

period + space   period space   space
↓   ↓   ↓
Author(s). "Title of Article." <u>Title of Journal</u> Volume

Number (Year Published): Page numbers.
↑   ↑   ↑   ↑
indent ½"   space   colon + space   period
or five spaces

- **Author.** Give the last name first, followed by a comma. Add the first name and any middle name or initial. End with a period.
- **Article title.** Give the full title in quotation marks, with the main words capitalized. Conclude with a period inside the quotation marks (unless the title ends in a question mark or an exclamation point).
- **Publication information.** Underline the journal or book title. Supply volume number (and sometimes issue number), year of publication, and page numbers. The volume number appears on the publication's title page or cover; use Arabic numerals even if the periodical uses Roman numerals. Introduce page numbers with a colon except for selections from books and in a few other situations shown in entries that follow. For page ranges, limit the second number to its two final numerals (14–21, 162–79) unless unclear (1498–1524).

23. Article in Journal Paginated by Volume

When each volume consists of several issues paginated continuously, give the volume number right after the journal's title.

> Rockwood, Bruce L. "Law, Literature, and Science Fiction: New
>
> Possibilities." <u>Legal Studies Forum</u> 23 (1999): 267-80.

24. Article in Journal Paginated by Issue

When the issues making up a volume are paginated separately, follow the volume number with a period and the issue number.

> Adams, Jessica. "Local Color: The Southern Plantation in Popular Culture."
>
> <u>Cultural Critique</u> 42.1 (1999): 171-87.

25. Article in Weekly Magazine

Note the day, month (abbreviated except for May, June, and July), and year followed by a colon. Give the sequence of page numbers (27–38). If the pages are not consecutive, give the first page with a plus sign (23+).

Conlin, Michelle. "Unmarried America." Business Week 20 Oct. 2003: 106+.

26. Article in Monthly Magazine

Jacobson, Doranne. "Doing Lunch." Natural History Mar. 2000: 66-69.

27. Article with No Author Given

Alphabetize by title, excluding *A*, *An*, and *The*.

"The Obesity Industry." Economist 27 Sept. 2003: 64+.

28. Article in Newspaper

Cite pages as you would for a magazine (see Entry 25), but add any section number or letter. Omit *The*, *A*, or *An* beginning a newspaper's name. For a local paper, add the city in brackets after the title unless it's named there.

Willis, Ellen. "Steal This Myth: Why We Still Try to Re-create the Rush of

the 60's." New York Times 20 Aug. 2000, late ed., sec. 2: AR1+.

29. Editorial

Start with the author or, if none, with the title.

"A False Choice." Editorial. Charlotte Observer 16 Aug. 1998: 2C.

30. Letter to the Editor

Larson, Dea. Letter. Wall Street Journal 28 Oct. 2003: A17.

31. Interview (Published)

Identify the person interviewed, not the interviewer, first. For untitled interviews, supply *Interview* (without underlining or quotation marks) in place of a title.

Stewart, Martha. "'I Do Have a Brain.'" Interview with Kevin Kelly. Wired

Aug. 1998: 114.

32. Review

Begin with the name of the reviewer or the title for an unsigned review. For an untitled review, follow the reviewer's name with *Rev. of* ("Review of"), the work's title, *by*, and the work's author.

> Muñoz, José Esteban. "Citizens and Superheroes." Rev. of The Queen of
>
> America Goes to Washington City, by Lauren Berlant. American
>
> Quarterly 52 (2000): 397-404.

> Hadjor, Kofi Buenor. Rev. of The Silent War: Imperialism and the Changing
>
> Perception of Race, by Frank Furendi. Journal of Black Studies 30
>
> (1999): 133-35.

33. Article in Encyclopedia or Reference Work

Begin with the author's name or an unsigned article's title. Note only the edition and date for a common reference work or series. If entries appear alphabetically, you may leave out the volume or page.

> Oliver, Paul, and Barry Kernfeld. "Blues." The New Grove Dictionary of
>
> Jazz. Ed. Barry Kernfeld. New York: St. Martin's, 1994.

> "The History of Western Theatre." The New Encyclopaedia Britannica:
>
> Macropaedia. 15th ed. 1987.

34. Chapter in Edited Book or Selection in Anthology

List the author of the selection or chapter, then its title (in quotation marks, but underline titles of novels, plays, and so on; see 51b, 55a). Next, provide the underlined title of the book containing the selection or chapter. If the book is edited, follow with *Ed.* and the names of the editors. Add publication information and page numbers for the selection.

> Atwood, Margaret. "Bluebeard's Egg." "Bluebeard's Egg" and Other Stories.
>
> New York: Fawcett-Random, 1987. 131-64.

For a reprinted selection, you may add the original source. Use *Rpt. in* ("Reprinted in") to introduce a subsequent reprint.

> Atwood, Margaret. "Bluebeard's Egg." "Bluebeard's Egg" and Other
>
> Stories. New York: Fawcett-Random, 1986. 131-64. Rpt. in Don't Bet
>
> on the Prince: Contemporary Feminist Fairy Tales in North America
>
> and England. Ed. Jack Zipes. New York: Methuen, 1987.
>
> 160-82.

35. More Than One Selection from Anthology or Collection

Include an entry for the collection. Use its author's name for cross-references from individual selections.

Goldberg, Jonathan. "Speculation: Macbeth and Source." Howard and

O'Connor 242-64.

Howard, Jean E., and Marion F. O'Connor, eds. Shakespeare Reproduced:

The Text in History and Ideology. New York: Methuen, 1987.

36. Preface, Foreword, Introduction, or Afterword

Identify the section as a preface, foreword, introduction, or afterword. Add the title of the work and its author, following *By*.

Tomlin, Janice. Foreword. The Complete Guide to Foreign Adoption. By

Barbara Brooke Bascom and Carole A. McKelvey. New York: Pocket,

1997.

37. Letter (Published)

Name the letter writer as the author. Include the letter's date or any collection number.

Garland, Hamlin. "To Fred Lewis Pattee." 30 Dec. 1914. Letter 206 of

Selected Letters of Hamlin Garland. Ed. Keith Newlin and Joseph B.

McCullough. Lincoln: U of Nebraska P, 1998.

38. Dissertation Abstract

For an abstract in *Dissertation Abstracts International (DAI)* or *Dissertation Abstracts (DA)*, include *Diss.* ("Dissertation"), the institution's name, and the date of the degree. Add publication information for that volume of abstracts.

Hawkins, Joanne Berning. "Horror Cinema and the Avant-Garde." Diss. U

of California, Berkeley, 1993. DAI 55 (1995): 1712A.

Field and Media Resources

39. Interview (Unpublished)

First identify the person interviewed and the type of interview: *Personal interview* (you conducted it in person), *Telephone interview* (you talked to the person over the telephone), or *Interview* (someone else conducted the interview, perhaps on radio or television). If the interview has a title, use it to replace *Interview*. Give the date of the interview or other detail.

> Schutt, Robin. E-mail interview. 7 Oct. 2005.
>
> Coppola, Francis Ford. Interview with James Lipton. <u>Inside the Actors</u>
>
>> <u>Studio</u>. Bravo, New York. 10 July 2001.

40. Survey or Questionnaire

MLA does not specify a form for these field resources. When citing your own research, you may wish to use this format.

> Figliozzi, Jennifer Emily, and Summer J. Arrigo-Nelson. Questionnaire on
>
>> Student Alcohol Use and Parental Values. U of Rhode Island,
>>
>> Kingston. 15-20 Apr. 2004.

41. Observation

Because MLA does not specify a form, you may wish to cite your field notes in this way.

> Ba, Ed. Ski Run Observation. Vail, CO. 26 Jan. 2006.

42. Letter or Memo (Unpublished)

Give the author's name, a brief description (*Memo to Jane Cote* or, for a letter to you, *Letter to the author*), and the date. For letters between other people, identify any library holding the letter in its collection.

> Hall, Donald. Letter to the author. 24 Jan. 1990.

43. Oral Presentation

Identify the speaker, title or type of presentation, and meeting details, including sponsor, place, and date.

> Johnson, Sylvia. "Test Fairness: An Oxymoron? The Challenge
>
>> of Measuring Well in a High Stakes Climate." Amer.
>>
>> Educ. Research Assn. Sheraton Hotel, New Orleans. 27 Apr.
>>
>> 2000.

44. Performance

Following the title of the play, opera, dance, or other performance, note the composer, director, writer, theater or location, city, and date. (Include actors when relevant.)

> <u>Cabaret</u>. By Joe Masteroff. Dir. Sam Mendes. Studio 54, New York. 2 July
>
>> 2001.

45. Videotape or Film

Alphabetize by title, and generally name the director. Name others important for identifying the work or for your discussion. Identify the distributor, date, and other relevant information.

> Rosencrantz and Guildenstern Are Dead. Dir. Tom Stoppard. Perf. Gary
>
> Oldman, Tim Roth, and Richard Dreyfuss. Videocassette. Buena Vista
>
> Home Video, 1990.
>
> Rosencrantz and Guildenstern Are Dead. Dir. Tom Stoppard. Perf. Gary
>
> Oldman, Tim Roth, and Richard Dreyfuss. Cinecom Entertainment,
>
> 1990.

46. Television or Radio Program

> "The Tour." I Love Lucy. Dir. William Asher. Nickelodeon. 2 July 2001.

47. Recording

Identify the form of the recording unless it is a compact disc.

> The Goo-Goo Dolls. Dizzy Up the Girl. Warner, 1998.
>
> Mozart, Wolfgang Amadeus. Symphony no. 40 in G minor. Vienna
>
> Philharmonic. Cond. Leonard Bernstein. Audiocassette. Deutsche
>
> Grammophon, 1984.

48. Artwork or Photograph

> Leonardo da Vinci. Mona Lisa. Louvre, Paris.
>
> Larimer Street, Denver. Personal photograph by author. 5 May 2006.

49. Map or Chart

> Arkansas. Map. Comfort, TX: Gousha, 1996.

50. Comic Strip or Cartoon

Provide the cartoonist's name, any title, and *Cartoon* or *Comic strip.*

> Cochran, Tony. "Agnes." Comic strip. Denver Post 9 May 2004: 4.

51. Advertisement

First, name the product or organization advertised.

> Toyota. Advertisement. GQ July 2001: 8.

25b
MLA

Online and Electronic Resources

MODEL FORMAT FOR ONLINE BOOK OR DOCUMENT

period + space   period space   colon + space
↓   ↓ ↓   ↓
Author(s). "Title of Page or Document." Place of Publication:

comma + space   period + space
↓   ↓
Publisher, Year Published. [for print book, if available]

period + space   period + space   comma
↓   ↓   ↓
Site Name. Date Posted or Updated. Sponsoring Organization,

period + space   space   period
↓   ↓   ↓
Institution. Your Access Date <URL>.

↑
indent ½" or five spaces

MODEL FORMAT FOR ONLINE ARTICLE

period + space   period space   space
↓   ↓ ↓   ↓
Author(s). "Title of Page or Document." Title of Journal Volume

space   colon + space   period + space
↓   ↓   ↓
Number (Year Published): Page Numbers. [for print article, if

period + space   period + space
↓   ↓
available] Site Name. Date Posted or Updated. Sponsoring

comma   period + space   space period
↓   ↓   ↓   ↓
Organization, Institution. Your Access Date <URL>.

↑
indent ½" or five spaces

25b
MLA

- **Author, title, and publication information.** Supply available information like that for a print source so a reader could identify or find the item.
- **Dates.** Give the date the material was posted, revised, or updated and then, just before the URL, the date you accessed the source.
- **Uniform resource locator (URL).** Enclose the complete URL (beginning with *http*, *gopher*, *telnet*, or *ftp*) in angle brackets (< >). Include the search page, path, links, or file name needed to reach the page or frame

you used, especially to avoid an unwieldy URL. Split the URL only after a slash; do not add a hyphen.

* **Page numbering.** Include any page, paragraph (*par.*, *pars.*), section (*sec.*), or screen numbers provided.

52. Professional Web Site

History of the American West, 1860–1920. 25 July 2000. Denver Public Lib.

16 Oct. 2001 <http://memory.loc.gov/ammem/award97/codhtml>.

53. Academic Home Page

Note the creator, title or description such as *Home page*, and sponsor.

Baron, Dennis. Home page. 16 Aug. 2000. Dept. of English, U of Illinois,

Urbana-Champaign. 10 Oct. 2003 <http://www2.english.uiuc.edu/

baron/Default.htm>.

54. Online Book

Add any available information about print publication.

London, Jack. The Iron Heel. New York: Macmillan, 1908. The Jack London

Collection. 10 Dec. 1999. Berkeley Digital Lib. SunSITE. 15 July 2001

<http://sunsite.berkeley.edu/London/Writing/IronHeel>.

55. Selection from Online Book

Muir, John. "The City of the Saints." Steep Trails. 1918. 17 July 2001

<http://encyclopediaindex.com/b/sttrl10.htm>.

56. Online Journal Article

Dugdale, Timothy. "The Fan and (Auto)Biography: Writing the Self in the

Stars." Journal of Mundane Behavior 1.2 (2000). 19 Sept. 2000

<http://www.mundanebehavior.org/issues/v1n2/dugdale.htm>.

57. Online Magazine Article

Wright, Laura. "My, What Big Eyes . . ." Discover 27 Oct. 2003.

4 Apr. 2004 <http://www.discover.com/web-exclusives-archive/

big-eyed-trilobite1027>.

25b
MLA

58. Online Newspaper Article

Mulvihill, Kim. "Childhood Obesity." <u>San Francisco Chronicle</u> 12 July 2001. 15 July 2001 <http://www.sfgate.com/search>.

59. Online Government Document

United States. Dept. of Commerce. Bureau of the Census. <u>Census Brief: Disabilities Affect One-Fifth of All Americans</u>. Dec. 1997. 18 July 2001 <http://www.census.gov/prod/3/97pubs/cenbr975.pdf>.

60. Online Editorial

"Mall Mania/A Measure of India's Success." Editorial. <u>startribune.com</u> Minneapolis-St. Paul 31 Oct. 2003. 14 Nov. 2003 <http://www.startribune.com/stories/1519/4185511.html>.

61. Online Letter to the Editor

Hadjiargyrou, Michael. "Stem Cells and Delicate Questions." Letter. <u>New York Times on the Web</u> 17 July 2001. 18 July 2001 <http://www.nytimes.com/2001/07/18/opinion/L18STEM.html>.

62. Online Interview

Rikker, David. Interview with Victor Payan. <u>San Diego Latino Film Festival</u>. May 1999. 20 Jan. 2002 <http://www.sdlatinofilm.com/video.html#Anchor-David-64709>.

63. Online Review

Chaudhury, Parama. Rev. of <u>Kandahar</u>, dir. Mohsen Makhmalbaf. <u>Film Monthly</u> 3.4 (2002). 19 Jan. 2002 <http://www.filmmonthly.com/Playing/Articles/Kandahar/Kandahar.html>.

64. Online Abstract

Prelow, Hazel, and Charles A. Guarnaccia. "Ethnic and Racial Differences in Life Stress among High School Adolescents." <u>Journal of Counseling & Development</u> 75.6 (1997). Abstract. 6 Apr. 1998 <http://www.counseling.org/journals/jcdjul197.htm#Prelow>.

25b
MLA

65. Online Database: General Entry

For entries from online databases to which libraries subscribe (through services such as EBSCO or LexisNexis), begin with the details of print publication, if any. Name the database, the service, the library, and your date of access. Then give the URL. If it is too long, give the URL of the search page for the site. Should the service give only the first page number of the printed text, follow it with a hyphen, space, and period, as in *223-*.

> Kallis, Giorgos, and Henri L. F. De Groot. "Shifting Perspectives
>
> on Urban Water Policy in Europe." European Planning Studies
>
> 11 (2003): 223-28. Academic Search Premier. EBSCO.
>
> Auraria Lib., Denver, CO. 19 Dec. 2003 <http://
>
> 0-web12.epnet.com.skyline.cudenver.edu>.

66. Online Database: Journal Article

> Stillman, Todd. "McDonald's in Question: The Limits of the Mass Market."
>
> American Behavioral Scientist 47 (2003): 107-18. Academic Search
>
> Premier. EBSCO. U of Rhode Island Lib. 15 Nov. 2003 <http://
>
> 0-ejournals.ebsco.com>.

67. Online Database: Article Abstract

> Lewis, David A., and Roger P. Rose. "The President, the Press, and the
>
> War-Making Power: An Analysis of Media Coverage Prior to the
>
> Persian Gulf War." Presidential Studies Quarterly 32 (2002): 559-71.
>
> Abstract. America: History and Life. ABC/CLIO. U of Rhode Island
>
> Lib. 1 Nov. 2003 <http://0-serials.abc-clio.com>.

68. Online Database: Magazine Article

> Barrett, Jennifer. "Fast Food Need Not Be Fat Food." Newsweek 13 Oct.
>
> 2003: 73-74. Academic Search Premier. EBSCO. U of Rhode Island
>
> Lib. 31 Oct. 2003 <http://0-ejournals.ebsco.com>.

69. Online Database: Newspaper Article

> Lee, R. "Class with the 'Ph.D. Diva.'" New York Times 18 Oct. 2003: B7.
>
> InfoTrac OneFile. InfoTrac. Providence Public Lib., RI. 31 Oct. 2003
>
> <http://infotrac.galegroup.com/menu>.

25b
MLA

70. Online Database: Summary of Research

Holub, Tamara. "Early-Decision Programs." <u>ERIC Digests</u>. ERIC
Clearinghouse on Higher Education. ERIC, the Educational Resources
Information Center. ED470540. 2002. U of Rhode Island Lib. 7 Nov.
2003 <http://www.ericfacility.net/ericdigests/ed470540.html>.

71. Online Database: Collection of Documents

"Combating Plagiarism." <u>CQ Researcher</u> 9 Sept. 2003. CQ P. U of Rhode Island
Lib. 12 Nov. 2003 <http://0-library.cqpress.com.helin.uri.edu:80/
cqresearcher/>.

72. Online Database: Personal Subscription Service

Include your access route (introduced by *Keyword* or *Path*).

"Native American Food Guide." <u>Health Finder</u>. 16 July 2001. America
Online. 16 July 2001. Keyword: Health.

73. Online Videotape or Film

Coppola, Francis Ford, dir. <u>Apocalypse Now</u>. 1979. <u>Film.com</u>. 17 July 2001
<http://ramhurl.film.com/smildemohurl.ram?file=screen/2001/
clips/apoca.smi>.

74. Online Television or Radio Program

Edwards, Bob. "Adoption: Redefining Family." <u>Morning Edition</u>. Natl.
Public Radio. 28-29 June 2001. 17 July 2001 <http://www.npr.org/
programs/morning/features/2001/jun/010628.cfoa.html>.

75. Online Recording

Malcolm X. "The Definition of Black Power." 8 Mar. 1964. <u>Great Speeches</u>.
2000. 18 July 2001 <http://www.chicago-law.net/speeches/
speech.html#1m>.

76. Online Artwork

<u>Elamite Goddess</u>. 2100 BC (?). Louvre, Paris. 16 July 2001 <http://
www.louvre.fr/louvrea.htm/search>.

77. Online Map or Chart

"Beirut [Beyrout] 1912." Map. <u>Perry-Castañeda Library Map Collection</u>.
16 July 2000. <http://www.lib.utexas.edu/maps/historical/
beirut2_1912.jpg>.

78. Online Comic Strip or Cartoon

Auth, Tony. "Spending Goals." Cartoon. <u>Slate</u> 7 Sept. 2001. 16 Oct. 2001
<http://cagle.slate.msn.com/politicalcartoons/pccartoons/
archives/auth.asp>.

79. Online Advertisement

Mazda Miata. Advertisement. 16 July 2001 <http://www.mazdausa.com/
miata/>.

80. Other Online Sources

When citing a source not shown here (such as a photo, painting, or
recording), adapt the nonelectronic MLA model.

NASA/JPL. "Martian Meteorite." <u>Views of the Solar System: Meteoroids
and Meteorites</u>. Ed. Calvin J. Hamilton. 1999. 13 June 1999
<http://spaceart.com/solar/eng/meteor.htm#views>.

81. FTP, Telnet, or Gopher Site

Treat a source obtained through FTP (file transfer protocol), telnet, or
gopher as you would a similar Web source.

Clinton, William Jefferson. "Radio Address of the President to the
Nation." 10 May 1997. 29 June 1999 <ftp://OMA.EOP.GOV.US/1997/
5/10/1.TEXT.1>.

25b
MLA

82. Email

Give the writer's name, message title or type, and date. Be sure to hyphenate *e-mail* in MLA style.

Trimbur, John. E-mail to the author. 17 Sept. 2000.

83. Online Posting

Aid readers (if you can) by citing an archived version.

Brock, Stephen E. "School Crisis." Online posting. 27 Apr. 2001. Special

Events Chat Transcripts. Lycos Communities. 18 July 2001

<http://clubs.lycos.com/live/Events/transcripts/

school_crisis_tscript.asp>.

84. Synchronous Communication

When citing material from a MUD, a MOO, or another form of synchronous communication, identify the speaker, the event, its date, its forum (such as *CollegeTownMOO*), and your access date. End with *telnet* and the address. Cite an archived version if possible.

Finch, Jeremy. Online debate "Can Proust Save Your Life?" 3 Apr. 1998.

CollegeTownMOO. 3 Apr. 1998 <telnet://next.cs.bvc.edu.7777>.

85. CD-ROM, Diskette, or Magnetic Tape

Note the medium (*CD-ROM*, *Diskette*, *Magnetic tape*), the name of the vendor, and the publication date.

Shakespeare, William. All's Well That Ends Well. William Shakespeare: The

Complete Works on CD-ROM. CD-ROM. Abingdon, Eng.: Andromeda

Interactive, 1994.

86. CD-ROM Abstract

Add information for any parallel printed source. Identify the database and medium (*CD-ROM*, *Diskette*), vendor, and publication date.

Straus, Stephen. Interview with Claudia Dreifus. "Separating Remedies

from Snake Oil." New York Times 3 Apr. 2001: D5+. Abstract.

CD-ROM. InfoTrac. 19 July 2001.

25c
MLA

25c Sample MLA paper

The *MLA Handbook* recommends beginning a research paper with the first page of the text, using the format shown on page 229. Refer to the features of Jenny Latimer's paper, noted in the margins, as you prepare your paper.

1" from top of page

½" from top

Latimer 1

1" margin on each side

Jenny Latimer

Professor Schwegler

Writing 101

7 November 2003

Heading format without title page

Double-spaced heading and paper

No, Thanks, I'll Pass on That

One night at work my friend Kate turned down my offer
of a red licorice stick after quickly checking the ingredients
on the bag. I asked her to explain why, and she replied that
they contained hydrogenated oils, which are, accordng to
research articles she had read, "silent killers." She went on
briefly to describe the horrors they do to your body, the
various foods that contain them, as well as the effort she makes
to avoid hydrogenated oils. I was shocked and intrigued by
this news and decided to explore the reality of what
she'd said.

A day or two later, while browsing through the shelves at
the supermarket, I started checking ingredients. To my
astonishment I couldn't seem to find a snack without these words
on the back. Whether followed by the word "coconut,"
"cottonseed," or "soy bean," there it was lurking amidst the other
ingredients--hydrogenated oil. I was horrified! Thinking these
scary oils couldn't be everywhere, I continued my search. A box of
toaster tarts, again yes. A can of soup, there it was. I picked up a
bag of pretzels, tossed it back on the shelf, and left the store in
frustration, needless to say without buying a snack. Returning
home I realized I needed to know the truth; I set out to find the
answers to my questions.

1

¶ indented
5 spaces or
½"

Anecdote
introduces
purpose of
research

2

Field
research
confirms
anecdote

25c
MLA

1" margin at bottom

Latimer 2

3

First research question

My first question was this: what exactly does it mean to hydrogenate an oil? This is where things get a little technical: to hydrogenate is to add hydrogen. During the hydrogenation process the hydrogen atoms of a fatty acid are moved to the opposite side of the double bond of its molecular structure (Roberts). According to

No page number given for general reference

Lewis Harrison, author of The Complete Fats and Oils Book, this changed fatty acid molecule can actually be toxic to the body. It can cause oxidative stress and damage the body in the same way as cigarette smoke and chemical toxins. It can alter the normal transport

Paragraph synthesizes several sources

of minerals and nutrients across cell membranes. As a result, foreign invaders may pass the cell membrane unchallenged; also, supplies and information important to the cell may not be allowed in. Good fats

Citation from book includes page number

that the body uses for many functions are not allowed to pass through the membrane while these fatty acids build up unused outside the cell, making us fat (Armstrong; Rudin and Felix 21).

4

Process summarized

To formulate hydrogenated oils, gas is fused into the oils using a metal catalyst (such as aluminum, cobalt, and nickel). These metals are needed to fuse the hydrogen into the oils. After hydrogenation these fatty acids are called trans-fatty acids or

Second research question

hydrogenated oils (Harrison 93). As a result, my licorice snacks were making me fat--which was a given--but not only that. They were actually disrupting the normal functions of my cells. What was this doing to me in the long run?

5

Historical background supplied

After production companies started using hydrogenated oils, which were first introduced in 1914 and fully part of the food production market by the mid-fifties, substantial increases in several diseases occurred rapidly within the span of a few years. According to information available from the National Institutes of

Latimer 3

Health, during 1973 to 1994 there was a 22% increase from 364 cancers of assorted types to 462 cancers for every 100,000 people. And from 1973 to 1992, those 364 cancers rose to 530 for every 100,000 people. This 31% increase was "an additional 9% increase from the previous years" (Dewey).

Dr. Andrew Weil, one of the nation's leading advocates of holistic medicine, claims that hydrogenated oils are "one of the most toxic substances Americans consume" (qtd. in Alter). Another article compared hydrogenated oils to inhaling cigarette smoke: "They will kill you--slowly over time, but surely as you breathe" (Armstrong). The US Food and Drug Administration and the American Heart Association agree that trans-fatty acids raise LDL ("bad") cholesterol levels and lower HDL ("good") cholesterol levels, therefore increasing the risk of coronary disease--a leading cause of death in the United States. The Institute of Medicine reported this year that trans fats may raise levels of lipoprotein, higher levels of which have been associated with a greater risk of heart and blood vessel disease (Roberts 17). Trans fats also have artery-clogging qualities (McCord and McVeigh).

Hydrogenated oils have also been shown to increase the risks of breast cancer. According to research by the Cancer Research Foundation of America, women with the highest levels of trans fatty acids were 40% more likely to develop breast cancer than those with lower levels (Cancer Research Foundation; Cancer Web Project). Some have speculated that hydrogenated oils are the cause of what is called non-insulin-dependent diabetes type II, wherein a person produces enough insulin, but it does not reduce the sugar levels in the blood. It is unknown what causes the insulin to be resistant (Dewey).

6
Discussion of risk continues

Indirect source (with quotation from someone else) identified

Group authors cited in sentence

7
Specific risks identified

**25c
MLA**

8

Opposing views acknowledged

On the other hand, according to James R. Marshall in an article for <u>Nutrition Reviews</u>, there is no conclusive evidence that trans fatty acids specifically are a cause of cancer; fats in general are known to cause cancer, but trans fatty acids are not directly responsible. Marshall maintains that "Any effort to lower the risks of heart diseases should be focused on decreasing total fat intake, and not on consuming less trans fat or saturated fat." Bruce Watkins, in an article for <u>Food Technology</u>, says that foods "should be evaluated based on their impact on overall health. For instance, total fat and not trans fat or saturated fat alone, is correlated with obesity and cancer."

9

Cause of situation discussed

So in today's health-conscious America, why do over 90% of our foods still contain hydrogenated oils? The answer is money. The process of hydrogenation increases the volume of the oil, thus making more oil available to sell. Hydrogenating creates a product that can exist at room temperature as either a solid or a liquid; therefore, any desired consistency is possible (Byers). Hydrogenated oils also give food products a rich flavor and texture at cheaper costs.

10

But most importantly for manufacturers, hydrogenated oils act as a preservative, which means a longer shelf life for products and fewer returns of spoiled products (Dewey). By using hydrogenated oils rather than other less health-threatening oils, food companies are saving money (Dewey). Juan Menjivar, vice president of global research and development at Rich Products, estimates that it will cost a few pennies more per pound of ingredients to eliminate trans fats (Haarlander). Research alone for a replacement for trans fats will cost companies tens of

25c
MLA

Latimer 5

millions of dollars (Dwyer). Up until now, companies have relied
on the ignorance or lack of concern of the public, along with
keeping their prices lower than those of healthier foods, to stay
in business.

This situation, however, is changing. By January 1, 2006, the
US Food and Drug Administration will require that the amount of
trans fatty acids in the product be listed on the label directly
under the line for saturated fats. This requirement is encouraging
companies to use healthier oils so as not to scare away consumers
(Haarlander). The entire food industry is researching options for
different oils and for ways of preparing new products, said
Stephanie Childs of the Grocery Manufacturers of America (Dwyer).

The reason the FDA is giving food companies three years is
because this is such a large change, and companies need time to
adjust. Because there will be a need for new products, these
products need time to grow. Food doesn't grow overnight. Many
countries have recognized the health issues of hydrogenated oils
for some time. In Denmark, the country with the lowest diagnosed
rates of heart disease, cancers, and diabetes, hydrogenated oils
have been banned for over forty years. Many other countries have
limitations on the amounts of hydrogenated oils in foods (Dewey).

So, until 2006, how can one avoid trans fats? Although trans
fats do occur naturally in tiny amounts in some dairy products and
meats, the majority of trans fats come from processed foods. In
addition to the many health food stores full of hydrogenated-free
foods, most supermarkets stock them in special sections. Although
the greater part of what you will find in your snack food, frozen
food, and ready-bake aisles will contain hydrogenated oils, some

11

Future
situation
identified

12

13

Advice
for
readers

25c
MLA

producers have already made the switch from trans fats: Frito-Lay Doritos, Jolly Time Pop Corn, Tostitos and Cheetos, Take Control Spread, I Can't Believe It's Not Butter products, some Kraft food products, and products from Jaret International, which makes Sour Patch Kids and Swedish Fish (Dwyer).

14

There are also ways to find the amount of trans fatty acids that are in a food. Where the words "hydrogenated oil" appear on the list of ingredients is a clue; the higher up on the list, the greater the content in the product. Take the amount of total fat listed on the label, and subtract all the other fats listed; chances are the remaining number is trans fat. The highest levels of trans fats are found in the foods that you might expect: French fries, doughnuts, cookies, cakes, margarine, single-serving soups such as ramen noodles, grilled foods, pizza, waffles, breaded fish sticks, pot pies, and many frozen convenience items ("Think"). As an alternative, try making things from scratch, using canned veggies and soups, having butter instead of margarine, going for broiled or baked over grilled or fried, and if you're craving a snack, choosing jelly beans or gummy bears over chocolate and cookies.

Article without author cited by title

15

So I return to the supermarket, and as I walk in, I am surrounded by processed-hydrogenated food, rows upon rows of cookies and candies, boxes and bags of tantalizing treats. But now that I've found the answers to my questions and know what is in the things I have been eating, I find it easy to resist temptation. Instead I walk to the small health-food section toward the back. More expensive--but worth it. Actually, I feel great. If giving up licorice sticks is what it takes to keep my body in good health, then that's a price I'm willing to pay.

Anecdote concludes with outcomes of research

Works Cited   Heading centered

Page numbers continue

Alter, Alexandra. "Alarms Raised Over Partially Hydrogenated Oil."

Columbia News Service 21 May 2003. 26 Oct. 2003 <http://

naturalhealthchiropractic.com/know_that.html#fats>.

Sources from paper listed alphabetically

American Heart Association. "Hydrogenated Fats." 2002. 26 Oct.

2003 <http://www.amhrt.org/presenter.jhtml?identifier=4662>.

Armstrong, Eric. "What's Wrong with Partially Hydrogenated Oils?"

Treelight Health.com. 2001. 30 Sept. 2003 <http://

www.treelight.com/health/PartiallyHydrogenatedOils.html>.

All lines double-spaced

Byers, Tim. "Hardened Fats, Hardened Arteries?" New England

Journal of Medicine 337 (1997): 1554. Abstract. Academic

Search Premier. EBSCO. U of Rhode Island Lib. 26 Oct. 2003

<http://0-web20.epnet.com>.

First line of each entry not indented

Cancer Research Foundation of America. "Trans Fatty Acids Linked

to Breast Cancer Risk." Aug. 1998. 10 Sept. 2003 <http://

www.dldewey.com/columns/breast2.htm>.

Additional lines indented 5 spaces (½")

Cancer WEB Project. "Hydrogenation." 9 Oct. 1977. On-Line Medical

Dictionary. Dept. of Medical Oncology, U of Newcastle upon

Tyne. 10 Sept. 2003 <http://cancerweb.ncl.ac.uk/cgi-bin/

omd?query=hydrogenation&action=Search+OMD>.

Dewey, David Lawrence. "Food for Thought: Hydrogenated Oils

Are Silent Killers." 18 Sept. 1998. 30 Sept. 2003

<http:www.dldewey.com/hydroil.htm>.

25c
MLA

Dwyer, Kelly Pate. "Frito-Lay Removes Trans Fats from Chips."

Knight Ridder/Tribune Business News 28 Sept. 2003.

InfoTrac OneFile. Gale. Providence Public Lib., RI. 26 Oct.

2003 <http://web4.galegroup.com>.

1" margin at bottom

Latimer 8

Haarlander, Lisa. "Nutrition: Getting the Fat Out." News Business
    Reporter 1 Sept. 2003. 24 Oct. 2003 <http://www.buffalo.com>.

Harrison, Lewis. The Complete Fat and Oils Book. New York: Avery-
    Penguin, 1996.

Marshall, James R. "Trans Fatty Acids in Cancer." Nutrition Reviews
    May 1996. Abstract. Health and Wellness Resource Center.
    Gale. U of Rhode Island Lib. 26 Oct. 2003 <http://
    galenet.galegroup.com>.

McCord, Holly, and Gloria McVeigh. "Smart Bites." Prevention Dec.
    2001. Academic Search Premier. EBSCO. U of Rhode Island
    Lib. 26 Oct. 2003 <http://0-web20.epnet.com>.

Roberts, Shauna S. "IOM Takes Aims at Trans Fats." Diabetes Forecast
    56 (2003): 17-18. Academic Search Premier. EBSCO. U of Rhode
    Island Lib. 26 Oct. 2003 <http://0-web20.epnet.com>.

Rudin, Donald, and Clara Felix. The Omega-3 Phenomenon. New York:
    Rawson Assoc., 1987.

"Think Before You Eat: Trans Fats Lurking in Many Popular Foods."
    Knight Ridder/Tribune News Service 8 Sept. 2003. InfoTrac
    OneFile. Gale. Providence Public Lib., RI. 26 Oct. 2003
    <http://web4.galegroup.com>.

United States Food and Drug Administration. "What Every
    Consumer Should Know About Trans Fatty Acids." 9 July
    2003. 23 Oct. 2003 <http://www.fda.gov/oc/initiatives/
    transfat/q_a.html>.

Watkins, Bruce A. "Trans Fatty Acids: A Health Paradox?" Food
    Technology 52 (1998): 120. Abstract. Health and Wellness
    Resource Center. Gale. U of Rhode Island Lib. 26 Oct. 2003
    <http://galenet.galegroup.com>.

Exercise 1   *(Answers appear on p. 508.)*

Rewrite the following sentences to include MLA-style in-text citations.

1. The article concludes that "a 10-percent permanent increase in the price of cigarettes reduces current consumption by 4 percent in the short run and by 7.5 percent in the long run."
   The quotation is from page 397 of an article by Gary S. Becker, Michael Grossman, and Kevin M. Murphy. It appeared in *American Economic Review.* The volume number was 84, the year was 1994, and the article ran from page 396 to page 418.

2. The original release of Neil Young's concert film *Rust Never Sleeps* in 1979 was a major event in the history of rock and roll and popular music. According to one critic, the DVD release provides continued evidence of its importance.
   The reference is to a review by LC Smith in *Rolling Stone* magazine titled "My, My, Hey, Hey: A Neil Young Treasure Resurfaces." The date is 10/17/2002 and it appears on page 39. It was accessed on 14 November 2003 through *Academic Search Premier*, an EBSCO database, through the University of Rhode Island Library: http://0-web11.epnet.com.helin.uri.edu/citation.asp?tb=1&_ug=dbs+0+ln+en%2Dus+sid+D0695035%2D68B1%2D42F6%2DAABC%2D8963F3EC6024%40sessionmgr3%2Dsessionmgr4+699B&_us=bs+San++Francisco++And+++sleep+db+0+ds+San++Francisco++And+++sleep+dstb+ES+fh+0+hd+0+hs+0+or+Date+ri+KAAACBTB00365969+sm+ES+ss+SO+302E&cf=1&fn=1&rn=6

3. In Samoa during the 1930s, girls separated socially from their siblings at about age seven and began to form close and lasting relationships with other girls their age.
   The reference is to Margaret Mead's discussion in *Coming of Age in Samoa*, originally published in 1928 and reprinted in 1961 by Morrow Publishers in their Morrow Quill paperback series. It cites the general discussion in Chapter 5, "The Girl and Her Age Group," on pages 59 through 73 of the 1961 edition.

Exercise 2   *(Answers appear on p. 508.)*

Create a list of works cited using MLA style, and include the following items:

1. A 368-page book by Peter Brazaitis titled *You Belong in a Zoo!* It was published in 2003 by Villard Books in New York.

2. A poem by Jorie Graham titled "Self-Portrait as Apollo and Daphne," available in her *The Dream of the Unified Field: Selected Poems, 1974–1994.* The book was published in 1995 by Ecco Press, and the poem appeared on pages 70–73.

25c
MLA

3. A review in the online magazine *Salon.com*. The title of the review is "The Matrix Revolutions," and it was written by Andrew O'Hehir. It was accessed on November 5, 2003 at http://salon.com/ent/movies/review/2003/11/5/matrix_revolutions/index_np.html. The date of publication is also November 5, 2003.

4. An abstract of an article titled "Understanding Sleep Disorders in a College Student Population." The article was written by Dallas R. Jensen. It appeared in the *Journal of College Counseling* in the Spring 2003 issue on pages 25–34. The abstract appeared in a research data-base, *Academic Search Premier*, created and maintained by EBSCO. It was accessed on November 15, 2003 through the University of Rhode Island Library at the URL http://0-search.epnet.com.helin.uri.edu:80/direct.asp?an=9744711&db=aph. It was first included in the database in 2003.

5. A book of 280 pages by Vera Rosenbluth titled *Keeping Family Stories Alive*. The subtitle is *A Creative Guide to Taping Your Family Life and Lore*. It was published in 1990 by Hartley and Marks, a publisher in Point Roberts, Washington.

PART 6

Documenting Sources: APA Style

26 APA Documentation Style

The documentation style developed by the APA (American Psychological Association) identifies a source by providing its author's name and its date of publication within parentheses. For this reason, the APA style is often called a name-and-date style. The information in the parenthetical citation (Kitwana, 2002) will guide readers to more detail about the source in a reference list at the end of the paper or report.

> Kitwana, B. (2002). *The hip hop generation: Young blacks and the crisis in African American culture.* New York: Basic Civitas.

26.1

STRATEGY   Decide when to use APA style.

ACADEMIC SETTINGS
When readers expect APA or a name-and-date style

WORK AND PUBLIC SETTINGS
When business or professional readers prefer a name-and-date system or want to see at once how current your sources are
When you need a simple way to identify sources and dates
When other writers or publications in your setting use APA style, modified APA style, or a similar informal system

For more on this documentation style, consult the *Publication Manual of the American Psychological Association* (5th ed., Washington, DC: APA, 2001). Updates are posted on the APA Web site at <http://www.apastyle.org>.

26a APA in-text citations

The APA system provides in-text parenthetical citations for quotations, paraphrases, summaries, and other specific information from a source. (For advice on what to document, see 22c–f.) APA style makes the year of publication part of an in-text citation which refers to a reference list.

DRAFT   The current argumentative climate impedes exchanges among those with differing ideas (Tannen).

EDITED   The current argumentative climate impedes exchanges among those with differing ideas (Tannen, 1998).

1. Author's Name in Parentheses

When you include both the author's name and the year of publication in parentheses, separate them with a comma. To specify the location of a quotation, paraphrase, summary, or other information, add a comma, *p.* or *pp.*, and the page number(s) on which the material appears in the source.

One recent study examines the emotional intensity of "the fan's link to the star" (Gitlin, 2001, p. 129).

2. Author's Name in Discussion

When you include an author's name in your discussion, give the date of the source in parentheses after the name. Provide the page number in the source following any quotation or paraphrase.

For Gitlin (2001), emotion is the basis of "the fan's link to the star" (p. 129).

3. Specific Reference

Indicate what you are citing: *p.* ("page"), *chap.* ("chapter"), *figure, para.* or ¶ (paragraphs) in electronic sources. Spell potentially confusing words. For classical works always indicate the part (chap. 5), not the page.

Teenagers who survive suicide attempts experience distinct stages of recovery (Mauk & Weber, 1991, Table 1).

4. One Author

You can vary your in-text citations as you present both the name and date in parentheses, both in the text, or the name in the text.

Dell's 2002 study of charter schools confirmed issues identified earlier (James, 1996) and also updated Rau's (1998) school classification.

26a
APA

5. Two Authors

In a parenthetical citation, separate the names with an ampersand (&); in your text, use the word *and*.

> Given evidence that married men earn more than unmarried men (Chun & Lee, 2001), Nakosteen and Zimmer (2001) investigate how earnings affect spousal selection.

6. Three to Five Authors

Include all the names, separated by commas, in the first citation. In parenthetical citations, use an ampersand (&) rather than *and*.

> Sadeh, Raviv, and Gruber (2000) related "sleep problems and neuropsychological functioning in children" (p. 292).

In any following references, give only the first author's name and *et al.* ("and others"): Sadeh et al. (2000) reported their findings.

7. Six or More Authors

In all text citations, follow the first author with *et al.*: (Berg et al., 1998). For your reference list, see Entry 2 on page 246.

8. Corporate or Group Author

Spell out the name of the organization, corporation, or agency in the first citation. Follow any cumbersome name with an abbreviation in brackets, and use the shorter form in later citations.

FIRST CITATION   Besides instilling fear, hate crimes limit where women live and work (National Organization of Women [NOW], 2001).

LATER CITATION   Pending legislation would strengthen the statutes on bias-motivated crimes (NOW, 2001).

9. No Author Given

Give the title or the first few words of a long title.

> These photographs represent people from all walks of life (*Friendship*, 2001).

Full title: *Friendship: Celebration of humanity.*

10. Work Cited More Than Once

When you cite the same source more than once in a paragraph, repeat the source as necessary to clarify a page reference or specify one of several sources. If a second reference is clear, don't repeat the date.

26a
APA

Much of the increase in personal debt can be linked to unrestrained use of credit cards (Schor, 1998, p. 73). In fact, according to Schor, roughly a third of consumers "describe themselves as either heavily or moderately in financial debt" (p. 72).

11. Authors with the Same Name

When your references include works by two authors who share the same last name, provide the author's initials for each in-text citation.

Scholars have examined the development of African American culture during slavery and reconstruction (E. Foner, 1988), including the role of Frederick Douglass in this process (P. Foner, 1950).

12. Personal Communications, Including Interviews and Email

In your text, cite letters, interviews, memos, email, telephone calls, and so on using the name of the person, the expression *personal communication*, and the full date. Readers have no access to such sources, so you can omit them from your reference list.

According to J. M. Hostos, the state no longer funds services duplicated by county agencies (personal communication, October 7, 2006).

13. Two or More Sources in a Citation

If you sum up information from several sources, include them all in your citation. Separate the authors and years with commas; separate the sources with semicolons. List the sources alphabetically, then oldest to most recent for several by the same author.

Several studies have related job satisfaction with performance (Faire, 2002; Hall, 1996, 1999).

14. Two or More Works by the Same Author in the Same Year

If you use works published in the same year by the same author or author team, alphabetize the works, and add letters after the year to distinguish them.

Gould (1987a, p. 73) makes a similar point.

15. Content Footnote

You may use a content footnote to expand material in the text. Place a superscript number above the related line of text; number the notes consecutively. On a separate page at the end, below the centered heading "Footnotes," present the notes in numerical order. Begin each with its superscript number. Indent five to seven spaces for the first line only of each note, and double-space all notes.

TEXT   I tape-recorded and transcribed all interviews.[1]

NOTE   [1]Although background noise obscured some parts of the tapes, these gaps did not substantially affect the material studied.

26b APA reference list

On a separate page at the end of your text (before notes or appendixes), provide a list of references to the sources you've cited.

- **Page format.** Allow a one-inch margin, and center the heading "References" without underlining or quotation marks.
- **Alphabetizing.** List the works alphabetically by author or by the first main word of the title if there is no author. Arrange two or more works by the same author from oldest to most recent, by year of publication.
- **Spacing.** Double-space within and between all entries.
- **Indentation.** Do not indent the first line, but indent all additional lines like paragraphs, consistently a half inch or five to seven spaces.

26.2

DRAFT   Carlson, NR., and Buskist, Wm. (1997), *Psychology: The Science of Behavior.* Boston, Allyn & Bacon.

EDITED   Carlson, N. R., & Buskist, W. (1997). *Psychology: The science of behavior* (5th ed.). Boston: Allyn & Bacon.

Books and Works Treated as Books

MODEL FORMAT FOR BOOKS AND WORKS TREATED AS BOOKS

period + period +   period +
space   space   space
↓   ↓   ↓
Author(s). (Date). *Title of work.* Place of

Publication: Publisher.
↑   ↑   ↑
indent ½″ or   colon + space   period
5–7 spaces

26b
APA

- **Author.** Give the author's last name followed by a comma and the *initials only* of the first and middle names. Use the same inverted order for all

Guide to APA Formats for References

the names of coauthors. Separate the names of coauthors with commas, and use an ampersand (&) before the name of the last author.

- **Date.** Put the year of publication in parentheses followed by a period.
- **Title.** Italicize the title, but capitalize only proper names and the first word of the main title and any subtitle.
- **Publication information.** Name the city (and the country or the state's postal abbreviation except for major cities) followed by a colon and a space. Supply the publisher's name without words such as *Inc.* or *Publishers.*

26b
APA

1. One Author

> Wilson, W. J. (1996). *When work disappears: The world of the new urban poor*. New York: Knopf.

2. Two or More Authors

List up to six authors; add *et al.* to indicate any others.

> Biber, D., Conrad, S., & Reppen, R. (1998). *Corpus linguistics: Investigating language structure and use*. Cambridge, England: Cambridge University Press.

3. Corporate or Group Author

Treat the group as an author. When author and publisher are the same, give the word *Author* after the place instead of repeating the name.

> Amnesty International. (2001). *Annual report 2001* [Brochure]. London: Author.

4. No Author Given

> *Boas anniversary volume: Anthropological papers written in honor of Franz Boas*. (1906). New York: Stechert.

5. More Than One Work by the Same Author

List works chronologically with the author's name in each entry.

> Aronowitz, S. (1993). *Roll over Beethoven: The return of cultural strife*. Hanover, NH: Wesleyan University Press.
>
> Aronowitz, S. (2000). *From the ashes of the old: American labor and America's future*. New York: Basic Books.

6. More Than One Work by the Same Author in the Same Year

If works by the same author appear in the same year, list them alphabetically based on the first main word in the title. Add lowercase letters after the dates to distinguish them in text citations: (Gould, 1987b).

> Gould, S. J. (1987a). *Time's arrow, time's cycle: Myth and metaphor in the discovery of geological time*. Cambridge, MA: Harvard University Press.

Gould, S. J. (1987b). *An urchin in the storm: Essays about books and ideas*. New York: Norton.

7. One or More Editors

Include (*Ed.*) or (*Eds.*) after the names of the editor or editors.

Bowe, J., Bowe, M., & Streeter, S. C. (Eds.). (2001). *Gig: Americans talk about their jobs*. New York: Three Rivers Press.

8. Translator

Bourdieu, P. (1990). *In other words: Essays towards a reflexive sociology*. (M. Adamson, Trans.). Stanford, CA: Stanford University Press.

9. Edition Following the First

Identify the edition in parentheses after the title (for example, *3rd ed.* or *Rev. ed.* for "revised edition").

Groth-Marnat, G. (1996). *Handbook of psychological assessment* (3rd ed.). New York: Wiley.

10. Reprint

Butler, J. (1999). *Gender trouble*. New York: Routledge. (Original work published 1990)

11. Multivolume Work

Strachey, J., Freud, A., Strachey, A., & Tyson, A. (Eds.). (1966-1974). *The standard edition of the complete psychological works of Sigmund Freud* (J. Strachey et al., Trans.) (Vols. 3-5). London: Hogarth Press and the Institute of Psycho-Analysis.

12. Anthology or Collection of Articles

Appadurai, A. (Ed.). (2001). *Globalization*. Durham, NC: Duke University Press.

13. Encyclopedia or Reference Work

Winn, P. (Ed.). (2001). *Dictionary of biological psychology*. London: Routledge.

26b
APA

14. *Diagnostic and Statistical Manual of Mental Disorders*

After an initial full in-text citation, you may use standard abbreviations: *DSM–III* (1980), *DSM–III–R* (1987), *DSM–IV* (1994), or *DSM–IV–TR* (2000).

American Psychiatric Association. (1994). *Diagnostic and statistical manual of mental disorders* (4th ed.). Washington, DC: Author.

15. Dissertation (Unpublished)

Gomes, C. S. (2001). *Selection and treatment effects in managed care.* Unpublished doctoral dissertation, Boston University.

16. Government Document

Select Committee on Aging, Subcommittee on Human Services, House of Representatives. (1991). *Grandparents' rights: Preserving generational bonds* (Com. Rep. No. 102-833). Washington, DC: U.S. Government Printing Office.

17. Report

Begin with the individual, group, or agency that has written the report. If the same body publishes the report, use *Author* in the publication information. If the report has a number, put it in parentheses after the title but before the period.

Dossey, J. A. (1988). *Mathematics: Are we measuring up?* (Report No. 17-M-02). Princeton, NJ: Educational Testing Service. (ERIC Document Reproduction Service No. ED300207)

Articles from Periodicals and Selections from Books

MODEL FORMAT FOR ARTICLES

period + space	period + space	period + space	comma + space
↓	↓	↓	↓

Author(s). (Date). Title of article. *Title of Periodical,*

Volume Number, Page numbers.

↑	↑	↑	↑
indent ½″ or 5–7 spaces	number italicized	comma italicized	period

- **Author.** Follow the author's last name and initials with a period.
- **Date.** Supply the date in parentheses followed by a period.

- **Title of article.** Capitalize only proper names and the first word of the title and any subtitle. Do not use quotation marks or italics. End with a period.
- **Title of journal, periodical, or book.** Italicize the journal title, with all main words capitalized, and the volume number. Follow with page numbers. Capitalize a book title like an article title, but italicize it.

18. Article in Journal Paginated by Volume

Omit the issue number when the page numbers run continuously throughout the different issues making up a volume.

> Klein, R. D. (2003). Audience reactions to local TV news. *American*
>
> *Behavioral Scientist, 46*, 1661-1672.

19. Article in Journal Paginated by Issue

When page 1 begins each issue, include the issue number in parentheses, but not italicized, directly after the volume number.

> Sadeh, A., Raviv, A., & Gruber, R. (2000). Sleep patterns and sleep
>
> disruptions in school-age children. *Developmental Psychology, 36*(3),
>
> 291-301.

20. Special Issue of Journal

Begin with the special issue's editor (if other than the regular editor). If no editor is indicated, begin with the title.

> Balk, D. E. (Ed.). (1991). Death and adolescent bereavement [Special
>
> issue]. *Journal of Adolescent Research, 6*(1).

21. Article in Weekly Magazine

> Adler, J. (1995, July 31). The rise of the overclass. *Newsweek, 126*, 33-34,
>
> 39-40, 43, 45-46.

22. Article in Monthly Magazine

> Dold, C. (1998, September). Needles and nerves. *Discover, 19*, 59-62.

23. Article with No Author Given

> True tales of false memories. (1993, July/August). *Psychology Today, 26*,
>
> 11-12.

26b
APA

24. Article in Newspaper

Use *p.* or *pp.* to introduce the article's page numbers.

Murtaugh, P. (1998, August 10). Finding a brand's real essence.

Advertising Age, p. 12.

25. Editorial or Letter to the Editor

Ellis, S. (2001, September 7). Adults are problem with youth sports

[Letter to the editor]. *USA Today,* p. 14A.

26. Interview (Published)

Although APA does not specify a form for published interviews, you may wish to employ the following form.

Dess, N. K. (2001). The new body-mind connection (John T. Cacioppo)

[Interview]. *Psychology Today, 34*(4), 30-31.

27. Review with Title

Following the title of the review, describe in brackets the kind of work (*book, film, television program*), and give the work's title.

McMahon, R. J. (2000). The Pentagon's war, the media's war [Review of

the book *Reporting Vietnam: Media and military at war*]. *Reviews in*

American History, 28, 303-308.

28. Review Without Title

Verdery, K. (2002). [Review of the book *The politics of gender after*

socialism]. *American Anthropologist, 104,* 354-355.

29. Article in Encyclopedia or Reference Work

Chernoff, H. (1978). Decision theory. In *International encyclopedia of*

statistics (Vol. 1, pp. 131-135). New York: Free Press.

30. Chapter in Edited Book or Selection in Anthology

Chisholm, J. S. (1999). Steps to an evolutionary ecology of mind. In A. L.

Hinton (Ed.), *Biocultural approaches to the emotions* (pp. 117-150).

Cambridge, England: Cambridge University Press.

31. Dissertation Abstract

Yamada, H. (1989). American and Japanese topic management strategies in business conversations. (Doctoral dissertation, City University of Hong Kong, 1989). *Dissertation Abstracts International, 50*(09), 2982B.

If you consult the dissertation on microfilm, end with the University Microfilms number in parentheses: (University Microfilms No. AAC–9004751).

Field and Media Resources

32. Unpublished Raw Data

When you use data from field research, briefly describe its topic within brackets, and end with *Unpublished raw data.*

Hernandez, J. (2003). [Survey of attitudes on unemployment benefits]. Unpublished raw data.

33. Interview (Unpublished)

If you have conducted an interview, cite it only in the text: (R. Gelles, personal communication, November 20, 2005).

34. Personal Communications (Including Email)

Cite letters, email, phone calls, and other communications unavailable to readers only in your text (see Entry 12 on p. 243).

35. Paper Presented at a Meeting

Nelson, J. S. (1993, August). *Political argument in political science: A meditation on the disappointment of political theory.* Paper presented at the annual meeting of the American Political Science Association, Chicago.

36. Videotape or Film

Musen, K. (Producer/Writer), & Zimbardo, P. (Writer). (1990). *Quiet rage: The Stanford prison study* [Motion picture]. (Available from Insight Media, New York)

37. Television or Radio Program

Siceloff, J. L. (Executive Producer). (2002). *Now with Bill Moyers* [Television series]. New York: WNET.

26b
APA

38. Recording

Begin with the name of the writer and the copyright date.

Freeman, R. (1994). Porscha [Recorded by R. Freeman & The Rippingtons].
On *Sahara* [CD]. New York: GRP Records.

Online and Electronic Resources

39. Web Site

Brown, D. K. (1998, April 1). *The children's literature Web guide.* Retrieved
August 23, 1998, from http://www.acs.UCalgary.ca/~dkbrown

40. Online Book or Document

If you can't pinpoint a date of publication, use *n.d.* ("no date").

Frary, R. B. (n.d.). *A brief guide to questionnaire development.*
Retrieved August 8, 1998, from http://ericae.net/ft/tamu/
upiques3.htm

41. Selection from Online Book or Document

Lasswell, H. D. (1971). Professional training. In *A pre-view of policy
sciences* (chap. 8). Retrieved March 28, 2006, from http://
www.policysciences.org/apreviewpolsci/pps_chapter8.pdf

42. Online Journal Article

Sheridan, J., & McAuley, J. D. (1998). Rhythm as a cognitive skill:
Temporal processing deficits in autism. *Noetica, 3*(8). Retrieved
December 31, 1998, from http://www.cs.indiana.edu/
Noetica/OpenForumIssue8/McAuley.html

43. Online Article Identical to Print Version

If online and print articles are identical, you may use the print format
but identify the online version you used.

Epstein, R. (2001). Physiologist Laura [Electronic version]. *Psychology
Today, 34*(4), 5.

If the online article differs in format or content, add your retrieval date with
the URL.

44. Online Newsletter Article

Cashel, J. (2001, July 16). Top ten trends for online communities. *Online Community Report*. Retrieved from http://www.onlinecommunityreport.com/features/10

45. Online Newspaper Article

Phillips, D. (1999, June 13). 21 days, 18 flights. *Washington Post Online*. Retrieved June 13, 1999, from http://www.washingtonpost.com/wp-srv/business/daily/june99/odyssey13.htm

46. Online Organization or Agency Document

Arizona Public Health Association. (n.d.). *Indigenous health section*. Retrieved September 6, 2001, from http://www.geocities.com/native_health_az/AzPHA.htm

47. Online Government Document

U.S. Department of Labor, Women's Bureau. (2001). *Women's jobs 1964-1999: More than 30 years of progress*. Retrieved September 7, 2001, from http://www.dol.gov/dol/wb/public/jobs6497.htm

48. Online Document from Academic Site

Cultural Studies Program. (n.d.). Retrieved September 9, 2001, from Drake University, Cultural Studies Web site: http://www.multimedia.drake.edu/cs/

49. Online Report

Amnesty International. (1998). *The death penalty in Texas: Lethal injustice*. Retrieved September 7, 2001, from http://www.web.amnesty.org/ai.nsf/index/AMR510101998

50. Online Report from Academic Site

Use "Available from" rather than "Retrieved from" if the URL will take your reader to access information rather than the source itself.

26b
APA

Vandell, D. L., & Wolfe, B. (2000). *Child care quality: Does it matter and does it need to be improved?* (Special Report No. 78). Available from University of Wisconsin, Institute for Research on Poverty Web site: http://www.ssc.wisc.edu/irp/sr/sr78.pdf

51. Online Abstract

Include the source of the original work.

National Bureau of Economic Research. (1998). Tax incentives for higher education. *Tax Policy and the Economy, 12*, 49-81. Abstract retrieved August 24, 1998, from http://www-mitpress.mit.edu/journal-editor .tcl?ISSN=08928649

52. Online Database: Journal Article

Piko, B. (2001). Gender differences and similarities in adolescents' ways of coping. *Psychological Record, 51*(2), 223-236. Retrieved August 31, 2001, from InfoTrac Expanded Academic database.

53. Online Database: Newspaper Article

Sappenfield, M. (2002, June 24). New laws curb teen sports drugs. *The Christian Science Monitor*. Retrieved June 26, 2002, from America Online: News Publications database.

54. Presentation from Virtual Conference

Brown, D. J., Stewart, D. S., & Wilson, J. R. (1995). *Ethical pathways to virtual learning*. Paper presented at the Center on Disabilities 1995 virtual conference. Retrieved September 7, 2001, from http://www.csun.edu/cod/95virt/0010.html

55. Email

Cite email only in your text. (See Entry 12, p. 243.)

56. Online Posting

Treat these as personal communications (see Entry 12, p. 243) unless they are archived and accessible.

Lanbehn, K. (2001, May 9). Effective rural outreach. Message posted to

State Independent Living Council Discussion Newsgroup, archived at

http://www.acils.com/silc

57. Computer Program

Begin with the name of an author who owns rights to a program or with its title (without italics).

Family Tree Maker (Version 9.0) [Computer software]. (2001). Fremont,

CA: Learning Company.

58. CD-ROM Database

Hall, Edward T. (1998). In *Current biography: 1940-1997*. Retrieved March

14, 1999, from Wilson database.

26c Sample APA paper

The APA manual recommends beginning a paper with a separate title page, as illustrated on page 256. The student also included an abstract before the paper and her questionnaire in the appendix following it.

26c
APA

**Number title page and all
others using short title**

Body Esteem   1

**Abbreviate title (50 characters
maximum) for heading**

Running head: BODY ESTEEM

Center title and all other lines

Body Esteem in Women and Men

**Supply
name and
institution**

Sharon Salamone

The University of Rhode Island

**Supply
course
information
and date if
requested
by your
instructor**

Professor Robert Schwegler

Writing 233

Section 2

April 30, 2003

26c
APA

Body Esteem   2

Center heading

Do not indent   Abstract

Begin on new page

Undergraduate students, male and female, were asked to complete

a Body Esteem Survey to report attitudes toward their bodies

(body images). Responses to the survey provided an answer to the

Summarize paper in one ¶, no more than 120 words

question of whether the men or the women had higher body

esteem. The mean responses for women and men indicated a

higher level of body esteem among men with a statistically

Double-space abstract and paper

significant difference in the means. Because the sample was

limited to college undergraduates and displayed little variety in

ethnicity (predominantly White), the findings of the study are

limited. Prior research on ethnicity and body image suggests that a

more ethnically varied sample might produce different results.

[Besides the abstract, typical sections in an APA paper
are Introduction, Method, Results, and Discussion.]

26c
APA

Body Esteem in Men and Women

1" margin on each side

The concept of beauty has changed over the years in Western society, especially for women. In past centuries the ideal was a voluptuous and curved body; now it is a more angular and thin shape (Monteath & McCabe, 1997). Lean, muscular bodies are currently held up as ideals for men, too. Ideals of physical appearance and attractiveness play an important role in the lives of people. Often, people considered attractive are preferred as working partners, as dating partners, or as job candidates (Lennon, Lillethun, & Buckland, 1999). Media images endorse particular body ideals as well; for example, "media in Western countries have portrayed a steadily thinning female body ideal" (Monteath & McCabe, 1997, p. 711).

Most of us assume that women are quite concerned about their weight and appearance--their body images--and that they often lack positive body esteem, perhaps as a result of media images and other cultural influences (Polivy & Herman, 1987; Rodin, Silberstein, & Striegel-Moore, 1984; Wilcox & Laird, 2000). But what about men? Are they concerned as well? Is their level of body esteem higher or lower than women's or about the same? In this paper I report on a study I undertook with a group of college undergraduates to compare the attitudes of men and women toward their bodies. In particular, I wanted to determine whether or not the men had a higher body esteem than the women had.

Indent ¶s and reference list consistently, ½" or 5–7 spaces

Problem and background introduced

1

2

Citation includes more than one source

Research questions identified

1" margin at bottom

26c
APA

Body Esteem   4

Center subheading   Introduction

Thinness is prized in contemporary society, especially for
women. In our culture, thinness, a statistical deviation, has
become the norm, leading millions of women to believe their
bodies are abnormal. Therefore, it is reasonable for women to be
concerned about their appearance and compare themselves to
others on the basis of what they believe to be the norm
(Lennon et al., 1999). As Lennon et al. point out, "Comparison
with such images may be related to negative outcomes such
as low self-esteem (Freedman, 1984), dissatisfaction with
appearance (Richens, 1991), eating disorders (Peterson, 1987;
Stice et al., 1994), and negative body image (Freedman, 1984)"
(p. 380).

Body image is basically made up of two important
components: one's perception and one's attitude toward body
image. Social factors can play a large role in determining both
components (Monteath & McCabe, 1997). Given the cultural
pressures on women to be thin, we might expect many women to
have somewhat negative body images. As Wilcox and Laird (2000)
put it, "To many observers, the media appear to be unwittingly
engaged in a campaign to make women feel badly about
themselves" (p. 279).

On the other hand, some researchers suggest that "men seem
less obsessed with and disturbed by being or becoming fat: thus,
the occurrence of pathogenic values related to eating and body size
is extremely low among men" (Demarest & Allen, 2000, p. 465).
Although there is some research, "the literature on body image

3
Background
including
prior
studies

4
Body image
and women
introduced

5
Body image
and men
introduced

26c
APA

perception in men is far more limited" than that on women
(Pope et al., 2000, p. 1297). Possible reasons to suspect that
men also suffer from distorted perceptions of body image
have been evident in two recent studies. First, men with eating
disorders believe that they are fatter than men of normal
weight believe. Also, recent studies have shown that athletes
perceive themselves to be small and frail when they are, in
fact, large and muscular (Pope et al., 2000). Moreover, in one
study, men indicated that they would prefer to have a body
with 27 pounds more muscle than they actually have
(Pope et al., 2000). Thus it seems reasonable to ask
whether men and women have clearly different levels of body
esteem.

Method

6

Procedure for study explained

To measure differences between men's and women's levels of
body esteem, I administered a Body Esteem Scale (BES) (Franzoi &
Sheilds, 1984). Participants in my study were 174 undergraduate
college students from a state university. I approached them and
asked them to complete the BES. I asked each willing participant to
read and sign an informed consent form before participating. This
form states that the participant may stop at any point if he or she
feels uncomfortable answering a particular question or group of
questions and reassures each person that he or she will remain
anonymous.

7

Participants described

The majority of the participants, between the ages of 18 and
59, were White, making up 81% of the sample. Blacks and African
Americans made up 6.3%; Asian/Pacific Islanders made up 3.4%;

26c
APA

Body Esteem   6

Latino/Latina, mixed race, and all others made up 2.9% each; and Native Americans made up .6% of the sample. The sample was equally divided between men and women.

The Body Esteem Scale consists of general questions (BES) (see Appendix) followed by three components (BES 1, BES 2, and BES 3). BES 1 makes up the Physical/Sexual Attractiveness part of the scale, focusing primarily on elements of the body; BES 3 consists of the Physical Condition component of the scale, covering such matters as stamina, physical condition, and strength. BES 1 and BES 3 have different forms and questions for women and men. For BES 2, the women's questionnaire constitutes the Weight Concern component of the scale while the men's questionnaire constitutes the Upper Body Strength component of the scale.

8 Questionnaire described with cross-reference to appendix

Results

I recorded the results from the questionnaires into an Excel spreadsheet. In order to determine whether women or men had higher levels of body esteem as measured by the BES, I calculated the average score for each group (statistical mean). The mean for women was lower than for men: for women, $M = 3.2304$; for men, $M = 3.6514$. From this I arrived at my preliminary conclusion that for this particular sample of college students, the men had clearly higher body esteem than did the women, by .4211, or approximately .4 on a scale of 1-5.

9 Findings explained

I realized, however, that results can occur by chance and that there are statistical procedures for determining the likelihood that chance was responsible for the difference between the two

10

26c
APA

groups. To determine whether the results were statistically significant (not occurring by chance), I had the spreadsheet program calculate an ANOVA (univariate analysis of variance) to compare the two body esteem indexes. The results indicated that the differences were significant, F (1.172) = 28.05, $p < .05$.

I conducted this study in order to determine whether men had higher, lower, or similar levels of body esteem compared with the levels women had, at least for the group of people (university undergraduates) I was studying. For this group, it is clear that men had higher levels of body esteem.

Main conclusion stated

Discussion

Comparing men's and women's body esteem is not as simple as this study might seem to suggest, however. The body esteem scales for men and women are certainly comparable, but they do not measure exactly the same things. According to Franzoi and Shields (1984), body esteem for women appears to consist of three primary components: sexual attractiveness, weight concern, and physical condition. The sexual attractiveness subscale consists of physical attributes that cannot generally be changed through exercise, but only through cosmetics. The physical appearance subscale includes body parts that can be altered through exercise of the control of food intake. The third subscale pertains to qualities such as stamina, agility, and strength. For men, the first subscale measures facial features and some aspects of the physique. The second subscale is composed of upper body parts and functions that can be altered through exercising. The third subscale is similar to the woman's physical subscale, consisting of stamina, agility, and strength.

Findings qualified

26c
APA

As social attitudes and values change, perhaps men's and women's versions of the BES may need to change too. As sports and physical strength become more important to women, parts of the BES may possibly need to be revised to be more parallel to the men's. Right now, however, the BES seems to provide some understanding of the different levels of bodily self-esteem held by women and men.

13 Possibilities for future research suggested

The great pressure on women in our society to be thin and physically attractive according to standards that do not represent a normal range of body types and sizes probably accounts for the difference between the women's and men's results. Franzoi and Shields (1984) made a comment that helps explain the higher body esteem of the males: "It appears that men associate these body parts and functions, not with how they and others assess them as static objects, but with how they will help or hinder physical activity" (p. 178).

14 Findings analyzed

My results are consistent with other research. For example, "in studies of body-shape perception, men typically have more positive body images than women do, regardless of their weight" (Demarest & Langer, 1996, p. 569). Overall, men are generally satisfied with their body sizes, although they misjudge what women think to be attractive (Demarest & Allen, 2000).

15

Gender is not the only factor that influences body image. Ethnicity is also very important, especially among women. In interviews conducted by Lopez, Blix, and Blix (1995) and by Rosen and Gross (1987), Black women seem to have more positive body images and less desire to be thin than White or Hispanic women

16

26c
APA

(Demarest & Allen, 2000). When compared to Black women, White women showed greater body dissatisfaction at lower body weights (Demarest & Allen). It has also been found that Black men were less likely than White men to refuse a date with a woman because she was overweight. According to Demarest and Allen, among the female participants, Black women have a more accurate view of the perception of men, whereas White women have a more distorted perception.

17   In my study, the majority of the sample consisted of White participants. This may have affected my results and my conclusions. Because ethnicity is important in a study such as this, a more varied sample would lead to stronger conclusions.

References

Begin on new page

Demarest, J., & Allen, R. (2000). Body image: Gender, ethnic, and age differences. *Journal of Social Psychology, 140,* 465-471.

Demarest, J., & Langer, E. (1996). Perception of body shape by underweight, average-weight, and overweight men and women. *Perceptual and Motor Skills, 83,* 569-570.

Franzoi, S. L., & Shields, S. A. (1984). The body esteem scale: Multidimensional structure and sex differences in a college population. *Journal of Personality Assessment, 407,* 173-178.

Lennon, S. J., Lillethun, A., & Buckland, S. S. (1999). Attitudes toward social comparison as a function of self-esteem: Idealized appearance and body image. *Family & Consumer Sciences Research Journal, 27,* 379-405.

Lopez, E., Blix, G., & Blix, A. G. (1995). Body image of Latinas compared to body image of non-Latina white women. *Health Values, 19,* 3-10.

Monteath, S. A., & McCabe, M. P. (1997). The influence of societal factors on female body image. *Journal of Social Psychology, 137,* 708-727.

Polivy, J., & Herman, C. P. (1987). The diagnosis and treatment of abnormal eating [Electronic version]. *Journal of Consulting and Clinical Psychology, 55,* 635-644.

Pope, H. G., Bureau, B., DeCol, C., Gruber, A. J., Hudson, J. I., Jouvent, R., et al. (2000). Body image perception among men in three countries. *American Journal of Psychiatry, 157,* 1297-1301.

Rodin, J., Silberstein, L., & Striegel-Moore, R. (1984). Women and weight: A normative discontent. In T. B. Sonderegger (Ed.),

26c
APA

Body Esteem   11

Nebraska symposium on motivation: Psychology and gender (pp. 267-307). Lincoln: University of Nebraska Press.

Rosen, J. C., & Gross, J. (1987). Prevalence of weight reducing and weight gaining in adolescent boys and girls. *Health Psychology, 6,* 131-147.

Wilcox, K., & Laird, J. D. (2000). The impact of media images of super-slender women on women's self-esteem: Identification, social comparison, and self-perception. *Journal of Research in Personality, 34,* 278-286.

Appendix

Body Esteem Scale for Adolescents and Adults:

Begin on new page

General Questions

Instructions: Indicate how often you agree with the following statements, ranging from "never" (0) to "always" (4). Circle the appropriate number beside each statement.

Never = 0   Seldom = 1   Sometimes = 2   Often = 3   Always = 4

1. I like what I look like in pictures.   0 1 2 3 4

2. Other people consider me good looking.   0 1 2 3 4

3. I'm proud of my body.   0 1 2 3 4

4. I am preoccupied with trying to change my
   body weight.   0 1 2 3 4

5. I think my appearance would help me get
   a job.   0 1 2 3 4

6. I like what I see when I look in the mirror.   0 1 2 3 4

7. There are lots of things I'd change about
   my looks if I could.   0 1 2 3 4

8. I am satisfied with my weight.   0 1 2 3 4

9. I wish I looked better.   0 1 2 3 4

10. I really like what I weigh.   0 1 2 3 4

11. I wish I looked like someone else.   0 1 2 3 4

12. People my own age like my looks.   0 1 2 3 4

13. My looks upset me.   0 1 2 3 4

14. I'm as nice looking as most people.   0 1 2 3 4

15. I'm pretty happy about the way I look.   0 1 2 3 4

16. I feel I weigh the right amount for my height. 0 1 2 3 4

17. I feel ashamed of how I look.   0 1 2 3 4

18. Weighing myself depresses me.   0 1 2 3 4

26c
APA

		Body Esteem	13
19. My weight makes me unhappy.		0 1 2 3 4	
20. My looks help me to get dates.		0 1 2 3 4	
21. I worry about the way I look.		0 1 2 3 4	
22. I think I have a good body.		0 1 2 3 4	
23. I'm looking as nice as I'd like to.		0 1 2 3 4	

Exercise 1   *(Answers appear on p. 508.)*

Turn to Exercise 1 in Chapter 25. Rewrite the items supplied there to add in-text citations in APA style.

Exercise 2   *(Answers appear on p. 509.)*

Turn to Exercise 2 in Chapter 25. Rewrite the items supplied there to create a list of references in APA style.

PART 7

Documenting Sources: CMS and CSE Style

27 CMS Documentation Style

The CMS (*Chicago Manual of Style*) outlines a system for references using endnotes or footnotes. These notes are less compact than parenthetical references and may distract a reader, but they allow detailed citations.

> **STRATEGY** Use CMS style in the arts and sciences to place citations in notes.
>
> **ACADEMIC SETTINGS**
> When readers expect "Turabian," "Chicago," or footnotes or endnotes
>
> **PUBLIC AND WORK SETTINGS**
> When your readers expect footnotes or endnotes
> When readers won't need to consult each note as they read and might be distracted by names, page numbers, or dates in parentheses
> When other writers or publications addressing your readers use CMS

27.1

The CMS style is one of two systems of documentation outlined in *The Chicago Manual of Style* (15th edition, Chicago: University of Chicago Press, 2003), a reliable guide often simply called "Chicago." Its Web site at <http://www.chicagomanualofstyle.org/cmosfaq.html> answers many questions for writers and editors who routinely use CMS. This style is detailed for students in Kate L. Turabian's *A Manual for Writers of Term Papers, Theses, and Dissertations* (6th ed., rev. John Grossman and Alice Bennett, Chicago: University of Chicago Press, 1996). This popular student manual accounts for the wide identification of CMS style as "Turabian."

27a Using CMS endnotes or footnotes

To indicate a reference in your text, add a superscript number above the line; number the references consecutively. Provide the details about the source at the end of the paper (in an endnote) or at the bottom of the page (in a footnote). (For advice on what to document, see 22c–f.)

TEXT   Wideman describes his impoverished childhood neighborhood as being not simply on "the wrong side of the tracks" but actually "*under* the tracks."[1]

NOTE   1. John Edgar Wideman, *Brothers and Keepers* (New York: Penguin Books, 1984), 39.

Most word-processing programs will position footnotes between the text and the bottom margin. Otherwise, you'll probably prefer endnotes. Most readers mark the endnote page for easy reference, but you should put all necessary information in the text, not the notes, in case a reader skips a note.

Place endnotes following your paper, after any appendix but before the bibliography, which alphabetically orders your sources. Supply the notes on a separate page with the centered heading "Notes." Indent the first line of each note like a paragraph; type its number on the line, followed by a period and a space. Do not indent any following lines. CMS suggests double-spacing all of your text, but Turabian suggests single-spaced notes. Although both alternatives appear in this chapter, we advise double-spacing for ease of reading.

Notes can also supply material of interest to only a few readers, but avoid excessive detail that may obscure a source reference.

TEXT Another potential source of workplace misunderstanding comes

from differences in the ways orders are given by men (directly) and

women (indirectly, often as requests or questions).[2]

NOTE 2. Deborah Tannen, "How to Give Orders Like a Man,"

New York Times Magazine, 18 August 1994, 46. Tannen provides

a detailed and balanced discussion of the ways men and women use

language in *Talking from 9 to 5* (New York: William Morrow, 1994).

27b Creating CMS endnotes or footnotes

A typical note provides the author's name in regular order, the title, publication information, and the page reference.

Guide to CMS Formats for Endnotes and Footnotes

Books and Works Treated as Books
1. One Author 272
2. Two Authors 272
3. Three Authors 272
4. Four or More Authors 272
5. No Author Given 272
6. One Editor 273
7. Two or More Editors 273
8. Author and Editor 273
9. Edition Following the First 273

10. Reprint 273
11. Multivolume Work 273

Articles from Periodicals and Selections from Books
12. Article in Journal Paginated by Volume 274
13. Article in Journal Paginated by Issue 274
14. Article in Magazine 274
15. Article in Newspaper 274

(Continued)

27b
CMS

27.2

Books and Works Treated as Books

MODEL FORMAT FOR BOOKS AND WORKS TREATED AS BOOKS

note
number space

comma
+ space space

colon
+ space

↓ ↓   ↓   ↓   ↓
1. Author(s), *Title* (Place of Publication: Publisher,
Year), Page number(s).
↑
comma + space

1. One Author

1. Bobby Bridger, *Buffalo Bill and Sitting Bull: Inventing the Wild West* (Austin: University of Texas Press, 2002), 297.

2. Two Authors

2. William H. Gerdts and Will South, *California Impressionism* (New York: Abbeville Press, 1998), 214.

3. Three Authors

3. Michael Wood, Bruce Cole, and Adelheid Gealt, *Art of the Western World* (New York: Summit Books, 1989), 206-10.

4. Four or More Authors

Follow the name of the first author with *and others.* (Generally supply all the names, up to ten, in the bibliography entry.)

4. Anthony Slide and others, *The American Film Industry: A Historical Dictionary* (New York: Greenwood Press, 1986), 124.

5. No Author Given

5. *The Great Utopia* (New York: Guggenheim Museum, 1992), 661.

6. One Editor

To emphasize the editor, translator, or compiler, begin with that name.

> 6. Robert H. Ferrell, ed., *Dear Bess: The Letters from Harry to Bess Truman 1910-1959* (New York: W. W. Norton, 1983), 71-72.

The word *by* with the author's name may follow the title but isn't needed if the name appears in the title.

7. Two or More Editors

> 7. Cris Mazza, Jeffrey DeShell, and Elisabeth Sheffield, eds., *Chick-Lit 2: No Chick Vics* (Normal, IL: Black Ice Books, 1996), 173-86.

8. Author and Editor

Name any editor (*ed.*), translator (*trans.*), compiler (*comp.*), or some combination of these after the title.

> 8. Francis Bacon, *The New Organon*, ed. Lisa Jardine, trans. Michael Silverthorne (Cambridge: Cambridge University Press, 2000), 45.

9. Edition Following the First

After the title, abbreviate the edition: *3rd ed.* ("third edition") or *rev. and enl. ed.* ("revised and enlarged edition").

> 9. Thomas E. Skidmore and Peter H. Smith, *Modern Latin America*, 5th ed. (New York: Oxford University Press, 2001), 243.

10. Reprint

Note original publication of a reprint or paperback edition.

> 10. Henri Frankfort and others, *The Intellectual Adventure of Ancient Man* (1946; repr., Chicago: University of Chicago Press, 1977), 202-4.

11. Multivolume Work

If you cite the whole work, include the total number of volumes after the title. Separate volume and page numbers for a specific volume with a colon. For a separately titled volume, give the volume number and name after the main title and only a page reference at the end.

> 11. Sigmund Freud, *The Standard Edition of the Complete Psychological Works of Sigmund Freud*, trans. James Strachey (London: Hogarth Press, 1953), 11:180.

Articles from Periodicals and Selections from Books

MODEL FORMAT FOR ARTICLES

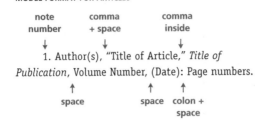

12. Article in Journal Paginated by Volume

When page numbers run continuously through the issues in a volume, give only the volume number. Supply specific page numbers for part or inclusive numbers for all of an article, such as 98–114.

12. Lily Zubaidah Rahim, "The Road Less Traveled: Islamic Militancy in Southeast Asia," *Critical Asian Studies* 35 (2003): 224.

13. Article in Journal Paginated by Issue

If each issue of a journal begins with page 1, give the volume number and *no.* ("number") with the issue number. If the issue is identified by month or season, include this inside the parentheses with the year: (Winter 1994) or (February 1996).

13. Jose Pinera, "A Chilean Model for Russia," *Foreign Affairs* 79, no. 5 (2000): 62-73.

14. Article in Magazine

Follow the magazine title with the date: November 25, 2001.

14. Joan W. Gandy, "Portrait of Natchez," *American Legacy*, Fall 2000, 51-52.

15. Article in Newspaper

Identify newspapers by date: February 4, 2002. Provide the section (*sec.*) number or letter but omit the page, which may change in different editions. Add the city, state, or country, as needed: *Westerly (R.I.) Sun*, *Times* (London).

15. Janny Scott, "A Bull Market for Grant, A Bear Market for Lee," *New York Times*, sec. A, September 30, 2000.

16. Chapter in Edited Book

Follow the title with *ed.* and the editor's name.

16. John Matviko, "Television Satire and the Presidency: The Case of *Saturday Night Live*," in *Hollywood's White House: The American Presidency in Film and History*, ed. Peter C. Rollins and John E. O'Connor (Lexington: University of Kentucky Press, 2003), 341.

17. Selection in Anthology

17. W. E. B. Du Bois, "The Call of Kansas," in *W. E. B. Du Bois: A Reader*, ed. David Levering Lewis (New York: Henry Holt, 1995), 113.

Field and Media Resources

18. Interview (Unpublished)

For unpublished interviews by someone else, supply the name of the person interviewed, *interview by*, the name of the interviewer, the date, any file number, the medium (such as *tape recording* or *transcript*), and the place where the interview is stored (*Erie County Historical Society, Buffalo, NY*). Identify interviews you conduct as *interview by author*; include the medium, place, and date of the interview.

18. LeJon Will, interview by author, May 22, 2003, transcript, Tempe, AZ.

19. Audio or Video Recording

Start with the title unless the recording features a particular individual. Give names and roles (if appropriate) of performers or others. Add any recording number (audio) after the company.

19. *James Baldwin*, VHS, directed by Karen Thorsen (San Francisco: California Newsreel, 1990).

Online and Electronic Resources

20. Online Book

20. Sharon Marcus, *Apartment Stories: City and Home in Nineteenth-Century Paris and London* (Berkeley: University of California Press, 1999), http://ark.cdlib.org/ark:13030/ft0d5n99jz/ (accessed October 15, 2003).

21. Online Older Book

For a book previously in print, include all standard information, the URL, and your access date if expected in the field.

21. Charles Darwin, *On the Origin of Species by Means of Natural Selection, or the Preservation of Favoured Races in the Struggle for Life* (1859;

Project Gutenberg, 1998), ftp://sailor.gutenberg.org/pub/gutenberg/ etext98/otoos10.txt (accessed November 1, 2003).

22. Online Journal Article

22. Alfred Willis, "A Survey of Surviving Buildings of the Krotona Colony in Hollywood," *Architronic* 8, no. 1 (1999), http:// architronic.saed.kent.edu/ (accessed September 29, 2000).

23. Online Magazine Article

23. Alexander Barnes Dryer, "Our Liberian Legacy," *The Atlantic Online*, July 30, 2003, http://www.theatlantic.com/unbound/flashbks/ liberia.htm (accessed October 24, 2003).

24. Online Newspaper Article

24. Joshua Klein, "Scaring up a Good Movie," *Chicago Tribune Online Edition*, October 28, 2003, http://www.chicagotribune.com/ (accessed October 28, 2003).

25. Web Site

25. Smithsonian Center for Folklife and Cultural Heritage, "2002 Smithsonian Folklife Festival: The Silk Road," Smithsonian Institution, http:// www.folklife.si.edu/CFCH/festival2002.htm (accessed October 27, 2003).

26. Online Posting

26. Justin M. Sanders, e-mail to alt.war.civil.usa, February 15, 2002, http://groups.google.com/groups?q=civil+war&hl= en&lr=&ie=UTF-8&selm= civil-war-usa/faq/part2_1013770939%40rtfm.mit.edu&rnum=1 (accessed October 21, 2003).

27. CD-ROM

Add the medium, *CD-ROM*.

27. Rose, Mark, ed., "Elements of Theater," *The Norton Shakespeare Workshop CD-ROM* (New York: Norton Publishing, 1997), CD-ROM, version 1.1.

Multiple Sources and Sources Cited in Prior Notes

28. Multiple Sources

Separate several references with semicolons. Give the entries in the order in which they are cited in the text.

28. See Greil Marcus, *Mystery Train: Images of America in Rock 'n Roll Music* (New York: E. P. Dutton, 1975), 119; Susan Orlean, "All Mixed Up," *New Yorker*, June 22, 1992, 90; and Cornel West, "Learning to Talk of Race," *New York Times Magazine*, August 2, 1992, 24.

27c
CMS

29. Work Cited More Than Once

In your first reference, provide full information. Later, provide only the author's last name, a short title, and the page.

29. Pinera, "Chilean," 63.

30. Wood, Cole, and Gealt, *Art*, 207.

If two notes in a row refer to the same source, you can use the traditional *ibid.* (Latin for "in the same place") for the second note. Add a new page reference if the specific page is different.

31. Tarr, "'A Man,'" 183.

32. Ibid.

33. Ibid., 186.

27c Creating a CMS bibliography

In addition to your notes, provide an alphabetical list of sources, titled "Selected Bibliography," "Works Cited," "References," or something similar. Place this list on a separate page at the end of your paper; center the title two inches from the top. Continue the page numbering used for the text. Although we show single-spaced entries below to conserve space, we recommend double-spacing throughout for ease of reading. (Check with your instructor.) Do not indent the first line, but indent any subsequent lines five spaces. Alphabetize by authors' last names or by the first word of the title, excluding *A*, *An*, and *The*, if the author is unknown.

Guide to CMS Formats for Bibliography Entries

Books and Works Treated as Books
1. One Author 278
2. Two Authors 278
3. Three Authors 278
4. Four or More Authors 278
5. No Author Given 278
6. One Editor 279
7. Two or More Editors 279
8. Author and Editor 279
9. Edition Following the First 279

10. Reprint 279
11. Multivolume Work 279

Articles from Periodicals and Selections from Books
12. Article in Journal Paginated by Volume 279
13. Article in Journal Paginated by Issue 280
14. Article in Magazine 280

(Continued)

Books and Works Treated as Books

MODEL FORMAT FOR BOOKS AND WORKS TREATED AS BOOKS

period +   period +   colon +
  space   space   space
   ↓   ↓   ↓

Author(s). *Title*. Place of Publication:

      Publisher, Date.

 ↑   ↑
indent   comma + space
5 spaces

1. One Author

Bridger, Bobby. *Buffalo Bill and Sitting Bull: Inventing the Wild West*.
Austin: University of Texas Press, 2002.

2. Two Authors

Gerdts, William H., and Will South. *California Impressionism*. New York:
Abbeville Press, 1998.

3. Three Authors

Wood, Michael, Bruce Cole, and Adelheid Gealt. *Art of the Western World*.
New York: Summit Books, 1989.

4. Four or More Authors

Slide, Anthony, Val Almen Darez, Robert Gitt, and Susan Perez Prichard.
The American Film Industry: A Historical Dictionary. New York:
Greenwood Press, 1986.

5. No Author Given

The Great Utopia. New York: Guggenheim Museum, 1992.

6. One Editor

Ferrell, Robert H., ed. *Dear Bess: The Letters from Harry to Bess Truman 1910-1959.* New York: W. W. Norton, 1983.

7. Two or More Editors

Mazza, Cris, Jeffrey DeShell, and Elisabeth Sheffield, eds. *Chick-Lit 2: No Chick Vics.* Normal, IL.: Black Ice Books, 1996.

8. Author and Editor

Bacon, Francis. *The New Organon.* Edited by Lisa Jardine. Translated by Michael Silverthorne. Cambridge: Cambridge University Press, 2000.

9. Edition Following the First

Skidmore, Thomas E., and Peter H. Smith. *Modern Latin America.* 5th ed. New York: Oxford University Press, 2001.

10. Reprint

Frankfort, Henri, H. A. Frankfort, John A. Wilson, Thorkild Jacobsen, and William A. Irving. *The Intellectual Adventure of Ancient Man.* 1946. Reprint, Chicago: University of Chicago Press, 1977.

11. Multivolume Work

Freud, Sigmund. *The Standard Edition of the Complete Psychological Works of Sigmund Freud.* Translated by James Strachey. Vol. 11. London: Hogarth Press, 1953.

Articles from Periodicals and Selections from Books

MODEL FORMAT FOR ARTICLES AND SELECTIONS

```
          period +
     space   period                    space    space
       ↓       ↓                         ↓        ↓
Author(s). "Title." Name of Publication Volume (Date): Pages.
                                               ↑
                                        colon + space
```

12. Article in Journal Paginated by Volume

Rahim, Lily Zubaidah. "The Road Less Traveled: Islamic Militancy in Southeast Asia." *Critical Asian Studies* 35 (2003): 209-32.

13. Article in Journal Paginated by Issue

Pinera, Jose. "A Chilean Model for Russia." *Foreign Affairs* 79, no. 5 (2000): 62-73.

14. Article in Magazine

Gandy, Joan W. "Portrait of Natchez." *American Legacy*, Fall 2000, 51-52.

15. Article in Newspaper

Scott, Janny. "A Bull Market for Grant, A Bear Market for Lee." *New York Times*, September 30, 2000, sec. A.

16. Chapter in Edited Book

Matviko, John. "Television Satire and the Presidency: The Case of *Saturday Night Live*." In *Hollywood's White House: The American Presidency in Film and History*, edited by Peter C. Rollins and John E. O'Connor, 341-60. Lexington: University of Kentucky Press, 2003.

17. Selection in Anthology

Du Bois, W. E. B. "The Call of Kansas." In *W. E. B. Du Bois: A Reader*, edited by David Levering Lewis, 101-21. New York: Henry Holt, 1995.

Field and Media Resources

18. Interview (Unpublished)

Generally treat this as a personal or informal communication, cited only in your notes. (See Entry 18, p. 275.)

19. Audio or Video Recording

James Baldwin. VHS. Directed by Karen Thorsen. San Francisco: California Newsreel, 1990.

Online and Electronic Resources

20. Online Book

Marcus, Sharon. *Apartment Stories: City and Home in Nineteenth-Century Paris and London*. Berkeley: University of California Press, 1999. http://ark.cdlib.org/ark:13030/ft0d5n99jz/ (accessed October 15, 2003).

21. Online Older Book

Darwin, Charles. *On the Origin of Species by Means of Natural Selection, or the Preservation of Favoured Races in the Struggle for Life.* 1859. Project Gutenberg, 1998. ftp://sailor.gutenberg.org/pub/ gutenberg/etext98/otoos10.txt (accessed November 1, 2003).

22. Online Journal Article

Willis, Alfred. "A Survey of Surviving Buildings of the Krotona Colony in Hollywood." *Architronic* 8, no. 1 (1999), http://architronic.saed.kent .edu/ (accessed September 29, 2000).

23. Online Magazine Article

Dryer, Alexander Barnes. "Our Liberian Legacy." *The Atlantic Online*, July 30, 2003. http://www.theatlantic.com/unbound/flashbks/liberia.htm (accessed October 24, 2003).

24. Online Newspaper Article

Klein, Joshua. "Scaring up a Good Movie." *Chicago Tribune Online Edition*, October 28, 2003. http://www.chicagotribune.com/(accessed October 28, 2003).

25. Web Site

Smithsonian Center for Folklife and Cultural Heritage. "2002 Smithsonian Folklife Festival: The Silk Road." Smithsonian Institution. http://www .folklife.si.edu/CFCH/festival2002.htm (accessed October 27, 2003).

26. Online Posting

Treat this as a personal or informal communication, cited only in your notes. (See Entry 26, p. 276.)

27. CD-ROM

Rose, Mark, ed. "Elements of Theater." *The Norton Shakespeare Workshop CD-ROM.* CD-ROM, Version 1.1. New York: Norton Publishing, 1997.

Multiple Sources

28. Multiple Sources

When a note mentions more than one source, list each one separately in your bibliography.

Exercise 1   *(Answers appear on p. 509.)*

> Turn to Exercise 1 in Chapter 25. Rewrite the items supplied there to add note numbers in CMS style. Then prepare the corresponding notes for these items.

Exercise 2   *(Answers appear on p. 509.)*

> Turn to Exercise 2 in Chapter 25. Rewrite the items supplied there to create a list of works cited in CMS style.

28 CSE Documentation Style

28.1

One widely used form of documentation in the sciences is the CSE (Council of Science Editors) style. CSE advocates a simplified international scientific style and presents three options for documentation: a name-and-year, a number, and a name system. This handbook focuses on the first two systems.

STRATEGY   Use CSE style in physical, life, and technical sciences.

ACADEMIC SETTINGS
When readers expect CSE or "scientific documentation"

PUBLIC AND WORK SETTINGS
When a professional group or company division expects you to use CSE or some type of scientific documentation
When readers prefer a name-and-year or number system
When other writers or publications addressing audiences like yours use CSE, modified CSE, or a similar style

---

CSE style tends to vary more than the other styles, mainly because different scientific and engineering fields have different requirements. Check expectations with your instructor or your readers. If you are advised to follow the style of a specific journal, find its guidelines for authors, or compare examples from it with general CSE advice. For more information, see *Scientific Style and Format: The CSE Manual for Authors, Editors, and Publishers* (7th ed.,

Reston, VA: Council of Science Editors, 2006) or the CSE Web site at <http://www.councilscienceeditors.org>.

28a CSE in-text citations

You can use one of two methods for CSE in-text references.

28.2

1 Use the name-and-year method

With this method, include the name of the author and the publication date in parentheses unless you mention the name in the text.

PARENTHETICAL   Decreases in the use of lead, cadmium, and zinc have resulted

in a "very large decrease in the large-scale pollution of the

troposphere" (Boutron 1991).

NAMED IN TEXT   Boutron (Boutron 1991) found that decreases in the use of lead,

cadmium, and zinc have resulted in a "very large decrease in

the large-scale pollution of the troposphere."

Distinguish several works by the same author, all dated in a single year, by letters (*a, b*, and so forth) after the date.

2 Use the number method

With this method, use numbers instead of names of authors. The numbers can be placed in parentheses in the text or raised above the line; they correspond to numbered works in your reference list.

Decreases in the use of lead, cadmium, and zinc have reduced pollution

in the troposphere (1).

Your first option is to number your in-text citations consecutively as they appear and to arrange them accordingly on the references page. Your second is to alphabetize your references first, number them, and then use the corresponding number in your paper. Because only the number appears in your text, you should mention the author's name if it is important.

28b CSE reference list

You may use "References" to head your list. The samples below follow the number method. If you use the consecutive number method, arrange your references according to which work comes first in your paper, which second, and so on. If you use the alphabetized number method, arrange your list alphabetically, and then number the entries. If you use the name-and-year method instead, alphabetize the references by the last name of the main author, and then order works by the same author by date of publication. Place the date after the author's name, followed by a period.

Guide to CSE Formats for References

Books and Works Treated as Books
1. One Author 285
2. Two or More Authors 285
3. Corporate or Group Author 285
4. Editor 285
5. Translator 285
6. Conference Proceedings 285
7. Report 285

Articles from Periodicals and Selections from Books
8. Article in Journal Paginated by Volume 286
9. Article in Journal Paginated by Issue 286

10. Article with Corporate or Group Author 286
11. Entire Issue of Journal 286
12. Chapter in Edited Book or Selection in Anthology 287
13. Figure from Article 287

Online and Electronic Resources
14. Patent from Database or Information Service 287
15. Online Article 287
16. Online Abstract 287
17. CD-ROM Abstract 287

Books and Works Treated as Books

MODEL FORMAT FOR BOOKS AND WORKS TREATED AS BOOKS

NAME-AND-YEAR METHOD

period + space   period + space   period + space
↓   ↓   ↓

Author(s). Date. Title of work. Place of
Publication: Publisher. Total pages.

↑   ↑
colon + space   period + space

NUMBER METHOD

period + space   period + space   period + space
↓   ↓   ↓

1. Author(s). Title of work. Place of
Publication: Publisher; Date. Total pages.

↑   ↑   ↑
colon + space   semicolon + space   period + space

1. One Author

Include the total number of pages at the end of the entry for a book.

> 1. Bishop RH. Modern control systems analysis and design using MATLAB and SIMULINK. Menlo Park (CA): Addison Wesley; 1997. 251 p.

2. Two or More Authors

> 2. Freeman JM, Kelly MT, Freeman JB. The epilepsy diet treatment: an introduction to the ketogenic diet. New York: Demo; 1994. 180 p.

3. Corporate or Group Author

If an organization is also the publisher, include the name in both places. You can replace the name with a well-known acronym.

> 3. Intergovernmental Panel on Climate Change. Climate change 1995: the science of climate change. Cambridge: Cambridge University Press; 1996. 572 p.

4. Editor

> 4. Dolphin D, editor. Biomimetic chemistry. Washington: American Chemical Society; 1980. 437 p.

5. Translator

If the work has an editor as well as a translator, place a semicolon after *translator*, name the editor, and add *editor*.

> 5. Jacob F. The logic of life: a history of heredity. Spillmann BE, translator. New York: Pantheon Books; 1982. 348 p.

6. Conference Proceedings

> 6. Witt I, editor. Protein C: biochemical and medical aspects. Proceedings of the International Workshop; 1984 Jul 9-11; Titisee, Germany. Berlin: De Gruyter; 1985. 195 p.

7. Report

Include the information a reader would need to order a report. Bracket a widely accepted acronym following an agency's name.

> 7. Environmental Protection Agency (US) [EPA]. Guides to pollution prevention: the automotive repair industry. Washington: US EPA; 1991. 46 p. Available from: EPA Office of Research and Development; EPA/625/7-91/013.

Articles from Periodicals and Selections from Books

MODEL FORMAT FOR ARTICLES

NAME-AND-YEAR METHOD

period + space period + space   period + space
↓   ↓   ↓
Author(s). Year. Title of article. Title of
Journal. Volume Number:Pages.
↑   ↑
period + space   colon + no space

NUMBER METHOD

period + space period + space   period + space
↓   ↓   ↓
1. Author(s). Title of article. Title of
Journal. Date;Volume Number:Pages.
↑   ↑   ↑
period   semicolon   colon +
+ space + no space   no space

8. Article in Journal Paginated by Volume

8. Yousef YA, Yu LL. Potential contamination of groundwater from Cu, Pb, and Zn in wet detention ponds receiving highway runoff. J Environ Sci Hlth. 1992;27:1033-44.

9. Article in Journal Paginated by Issue

Give the issue number in parentheses with no space after the volume number.

9. Boutron CF. Decrease in anthropogenic lead, cadmium and zinc in Greenland snows since the late 1960's. Nature. 1991;353(6340):153-5, 160.

10. Article with Corporate or Group Author

10. Derek Sims Associates. Why and how of acoustic testing. Environ Eng. 1991;4(1):10-12.

11. Entire Issue of Journal

11. Savage A, editor. Proceedings of the workshop on the zoo-university connection: collaborative efforts in the conservation of endangered primates. Zoo Biol. 1989;1(Suppl).

12. Chapter in Edited Book or Selection in Anthology

The first name and title refer to the selection and the second to the book in which it appears.

> 12. Moro M. Supply and conservation efforts for nonhuman primates. In: Gengozian N, Deinhardt F, editors. Marmosets in experimental medicine. Basel: S. Karger AG; 1978. p 37-40.

13. Figure from Article

Identify a figure (or graphic) by name, number, and page.

> 13. Kanaori Y, Kawakami SI, Yairi K. Space-time distribution patterns of destructive earthquakes in the inner belt of central Japan. Eng Geol. 1991;31(3-4):209-30 (p 216, table 1).

Online and Electronic Resources

CSE recommends following the National Library of Medicine formats for Internet sources, reflected here and available through the CSE Web site.

14. Patent from Database or Information Service

> 14. Collins FS, Drumm ML, Dawson DC, Wilkinson DJ, inventors. Method of testing potential cystic fibrosis treating compounds using cells in culture. United States patent US 5,434,086. 1995 Jul 18. Available from: Lexis/Nexis/Lexpatlibrary/ALLfile.

15. Online Article

> 15. Grolmusz V. On the weak mod m representation of Boolean functions. Chi J Theor Comp Sci [serial online] 1995 [cited 1996 May 3]; 100-5. Available from: http://www.csuchicago.edu/publication/cjtcs/articles/1995/2/contents.html.

16. Online Abstract

> 16. Smithies O, Maeda N. Gene targeting approaches to complex genetic diseases: atherosclerosis and essential hypertension [abstract]. Proceedings of the Natl Acad Sci USA [serial online]. 1995 [cited 1996 Jan 21]; 92(12):5266-72. 1 screen. Available from: Lexis/Medline/ABST.

17. CD-ROM Abstract

> 17. MacDonald R, Fleming MF, Barry KL. Risk factors associated with alcohol abuse in college students [abstract]. Am J Drug and Alc Abuse [CD-ROM]. 2001;17:439-49. Available from: SilverPlatter File: PsycLIT Item: 79-13172.

Exercise 1

Turn to Exercise 1 in Chapter 25. Rewrite the items supplied there to add note numbers in CSE style. Then prepare the corresponding notes for these items.

Exercise 2

Turn to Exercise 2 in Chapter 25. Rewrite the items supplied there to create a list of works cited in CSE style.

PART 8

Editing Grammar

29 Words Working in Sentences

To edit effectively, you need to recognize sentence components and their working relationships. At the simplest level, sentences consist of different types of words, often called *parts of speech.*

29a
gr

29a Nouns and articles

To identify a **noun**, look for a word that names a person, a place, an idea, or a thing. Most nouns form the **plural** (two or more) by adding -s or -es to the **singular** (one): *cow* + -s = *cows*; *gas* + -es = *gases*. Some are irregular: *child, children; deer, deer.* A noun's **possessive** form expresses ownership.

SINGULAR	SINGULAR POSSESSIVE ('S)	PLURAL	PLURAL POSSESSIVE (')
student	student's	students	students'

A noun often requires an **article**: *the, a* (before a consonant sound), or *an* (before a vowel sound).

<u>An</u> **intern** prepared <u>a</u> **report** for <u>the</u> **doctor** at **Hope Hospital**.

TYPES OF NOUNS	
Count noun	Names individual items that can be counted: <u>four</u> cups, <u>a hundred</u> beans
Noncount noun (mass noun)	Names material or abstractions that cannot be counted: *flour, water, steel*
Collective noun	Names a unit composed of more than one individual or thing (see 33b-2 on agreement): *group, board of directors, flock*
Proper noun	Names specific people, places, titles, or things (see 54b on capitalizing): *Miss America; Tuscaloosa, Alabama; Microsoft Corporation*
Common noun	Names nonspecific people, places, or things (see 54b on capitalizing): *children, winner, town, mountain, company, bike*

ESL ADVICE: NOUNS AND THE USE OF ARTICLES

Notice how to use the **indefinite articles** (*a* or *an*) and the **definite article** (*the*). Remember that you'll still communicate your meaning even if you choose the wrong article or forget one.

29a
gr

- **Singular proper nouns** generally use no article, and **plural proper nouns** usually use *the*.

  SINGULAR   Rosa Parks helped initiate the civil rights movement.

  PLURAL   **The** Everglades have abundant wildlife and plants.

- **Singular count nouns** use *a*, *an*, or *the* and cannot stand alone.

  SINGULAR   **The** pig is **an** intelligent animal.

- **Plural count nouns** use either no article (to show a generalization) or *the* (to refer to something specific).

  GENERALIZATION   Books are the best teachers. [books in general]

  SPECIFIC   **The** books on his desk are due Monday. [specific books]

- **Noncount (mass) nouns** use either no article or *the*, never *a* or *an*. **General noncount nouns** sometimes stand alone. **Specific noncount nouns**, which have been limited in some way, use *the*.

  DRAFT   A laughter is good medicine.

  GENERAL   Laughter is good medicine. [laughter in general]

  SPECIFIC   **The** laughter of children is good medicine. [specific type of laughter]

Follow these guidelines when you select *a*, *an*, or *the*.

- Use *a* or *an* when you are not referring to any specific person or thing (using a nonspecific, singular count noun). Use *a* before a consonant sound and *an* before a vowel sound.

  I need **a** car to go to work. [unknown, nonspecific car or any car]

- Use *the* when you are referring to an exact, known person or thing (using a specific, singular noun).

  I need **the** car to go to work. [specific, known car]

  The car that she bought is metallic gray. [specific, known car]

- Generally use no articles with plural count and noncount nouns.

  COUNT <u>Airline tickets</u> to Chicago are at half price.

  NONCOUNT <u>Information</u> about flights to Chicago is available.

- Use *the* when a plural count noun or a noncount noun is followed by a modifier, such as an adjective clause (see 30c-1) or prepositional phrase (see 30b-1), that makes the noun specific.

29c
gr

  COUNT **The** <u>airline tickets</u> <u>that you bought</u> are at half price.

  NONCOUNT **The** <u>information</u> <u>on the flight board</u> has changed.

29b Pronouns

29.1

To identify a **pronoun**, look for a word like *them*, *she*, *his*, or *it* that takes the place of a noun and can play the same roles in a sentence. You can use a pronoun to avoid repeating a noun, but the pronoun's meaning depends on a clear relationship to the noun to which it refers—its **antecedent** or **headword**. (See 33d on agreement and 37a on pronoun reference.)

  antecedent   pronoun
  Jean presented **her** proposal to the committee.

You can also use a pronoun to modify a noun or another pronoun.

  This <u>part</u> has been on order for a month, and **that** <u>one</u> for a week.

A pronoun changes form to show number (singular or plural), gender (masculine, feminine, or neuter), and role in a sentence—subject, object, or possessive (see 30a on sentence structure and 32a on pronoun form).

29c Verbs

To identify **verbs**, look for words that express actions (*jump*, *build*), occurrences (*become*, *happen*), and states of being (*be*, *seem*). Change a verb's form to reflect person and number (see 33a on agreement) and to signal relationships in time (see 31a–g on **tense**).

29.2

PERSON	<u>She</u> **restores** furniture.	<u>They</u> **restore** furniture.
NUMBER	The <u>copier</u> **makes** noise.	The <u>copiers</u> **make** noise.
TENSE	They **prepare** the invoices.	They **prepared** the invoices.

Other forms show voice (see 31i and 43b-3) and mood (see 31h).

ACTIVE VOICE	The pump **cleans** the water.
PASSIVE VOICE	The water **is cleaned** by the pump.
INDICATIVE MOOD	The report **was** on the desk.
SUBJUNCTIVE MOOD	If the report **were** on the desk, I would have found it.

PRONOUNS AND THEIR FUNCTIONS

Personal pronouns	Designate persons or things using a form reflecting the pronoun's role in the sentence (see 32a)
SINGULAR	*I, me, you, he, him, she, her, it*
PLURAL	*we, us, you, they, them*
Possessive pronouns	Show ownership (see 32a on pronouns and 50a on apostrophes)
SINGULAR	*my, mine, your, yours, her, hers, his, its*
PLURAL	*our, ours, your, yours, their, theirs*
Relative pronouns	Introduce clauses that modify or add information to a main clause (see 30c and 42b on subordination)
	who, whom, whose, which, that
Interrogative pronouns	Introduce questions
	who, which
Reflexive and intensive pronouns	End in *-self* or *-selves*; enable the subject or doer also to be the receiver of an action (reflexive); add emphasis (intensive)
SINGULAR	*myself, yourself, herself, himself, itself*
PLURAL	*ourselves, yourselves, themselves*
Indefinite pronouns	Refer to people, things, and ideas in general rather than a specific antecedent (see 33c-5)
SINGULAR	*anybody, each, every, neither, none, something*
PLURAL	*both, few, fewer, many, others, several*
VARIABLE	*all, any, enough, more, most, some*
Demonstrative pronouns	Point out or highlight an antecedent; can refer to a noun or pronoun or sum up a phrase or clause
	this, that, these, those
Reciprocal pronouns	Refer to individual parts of a plural antecedent
	one another, each other

Use a main verb alone or with **helping (auxiliary) verbs** (forms of *be*, *do*, and *have*). A helping verb and a main verb form a **verb phrase**. You can use **modal auxiliary verbs** as helping verbs but not as main verbs. They include *will/would*, *can/could*, *shall/should*, *may/might*, *must*, and *ought*. (See 31d.)

MAIN VERB   The city **welcomes** tourists all year round.

HELPING + MAIN   The tourist agency **is planning** a video.

MODAL + MAIN   They **might decide** to include the Old Courthouse.

Use **action verbs** to show action or activity: *swim*, *analyze*, *dig*, *turn*. Use **linking verbs** (or **state-of-being verbs**) to express a state of being or an occurrence: *is*, *seems*, *becomes*, *grows*. These verbs link a subject with a **complement** that renames or describes it.

ACTION   The company and the union **negotiated** a contract.

LINKING   The flowers **smelled** musky.

A **phrasal verb** includes a verb plus a closely associated word that seems like a preposition but is known as a **particle**, as in *throw up* ("regurgitate"). The meaning of a phrasal verb differs from that of the separate words. For example, *clear out* means "depart" and *run by* means "consult." In contrast, a verb *plus* a preposition is the sum of its parts: *run* (action) + *by* (direction).

phrasal verb	verb + preposition
I **ran** the idea **by** the committee.	I **ran by** the house.

29d Adjectives

To identify **adjectives**, look for words that modify nouns, pronouns, or word groups acting as nouns. Adjectives come in three degrees of comparison: *high*, *higher*, *highest*; *crooked*, *more crooked*, *most crooked*. Adjectives answer questions like "How many?" "Which one?" or "What kind?" (See also Chapter 34.)

HOW MANY?   The **two** reports reached different conclusions.

WHICH ONE?   Our report is the **last** one.

WHAT KIND?   Their proposal was **unrealistic**.

ESL ADVICE: ADJECTIVE FORMS

Adjectives in English never use a plural form.

DRAFT   Santo Domingo is renowned for beautifuls beaches.

EDITED   Santo Domingo is renowned for beautiful beaches.

29e Adverbs

To identify **adverbs**, look for words that modify verbs, adjectives, other adverbs, or entire sentences. They answer questions such as "When?" "Where?" "Why?" "How often?" "Which direction?" "What conditions?" and "What degree?"

WHEN?	Our committee met **yesterday**. [modifies verb *met*]
WHAT DEGREE?	We had a **very** long meeting. [modifies adjective *long*]
HOW OFTEN?	I attend board meetings **quite** frequently. [modifies adverb *frequently*, which modifies verb *attend*]

Adverbs may consist of an adjective plus *-ly* (*quickly, blindly, frequently*) although some adjectives also end in *-ly* (*neighborly, lovely*). Other common adverbs include *very, too, tomorrow, not, never, sometimes,* and *well.* Adverbs come in three degrees of comparison: *frequently, more* (or *less*) *frequently, most* (or *least*) *frequently* (see 34a).

You can use **conjunctive adverbs** such as *however, moreover, thus,* and *therefore* to indicate logical relationships. (See 42a for a list.)

They opposed the policy; **nevertheless,** they implemented it.

29f Prepositions

To recognize a **preposition**, look for a word like *in* or *at* followed by a noun or pronoun, forming a **prepositional phrase** (see 30b-1). The phrase adds precise, detailed information to a sentence.

The office <u>in</u> **this region** sells homes priced <u>above</u> **$150,000**.

COMMON PREPOSITIONS				
about	at	despite	near	to
above	before	down	of	toward
across	behind	during	off	under
after	below	except	on	until
against	beneath	for	out	up
along	between	from	outside	upon
among	beyond	in	over	with
around	by	into	past	within
as	concerning	like	through	without

29.3

ESL ADVICE: PREPOSITIONS

29f
gr

In general, use prepositional phrases in this order: place, then time.

place + time
The runners will start **in the park** <u>on Saturday</u>.

PREPOSITIONS OF PLACE: *AT, ON, IN,* AND NO PREPOSITION

AT	ON	IN	NO PREPOSITION
the mall*	the bed*	(the) bed*	downstairs
home	the ceiling	the kitchen	downtown
the library*	the floor	the car	inside
the office	the horse	(the) class*	outside
school*	the plane	the library*	upstairs
work	the train	school*	uptown

*You may sometimes use different prepositions for these locations.

PREPOSITIONS OF PLACE: *AT, ON,* AND *IN*

Use *at* for specific addresses; use *on* for names of streets, avenues, and boulevards; use *in* for names of areas of land—states, countries, continents.

She works **at** 99 Tinker Street **in** Dayton.

***TO* OR NO PREPOSITION TO EXPRESS GOING TO A PLACE**

When you express the idea of going to a place, use the preposition *to*.

I am going **to** work.   I am going **to** the office.

In the following cases, use no preposition.

I am going home.   I am going downstairs (downtown, inside).

PREPOSITIONS OF TIME: *AT, ON,* AND *IN*

Use *at* for a specific time; use *on* for days and dates; use *in* for nonspecific times during a day, month, season, or year.

Brandon was born **at** 11:11 a.m. **on** a Monday **in** 1991.

***FOR* AND *SINCE* IN TIME EXPRESSIONS**

Use *for* with an amount of time (minutes, hours, days, months, years) and *since* with a specific date or time.

The housing program has operated **for** many years.

The housing program has operated **since** 1971.

PREPOSITIONS WITH NOUNS, VERBS, AND ADJECTIVES

NOUN + PREPOSITION	He has an <u>understanding</u> **of** global politics.
VERB + PREPOSITION	Managers <u>worry</u> **about** many things.
ADJECTIVE + PREPOSITION	Life in your country is <u>similar</u> **to** life in mine.

NOUN + PREPOSITION COMBINATIONS

approval of	confusion about	hope for	participation in
awareness of	desire for	interest in	reason for
belief in	grasp of	love of	respect for
concern for	hatred of	need for	understanding of

VERB + PREPOSITION COMBINATIONS

ask about	differ from	pay for	study for
ask for	grow into	prepare for	think about
belong to	look at	refer to	trust in
care for	participate in	step into	work for

29g
gr

ADJECTIVE + PREPOSITION COMBINATIONS

afraid of	careless about	interested in	similar to
angry at	familiar with	made of	sorry for
aware of	fond of	married to	sure of
capable of	happy about	proud of	tired of

29g Conjunctions

To identify **conjunctions**, look for words that join other words or word groups, signaling their relationships.

Coordinating conjunctions. Use *and, but, or, nor, for, yet,* and *so* to link grammatically equal elements (see 42a).

WORDS   analyze **and** discuss, compare **or** contrast

PHRASES   over past sales **yet** under current goals

CLAUSES   They petitioned the board, **but** they lost their appeal.

Subordinating conjunctions. Use words such as *because* or *if* to create a **subordinate** (or **dependent**) **clause**. Such a clause cannot stand on its own as a sentence; you need to attach it to a **main** (or **independent**) **clause** that it qualifies or limits. (See 42b for a list of conjunctions.)

        main clause   subordinate clause
Li spoke persuasively, **though** the crowd favored her opponent.

Correlative conjunctions. These pairs include *not only . . . but also, either . . . or, both . . . and,* and similar combinations. They join sentence elements that are grammatically equal. (See 41b on parallelism.)

29h Interjections

To identify **interjections**, look for expressions that convey a strong re-action or emotion, such as surprise (*Hey!*) or disappointment (*Oh, no!*). They may stand alone or be loosely related to the rest of a sentence.

Exercise 1

Underline each noun in the following selection *once* and each pronoun *twice*.

Seconds later the Help Desk received a call from another user with the same problem. The switchboard lit up. There were callers from all over the company, all with the same complaint: their comput-ers were making odd noises. It might be a tune, one of the callers added helpfully, coming from the computer's small internal speaker. The sixth caller recognized the melody. The computers were all playing tinny renditions of "Yankee Doodle."

—PAUL MUNGO AND BRYAN CLOUGH, "The Bulgarian Connection"

Exercise 2

In the following sentences, underline each main verb once and each helping verb twice.

EXAMPLE
The new construction in Maple Valley has created some problems.

1. The power company's engineers began studying a map of the area.
2. They had thought about using underground cables.
3. A field test revealed a large rock ledge, so the engineers decided that underground lines would be too expensive.
4. They proposed cutting a path through the woods for the power lines, but the contractor claimed that potential homebuyers might not like the effect on the scenery.
5. They strung the power lines on poles along the main road into the development.

Exercise 3

In the following passage, underline all adjectives once and all adverbs twice.

Back in Chicago, Sereno's analysis of his new dinosaur's skele-ton convinces him it is indeed more primitive than *Herrerasaurus*. It lacks a flexible jaw that let *Herrerasaurus* and later carnivores snag and trap struggling prey. Thus Sereno believes this new creature is the closest fossil we have to the first dinosaur.

"I call it 'Eoraptor,'" he says. "Eos was the Greek goddess of dawn. Raptor means thief. It was a light-bodied little rascal. And it may have been a thief, dashing in to grasp scraps of someone else's kill."

—RICK GORE, "Dinosaurs"

Exercise 4

Expand the following sentences by adding details and information in the form of adjectives and adverbs.

EXAMPLE

generally   deep, extended

The term *coma* refers to a state of unconsciousness.

1. Accidents leave people in comas.
2. Comas are serious medical problems.
3. Newspapers contain reports of people awakening from comas.
4. Long comas are dangerous.
5. They cause irreversible damage.

Exercise 5

Underline all the prepositions in the following sentences. Circle all the prepositional phrases.

EXAMPLE

At eighteen minutes after one o'clock, the emergency number received a call from Mrs. Serena Washington.

1. From its station near city hall, the rescue truck drove to Briar Brook Avenue.
2. Along the way, it narrowly missed colliding with a bread truck that failed to pull to the side of the road.
3. Despite the near accident, the rescue team arrived at the Washingtons' home in less than five minutes.
4. Mr. Washington was complaining of pain in his chest and back and displaying other symptoms of a heart attack.
5. By its quick response to the emergency call, the rescue team may have saved a life.

Exercise 6

For each of the following word groups, create two sentences, one using the words as a verb plus preposition, the other using the words as a phrasal verb (see 29c). Then rewrite the sentence that contains the phrasal verb, substituting another word or words for the phrasal verb.

29
gr

EXAMPLE: TEAR OUT

Brian tore out the door.
Brian tore out the old shelving.
Brian removed the old shelving.

cut down	hang around	run up
fill in	put up with	call up

Exercise 7

Underline all the conjunctions in the following passage. Indicate whether each is a coordinating, subordinating, or correlative conjunction.

Thirty-five years ago, E. R. Guthrie and G. P. Horton described an experiment in which cats were placed in a glass-fronted puzzle box and trained to find their way out by jostling a slender vertical rod at the front of the box, thereby causing a door to open. What interested these investigators was not so much that the cats could learn to bump into the vertical rod, but that before doing so each animal performed a long ritual of highly stereotyped movements, rubbing their heads and backs against the front of the box, turning in circles, and finally touching the rod. The experiment has ranked as something of a classic in experimental psychology, even raising in some minds the notion of a ceremony of superstition on the part of cats: before the rod will open the door, it is necessary to go through a magical sequence of motions.   —LEWIS THOMAS, "Clever Animals"

30   Sentence Parts and Patterns

Careful editing depends on your ability to recognize the different parts of sentences so that you can choose among alternative patterns. See also Chapter 29, which reviews the functions of the words in sentences.

30a Subjects and predicates

A **subject** names the topic or doer of a sentence. A **predicate** indicates an action or a relationship expressed in a sentence. It may specify consequences or conditions.

1 Look for sentence subjects

To identify a **simple subject**, look for one or more nouns (or pronouns) naming the doer or the topic. To identify a **complete subject**, find the simple subject *plus* all its modifying words.

SIMPLE SUBJECT	**Email** has changed business communication.
COMPLETE SUBJECT	**All the sales staff on this floor** left early.

A subject may be singular, plural, or compound (linked by *and* or *or*).

SINGULAR SUBJECT	**She** put the monitor on the desk.
PLURAL SUBJECT	**These pills** are difficult to swallow.
COMPOUND SUBJECT	**John and Chifume** are medical students.

In most sentences, the subject comes before the verb. There are exceptions to this pattern. An **expletive construction** (*there is/are* or *here is/are*) allows you to delay the subject until after the verb (see 43b-2).

USUAL ORDER	**Homeless people** <u>camped</u> here.
EXPLETIVE	There <u>were</u> **homeless people** camping here.

For emphasis, you can reverse (invert) the subject and verb.

INVERTED	In this tiny house <u>was born</u> **a leader**.

Questions often place the subject between helping and main verbs.

QUESTION	<u>Did</u> **the board** <u>approve</u> the light-rail proposal?

In an **imperative** sentence expressing a request or command, the subject *you* generally is implied, not stated (see 30d).

IMPERATIVE	**[You]** <u>Put</u> the insulation around the door frame.

2 Look for sentence predicates

A **simple predicate** includes only a verb (see 29a) or verb phrase (see 31d).

VERB	The bus **stopped**.	VERB PHRASE	The bus **might stop**.

The verb may be single or compound (linked by *and* or *or*).

SINGLE	The client **slipped**.	COMPOUND	The client **slipped and fell**.

To recognize a **complete predicate**, look for a verb or verb phrase *plus* modifiers and other words that receive the action or complete the verb.

COMPLETE PREDICATE	The lab tech **gave me the printout**.

30.1

FIVE BASIC PREDICATE PATTERNS

Most sentences employ one of these predicate structures, often in expanded or combined form.

1. Subject + intransitive verb

Our team **lost**.   Last week, the ferryboat **sank**.

An **intransitive verb** doesn't take an object or a complement (see below); neither is needed to complete the meaning.

OBJECT PATTERNS

2. Subject + transitive verb + direct object

The bank officer **approved** <u>the loan</u>.

A sentence with a **transitive verb** can include a **direct object** in the predicate, telling *who* or *what* receives the action.

3. Subject + transitive verb + indirect object + direct object

The Marine Corps reserve **gives** <u>needy children</u> toys.

A sentence with a transitive verb can also include an **indirect object**, a noun or pronoun telling readers *to whom* or *for whom* the action is undertaken.

4. Subject + transitive verb + direct object + object complement

NOUN   His coworkers elected <u>Jim</u> <u>project leader</u>.

ADJECTIVE   Critics judged **the movie** <u>inferior</u>.

An **object complement**, a noun or adjective that renames or describes the direct object, adds information to a sentence predicate.

SUBJECT COMPLEMENT PATTERNS

5. Subject + linking verb + subject complement

The grant proposal **is** <u>too complicated</u>.

A sentence with a **linking verb**, such as *is*, *seems*, or *feels* (see 29c), can include a **subject complement**, "completing" the subject by describing or renaming it.

30b Phrases

30.2

A **sentence** is a word group with a subject and a predicate that can stand alone (see 30d). In contrast, a **phrase** is a word group that lacks a subject, a predicate, or both. A phrase cannot stand alone and must be integrated within a freestanding sentence. If you capitalize and punctuate a phrase as if it were a sentence, you create a fragment (see 35a).

1 Look for prepositional phrases

To recognize a **prepositional phrase**, look first for a **preposition**—a word like *at, for, under,* or *except* (see the list in 29f). Then identify the **object of the preposition**—the noun, pronoun, or word group that follows the preposition.

to <u>the beach</u>   **near** <u>her</u>   **after** <u>a falling out</u>   **inside** <u>the case</u>

A prepositional phrase can act as an adjective or as an adverb.

AS ADJECTIVE   The coupons **in the newspaper** offer savings **on groceries**.

AS ADVERB   Her watch started beeping **during the meeting**.

During the meeting, her watch started beeping.

2 Look for absolute phrases

An **absolute phrase** modifies a sentence as a whole. It includes a noun (or a pronoun or word group acting as a noun) plus a present or past participle and any modifiers.

They fought the fire, **the dense smoke slowing their efforts**.

3 Look for appositive phrases

An **appositive** adds information by renaming a noun or pronoun. An appositive plus its modifiers is an **appositive phrase**. (see also 48c).

Ken Choi, **my classmate**, won an award for his design.

He uses natural materials, **berry dyes**, for example.

4 Look for verbal phrases

Verb parts, known as **verbals**, are participles, gerunds, or infinitives. These can function as nouns, adjectives, or adverbs—but never stand alone as verbs. A **verbal phrase** is a verbal plus its modifiers, object, or complements.

Participial phrases. Use the *-ing* (present participle) or *-ed/-en* (past participle) forms of a verbal in a **participial phrase** acting as an adjective to modify a noun or pronoun.

Few neighbors **attending the meeting** owned dogs.

They signed a petition **addressed to the health department**.

Gerund phrases. Use the *-ing* form of a verbal (present participle) in a **gerund phrase** acting as a noun in a subject, object, or subject complement.

sentence subject   object of preposition
Closing the landfill may keep it from **polluting the bay**.

Infinitive phrases. Use the *to* form of a verbal in an **infinitive phrase** acting as an adjective, adverb, or noun.

30b
gr

ADVERB   He used organic methods **to raise his garden**.

NOUN (SUBJECT)   **To live in the mountains** was his goal.

ESL ADVICE: VERBALS

GERUNDS

Use a gerund, not an infinitive, after some verbs, as in this sentence: Children **enjoy** <u>reading</u> fairy tales.

COMMON VERBS TAKING GERUNDS

admit	consider	finish	postpone
anticipate	delay	imagine	practice
appreciate	deny	keep	quit
avoid	discuss	mind	recommend
can't help	enjoy	miss	suggest

GERUNDS WITH IDIOMATIC EXPRESSIONS

* After *go* (any tense): I **go** <u>swimming</u>.   I **went** <u>kayaking</u>.
* After *spend time*: Volunteers **spend** a lot of **time** <u>helping</u> others.
* After *have* + noun: Pilots **have difficulty** <u>flying</u> in bad weather.
* After a preposition: Midwives are trained **in** <u>assisting</u> at childbirth.

GERUNDS WITH *TO* ACTING AS A PREPOSITION

In each of the following examples, *to* is not part of an infinitive. *To* acts like a preposition and must be followed by a gerund ending in *-ing*.

I look **forward** to <u>working</u> at the museum.

He is **accustomed** to <u>designing</u> exhibits.

Patrons are **used** to <u>viewing</u> complex displays.

INFINITIVES

Some verbs take only an infinitive, not a gerund, as in this sentence: Some students **need** <u>to work</u> part time.

COMMON VERBS TAKING AN INFINITIVE

agree	expect	need	refuse
ask	fail	offer	seem
choose	hope	plan	venture
claim	intend	pretend	want
decide	manage	promise	wish

30b
gr

COMMON VERBS TAKING AN OBJECT + INFINITIVE

Other verbs take an object and an infinitive.

Doctors often **advise** <u>their patients</u> <u>to eat</u> well.

advise	encourage	need	teach
allow	expect	permit	tell
ask	force	persuade	urge
convince	help	require	want

When *make*, *let*, and *have* suggest "caused" or "forced," they use the infinitive without *to* (the base form).

She	**made/let/had** me	clean my room.

Certain adjectives are also followed by infinitives.

I	**am**	<u>delighted</u>	<u>to meet</u> you.
The report	**is**	<u>easy</u>	<u>to understand.</u>
The volunteers	**are**	<u>pleased</u>	<u>to help.</u>

GERUNDS OR INFINITIVES

The meaning stays the same when you use most verbs that can be followed by either a gerund or an infinitive.

GERUND   Developers prefer **working** with local contractors.

INFINITIVE   Developers prefer **to work** with local contractors.

COMMON VERBS TAKING EITHER GERUNDS OR INFINITIVES

begin	hate	like	start
can't stand	intend	love	stop
continue	learn	prefer	try

Remember, forget, regret, and *stop* change meaning with a gerund or an infinitive.

GERUND	I **remembered** <u>meeting</u> Mark. [I recall an event in the past.]
INFINITIVE	I **remembered** <u>to meet</u> Mark. [I did not forget to do this in the past.]
GERUND	I will never **forget** <u>visiting</u> Texas. [I recall a past event.]
INFINITIVE	I never **forget** <u>to study</u> for exams. [I remember to do something.]
GERUND	I **regret** <u>telling</u> you about her. [I'm sorry I told you in the past.]
INFINITIVE	I **regret** <u>to tell</u> you that you were not hired. [I'm sorry to tell you now.]
GERUND	I **stopped** <u>smoking</u>. [I do not smoke anymore.]
INFINITIVE	I **stopped** <u>to smoke</u>. [I paused to smoke.]

30c Subordinate clauses

A **main clause** is a word group that includes a subject and a verb and can stand alone as a complete sentence. (A main clause is sometimes called an **independent clause**.)

MAIN CLAUSE	I had many appointments last Friday.

In contrast, a **subordinate** (or **dependent**) **clause** contains both a subject and a predicate yet cannot stand on its own as a sentence. It begins with a subordinating word such as *if*, *that*, or *although* that prevents the clause from standing on its own. (See the list of subordinating words in 42b.) A subordinate clause must be attached to a main clause.

SUBORDINATE CLAUSE	**because** I was busy
CONNECTED TO SENTENCE	**Because I was busy**, I didn't call.

Don't punctuate a subordinate clause as a sentence. If you do, you create a fragment (see 35a).

1 Look for subordinate clauses as adjectives

If you begin a subordinate clause with a word like *who*, *which*, *that*, *whom*, or *whose* (**relative pronouns**) or with *when* or *where* (**relative adverbs**), you can use the clause as an adjective to modify a noun or pronoun.

Generally, you put the modifying clause right after the noun or pronoun it modifies.

Many people **who live in Erie** came to the meeting.

They opposed the road **that the county plans to approve**.

Who, whom, whose, and *that* modify people. *Which, whose,* and *that* modify animals, places, and things. In spoken English *whom* generally is optional, but it is used in formal writing, especially in the academic community.

30c
gr

STRATEGY	Use adjective clauses to combine short sentences.
CHOPPY	I have an aunt. Her book is on the best-seller list.
COMBINED	I have an aunt **whose** book is on the best-seller list.

2 Look for subordinate clauses as adverbs

If you begin a clause with a subordinating conjunction such as *because, although, since,* or *while* (see list in 42b), you can use the subordinating clause as an adverb (modifying verbs, adjectives, or adverbs).

WHY?	She volunteered **because she supports the zoo**.
WHEN?	**As the rally continued**, Jean joined the picket line.

3 Look for subordinate clauses as nouns

Noun clauses begin with *who, whom, whose, whoever, whomever, what, whatever, when, where, why, whether,* or *how.* Look for them in the roles of nouns: subject, object, object of a preposition, or complement.

SENTENCE SUBJECT	**What she said** is interesting.
DIRECT OBJECT	You should pack **what you need for the trip**.

ESL ADVICE: ADJECTIVE, ADVERB, AND NOUN CLAUSES

ADJECTIVE CLAUSES

You may include or drop a relative pronoun if it is not the subject of the clause. Either way is correct.

INCLUDED	The Web site **that** we designed was very popular.
OMITTED	The Web site we designed was very popular.

When a relative pronoun is the subject of an adjective clause, the clause can be changed to an **adjective phrase**. In a clause with a *be* verb, omit the relative pronoun and the *be* verb.

	X X
CLAUSE (WITH *BE*)	He is the man **who is studying German**.
PHRASE	He is the man **studying German**.

With another verb, omit the relative pronoun, and change the verb to a present participle. (See 30b-4 on participial phrases.)

	X
CLAUSE (NOT *BE*)	He is the man **who wants to study German**.
PHRASE	He is the man **wanting to study German**.

ADVERB CLAUSES

TIME	**When** the weather changes, the malls stock winter clothes.
REASON	It is difficult to buy shorts **because** winter has started.
CONTRAST	**Although** some shoppers turn to catalogs, others do not.
CONDITION	Our online customers may do the same **unless** we expand our inventory.

SOME WORDS TO INTRODUCE ADVERB CLAUSES

TIME	REASON	CONTRAST	CONDITION
after	as	although	as long as
as, while	because	even though	even if
before	now that	though	if
once	since	while	only if
since	whereas		provided that
until			unless
when			

NOUN CLAUSES

When you form a complex sentence by combining a noun clause with other sentence parts, the clause acts like a noun in the sentence.

***THAT* CLAUSE**	I believe **that** life exists in other solar systems.
***YES/NO* QUESTION CLAUSE**	I wonder **if** life exists in other solar systems.
	I wonder **whether** life exists in other solar systems.
***WH-* QUESTION CLAUSE**	I wonder **where** signs of other life may be found.

When the noun clause follows an introductory clause, the noun clause uses question word order.

QUESTION   Who discovered the fire?

NOUN CLAUSE   Do you know **who discovered the fire?** [question word order]

Change to statement order when the question includes a form of *be* and a subject complement, a modal, or the auxiliary *do, does, did, have, has,* or *had.* Also use statement word order with *if* and *whether* clauses.

QUESTION   Who **are** your friends?

NOUN CLAUSE   I wonder who your friends **are**. [statement word order]

QUESTION   How **can** I meet them?

NOUN CLAUSE   Please tell me how I **can** meet them. [statement word order]

30d Different types of sentences

Sentences vary according to the kind and number of clauses they contain (sentence structure) and the relationships they establish with readers (purpose).

30.3

1 Look for sentence structures

A sentence with one main (independent) clause and no subordinate (dependent) clauses is a **simple sentence.**

The mayor proposed an expansion of city hall.

A sentence with two or more main (independent) clauses and no subordinate (dependent) clauses is a **compound sentence.** (See 42a on coordination.)

       main clause   main clause
Most people praised the plans, yet **some found them dull.**

A sentence with one main (independent) clause and one or more subordinate (dependent) clauses is a **complex sentence.** (See 42b on subordination.)

     subordinate clause   main clause
Because people objected, **the architect revised the plans.**

A sentence with two or more main (independent) clauses and one or more subordinate (dependent) clauses is a **compound-complex sentence.**

subordinate clause   subordinate clause

<u>Because he wanted to make sure</u> <u>that the expansion did not damage</u>

main clause

<u>the existing building</u>, **the architect examined the frame of the older**

main clause

structure, and **he asked the contractor to test the soil stability**.

2 Look for sentence purposes

A **declarative sentence** makes a statement. An **interrogative sentence** poses a question. An **imperative sentence** requests or commands. An **exclamatory sentence** exclaims.

DECLARATIVE	The motor is making a rattling noise.
INTERROGATIVE	Have you checked it for overheating?
IMPERATIVE	Check it again.
EXCLAMATORY	It's on fire!

Exercise 1   *(Answers appear on p. 510.)*

In each of the following sentences, circle the complete subjects and draw a wavy line under the complete predicates.

EXAMPLE

(Stories about Mount Everest) often mention people known as Sherpas.

1. The Sherpas are well-known guides for mountain-climbing expeditions in the Himalayas.
2. They are a group of about 35,000 people who live in the country of Nepal.
3. The Sherpas, who are primarily Buddhists, live in a country dominated by Hindus.
4. Before the early 1900s, most Sherpas did not attempt to scale the mountains in their homeland.
5. In the early part of this century, however, Westerners wishing to climb the mountains gave many Sherpas jobs as guides and laborers.

Exercise 2

First, identify all the phrases in the following passage, and tell whether each is a prepositional, verbal, absolute, or appositive phrase.

Without electricity, we would perish. We could learn to do without the flow of electrons that power VCRs and food processors, but the currents inside our bodies are vital. The brain needs electricity to issue its commands from neuron to neuron. When these signals reach a muscle, they set up a wave of electrical excitation in the fibers, which in turn triggers the chemical reactions that make the fibers contract or relax. The most important muscle is the heart; it shudders under a wave of electricity about once each second.

—CARL ZIMMER, "The Body Electric"

Next, combine the following sentences to create a paragraph that might follow the one above. Try to create a variety of phrases.

The heart has an electric field. The field radiates into the chest cavity. The field sends clues. The clues are about the heart's function. The clues go toward the skin. Cardiologists can get a peek at the heart. They are taping electrodes. The electrodes are taped to a person's torso. Each electrode produces a familiar squiggle. The squiggles are on an electrocardiogram. The electrocardiogram shows how the voltage changes at that single point. The point is on the body. Cardiologists spend years learning. They learn to infer heart function from these signals. They learn to recognize the telltale signs. The signs are in EKG readings. The signs tell of dangerous heart conditions.

Exercise 3   (Answers appear on p. 510.)

Underline all subordinate clauses in the following passage.

Because the tax laws have gotten more complex recently, we have published a guide to tax preparation that highlights new features of the tax code. In addition, the guide provides step-by-step instruction for tax forms, which should be helpful even if a person has considerable experience filling out the forms. Anyone who plans to file taxes for a small business will be interested in the special section on business tax laws. Although many professionals and businesspeople rely on accountants when tax time arrives, they will nonetheless find that the guide provides money-saving advice.

31   Using Verbs

In casual speech, many different verb forms may be acceptable to listeners, especially those within your own dialect community.

CASUAL SPEECH   My daddy **be pushin'** me to do good in school.

Jimmy **should'a went** with them.

We **were fixin'** to eat dinner.

You **might could carpool** to work with Don.

LISTENER'S REACTION: **What sounds fine when we talk might not be correct in a paper.**

In your writing, however, nonstandard verb forms may distract readers who expect you to write fluently in standard English. Some readers may even assume that you are uneducated or careless if you don't edit the verb forms in your final drafts. Adjust to the expectations of your readers. After all, the formal language of the academic community is as inappropriate on the street corner as casual language is in a history paper or marketing report.

31b
verb

31a Simple present and past tense verbs

When you use a simple verb in a sentence, you put that verb into the **present tense** for action occurring *now* or the **past tense** for action that has *already occurred*. Most verbs form the past tense by adding *-ed* to the present tense form, also called the **base form**. Depending on the verb, this addition may be pronounced as *-t* (*baked*), *-d* (*called*), or *-ed* (*defended*).

ESL ADVICE: SIMPLE PRESENT AND SIMPLE PAST

Only these two tenses stand alone with no helping verbs. (See 31d.)

SIMPLE PRESENT   They **live** in the new dormitory.

SIMPLE PAST   They **lived** in an apartment last semester.

31b Editing present tense verbs

You need no special ending to mark the present tense *except* in the third person singular form (with *he*, *she*, or *it* or a singular noun). Use *-s* or *-es* for the third person singular.

The cafeteria **opens** at eight o'clock.

For plurals in the third person (*I*, *you*, *we*, *they* or a plural noun), you do not use *-s* or *-es*. This can be confusing because plural nouns often end in *-s* or *-es* but the verb should not (*customers* + *wait*).

The customers **wait** in line until the cafeteria **opens**.

PRESENT TENSE IN ACADEMIC SETTINGS

In the academic community, readers may expect special uses of the present tense. When writing for your humanities courses, use the present tense to discuss a piece of literature, a film, an essay, a painting, or a similar creative production. Treat events, ideas, characters, or statements from such works as if they exist in an ongoing present tense.

In Erdrich's *Love Medicine*, Albertine **returns** to the reservation.

In the social sciences and sciences, use the present tense to discuss the results and implications of a current study or experiment, but use the past tense to review the findings of earlier researchers.

Although Maxwell (1991) **identified** three crucial classroom interactions, the current survey **suggests** two others as well.

31c
verb

ESL ADVICE: THE THIRD PERSON *-S* OR *-ES* ENDING

Be sure to add an *-s* or *-es* to verbs that are third person singular.

SUBJECT	VERB	SUBJECT	VERB + *-S*
I/you/we/they	**write**	he/she/it (animal, thing, concept)	**writes**

31c Editing past tense verbs

When you write the past tense of a regular verb, you usually add *-ed* to its base form. Sometimes you may leave off the *-ed* if you don't "hear" it, especially when a word beginning in *d* or *t* follows the verb.

DRAFT   The company **use** to provide dental benefits.

EDITED   The company **used** to provide dental benefits.

About sixty **irregular verbs** are exceptions to the "add *-ed*" rule; most change an internal vowel in the simple past tense (*run, ran*).

DRAFT   The characters in the movie **sweared** constantly.

EDITED   The characters in the movie **swore** constantly.

31.1

31c
verb

COMMON IRREGULAR VERBS

PRESENT	PAST	PAST PARTICIPLE
arise	arose	arisen
am/is/are	was/were	been
bear	bore	borne
begin	began	begun
bite	bit	bitten/bit
blow	blew	blown
break	broke	broken
bring	brought	brought
buy	bought	bought
catch	caught	caught
choose	chose	chosen
come	came	come
creep	crept	crept
dive	dived/dove	dived
do	did	done
draw	drew	drawn
dream	dreamed/dreamt	dreamt
drink	drank	drunk
drive	drove	driven
eat	ate	eaten
fall	fell	fallen
fight	fought	fought
fly	flew	flown
forget	forgot	forgotten
forgive	forgave	forgiven
get	got	got/gotten
give	gave	given
go	went	gone
grow	grew	grown
hang (person)	hanged/hung	hanged/hung
hang (object)	hung	hung
hide	hid	hidden
know	knew	known
lay	laid	laid
lead	led	led
lie	lay	lain
light	lit/lighted	lit
lose	lost	lost
prove	proved	proved/proven
ride	rode	ridden
ring	rang	rung

PRESENT	PAST	PAST PARTICIPLE
rise	rose	risen
run	ran	run
see	saw	seen
seek	sought	sought
set	set	set
shake	shook	shaken
sing	sang/sung	sung
sink	sank/sunk	sunk
sit	sat	sat
speak	spoke	spoken
spring	sprang	sprung
steal	stole	stolen
strike	struck	struck
swear	swore	sworn
swim	swam	swum
take	took	taken
tear	tore	torn
throw	threw	thrown
wake	woke/waked	woken/waked/woke
wear	wore	worn
write	wrote	written

31d
verb

31d Complex tenses and helping verbs

To recognize complex tenses, look for a **helping** or **auxiliary verb** (such as *is* or *has*) with a main verb in the form of the **past participle** (the *-ed/-en* form) or the **present participle** (the *-ing* form).

The **present participle** is formed by adding *-ing* to the base form of the verb (the form with no endings or markers).

	helping verb	main verb (present participle)
He	was/will be/had been	**loading** the truck.

The **past participle** of most verbs is just like the simple past tense (base form + *-ed*). Because this form can be irregular, check the chart on irregular verbs (see 31c) or the dictionary if you are uncertain of the form.

	helping verb	main verb (past participle)
REGULAR VERB	Mike has/had	**rented** the truck.
IRREGULAR VERB	The copier has/had	**broken** down.

ESL ADVICE: PRINCIPAL PARTS OF VERBS AND HELPING VERBS

PRINCIPAL PARTS OF VERBS

BASE FORM	PAST	PRESENT PARTICIPLE	PAST PARTICIPLE
REGULAR VERBS			
live	lived	living	lived
want	wanted	wanting	wanted
IRREGULAR VERBS			
eat	ate	eating	eaten
run	ran	running	run

HELPING VERBS AND VERB PHRASES

Most verbs combine one or more helping verbs (also called auxiliary verbs) with a main verb to form a **verb phrase**.

HELPING VERB	I **was walking** to school during the snowstorm.
HELPING VERBS	I **have been walking** to school for many years.

Helping verbs include *am, is, are, will, would, can, could, have, has, had, was, were, should, might, may, must, do, does,* and *did.* These words may be combined, as in *have been, has been, had been, will be, will have,* and *will have been.*

VERB AND HELPING VERB FORMS FOR *BE* AND *HAVE*

PROGRESSIVE FORMS OF *BE*

PAST subject + *was/were* + present participle
I **was** working in my studio yesterday.

PRESENT subject + *am/is/are* + present participle
I **am** working in my studio right now.

FUTURE subject + *will* (modal) + *be* + present participle
I **will be** working in my studio tomorrow.

PERFECT FORMS OF *HAVE*

PAST subject + *had* + past participle
I **had** tried to call you all day yesterday.

PRESENT subject + *have/has* + past participle
I **have** tried to call you all day today.

FUTURE subject + *will* (modal) + *have* + past participle
I **will have** called you by midnight tonight.

31e Editing progressive and perfect tenses

When you use the **present, past,** and **future progressive** tenses, you can show an action in progress at some point in time.

PRESENT PROGRESSIVE   The carousel **is turning** quickly.

PAST PROGRESSIVE   The horses **were bobbing** up and down.

FUTURE PROGRESSIVE   The children **will be laughing** from the thrill.

31e
verb

In progressive tenses, the main verb must take the *-ing* ending. In the future progressive tense, the verb must also include *be.*

Indicating the order of events. Turn to the three **perfect tenses** to show the order in which events take place.

Use the **past perfect tense** for the first event to indicate that it had already happened before something else took place.

The fire **had burned** for an hour before the brigade arrived.

Avoid substituting simple past tense for the past participle.

MISTAKEN PAST   The band **had forgot** the first tour.

EDITED   The band **had forgotten** the first tour.

Use the **present perfect tense** much like the past perfect, showing action that has happened before without a specific time marker or that you insist has already occurred.

I **have reported** the burglary already.

The present perfect also shows action begun in the past and continuing into the present. It differs from the simple past, which indicates an action already completed or specified in time.

PRESENT PERFECT   I **have lived** in St. Louis for three weeks.

SIMPLE PAST   I **lived** in St. Louis in 1998.

Select the **future perfect tense** to show that something will have happened by the time something else will be taking place.

The chef **will have baked** all the cakes before noon.

ESL ADVICE: SIMPLE PRESENT AND PRESENT PROGRESSIVE TENSES

31e
verb

PRESENT TENSE HABITUAL ACTIVITIES

Use the **simple present** tense to describe factual or habitual activities. These occur in the present but are not necessarily in progress.

SHOWS FACT   The planets **revolve** around the sun.

SHOWS HABIT   The bus usually **arrives** late.

These common time expressions indicate present tense habitual activities.

all the time	every holiday	every year	rarely
always	every month	frequently	sometimes
every class	every semester	most of the time	usually
every day	every week	often	never

ACTIVITIES IN PROGRESS

Use the **present progressive** tense to describe activities in progress. If you wish, you can add expressions to pinpoint the time of the activity.

am/is/are + present participle
DeVaugh **is testing** the process.

DeVaugh **is testing** the process **this month**.

These common time expressions indicate activities in progress.

at the moment	this afternoon	this month	this year
right now	this evening	this morning	today

When you choose between the simple present and present progressive tenses, think about the time of the activity. Is it happening only at the moment (present progressive) or all the time as a fact or habit (simple present)?

PRESENT (FACT)   All people communicate in some language.

PRESENT (HABIT)   The students speak their own languages at home.

PRESENT PROGRESSIVE   Kim is studying Spanish this term.
(AT THE MOMENT)

VERBS THAT ARE TROUBLESOME IN PROGRESSIVE TENSES

	EXAMPLE	OTHER USAGES AND MEANINGS
SENSES		
see	I **see** the beauty.	I **am seeing** that doctor. (meeting with, visiting, dating)

hear	I **hear** the birds.	I **have been hearing** about the problem for a while. (receiving information)
smell	The flowers **smell** strong.	I **am smelling** the flowers. (action in progress)
taste	The food **tastes** good.	The cook **is tasting** the soup. (action in progress)

POSSESSION

have	We **have** many friends.	We **are having** a lot of fun. (experiencing)
own	They **own** many cars.	
possess	She **possesses** wealth.	
belong	The book **belongs** to me.	

31e
verb

STATES OF MIND

be	I **am** tired.	
know	I **know** the city well.	
believe	She **believes** in God.	
think	I **think** it is true. (know, believe)	I **am thinking** about moving. (having thoughts about)
recognize	She **recognizes** him. (knows)	
understand	The professor **understands** the equation.	
mean	I **don't mean** to pry. (don't want)	I **have been meaning** to visit. (planning, intending)

WISH OR ATTITUDE

| want | We **want** peace. | |
| desire | He **desires** freedom. | |

WISH OR ATTITUDE

need	We **need** rain.	
love	Children **love** snow.	I **have been loving** this book. (enjoying)
hate	Dan **hates** mowing.	
like	Lee **likes** skiing.	
dislike	She **dislikes** tests.	
seem	They **seem** kind.	
appear	He **appears** tired. (seems to be)	He **is appearing** at the theater. (acting, performing)
look	He **looks** tired. (seems to be)	We **are looking** at the map. (action of using eyes)

31f Editing troublesome verbs (*lie, lay, sit, set*)

Here are a few verbs confused even by experienced writers.

VERB	PRESENT	PAST	PARTICIPLE
lie (oneself)	lie	lay	lain
lay (an object)	lay	laid	laid
sit (oneself)	sit	sat	sat
set (an object)	set	set	set

DRAFT   I **laid** down yesterday for a nap. I **have laid** down every afternoon this week.

EDITED   I **lay** down yesterday for a nap. I **have lain** down every afternoon this week.

DRAFT   First Eric and Lisa **sat** the projector down on the table. Then they **set** down as the meeting began.

EDITED   First Eric and Lisa **set** the projector down on the table. Then they **sat** down as the meeting began.

31g Clear tense sequence

Conversation can jump from tense to tense with little warning. In writing, however, readers expect you to stick to one tense or to follow a clear **sequence of tenses** that relates events and ideas in time (see 39b).

             present   past

LOGICAL   People **forget** that four candidates **ran** in 1948.

            future   present

LOGICAL   I **will accept** your report even if it **is** a bit late.

            past

LOGICAL   The accountant **destroyed** crucial evidence because no one
          past perfect
had asked him to save the records.

            past perfect

LOGICAL   None of the crew **had realized** that food stored in cans sealed
      present (for generally true statement)
with lead solder **is** poisonous.

31h Subjunctive mood

Sentences can be classified by **mood**, the form of a verb that reflects the speaker's or writer's attitude. Most sentences are in the **indicative** (statements intended as truthful or factual like "The store closed at 10") or the **imperative** (commands like "Stop!"). Occasionally the **subjunctive** expresses uncertainty—supposition, prediction, possibility, desire, or wish.

SUBJUNCTIVE   **Were** the deadline today, our proposal would be late.

The subjunctive has faded from most casual speech and some writing. It is still expected by many readers in formal writing using **conditional statements**, often beginning with *if* and expressing the improbable or hypothetical.

31.2

DRAFT (PAST)   If fuel efficiency **was** improved, driving costs would go down.

EDITED   If fuel efficiency **were** improved, driving costs would go down.
(SUBJUNCTIVE)

31h
verb

Don't add *would* to the *had + verb* structure in the conditional clause, even if *would* appropriately appears in the **result clause** that follows the conditional.

EXTRA *WOULD*   If fuel efficiency **would have improved**, driving costs **would have gone** down.

EDITED   If fuel efficiency **had improved**, driving costs **would have gone** down.

Finally, some clauses with *that* require a subjunctive verb when they follow certain verbs that make demands or requests.

DRAFT (PAST)   The judge <u>asked</u> <u>that</u> the witnesses **be swore** in.

EDITED   The judge asked that the witnesses **be sworn** in.

Use the present tense form with *that*, even in the third person singular.

The court ordered that   I/you/he/she/it/we/they   appear.

For the verb *is*, the forms are *be* (present) and *were* (past).

ESL ADVICE: TYPES OF CONDITIONAL STATEMENTS

TYPE I: TRUE IN THE PRESENT

IF CLAUSE   RESULT CLAUSE
• **Generally true in the present as a habit or as a fact**

  if + subject + present tense   subject + present tense
  If I drive to school every day,   I get to class on time.

• **True in the future as a one-time event**

  if + subject + present tense   subject + future tense
  If I drive to school today,   I will get to class on time.

- **Possibly true in the future as a one-time event**

| *if* + subject + present tense | subject + modal + base form verb |
| If I drive to school today, | I may/should get to class on time. |

TYPE II: UNTRUE IN THE PRESENT

IF CLAUSE	RESULT CLAUSE
if + subject + past tense	subject + *would/could/might* + base form verb
If I drove to school,	I would arrive on time.
If I were a car owner,	I could arrive on time.

With Type II, the form of the verb *be* in the *if* clause is always *were*.

TYPE III: UNTRUE IN THE PAST

IF CLAUSE	RESULT CLAUSE
if + subject + past perfect tense	subject + *would/could/might* + *have* + past participle
If I had driven to school,	I would not have been late.

31i Active and passive voice

To recognize a verb in the **active voice**, look for a sentence in which the agent or doer of an action is the subject of the sentence (see 43b-3).

	AGENT (SUBJECT)	ACTION (VERB)	GOAL (OBJECT)
ACTIVE	The car	**hit**	the lamppost.
ACTIVE	Dana	**distributed**	the flyers.

In contrast, when a verb is in the **passive voice**, the goal of the sentence appears in the subject position, and the doer may appear in the object position, after the word *by* (in an optional prepositional phrase). The verb itself adds a form of *be* as a helping verb to the participle form.

	GOAL (SUBJECT)	ACTION (*BE* FORM + VERB)	[AGENT: PREPOSITIONAL PHRASE]
PASSIVE	The lamppost	**was hit**	[by the car].
PASSIVE	The flyers	**were distributed**	[by Dana].

The active and passive versions of a sentence create different kinds of emphasis because they use different words as sentence subjects.

ACTIVE	The city council **banned** smoking in restaurants.
PASSIVE	Smoking in restaurants **was banned** by the city council.
AGENT OMITTED	Smoking in restaurants **was banned**.

ESL ADVICE: PASSIVE VOICE

All tenses can appear in the passive voice *except* these progressive forms: present perfect, past perfect, future, future perfect. In the following sentences, the agent or doer of the action is not the subject *food*, but rather *chef*.

TENSES	SUBJECT + *BE* FORM + PAST PARTICIPLE
PRESENT	The food **is prepared** by the chef.
PRESENT PROGRESSIVE	The food **is being prepared** by the chef.
PAST	The food **was prepared** by the chef.
PAST PROGRESSIVE	The food **was being prepared** by the chef.
PRESENT PERFECT	The food **has been prepared** by the chef.
PAST PERFECT	The food **had been prepared** by the chef.
FUTURE	The food **will be prepared** by the chef.
FUTURE PERFECT	The food **will have been prepared** by the chef.

31i
verb

Each passive verb must have a form of *be* and a past participle (ending in *-ed* for regular verbs). Sometimes the *-ed* ending is hard to hear when spoken, so edit carefully for it.

MISSING *-ED*	The young man was **call** to the conference room.
EDITED	The young man was **called** to the conference room.

Exercise 1   *(Answers appear on p. 510.)*

In each of the following sentences, a correct or incorrect irregular verb form appears in parentheses. Edit each sentence to make it correct, or indicate that it's already correct. If necessary, consult the list on pages 314–15 or look in a dictionary for the principal parts of a particular verb.

EXAMPLE

       had fallen
The rain (~~had falled~~) all night.
       ^

1. Jeremy (*had chose*) to work along the levee as part of the volunteer corps.
2. The floodwater (*had rised*) rapidly during the night.
3. The work team (*had heaved*) sandbags on top of the levee for almost twenty-four hours.
4. Jim O'Connor and Rebecca Gomez (*had hung*) plastic sheeting up to plug a leak.
5. By eight o'clock in the morning, people (*had woke*) up to find that the river (*had fell*) by six inches and the town was safe.

Exercise 2

For each sentence, circle the appropriate verb from the choices within parentheses.

EXAMPLE

A fire last Saturday (*lead*,*(led)*)to Sandy's first big assignment as a reporter.

1. Sandy (*laid/lay*) the article for the newspaper on her editor's desk.
2. To get information for the article, she (*sat/set*) in the waiting room of the fire commissioner's office for three days.
3. During the interview, she (*layed/lay/laid*) on his desk a copy of the report criticizing the fire department's performance during the Brocklin Warehouse fire.
4. The commissioner looked the report over and then (*sat/set*) it next to the other report, which praised the department's performance.
5. After she had (*lead/led*) the three-hour discussion with the commissioner, Sandy was convinced that the department had done an adequate job at the fire.

Exercise 3   *(Answers appear on p. 510.)*

Decide whether the complex verb forms highlighted in the following sentences are correct. Edit those that are not; explain why you left any as they appear.

EXAMPLE

The team leader **is planning** to ask for reports just after the produc-
                begins.
tion meeting **will begin**.
                ^

1. Kamal **is finished** testing the circuit board by the time the production meeting **had started**.
2. The team members **will ask** Kamal if he **was planning** to test the remainder of the circuit boards.
3. As I prepare this report on the project, Michelle **is assembling** the prototype using the circuit boards.
4. The other people **will assemble** the extra machines as soon as the delivery van **arrived**.
5. If our customers **will be able** to recognize the advantages of our product, they **would order** more of the machines.

Exercise 4

Rewrite each of the following sentences in the tense or mood indicated in brackets by substituting appropriate main verb forms and any necessary helping verbs for the verb in parentheses.

31
verb

EXAMPLE

has been failing

The airplane assembly plant *(fail)* for several years. [present perfect progressive]

1. First, the recession (hurt) the market for small airplanes. [past perfect]
2. Then a new management team announced, "We (*close*) the plant unless productivity increases." [future]
3. At the same time, the company (*lose*) a product liability lawsuit. [past progressive]
4. This week, the company president (*announce*), "Unless we get some new orders in a few days, we (*declare*) bankruptcy." [simple past; future progressive]
5. If the plant (*be*) closed, three hundred workers would lose their jobs. [past subjunctive]

Exercise 5   *(Possible answer appears on p. 511.)*

Edit the following passage by rewriting unnecessary uses of the passive voice into the active voice. In rewriting passive voice sentences that do not indicate an agent (doer), fill in the names of the person(s) or thing(s) you consider responsible for the action.

Having cash registers full of change was found to increase the likelihood of a late-night robbery. In one example, a store clerk was held up at gunpoint. It was decided by management that requiring full payment for gasoline in advance of a purchase would minimize the risk of further holdups. This course of action had been voted on by the board of directors prior to implementation. The decision was posted at each location. Following implementation, it was discovered that holdups were not minimized unless large signs indicating the clerk's lack of available cash were placed in plain view. Once this was done, fewer holdups were experienced, and the turnover of late-night personnel was decreased.

32 Using Pronouns

Readers count on you to use different forms of pronouns to guide them through your sentences. The wrong choices can mislead or irritate them.

DRAFT   **Him** and **me** will make a strong management team.

READER'S REACTION: *Him* **and** *me* **makes the writer sound careless and un-educated.**

EDITED   **He** and **I** will make a strong management team.

Although most pronouns won't give you trouble, at times you may struggle with choices between *we* or *us*, *her* or *she*, and *who* or *whom*.

32a Pronoun forms

A pronoun changes form according to its role in a sentence: subject, object, or possessive, showing possession or ownership. (See also 29b.)

subjective possessive   objective
He and **his** design team created the furniture for **us**.

1 Choosing subjective forms

Choose a subjective form if a pronoun acts as the subject of all or part of a sentence or if it renames or restates a subject.

She wants to know why the orders have not been filled.

Because **they** were unable to get a loan, the business failed.

Atco will be hiring people **who** are willing to work the night shift.

I attend class more regularly than **he** [does].

When you use a pronoun to rename the subject following a form of the verb *be* (*is*, *am*, *are*, *was*, *were*) you create a **subject complement** (see 30a-2). Choose the subjective form because you are restating the subject.

SUBJECTIVE FORM   **The last art majors** to get jobs were Becky and **I**.

In conversation, people may use the objective form. In writing, however, use the correct form. If it sounds stilted or unnatural, rewrite the sentence.

CONVERSATION   The new traffic reporter is **him**.

STILTED   The new traffic reporter is **he**.

REWRITTEN   **He** is the new traffic reporter.

FORMS OF PRONOUNS

PERSONAL PRONOUNS

	SUBJECTIVE		OBJECTIVE		POSSESSIVE	
	SINGULAR	PLURAL	SINGULAR	PLURAL	SINGULAR	PLURAL
First person	I	we	me	us	my	our
					mine	ours
Second person	you	you	you	you	your	your
					yours	yours
Third person	he	} they	him	} them	his	} their
	she		her		her	theirs
					hers	
	it		it		its	

RELATIVE AND INTERROGATIVE PRONOUNS

SUBJECTIVE	OBJECTIVE	POSSESSIVE
who	whom	whose
whoever	whomever	
which	which	
that	that	
what	what	

INDEFINITE PRONOUNS

SUBJECTIVE	OBJECTIVE	POSSESSIVE
anybody	anybody	anybody's
everyone	everyone	everyone's

32a
pron

2 Choosing objective forms

When you make a pronoun the direct (or indirect) object of an entire sentence, use the objective form. Also use it for pronouns playing other object roles in a sentence.

indirect object   direct object
The company bought **her** __an antivirus program__.

STRATEGY Choosing objective forms.

As you edit, check whether a pronoun is acting as an object within some part of a sentence. Check also whether it renames or restates an object. If it plays either role, choose the word's objective form.

object of preposition
The rest of **them** had to wait several months for the software.

object in relative clause
An accountant **whom** the firm hired helped her out.

object in gerund phrase
Mr. Pederson's research for the report included interviewing **them**.

object in participial phrase
Having interviewed **us**, too, Mr. Pederson had a lot of material to summarize.

The report contained interviews with the two dissatisfied workers,
appositive renames object
her and him.

32a
pron

You may find pronouns used with infinitives (*to* + a verb) tricky so keep the following example in mind.

OBJECTIVE FORM   Mr. Pederson asked **us** to review the minutes.

Us might seem the subject of the phrase *to review the minutes*. It is the direct object of the sentence, however (*Mr. Pederson asked **us***). The objective form is correct.

3 Choosing possessive forms

When you use a pronoun to show possession, choose the possessive form. The particular form you use depends on whether the pronoun appears *before a noun* or *in place of a noun*.

BEFORE NOUN   The Topeka office requested a copy of **her** report.

REPLACING NOUN   **Hers** was the most up-to-date study available.

You should also use the possessive form before gerunds (-*ing* verb forms that act as nouns). Because this use of the possessive is often ignored in speech, you may need to practice writing it until it begins to "sound right" to you.

CONVERSATION   Them requesting the report pleased our supervisor.

EDITED   **Their** requesting the report pleased our supervisor.

English nouns also vary in form to show possession, signaled by an apostrophe ('s or '): *the study/the study's conclusions*. (See 50a–b.) Don't confuse nouns and pronouns by adding an apostrophe to a possessive pronoun.

> **STRATEGY** Choosing between *its* and *it's*.
>
> *Its*, not *it's*, is the form of the possessive pronoun. Test which you need by replacing the pronoun with *it is* (the expansion of *it's*). If *it is* fits, keep the apostrophe. If *it is* doesn't fit, omit the apostrophe.
>
> | | |
> |---|---|
> | **DRAFT** | The food pantry gave away (*its/it's*) last can of tuna. |
> | **REPLACEMENT TEST** | The food pantry gave away **it is** last can of tuna. *It is* **doesn't make sense.** |
> | **USE POSSESSIVE** | The food pantry gave away **its** last can of tuna. |

32b Editing common pronoun forms

Many problems with pronoun forms occur at predictable places. Pay attention to the following troublesome constructions.

32.1

1 Compound subjects and objects

When you use a compound subject such as *the committee and I* or *Jim and me*, the rule is simple: Use the same case for the pronoun in the compound that you would use for a single pronoun in the same role.

COMPOUND SUBJECT	Denise or (*he? him?*) should check the inventory.
SUBJECTIVE FORM	Denise or **he** should check the inventory.
COMPOUND OBJECT	The coach selected (*she? her? and he? him?*) as captains.
OBJECTIVE FORM	The coach selected **her and him** as captains.

> **STRATEGY** Focus-imagine-choose.
>
> * **Focus** on the pronoun whose form you need to choose.
>
> | | |
> |---|---|
> | **DRAFT** | Anne-Marie and **me** will develop the videotape. *FOCUS: I or me?* |
>
> * **Imagine** each choice for the pronoun as the subject (or object).
>
> | | |
> |---|---|
> | **#1 (INCORRECT)** | **Me** will develop the videotape. |
> | **#2 (CORRECT)** | **I** will develop the videotape. |
>
> * **Choose** the correct form for the compound subject (or object).
>
> | | |
> |---|---|
> | **EDITED** | Anne-Marie and **I** will develop the videotape. |

If the appropriate form is not immediately clear to you, see the chart in 32a. Choosing what "sounds right" may not work with compounds.

2 Pronouns that rename or are paired with nouns

When you rename a preceding noun or pronoun in an **appositive**, match the form of the word being renamed. If you pair pronouns like *we* or *us* with nouns, identify the role of the noun and match the pronoun form with it—*we, they* (subjective) or *us, them* (objective).

STRATEGY   Test alternatives.

- For appositives, imagine alternative versions of the sentence without the noun (or pronoun) that was renamed.

SENTENCE	The two book illustrators on the panel, (*she? her?*) and (*I? me?*), discussed questions from the audience.
#1 (INCORRECT)	**Her** and **me** discussed questions from the audience.
#2 (CORRECT)	**She** and **I** discussed questions from the audience.
EDITED	The two book illustrators on the panel, **she** and **I**, discussed questions from the audience.

- For pronoun-noun pairs, imagine alternatives without the noun.

SENTENCE	The teaching evaluation should be conducted by (*us? we?*) students, not by the faculty or administration.
#1 (INCORRECT)	The teaching evaluation should be conducted by **we**. . . .
#2 (CORRECT)	The teaching evaluation should be conducted by **us**. . . .
EDITED	The teaching evaluation should be conducted by **us** students, not by the faculty or administration.

3 Comparisons with *than* or *as*

When creating a comparison with *than* or *as* followed by a pronoun, make sure the pronoun form you choose accurately signals the information left out. A pronoun in the subjective case acts as the subject of the implied statement; a pronoun in the objective case acts as the object.

SUBJECTIVE	I gave her sister more help than **she** [did].
OBJECTIVE	I gave her sister more help than [I gave] **her**.

If readers may miss the grammatical signals, rewrite the sentence.

MAY BE AMBIGUOUS	I like working with Aisha better than she.
	READER'S REACTION: Does this mean that you prefer to work with Aisha? Or that you like to work with Aisha better than someone else does?
REWRITTEN	She doesn't like working with Aisha as much as I do.

4 *Who* and *whom*

You often use the pronouns *who* and *whom*, *whoever* and *whomever* to begin subordinate clauses known as **relative clauses** or **adjective clauses** (see 30c). Choose *who* and *whoever* when you use the pronouns as subjects; choose *whom* and *whomever* when you use them as objects.

SUBJECT   The boy **who wins the race** should get the prize.

OBJECT   Give this delicate assignment to **whomever you trust**.

Choose between *who* and *whom* according to the role the pronoun plays *within the relative clause*. Ignore the role the clause plays *within the sentence*.

DRAFT   The fine must be paid by **whomever** <u>holds the deed</u>.
> **Although the whole clause is the object of the preposition *by*, within the clause the pronoun acts as a subject, not an object.**

EDITED   The fine must be paid by **whoever** holds the deed.

At the beginning of a question, you should use *who* when the pronoun is the subject of the sentence and *whom* when the pronoun is an object.

SUBJECT   **Who** is most likely to get the reader's sympathy at this point in the novel, Huck or Jim?

OBJECT   **Whom** can Cordelia trust at the end of the scene?

32b
pron

Exercise 1   *(Answers appear on p. 511.)*

In each of the following sentences, choose the correct pronoun from the pair within parentheses. Then indicate whether the pronoun form is subjective, objective, or possessive.

EXAMPLE

Ruth and (*I*/me) are planning to open a children's clothing store.
subjective

1. The design for the new store was prepared by (*she/her*).
2. The city requires (*we/us*) to submit plans for remodeling the store we plan to rent.
3. Having interviewed Ruth and (*I/me*) about our marketing plan, the bank's officer approved our loan.
4. The person who will choose the stock for our store is (*she/her*).
5. I will supervise the salespeople (*who/whom*) we hire.

Next, revise the following sentences by correcting any errors in pronoun form.

EXAMPLE

her

The foundation sent copies of the grant proposal to ~~she~~ and me.
                                                        ^

1. Her and three other people worked for three weeks preparing the grant proposal.
2. The original grant-writing team included two other people, Kristen and she.
3. Because I spent more time working on the grant, I think I ought to get more credit for its success than him.
4. It is me who will have to supervise research work done under the grant.
5. Responsibility for budgeting the grant money is your's.

Exercise 2   *(Answers appear on p. 512.)*

Correct any errors in pronoun form in the following sentences.

EXAMPLE   *she*

Denise and ~~her~~ joined the Disney film group in our class.
               ^

1. The rest of us team members decided we should use recent animated movies as the subject of our project.
2. Because their parents own a video store, her brother and her brought in tapes of the movies we planned to study.
3. Bill and I decided to take notes on *Aladdin*; Pat and her chose to study *Beauty and the Beast*.
4. I thought the notes we took were more detailed and better than they.
5. Writing the final paper led to disagreements between the other members and myself.

Exercise 3   *(Answers appear on p. 512.)*

A. Correct any errors in pronoun form in the following sentences.

EXAMPLE

Whoever

~~Whomever~~ has taken an IQ test probably remembers the score.
           ^

1. In the past, psychologists assumed that whomever scored well on IQ tests was likely to succeed at school and work.
2. Recent studies of IQ tests have produced evidence of them being unable to predict success.
3. A test of constructive thinking skill may tell more about your or mine ability to meet challenges.
4. Reporting on research conducted by he and two of his colleagues, Robert Sternberg points out that "the ability to sell" is an important part of practical intelligence.

5. Other psychologists claim that personal qualities like self-confidence and optimism may by theirselves have as much to do with our mental abilities as IQ does.

B. Identify the pronouns in the following passage and correct any mistakes in case. Keep a record of those identifications and corrections you found most difficult, and be ready to try to explain why you found them difficult.

For we humans, yawning is a familiar activity. You and me probably yawn when we stretch, though not always. Boredom is also a likely cause for us yawning. People often think that no one yawns as much as them, but this is seldom true. We all yawn frequently during a day. We may even start yawning ourselves when we notice someone else whom is yawning.

33 Making Sentence Parts Agree

Readers get mixed signals when sentence parts are not coordinated.

INCONSISTENT   The city council and the mayor is known for her skillful responses to civic debate.

> READER'S REACTION: I thought the sentence was about two things—the city council and the mayor—but when I read *is* and *her*, it seemed to be about only one, the mayor.

EDITED   The city council and the mayor **are** known for **their** skillful responses to civic debate.

Readers expect you to help them understand how the ideas in a sentence relate by making the parts of a sentence work together grammatically—by showing **agreement** in number, person, and gender.

33a Agreement

Within a sentence, a subject and verb should agree in **number** (singular or plural) and **person** (first, second, or third).

<u>You</u> **know** our client. <u>She</u> **wants** to see the design next week.

In addition, each pronoun should agree with its **antecedent**, the noun or other pronoun to which it refers, in **number** (singular, plural), **person** (first, second, third), and **gender** (masculine, feminine, neuter).

The **crews** riding their snowplows left early; the **airport** needed its runways cleared.

33b
s-v agr

AGREEMENT: NUMBER, PERSON, AND GENDER

- *Number* shows whether words are singular (one person, animal, idea, or thing) or plural (two or more) in meaning.

  SINGULAR   This **community** needs its own recreation center.

  PLURAL   Local **communities** need to share their facilities.

- *Person* indicates the speaker or subject being spoken to or about.

  First person (speaker): *I, we*

  I operate the compressor.   **We** operate the compressor.

  Second person (spoken to): *you*

  You operate the forklift.

  Third person (spoken about): *he, she, it, they*; nouns naming things, people, animals, ideas

  He/she/it operates the drill.   **They** operate the drill.

- *Gender* refers to masculine (*he, him*), feminine (*she, her*), or neuter (*it*) qualities attributed to a noun or pronoun.

  MASCULINE/FEMININE
  The future father rushed for **his** car keys, while his wife packed **her** bag.

  NEUTER
  Despite **its** recent tune-up, the car stalled near the hospital.

33b Creating simple subject-verb agreement

To make subjects and verbs agree, make sure they are aligned in two ways: **number** (singular or plural) and **person** (first, second, or third). Keeping them aligned helps your sentences convey consistent, clear meaning.

1 Check subjects, then verbs

First look for the subject. Identify its number (singular or plural) and person (first, second, or third). Then edit the verb so that it agrees.

DRAFT	The clients is waiting.
BOTH PLURAL	The **clients** <u>are</u> waiting.
BOTH SINGULAR	The **client** <u>is</u> waiting.

2 Watch out for plurals

Most plural nouns end in -s or -es, yet exactly the opposite is the case for present tense verbs.

	33b
	s-v agr

*   **Look for a plural subject:** nouns ending in -s or -es; plural pronouns such as *they* and *we*.

    EXCEPTIONS
*   Nouns with irregular plurals (*person/people* or *child/children*)
*   Nouns with the same form for singular and plural (*moose/moose*)

SINGULAR	The dam prevent**s** flooding.
PLURAL	The dam**s** prevent flooding.

*   **Check for a plural verb:** -s or -es in present tense.

    EXCEPTIONS
*   Verbs with irregular forms, including *be* and *have* (see 31c)

*   **Check the verb again.** If you find a main verb *plus* a helping verb, re-member this: the helping verb *sometimes* changes form for singular and plural, but the main verb remains the same (see 31d).

	HELPING VERB CHANGES FORM	HELPING VERB DOES NOT CHANGE
SINGULAR	The **park** <u>does seem</u> safer.	The **park** <u>might seem</u> safer.
PLURAL	The **parks** <u>do seem</u> safer.	The **parks** <u>might seem</u> safer.

ESL ADVICE: SUBJECT-VERB AGREEMENT WITH *BE*, *HAVE*, AND *DO*

Some troublesome verbs change form according to person or tense.

SERIOUS
ERROR

*   *Be* **verbs** (present and past)
    I **am/was.**   He/She/It **is/was.** You/We/They **are/were.**
*   **Helping verb** *be* (present progressive and past progressive tenses)

I	**am** talking.	I/He/She/It	**was talking.**
You/We/They	**are** talking.	We/You/They	**were talking.**
He/She/It	**is** talking.		

*   *Have* **verbs** (present)
    I/You/We/They **have** a new home.   He/She/It   **has** a new home.

• **Helping verb** *have* (present perfect and present perfect progressive tenses)

I/You/We/They	**have** lived here for years.	**have** been living here since May.
He/She/It	**has** lived here for years.	**has** been living here since May.

• *Do* or *does* to show emphasis

I/You/We/They	**do** want the job.	He/She/It	**does** want it.

• *Doesn't* or *don't* to show the negative

I/You/We/They	**don't** exercise enough.	He/She/It	**doesn't** exercise enough.

33c Creating complex subject-verb agreement

Checking for subject-verb agreement sometimes becomes complicated. Try to remember the words and structures that cause problems, and be ready to look up the editing strategies below.

33.1

1 Watch for collective nouns or plural nouns with singular meanings

A **collective noun** is singular in form yet identifies a group of individuals (*audience, mob, crew, troop, tribe,* or *herd*). When the group acts as a single unit, choose a singular verb. When group members act individually, choose a plural verb.

ONE SINGLE UNIT   The **staff** <u>is</u> hardworking and well trained.

INDIVIDUAL MEMBERS   The **staff** <u>have earned</u> the respect of our clients.

Nouns with plural forms and singular meanings. Nouns like *politics, physics, statistics, mumps,* and *athletics* have *-s* endings but are singular.

Mathematics <u>is</u> an increasingly popular field of study.

Titles and names. When your sentence subject is a book title or company name, choose a singular verb even if the name or title is plural. Think to yourself, "The *company* pays . . ." or "The *book* is. . . ."

Home Helpers **pays** high wages and **has** excellent benefits.

The White Roses **is** second on the best-seller list this month.

Numbers. A measurement or figure (even one ending in *-s*) may still be singular if it names a quantity or unit as a whole. When it refers to individual elements, treat it as a whole.

Four years <u>is</u> the amount of time she spent studying stress.

Decide which pronoun accurately represents a complicated subject: *he, she,* or *it* (singular) or *they* (plural). Read your sentence aloud using this replacement pronoun; edit the verb to agree.

DRAFT The **news** about the job market _____ surprisingly good.
PRONOUN TEST: **I could replace "The news" with "It" and say "It is."**

EDITED The **news** about the job market **is** surprisingly good.

2 Check subjects linked by *and, or,* and *nor*

And creates a compound subject; *or* and *nor* create alternative subjects.

Compound subjects. Because *and* or *both . . . and* make the subject plural (even if its parts are singular), you generally need to choose a plural verb.

PLURAL Ham and eggs <u>are</u> ingredients in this casserole.

TWO PEOPLE My friend and my coworker <u>have</u> paintings in the show.

If the parts should be taken as a unit or if the parts designate a single person, thing, or idea, you need to choose a singular verb.

UNIT (SINGULAR) Ham and eggs <u>is</u> still my favorite breakfast.

ONE PERSON My friend and coworker <u>has</u> paintings in the show.

Both . . . and always needs a plural verb, whether the elements joined are singular or plural.

Both the president **and** her advisor <u>are</u> in Tokyo this week.

Both the president **and** her advisors <u>are</u> in Tokyo this week.

Alternative subjects. When you use *or* or *nor* (*either . . . or, neither . . . nor*) to connect alternative parts of the subject, the verb agrees with the closer part. Putting the plural element closer to the verb often is less awkward.

PLURAL CLOSE TO VERB The auditor or **the accountants** <u>review</u> each report.

SINGULAR CLOSE TO VERB False records or **late reporting** <u>weakens</u> the review process.

Either . . . or, neither . . . nor, and *not only . . . but also* may take either a singular or a plural verb, depending on the subject closer to the verb.

Either the president **or** her <u>advisor</u> <u>is</u> in Tokyo.

Neither the president **nor** her <u>advisors</u> <u>are</u> in Tokyo.

3 Pay attention to separated subjects and verbs

When you insert words between the subject and verb of a sentence, you may be tempted to make the verb agree with one of the intervening words rather than the actual subject.

To find the real subject, imagine the subject without intervening words or phrases. Then check that the subject and verb agree.

33c
s-v agr

DRAFT   The new trolley system, featuring expanded routes and lower fares, are especially popular with senior citizens.

FAULTY
AGREEMENT   The new **trolley system** . . .
are especially popular with senior citizens.

EDITED   The new **trolley system**, featuring expanded routes and lower fares, is especially popular with senior citizens.

ESL ADVICE: SEPARATED SUBJECTS AND VERBS

PHRASE SEPARATES   A person **with sensitive eyes** has to wear sunglasses.

CLAUSE SEPARATES   A person **whose eyes are sensitive** has to wear sunglasses.

When the subject is the same in both the main and subordinate clauses, the verbs must agree.

SAME SUBJECT   A **person** who **wants** to protect her eyes **wears** sunglasses.

If you mistake a phrase like *as well as, in addition to, together with,* or *along with* for *and,* you may be tempted to treat a noun following it as the subject.

The **provost**, as well as the deans, has issued new guidelines.

If you mean *and,* use the word itself.

REWRITTEN   The provost **and** the deans have issued new guidelines.

DRAFT   A regular tune-up, along with frequent oil **changes**, prolong the life of your car.
    IMAGINE: **A regular tune-up . . . prolongs the life of your car.**

EDITED   A regular **tune-up**, along with frequent oil changes, prolongs the life of your car.

4 Recognize unusual word order

When you alter typical word order to create emphasis or ask a question, make sure the verb still agrees with the subject. The verb and subject should agree even with inverted (reversed) word order.

33.2

QUESTION   Are popular comedy and action films mere escapism?

EMPHASIS   After victory comes overconfidence for many teams.

There is, there are. Expletive constructions such as *there are* and *it is* invert (reverse) the usual subject-verb sentence order, allowing you to put the subject *after* the verb (see 43b-2). Then the verb agrees with the subject that follows it.

33c
s-v agr

SINGULAR   There is opportunity for people starting service industries.

PLURAL   There are many opportunities for service industries.

Is, appears, feels, and other linking verbs. When you build a sentence around *is, appears, feels* or another linking verb (see 29c), make sure the verb agrees with the subject. You may be tempted to make it agree with the noun or pronoun renaming the subject (the complement, see 29c), but edit carefully to avoid this problem.

                          subject   verb   complement
DRAFT   The chief obstacle to change are the mayor and her allies.

EDITED   The chief obstacle to change is the mayor and her allies.

ESL ADVICE: SUBJECT-VERB AGREEMENT

- Check for agreement with compound verbs (more than one verb) in a simple sentence.

  The clerk collects, sorts, and files reports.

- Check for subject-verb agreement in a complex sentence (see 30d).

  ADVERB CLAUSE   When the snow falls, we enjoy the scenery.

  ADJECTIVE   The young man that I work with lives in town.
  CLAUSE
                  The young man that works with me lives in town.

- Check for correct selection of helping verbs.

  THIRD PERSON   That restaurant does give special dinner discounts.
  DOES
  MODAL   The president might give a speech this evening.

5 Pay attention to troublesome words

Watch for words such as *all*, *everybody*, *who*, *that*, and *each*.

All, everybody, none. *All*, *everybody*, and *none* (and other indefinite pronouns) do not refer to specific ideas, people, or things. Most have clearly singular meanings and require singular verbs.

Someone <u>is</u> mailing campaign flyers.

Everybody <u>has</u> the duty to vote.

You can treat a few pronouns, such as *all*, *any*, *most*, *none*, and *some*, as either singular or plural according to meaning.

33c
s-v agr

SOME INDEFINITE AND RELATIVE PRONOUNS

GENERALLY SINGULAR		PLURAL	EITHER SINGULAR OR PLURAL
another	neither	both	all
anybody	nobody	few	any
anyone	none	many	enough
anything	no one	others	more
each	nothing	several	most
either	one		some
every	other		that
everybody	somebody		which
everyone	someone		who
everything	something		whose
much			

STRATEGY Ask "Can it be counted?"

Does the pronoun refer to something that *cannot be counted*? Choose singular.

SINGULAR **All** of the <u>food</u> **is** for the camping trip next week.
food = food in general (not countable); *all* = singular

Does the pronoun refer to two or more elements of something that *can be counted*? Choose plural.

PLURAL **All** of the <u>supplies</u> **are** for the camping trip next week.
supplies = many kinds of supplies (countable), such as baking mixes, bottled water, and dried fruit; *all* = plural

Who, which, and that. *Who, which,* and *that* (relative pronouns, see 29b) do not have singular and plural forms, yet the words to which they refer (antecedents) generally do. Choose a singular or plural verb according to the number of the antecedent.

SINGULAR   He likes **a film** that **focuses** on the characters.

PLURAL   I prefer **films** that **combine** action and romance.

Make a habit of noticing the phrases *one of* and *the only one of.* They can create agreement problems when they come before *who, which,* or *that.*

33c
s-v agr

Dr. Tazu is **one** of the engineers who <u>design</u> storage systems.

Who refers to the plural *engineers;* the verb, *design,* is plural. There are other engineers like Dr. Tazu.

Dr. Tazu is **the only one** of the engineers who <u>designs</u> storage systems.

Who refers to the singular *Dr. Tazu;* the verb, *designs,* is singular. Dr. Tazu is the only one who designs storage systems.

Each and every. Your placement of *each* or *every* can create a singular (*each one*) or plural (*they each*) meaning.

Each before compound subject + singular verb
Each supervisor and manager <u>checks</u> the logs daily.

Each after compound subject + plural verb
The supervisors and managers **each** <u>check</u> the logs daily.

ESL ADVICE: QUANTIFIERS

A **quantifier**—a word like *each, one,* or *many*—indicates the amount or quantity of a subject.

EXPRESSIONS FOLLOWED BY A PLURAL NOUN **+** A SINGULAR VERB
Each of/Every one of/One of/None of   the **students** <u>lives</u> on campus.

EXPRESSIONS FOLLOWED BY A PLURAL NOUN **+** A PLURAL VERB
Several of/Many of/Both of   the **students** <u>live</u> off campus.

In some cases, the noun after the expression determines the verb form.

EXPRESSIONS FOLLOWED BY EITHER A SINGULAR OR A PLURAL VERB

noncount noun + singular verb
Some of/Most of/All of/A lot of   the **produce** <u>is</u> fresh.

	plural noun + plural verb
Some of/Most of/All of/A lot of	the **vegetables** <u>are</u> fresh.

MUCH AND MOST (NOT *MUCH OF* OR *MOST OF*) WITH NONCOUNT AND PLURAL NOUNS

NONCOUNT NOUN   Much traffic <u>occurs</u> during rush hour.

PLURAL NOUN   Most Americans <u>live</u> in the cities or suburbs.

OTHER, OTHERS, AND *ANOTHER* AS PRONOUNS OR ADJECTIVES

PRONOUNS
Others + **plural verb:** adds points about a topic; there may be more points.

I enjoy Paris for many reasons. Some reasons are the architecture and gardens; **others are** the wonderful people, culture, and language.

The others **(plural) + plural verb;** *the other* **(singular) + singular verb:** adds the last point or points about the topic; there are no more.

Some hikers favor Craig's plan; **the others want** to follow Tina's.

ADJECTIVES
Another + **singular noun:** adds an idea; there may be more ideas.
Other + **plural noun:** adds more ideas; there may be more ideas.

One strength of our engineering team is our knowledge of the problem. **Another strength** is our experience. **Other strengths** include our communication skills, teamwork, and energy.

The other + **singular or plural noun:** adds the final point or points to be discussed.

Of the two very important sights to see in Paris, one is the Louvre Museum, and **the other one** is the Cathedral of Notre Dame.

One of the major sights in Paris is the Louvre Museum. **The other sights** are the Eiffel Tower, the Champs-Élysées, the Cathedral of Notre Dame, and the Arc de Triomphe.

33d Creating pronoun-antecedent agreement

Agreement between a pronoun and its antecedent (in **number, person,** and **gender**—see 33a) helps readers recognize the link between them.

plural antecedent	pronoun

Campers should treat **their** tents with a mildew-preventing spray.

| **STRATEGY** | **Find the specific word to which a pronoun refers.** |

If you are uncertain about which pronoun form to use, circle or mark the specific word (or words) to which it refers. Then edit either the pronoun or the antecedent so that the two elements match.

INCONSISTENT   Proposals should address its audience.

CLEAR   **Proposals** should address **their audiences**.

CLEAR   **A proposal** should address **its audience**.

33d
p-a agr

A **collective noun** such as *team*, *group*, *clan*, *audience*, *army*, or *tribe* can act as a singular or plural antecedent, depending on whether it refers to the group as a whole or to the members acting separately.

SINGULAR   The **subcommittee** submitted **its** revised report.

PLURAL   The **subcommittee** discussed **their** concerns.

1 Check antecedents linked by *and*, *or*, and *nor*

When a pronoun refers to several things (Luis *and* Jennifer, for example), the pronoun form you choose usually depends on the word that links the elements of the antecedent.

Antecedents joined by *and*. When you form a **compound antecedent** by joining two or more antecedents with *and*, refer to them with a plural pronoun (such as *they*), even if one or more are singular.

Luis and Jenni said that the lab tests <u>they</u> ran were conclusive.

The other students and I admit that the tests <u>we</u> ran were not.

This guideline has two exceptions.

- If a compound antecedent refers to a single person, thing, or idea, use a singular pronoun.

  My colleague and coauthor is <u>someone</u> skilled at lab analysis.

- If you place *each* or *every* before a compound antecedent to single out the individual members of the compound, use a singular pronoun.

  Each of the soil and water samples arrives in <u>its</u> own container.

Antecedents joined by *or* or *nor*. When you join the parts of an antecedent with *or* or *nor* (or *either . . . or, neither . . . nor*), make sure the pronoun agrees with the part closer to it.

Neither the manager **nor** the **engineers** wrote their reports on time.

If one part is singular and the other plural, try putting the plural element second or rewriting to avoid an awkward or confusing sentence.

33d
p-a agr

CONFUSING | Either Jim and Al or Dalhat will include the projections in his report.
READER'S REACTION: **Will Jim and Al add to Dalhat's report? Or will the projections go into one of two reports, Dalhat's or Jim and Al's?**

EDITED | Either Dalhat or **Jim** and **Al** will include the projections in their report.

REWRITTEN | Either Dalhat will include the projections in his report, or Jim and Al will include them in theirs.

REWRITTEN | Either Dalhat or Jim and Al will include the projections in the team's report.

2 Watch for pronouns that refer to other pronouns

Many words like *somebody* and *each* (indefinite pronouns; see 29b-5) are singular. The pronouns that refer to them should also be singular.

Somebody on the team left her racket on the court.

Each of the men has his own equipment.

To avoid either sexist language (see 46a) or inconsistency, use *both* a plural pronoun and a plural antecedent, especially when writing for the academic community.

SEXIST | **Everybody** included charts in **his** sales **talk**.

INFORMAL (SPOKEN) | **Everybody** included charts in **their** sales **talks**.

WRITTEN | **All presenters** included charts in **their** sales **talks**.

ESL ADVICE: DEMONSTRATIVE ADJECTIVES OR PRONOUNS

Demonstrative adjectives or **pronouns** are either singular (*this, that*) or plural (*these, those*), depending on the noun being modified. (See 29b.)

INCONSISTENT | This crystals of water make snowflakes.

BOTH PLURAL | **These crystals** of water make snowflakes.

INCONSISTENT | Those snowflake crystal is made of frozen water.

BOTH SINGULAR | **That snowflake crystal** is made of frozen water.

Exercise 1 *(Answers appear on p. 512.)*

Fill in the blanks in the following sentences with verbs that agree in number and person with their subject.

EXAMPLE

Every day I _walk_ past the Valois Cafeteria.

1. The retired men in the neighborhood _____ lunch at the cafeteria.
2. The cafeteria's motto, "See What You Eat," _____ on the sign above the entrance.
3. The restaurant _____ run down.
4. Nonetheless, it _____ a clean and safe place.
5. A sociologist has studied the ways people of different races and cultures _____ with each other at the cafeteria.

33d
p-a agr

Exercise 2

In each of the following sentences, choose the word inside the parentheses that creates subject-verb agreement.

EXAMPLE

The mayor, as well as members of the city council, (has/have) been searching for better ways to fund the zoo.

1. Several large lizards and an eight-foot python (*makes/make*) up the main attractions in the reptile building of the tiny zoo.
2. The displays as well as the building itself (*appears/appear*) well designed and well maintained.
3. The animals each (*displays/display*) good health and behavior.
4. Neither the zoo's overseers nor its director (*is/are*) satisfied with the reptile building and the number of animals on display.
5. Of the zoo's visitors, three-quarters (*says/say*) that the collection should be enlarged.
6. This year the Cajun and Bluegrass Festival (*features/feature*) several new bands.
7. The group *Beausoleil* (*appears/appear*) twice on the program.
8. The Cajun food, along with more familiar snacks, (*does/do*) draw many people to the refreshment tent.
9. The festival staff (*wears/wear*) buttons saying "Ask me for help."
10. Both the dancing lessons and the crafts display (*occupies/occupy*) the same tent.

Exercise 3 *(Answers appear on p. 513.)*

A. For each of the following sentences, give the correct present tense form of the infinitive verb indicated in parentheses.

EXAMPLE

None of the department heads (to have) the same administrative style.

1. Frieda O'Connor is one of those managers who (*to lead*) by example.
2. All the other department heads (*to respect*) her leadership ability.
3. She knows each of the employees who (*to work*) in her department.
4. Each year, Alberti and Campos Design Associates (*to give*) a plaque and a bonus to the employee with the highest rating on a peer survey.
5. The award, both the plaque and the money, (*to be*) given to Frieda almost every other year.

33
agr

B. Correct the errors that have been introduced into the following passage from Thomas R. McDonough's "Is Anyone Out There?" Not all the sentences contain an error, and some may have more than one. If correcting an error results in an awkward sentence, rewrite, but do not do so simply to avoid dealing with an agreement problem.

Each of the scientists involved in the search are pretty sure something is out there. A lot of numbers, some high and some low, is thrown around to express the probability of intelligent life somewhere else in the universe. Here is some figures that are middle-of-the-road. There is an estimated four hundred billion stars in the Milky Way. Planets may be fairly common, so you can figure one out of every ten of these stars have planets, which equals forty billions stars with planets. But how many of these places seems suitable for life? Neither too hot nor too cold is the conditions needed for life forms similar to our own. An atmosphere along with some water are also necessary. In our solar system only Earth qualifies, though Mars and Venus each comes close. Let us be conservative and estimate that only one of each solar system's planets fit the pattern. That's still forty billion habitable planets.

Exercise 4

Correct any errors in pronoun-antecedent agreement in the following sentences. You may need to change other parts of a sentence besides the pronoun or the antecedent. Each sentence can be corrected in more than one way.

EXAMPLE

        People   *like*

~~A person~~ who ~~likes~~ camping should no longer feel they are unusual.

1. In any circle of friends, several are likely to say that he or she enjoys camping.
2. Everyone who goes camping needs to pay attention to their equipment.
3. All hikers should select good shoes and socks to protect your feet.

4. A camper or a hiker needs to choose their clothing carefully, paying attention to comfort, durability, and protection as well as style.
5. Both regular campers and occasional campers should be willing to put his or her money into well-designed tents, sleeping bags, and cooking equipment.
6. Each store or chain of stores in the retail camping industry meets the needs of their customers in a different way.
7. A store catering to campers and the hiker usually offers him or her a wide choice of equipment at different prices.
8. Eddie Bauer or L. L. Bean provides mail-order service to his customers.
9. A camping supplies and athletic equipment store may provide a narrower range of choices to their customers because of the need to stock sporting goods as well as camping equipment.
10. Nonetheless, any of these businesses should be able to provide you and their other customers with good, safe camping equipment.

34 Using Adjectives and Adverbs

If you confuse adjectives and adverbs or use them improperly, many readers will notice these errors.

DRAFT   The new medication acts **quick**.

> **READER'S REACTION:** *Quick* doesn't fit here. Maybe the writer is careless or doesn't know what to use.

EDITED   The new medication acts **quickly**.

Academic readers may be especially alert to these differences, but use modifiers carefully in formal contexts, whatever the community.

34a What adjectives and adverbs do

Adjectives and adverbs modify—add to, qualify, focus, limit, or extend the meaning of—other words and thus are called **modifiers**.

34.1

FEATURES OF ADJECTIVES AND ADVERBS

ADJECTIVES

- Modify nouns and pronouns
- Answer "How many?" "What kind?" "Which one (or ones)?" "What size, color, or shape?"
- Include words like *blue*, *complicated*, *good*, and *frightening*
- Include words created by adding endings like *-able*, *-ical*, *-less*, *-ful*, and *-ous* to nouns or verbs (such as *controllable*, *sociological*, *seamless*, *careful*, *nervous*)

ADVERBS

- Modify verbs, adjectives, and other adverbs
- Modify phrases (*almost* beyond the building), clauses (*soon after* I added the last ingredients), and sentences (*Remarkably*, the mechanism was not damaged.)
- Answer "When?" "Where?" "How?" "How often?" "Which direction?" "What degree?"
- Consist mostly of words ending in *-ly*, like *quickly* and *carefully*
- Include some common words that do not end in *-ly*, such as *fast*, *very*, *well*, *quite*, and *late*

You can use most modifiers in three forms, depending on how many things you compare—no other things, two things, or three or more.

POSITIVE	The cab drove **quickly** on the **smooth** road.
COMPARATIVE (2)	The cab drove **more quickly** on the **smoother** road.
SUPERLATIVE (3+)	The cab drove **most quickly** on the **smoothest** road.

ESL ADVICE: ADJECTIVES IN A SERIES

When you use two or more adjectives in a series, you need to place them in the appropriate order before the main noun.

DETERMINER	QUALITY	PHYSICAL DESCRIPTION	NATIONALITY	MATERIAL	QUALIFYING NOUN	MAIN NOUN
that	expensive	smooth black	German	fiberglass	racing	car
four	little	round white		plastic	Ping-Pong	balls
several	beautiful	young red	Japanese		maple	trees

34.2

COMPARATIVE AND SUPERLATIVE FORMS

ADJECTIVES

ONE SYLLABLE
Most add -*er* and -*est* (*pink, pinker, pinkest*).

TWO SYLLABLES
Many add -*er* and -*est* (*happy, happier, happiest*).
Some add either -*er* and -*est* or *more* and *most* (*foggy, foggier, foggiest; foggy, more foggy, most foggy*).

THREE (OR MORE) SYLLABLES
Add *more* and *most* (*plentiful, more plentiful, most plentiful*).

ADVERBS

ONE SYLLABLE
Most add -*er* and -*est* (*quick, quicker, quickest*).

TWO (OR MORE) SYLLABLES
Most add *more* and *most* (*carefully, more carefully, most carefully*).

NEGATIVE COMPARISONS

ADJECTIVES AND ADVERBS
Use *less* and *least* (*less agile, least agile; less clearly, least clearly*).

34a
adj/
adv

IRREGULAR COMPARATIVES AND SUPERLATIVES

ADJECTIVE	COMPARATIVE	SUPERLATIVE
bad	worse	worst
good	better	best
ill (harsh, unlucky)	worse	worst
a little	less	least
many	more	most
much	more	most
some	more	most
well (healthy)	better	best

ADVERB		
badly	worse	worst
ill (badly)	worse	worst
well (satisfactorily)	better	best

34b Editing adjectives and adverbs

Because not all adverbs end in -*ly* and some adjectives do (*friendly*, *lonely*), you can't always rely on -*ly* to help you choose a modifier.

1 Figure out what a modifier does in a sentence

First try to analyze what the modifier will do in your sentence.

- Do you need an adjective? Adjectives answer the questions "How many?" "What kind?" "Which one (or ones)?" or "What size, color, or shape?"
- Or do you need an adverb? Adverbs answer the questions "When?" "Where?" "How?" "How often?" "Which direction?" or "What degree?"

DRAFT   Write **careful** so that the directions are clear.

QUESTION: **Write *how*? This word answers an adverb question.**

EDITED   Write **carefully** so that the directions are clear.

The word modified also can tell you whether to use an adverb or adjective.

STRATEGY **Draw an arrow.**

Point to the word that is modified. If this word acts as a noun or pronoun, modify it with an adjective; if it acts as a verb, adjective, or adverb, modify it with an adverb.

DRAFT   The insulation underwent **remarkable** quick deterioration.

CONNECTION: *Remarkable* modifies *quick* (and answers the adverb question "How quick?"). *Quick* in turn modifies *deterioration* (and answers the adjective question "What kind of deterioration?") Replace *remarkable* with an adverb.

EDITED   The insulation underwent **remarkably** quick deterioration.

2 Check the sentence pattern

Verbs such as *look*, *feel*, and *prove* can show both states of being (**linking verbs**) and activities (**action verbs**). The verb *is* always acts as a linking verb. Choose an adjective for a state of being; choose an adverb for an action or activity.

subject	linking verb	complement (adjective)
The room	smelled	musty.
The procedure	proved	unreliable.

ADJECTIVE (BEING)	The metal cover over the motor <u>turned</u> **hot**.
ADVERB (ACTION)	The large wheel <u>turned</u> **quickly**.
ADJECTIVE	The movement <u>grew</u> **rapid**. [The motion became quick.]
ADVERB	The movement <u>grew</u> **rapidly**. [The group spread its ideas.]

3 Pay special attention to *real/really, sure/surely, bad/badly,* and *good/well*

34b adj/ adv

Common uses of *real/really, sure/surely, bad/badly,* and *good/well* may be acceptable in speech but not in other settings.

INFORMAL SPEECH   I feel **badly** that our group argues so much.

READER'S REACTION: **Someone who *feels badly* has a poor sense of touch.**

BAD/BADLY; GOOD/WELL

- Use *bad* (adjective) with linking verbs such as *is, seems,* or *appears* (see 29c, 30a-2).

  I feel **bad** that our group argues so much. [not *badly*]

- Use *badly* (adverb) with action verbs.

  The new breathing apparatus <u>works</u> **badly**. [not *bad*]

- Use *good* (adjective) with linking verbs.

  The chef's new garlic dressing <u>tastes</u> **good**. [not *well*]

- Use *well* (adverb) with action verbs unless it refers to health.

  The new pump <u>works</u> **well**. [not *good*]

REAL/REALLY; SURE/SURELY

- Use *really* (adverb) to modify an adjective like *fast, efficient,* or *hot*.

  Lu Ming is **really** <u>efficient</u>. [not *real*]

  Lu Ming works **really** <u>efficiently</u>. [not *real*]

- Use *surely* (adverb) to modify adjectives like *misleading, outdated,* or *courageous*.

  This diagram is **surely** <u>misleading</u>. [not *sure*]

4 Pay attention to comparisons and double negatives

Someone with only two children may say, "She's my oldest." In writing, however, you need to be more precise.

To compare two things, use the **comparative form** (*-er* or *more*); to compare three or more, use the **superlative form** (*-est* or *most*).

INACCURATE   The survey covered four age groups: 20–29, 30–44, 45–59, and 60+. Those in the older group smoked least.

> **READER'S REACTION:** Does this mean that the people in the older *groups* smoked least or that the people in the *oldest* group smoked least?

PRECISE   The survey covered four age groups: 20–29, 30–44, 45–59, and 60+. Those in the **oldest group** smoked least.

Double comparatives. Most readers will not accept a double comparative (combining the *-er* form and *more*) or a double superlative (combining the *-est* form and *most*).

DRAFT   Jorge is the **most agilest** athlete in the squadron.

EDITED   Jorge is the **most agile** athlete in the squadron.

Illogical comparatives. Some adjectives and adverbs such as *unique*, *impossible*, *pregnant*, *dead*, *gone*, *perfectly*, and *entirely* cannot logically take comparative or superlative form.

ILLOGICAL   Gottlieb's "Nightscape" is a **most unique** painting.

> **READER'S REACTION:** How can a thing be *more* or *most* if it is unique— the only one?

LOGICAL   Gottlieb's "Nightscape" is a **unique** painting.

SERIOUS ERROR

Double negatives. Informal speech and dialects may combine negatives such as *no*, *none*, *not*, *never*, *hardly*, *scarcely*, and *haven't* and *don't* (formed with *n't*, abbreviating *not*). In writing, however, readers are likely to feel that two negatives used together—a **double negative**—cancel each other out.

DRAFT   The nurses **can't hardly** manage routine care, much less emergencies.

> **READER'S REACTION:** This sounds more like a conversation than a staffing report.

EDITED   The nurses **can hardly** manage routine care, much less emergencies.

PART 9

Editing Sentence Problems

35 Sentence Fragments

If you punctuate a group of words as a sentence when they do not actually form a complete sentence, you are likely to irritate readers and undermine your authority as a writer.

PARTS MISSING   The insurance company processing the claim.

> READER'S REACTION: **Something is missing. What did the company *do*?**

EDITED   **The insurance company** processing the claim <u>sent</u> a check.

Despite having a capital letter at the beginning and a period at the end, a **sentence fragment** is only part of a sentence, not a complete sentence.

A fragment is considered the most serious sentence-level error by many college instructors as well as workplace and public readers. On occasion, an **intentional fragment** may create emphasis or a change of pace, especially in imaginative writing (see 35c). An unintentional fragment, however, forces readers to do the writer's job, mentally reattaching a word group to a nearby sentence or supplying missing information. If you make readers do your work, they may be too distracted to attend to your ideas and may harshly judge your writing (and you as a writer).

35a
frag

SERIOUS ERROR

35a Sentence fragments

Before you can edit fragments effectively, you need to be able to distinguish complete sentences from word groups missing a subject or a verb (see 30a) and from clauses detached from sentences to which they belong.

1 Look for a subject and a verb

A **complete sentence** contains both a subject and a complete verb, expressed or implied. If a word group lacks either, it's a fragment.

> **STRATEGY**   Ask questions.
>
> **Sentence Test 1:** Ask *Who* (or *what*) *does*? Or *Who* (or *what*) *is*?
>
> • Does a word group answer "Who?" or "What?" If not, it *lacks a subject* and is a fragment.

FRAGMENT   Also needs a family counselor.

> READER'S REACTION: **I can't tell *who* (or *what*) needs a counselor.**

EDITED   **Hope Clinic** also needs a family counselor.

In an imperative sentence (see 30d-2), the subject *you* is understood and needn't be stated.

IMPERATIVE   [**You**] Use the spectrometer to test for the unknown chemical.

• Does a word group answer "Does?" or "Is?" If not, it *lacks a verb* and is a fragment.

FRAGMENT   The new policy to provide health care coverage on the basis of hours worked each week.

READER'S REACTION: **I can't tell what the new policy *does* or *is*.**

EDITED   The new policy **provides** health care coverage on the basis of hours worked each week.

Sentence Test 2: See if you can turn a word group into a question that can be answered *yes* or *no*. If you can, the word group is a sentence.

WORD GROUP   They bought a van to carry the equipment.

QUESTION   Did they buy a van to carry the equipment?

CONCLUSION   The word group is a sentence.

WORD GROUP   Bought the building for a warehouse.

QUESTION   Did _____ buy the building for a warehouse?

CONCLUSION   The question doesn't have a subject, so the word group is a fragment.

EDITED   **Johnson Plumbing** bought the building for a warehouse.

WORD GROUP   The company providing repairs for our computers.

QUESTION   Does the company **providing** repairs for our computers?

CAUTION: **Do not begin the question with *is*, *are*, *has*, or *have*, or you may unintentionally provide a verb for the word group being tested.**

CONCLUSION   *Providing* can't act as the verb in its current form, so this is a fragment.

EDITED   The company **is** providing repairs for our computers.

35a
frag

Confusing verbs and verbals. In checking for fragments, be careful not to mistake a **verbal** for a verb. Verbals include participles (*testing, tested*), infinitives (*to test*), and gerunds (*testing*) (see 30b-4). A verbal alone can never act as the verb in a sentence. If you add words like *is, has, can,* or *should* (helping verbs, see 31d), you can turn verbals into verbs (*was testing, should test*).

RECOGNIZING A SENTENCE

A **sentence**—also called a **main** (or **independent**) **clause**—is a word group with a subject and verb that can stand alone.

SENTENCE   **The hungry bears** were hunting food.

SENTENCE   Because spring snows had damaged many plants, **the hungry bears** were hunting food in urban areas.

A **subordinate** (or **dependent**) **clause** has a subject and a predicate, yet it cannot stand on its own as a sentence because it begins with a subordinating word like *because, although, which,* or *that* (see 42c).

FRAGMENT   Because **spring snows** had damaged many plants.

A **phrase** is a word group that lacks a subject, a predicate, or both. It cannot stand alone.

FRAGMENTS   were hunting   in urban areas   the hungry bears

35a
frag

2 Look for words like *although, because, that,* and *since*

Pay attention to word groups containing a subject and a verb but beginning with subordinators such as *although, if, because,* or *that* (see the list in 42c). These words tell readers to regard the clause that follows as part of a larger statement.

Once you have identified a word group beginning with a subordinator or with a relative pronoun (*that, what, which,* or *who;* see 32a), check whether it is attached to a main clause—a cluster of words that can stand on its own as a sentence (see box, above). If the word group is unattached, it is a fragment.

FRAGMENT   Residents love the mild climate. Which **has encouraged outdoor events**.

EDITED   Residents love the mild climate, **which** has encouraged outdoor events.

3 Pay attention to *for example* and verbal fragments

Word groups beginning with phrases like *for example, such as,* or *for instance* are sometimes disconnected from sentences and mistakenly made to stand on their own. Often, too, verbal phrases (verbal plus object and modifiers, 30b-4) are detached from related sentences and asked, inappropriately, to stand on their own.

35b Editing sentence fragments

SERIOUS
ERROR

You can correct sentence fragments in four ways.

1 Supply the missing element

35.1

FRAGMENT **The judge allowing adopted children to meet their natural parents.**

EDITED
(VERB ADDED) The judge **favors** allowing adopted children to meet their natural parents.

2 Attach the fragment to a nearby main clause. Rewrite if necessary

FRAGMENT Trauma centers give prompt care to heart attack victims. Because **rapid treatment can minimize heart damage.**

ATTACHED Trauma centers give prompt care to heart attack victims **because** rapid treatment can minimize heart damage.

FRAGMENT **Introducing competing varieties of crabs into the same tank.** He did this in order to study aggression.

REWRITTEN He **introduced** competing varieties of crabs into the same tank in order to study aggression.

35b
frag

3 Drop a subordinating word, turning a fragment into a sentence

FRAGMENT **Although** several people argued against the motion. It still passed by a majority.

EDITED Several people argued against the motion. It still passed by a majority.

4 Rewrite a passage to eliminate a fragment

FRAGMENT Some sports attract many participants in their fifties, sixties, and even seventies. **For example, tennis and bowling**.

EDITED
(ATTACHED) Some sports, **such as tennis and bowling,** attract many participants in their fifties, sixties, and even seventies.

REWRITTEN
(EMPHASIZED) Some sports attract many participants in their fifties, sixties, and even seventies. For example, **tennis and bowling appeal to older adults year-round.**

35c Using partial sentences

In magazines, campaign literature, advertisements, and even well-written essays, you may encounter **partial sentences**—sentence fragments used intentionally, effectively, but sparingly. Partial sentences can call attention to details ("Deep rose, not red."), emphasize ideas ("Wilson. For the future."), heighten contrasts ("And in the last lane, my brother."), or add transition ("Next, the results."). Other uses include informal questions and answers ("Where?" "On my desk.") and exclamations ("Too bad!").

- Use partial sentences only when readers are likely to accept them.
- When in doubt, seek a reader's advice, or look at comparable writing.
- Have a clear purpose—describing, emphasizing, or contrasting.
- Be sure readers can supply missing elements or connect word groups.
- Make sure readers won't mistake your partial sentence for a fragment.

Exercise 1

Indicate which of the following word groups are sentence fragments and which are complete sentences. Correct the sentence fragments by supplying any information necessary to make complete sentences.

EXAMPLE

is

Our job ˄ to find a new head for nursing services.

1. Several people applying for the job.
2. The job description in the newspaper asks for someone who is a good administrator and also an innovator.
3. Is able to convince fellow workers to develop their own innovative staffing plan and present it to the hospital administration.
4. Julie Kim, the prior head of nursing services responsible for so much turmoil during her time in the job and also so many improvements in the way nurses interact with patients and physicians.
5. A study suggesting that nursing administrators develop in-service programs to create improved morale among the professional staff and also better patient care.

Exercise 2   *(Answers appear on p. 513.)*

Indicate which of the following word groups are sentence fragments and which are complete sentences. Correct all the sentence fragments by supplying any information necessary to make complete sentences or by attaching a fragment to an adjacent main clause.

EXAMPLE

Although many people think that afternoon sleepiness is caused by a heavy lunch, ˄Researchers say this is not true.

1. People such as interns and truck drivers often feel drowsy. Even though they are aware of a need to stay awake and alert.
2. Having an afternoon nap can greatly increase your alertness. Whether or not you got enough sleep the night before.
3. Almost accidentally, researchers started becoming aware of the importance of naps while they were mapping cycles of drowsiness and alertness we each go through during an entire day.
4. Almost everyone experiences sleepiness and a decline in mental alertness during the afternoon. Because our internal clocks tell us it is time to nap and get out of the sun's strongest rays.
5. Despite a widespread belief that siestas and naps are cultural customs. They actually have a biological base.

Exercise 3

Look through one or more popular magazines, focusing on either the advertising or the articles. Identify ten sentence fragments and list them. Indicate which fragments lack a subject or a verb (or both), and indicate which fragments are modifying clauses that contain a subject and a verb but are controlled by a subordinating word.

Exercise 4 *(Answers appear on p. 513.)*

Correct each of the fragments in the following passages in two different ways.

EXAMPLE

Some innovative rock groups have been touring this year. Drawing large crowds.

Some innovative rock groups have been touring this year. They have been drawing large crowds.

Some innovative rock groups have been touring this year, drawing large crowds.

1. Realizing that musical tastes are probably changing. Many record companies have decided to explore new and newly rediscovered kinds of music.
2. Some formerly popular musical artists no longer have recording contracts. Their sales of CDs having dropped drastically.
3. In recent campus concerts, jazz artists have attracted large and enthusiastic audiences. Because of their innovative melodies and sounds.
4. The rhythm section of one group consists of a single unusual instrument. An electronic instrument making sounds like a drum but looking like a guitar.
5. Undecided about whether to sign new groups to long-term contracts. Some companies agree to produce and sell a single CD with an option for future recordings.

35
frag

Exercise 5

Correct each of the fragments in the following passages in two different ways.

EXAMPLE

Living and working in another country creates many challenges for families. For example, arranging for children's schooling.

Living and working in another country creates many challenges for families. Arranging for children's schooling is one such challenge.

1. The armed forces run elementary and secondary schools around the world. To provide education for dependents.
2. Japanese executives working in North America worry about educating their children in the Japanese language. And worry about whether they will fit into Japanese culture when they are adults.
3. Americans and Canadians working outside North America often look for schools conducted in English. To make sure their children will be prepared to attend college when the families return home.
4. The modern world makes many demands on parents. Who must spend considerable time and energy educating their children.
5. Whoever grows up with knowledge of two different cultures. I think that person will have some distinct advantages.

Exercise 6

Identify the fragments in the following word groups. Then combine word groups to form a paragraph consisting of complete sentences. Feel free to alter wording or add information necessary to make the paragraph interesting and clear.

1. One store chain asks people to provide an address when cashing a check. And uses the information to create a mailing list for its advertising.
2. As a result, people who buy two pairs of pants and a few blouses are going to be receiving something in the mail each week for the next few months. For instance, a colorful flyer about home furnishings or automobile accessories.
3. Some people resent this marketing strategy. And complain to the post office or the company itself.
4. Lots of people consider advertising brochures fun to read. And a way to make shopping easier.
5. I think they are one of the many small irritations we encounter every day. Such as free samples of useless products and computerized telephone calls.

36 Comma Splices and Fused Sentences

You can easily confuse and annoy readers if you inappropriately join two or more sentences using either a comma only (**comma splice**) or no punctuation at all (**fused sentence**). If you don't clearly mark the parts and boundaries of a sentence, readers may have to puzzle over its meaning.

36.1

COMMA SPLICE CBS was founded in 1928 by William S. Paley, his uncle and his father sold him a struggling radio network.

> READER'S REACTION: **At first I thought CBS had three founders: Paley, his uncle, and his father. Then I realized that Paley probably bought the network from his relatives.**

EDITED CBS was founded in 1928 by William S. Paley ; his uncle and his father sold him a struggling radio network.

36a
cs/fs

FUSED SENTENCE The city had only one swimming pool without an admission fee the pool was poorly maintained.

> READER'S REACTION: **I can't decide whether the single pool in town is poorly maintained or the only free pool is in bad shape.**

EDITED The city had only one swimming pool , but without an admission fee, the pool was poorly maintained.

A **comma splice** links what could be two sentences (two main or independent clauses) by a comma alone. A **fused sentence** (or **run-on sentence**) joins what could be two sentences without any punctuation mark or connecting word to establish clear sentence boundaries. These errors are likely to occur when you draft quickly or when you write sentences with the same subject, with related or contrasting ideas, or with one illustrating the other.

36a Comma splices

To find comma splices, look for commas scattered between word groups that could stand on their own as sentences. Join these word groups by more than a comma alone.

COMMA SPLICE The typical Navajo husband serves as a trustee, the wife and her children own the family's property.

EDITED The typical Navajo husband serves as a trustee , but the wife and her children own the family's property.

> READER'S REACTION: **Until you added *but*, I missed your point about the woman playing a more important role than the man.**

36b Fused sentences

Fused sentences may be any length, but look especially for long sentences with little or no internal punctuation. If your sentence seems to contain more than one statement, check for appropriate punctuation and connecting words.

FUSED SENTENCE   The scientists had trouble identifying the fossil skeleton it resembled that of both a bird and a lizard.
WRITER'S REACTION: **I've made two statements here.**

EDITED   The scientists had trouble identifying the fossil skeleton **because** it resembled that of both a bird and a lizard.
READER'S REACTION: **Adding *because* separates the two main points and makes the ideas easier to understand.**

36c Editing comma splices and fused sentences

36c
cs/fs

Here are six strategies for correcting comma splices and fused sentences. Choose a strategy that highlights your ideas and creates emphasis.

1 Create separate sentences. (____. ____.)

COMMA SPLICE   The sport calls for a total of fourteen people (or twelve people and two dogs) divided into two teams, they throw a disk called a Frisbee up and down a field.

EDITED   The sport calls for a total of fourteen people (or twelve people and two dogs) divided into two teams● They throw a disk called a Frisbee up and down a field.

FUSED SENTENCE   Football does not cause the most injuries among student athletes gymnastics is the most dangerous sport.

EDITED   Football does not cause the most injuries among student athletes● Gymnastics is the most dangerous sport.

2 Use a comma plus *and, but, or, for, nor, so,* or *yet.* (____ , and ____.)

When main clauses convey equally important ideas, try linking them with a comma plus a coordinating conjunction telling how they relate.

COMMA SPLICE   The finance department has reviewed the plan, the operations department is still analyzing it.

EDITED   The finance department has reviewed the plan● **but** the operations department is still analyzing it.

FUSED SENTENCE	The emergency room is understaffed it still performs well.
EDITED	The emergency room is understaffed **,** **yet** it still performs well.

Three or more closely related clauses can be punctuated as a series to emphasize their connection. Especially for the academic community, include both a comma and a coordinating conjunction before the last item (see 48d).

SERIES OF CLAUSES	We collected the specimens, we cleaned them **,** **and** we measured them.

3 Make one clause subordinate. (*Because ____, ____.*)

Subordinators such as *although, when, because, until, where,* and *unless* (see 42c) can specify a range of relationships between clauses, as can relative pronouns such as *who, which,* or *that* (see 30a). A **subordinate clause** includes the subordinator plus a subject and a verb; it cannot stand alone as a sentence.

COMMA SPLICE	Automobiles are increasingly complex, skilled mechanics may spend several weeks a year in training.
EDITED	**Because** automobiles are increasingly complex **,** skilled mechanics may spend several weeks a year in training.
FUSED SENTENCE	Margaret Atwood is best known for her novels her essays and poems are also worth reading.
EDITED	**Although** Margaret Atwood is best known for her novels **,** her essays and poems are also worth reading.

36c
cs/fs

4 Use a semicolon. (____; ____.)

Use a semicolon to join two main clauses and emphasize their similar importance. (See 49a.)

COMMA SPLICE	An autopilot is a device that corrects drift, the system senses and reacts to changes in the aircraft's motion.
EDITED	An autopilot is a device that corrects drift **;** the system senses and reacts to changes in the aircraft's motion.
FUSED SENTENCE	Most colleges offer alternatives to four years on campus study abroad, exchange programs with other schools, and cooperative programs are common.
EDITED	Most colleges offer alternatives to four years on campus **;** study abroad, exchange programs with other schools, and cooperative programs are common.

36.2

5 Use wording like *however, moreover, for example,* and *in contrast* plus a semicolon. (___; however, ___.)

However, consequently, moreover, and other **conjunctive adverbs** (see 42a–b) specify relationships between clauses. You can use transitional expressions such as *in contrast* and *in addition* for similar purposes.

COMMA SPLICE   To draw the human body, you must understand it, therefore, art students sometimes dissect cadavers.

EDITED   To draw the human body, you must understand it; therefore, art students sometimes dissect cadavers.

FUSED SENTENCE   Chickens reach market size within months the lobster takes six to eight years.

EDITED   Chickens reach market size within months; in contrast, the lobster takes six to eight years.

Conjunctive adverbs and transitional expressions can begin the second main clause or appear within it. Set them off with a comma or commas; join the clauses with a semicolon (see 49a-1).

BEGINNING OF CLAUSE   The Great Lakes were once heavily polluted; however, recently fish and other wildlife have returned.

MIDDLE OF CLAUSE   The Great Lakes were once heavily polluted; recently, however, fish and other wildlife have returned.

END OF CLAUSE   The Great Lakes were once heavily polluted; recently fish and other wildlife have returned, however.

6 Use a colon. (___: ___.)

When a clause summarizes, illustrates, or restates a preceding clause, you can join the two with a colon. (See 49b-3.)

COMMA SPLICE   Foreign study calls for extensive language preparation, vaccinations and a passport are not enough.

EDITED   Foreign study calls for extensive language preparation: vaccinations and a passport are not enough.

ESL ADVICE: *BECAUSE* AND *BECAUSE OF*

The subordinator *because* introduces a clause with a subject and verb; the preposition *because of* introduces a phrase with its object.

DRAFT	Because of the pay is low, José must look for another job.
EDITED	**Because** the pay is low, José must look for another job.
EDITED	**Because of** the low pay, José must look for another job.

ESL ADVICE: CONNECTING WORDS WITH THE SAME MEANING

Connecting words may have the same meaning but need different punctuation.

COORDINATOR	José likes his job **,** **but** it doesn't pay enough.
CONJUNCTIVE ADVERB	José likes his job **;** **however,** it doesn't pay enough.

36c
cs/fs

Exercise 1

First, use the strategies discussed in 36a and 36c to identify the comma splices in the following passage.

The subarctic region provides little variety in food, therefore, Eskimo diet includes large quantities of meat such as seal and caribou. The cold weather and the available materials determine dressing habits, a loose shirt with a hood, trousers, stockings, and mittens (often made of caribou skin and fur) are a common outfit for men, women, and children alike. Social affairs are important in Eskimo communities, favorite gatherings include carnivals, Christmas parties, and feasts of game brought in by hunters. Children in Eskimo communities begin school at the age of five or six, most quit by the time they are twelve in order to go to work. Boys usually go hunting with their fathers, girls learn to sew and cook.

Next, draw a double vertical line between each of the independent (main) clauses making up the following fused sentences.

EXAMPLE

Casinos used to operate legally in only a few states // they are now springing up all over the country as states make casino gambling legitimate.

1. The gaming industry is one of the fastest-growing industries in some areas it is a major employer.
2. Legalized gambling takes many forms bingo, lotteries, casinos, and video games are run under government supervision in many states.

3. State lotteries are popular they may also encourage people to gamble unwisely.
4. The economic and law enforcement objections to legalized gambling get the most public attention the moral and psychological objections may deserve the most attention.
5. Legalized gambling now goes beyond people in casinos betting on roulette or sports events it includes people playing bingo at a charity event or playing video poker in a family restaurant.

Exercise 2   *(Answers appear on p. 514.)*

Identify and edit in *two* ways each of the following comma splices and fused sentences. Use the methods of revision indicated in brackets after each sentence.

EXAMPLE

Children often fight among themselves, these conflicts pose many challenges for parents. [comma plus coordinating conjunction; semicolon]

Children often fight among themselves, and these conflicts pose many challenges for parents.

Children often fight among themselves; these conflicts pose many challenges for parents.

1. Some parents refuse to become involved in their children's squabbles, they fear the children will resent the interference. [subordination; semicolon]
2. Siblings have special reasons to fight competing for space and playthings or for attention from a parent can turn playmates into rivals. [colon; semicolon plus transitional phrase]
3. Sibling fights offer an opportunity for children to become sensitive to the feelings of others, the arguments pose dangers as well. [comma plus coordinating conjunction; semicolon plus conjunctive adverb]
4. Bickering is common and normal excessive fighting can be a sign of more serious trouble. [semicolon plus conjunctive adverb; separate sentences]
5. By adolescence, most children have worked out compatible relationships with their siblings, they may still occasionally argue. [subordination; comma plus coordinating conjunction]

Exercise 3

Edit each of the following sentences in two ways, using strategies discussed in 36c. You may need to make changes in wording or punctuation.

36
cs/fs

1. One group claims that cattle raising is hard on the environment another group argues that raising wheat and other cereal grains causes water pollution and destroys topsoil.
2. In Central Florida, cattle waste has polluted Lake Okeechobee runoff from fertilizer has greatly increased the growth of algae in the lake.
3. The waters of Long Island's south shore are also polluted the main culprit is lawn fertilizer.
4. In my state, pesticides from potato farming have polluted the groundwater pig and chicken farming have caused problems.
5. Our large population makes a massive farming industry necessary we are going to have to deal with the problems caused by large-scale farming and livestock raising.

37 Pronoun Reference

Readers expect pronouns to make a sentence less repetitive and easier to understand by taking the place of nouns (or other pronouns). For this substitution to work effectively, your readers must recognize the word to which a pronoun refers so they can tell exactly what the sentence means.

AMBIGUOUS REFERENCE   Much of my life with the circus consisted of leading the elephants from the cages and hosing **them** down.

READER'S REACTION: What got hosed down? elephants? cages? both?

EDITED   Much of my life with the circus consisted of hosing the elephants down after leading **them** from **their** cages.

The word to which the pronoun refers is known as its **antecedent** (or **headword**). When **pronoun reference**—the connection between pronoun and antecedent—isn't clear and specific, readers may be confused. By creating clear pronoun reference, you tie ideas and sentences together, clarify their relationships, and focus readers' attention.

37a Unclear pronoun reference

SERIOUS ERROR

If readers say they "get lost" reading your work or "can't figure out what you are saying," make sure each pronoun refers *clearly* to one specific antecedent, either one word or several words acting as a unit.

1 Watch for ambiguous or distant pronoun reference

A pronoun may seem to refer to more than one possible antecedent (**ambiguous reference**) or may be too distant from its antecedent (**remote reference**) for a reader to recognize the connection.

AMBIGUOUS REFERENCE
Robespierre and Danton disagreed over the path the French Revolution should take. **He** believed that the Revolution was endangered by internal enemies.

READER'S REACTION: **I'm lost. Who's *he*? Robespierre or Danton?**

EDITED
Robespierre and Danton disagreed over the path the French Revolution should take. **Robespierre** believed that the Revolution was endangered by internal enemies.

2 Look for vague or implied pronoun reference

If readers have to guess what a pronoun refers to, you may have referred to the entire idea of an earlier passage (**vague** or **broad pronoun reference**) or to an **implied antecedent**, suggested but not stated.

37b
pr ref

IMPLIED ANTECEDENT
A hard frost damaged most of the local citrus groves, but **it** has not yet been determined.

READER'S REACTION: **I'm not sure what *it* means, though I guess it's related to the frost damage.**

STATED
A hard frost damaged most of the local citrus groves, but **the extent of the loss** has not yet been determined.

Certain words—*it, they, you, which, this,* or *that*—are especially likely to refer to vague, implied, or indefinite antecedents. To spot imprecise references, search for these pronouns. In each case, see if you can find an antecedent stated in the passage.

SERIOUS ERROR

37b Editing for clear pronoun reference

Your choices for editing pronoun reference will depend on the particular problem you are trying to correct.

37.1

1 Correcting ambiguous or distant reference

When a pronoun threatens to confuse readers because it refers to two or more possible antecedents (ambiguous reference), you can correct the problem in two ways.

1. **Replace** the troublesome pronoun with a noun.
2. **Reword** the sentence.

AMBIGUOUS REFERENCE	Detaching the measuring probe from the glass cylinder is a delicate job because **it** breaks easily.
	READER'S REACTION: **Which is so fragile, the probe or the cylinder?**
REPLACED WITH NOUN	Detaching the measuring probe from the glass cylinder is a delicate job because **the probe** breaks easily.
REWORDED	Because the measuring probe breaks easily, detaching it from the glass cylinder is a delicate job.

If a pronoun is too far away from its antecedent to refer to it clearly, either move the pronoun closer or replace it with a noun.

2 Editing vague or implied reference

Keeping pronouns and antecedents together is especially important for word groups beginning with *who*, *which*, and *that* (relative pronouns). Avoid confusion by placing the pronoun right after its antecedent.

CONFUSING	In my old bedroom, I saw a stale piece of the bubble gum under **the dresser that I loved to chew as a boy.**
EDITED	In my old bedroom, I saw under the dresser a stale piece of **the bubble gum that I loved to chew as a boy.**

37b
pr ref

Sometimes you need to follow *which*, *this*, or *that* with an explanation of the pronoun's referent.

VAGUE REFERENCE	Redfish have suffered from oil pollution and the destruction of their mangrove swamp habitat. **This** has led to a rapid decline in the redfish population.
	READER'S REACTION: **Does *this* refer to the destruction of habitat, to oil pollution, or to both?**
SPECIFIED	Redfish have suffered from oil pollution and the destruction of their mangrove swamp habitat. **This combination** has led to a rapid decline in the redfish population.
EXPLAINED	Redfish have suffered from oil pollution and the destruction of their mangrove swamp habitat. **That increasingly serious pair of challenges** has led to a rapid decline in the redfish population.

You is commonly accepted in letters, emails, and other kinds of writing where it means, "you, the reader" (see 39a). When *you* refers to people and situations in general, however, it may lead to imprecise sentences.

INDEFINITE ANTECEDENT	In Brazil, **you** pay less for an alcohol-powered car than for a gasoline-powered one.
	READER'S REACTION: **Who is *you*? I'm not likely to buy a car in Brazil.**

REPLACED WITH NOUN	In Brazil, **consumers** pay less for an alcohol-powered car than for a gasoline-powered one.
REWRITTEN	In Brazil, alcohol-powered cars cost less than gasoline-powered ones.

3 Clarifying the antecedent to which the pronoun refers

Many academic readers will consider a possessive noun used as an antecedent an error, although the pattern is common in informal writing. Pair a possessive noun with a possessive pronoun (*Kristen's . . . hers*), or rewrite to eliminate the possessive noun.

UNCLEAR	The **company's** success with a well-known jazz fusion artist led **it** to contracts with other musicians.
EDITED (POSSESSIVE PAIR)	The **company's** success with a well-known jazz fusion artist led to **its** contracts with other musicians.
EDITED (NO POSSESSIVE)	Success with a well-known jazz fusion artist led the company to other contracts.
INAPPROPRIATE	In William Faulkner's *The Sound and the Fury*, he begins the story from the point of view of a mentally retarded person.
EDITED	In *The Sound and the Fury*, **William Faulkner** begins the story from the point of view of a mentally retarded person.

37b
pr ref

4 Reworking a passage to create a reference chain

You can guide readers through a passage using a chain of pronouns to connect sentences. A **reference chain** begins with a statement of your topic, which is then linked to pronouns (or nouns) later in the passage.

UNCLEAR

Sand paintings were a remarkable form of Pueblo art. An artist would sprinkle dried sand of different colors, ground flower petals, corn pollen, and similar materials onto the floor to create **them**. The sun, moon, and stars as well as animals and objects linked to the spirits were represented in the figures **they** contained. Encouraging the spirits to send good fortune to humans was **their** purpose.
Because *them* and *they* are buried at the ends of sentences in the middle of the paragraph, readers may lose sight of the topic, sand paintings.

EDITED TO CREATE A REFERENCE CHAIN

Sand paintings were a remarkable form of Pueblo art. To create **them**, an artist would sprinkle dried sand of different colors, ground flower petals, corn pollen, and similar materials onto the floor. **They** contained figures representing the sun, moon, and stars as well as animals and objects linked to the spirits. **Their** purpose was to encourage the spirits to send good fortune to humans.

STRATEGY   Techniques for developing a reference chain.

• State the antecedent clearly in the opening sentence.
• Link the antecedent to pronouns in sentences that follow.
• Be sure no other possible antecedents interrupt the links in the chain.
• Don't interrupt the chain and then try to return to it later.
• Call attention to the links by giving the pronouns prominent positions (usually beginning sentences); vary their positions only slightly.

Exercise 1   *(Possible answers appear on p. 515.)*

Rewrite each of the following sentences to create clear pronoun reference.

EXAMPLE

Someone needs to pick up the weekend shipment ~~at the airport~~ that
          at the airport
may arrive late Saturday night.
              ∧

37b
pr ref

1. Both Carlo and Andy agree that he will be responsible for getting the cartons of replacement parts from the air terminal.
2. The accountant has told his client that he will be answerable for any problems with billing.
3. Airfreight offers weekend shipment and is cheaper, which means that work doesn't have to stop on Monday morning while workers wait for delivery of the replacement parts.
4. The van used to pick up shipments is the old one the company's owner purchased right after her divorce which is covered with rust spots.
5. The sales projections used to order supplies are often inaccurate because the sales manager calculates them using a formula on a spreadsheet that is overly optimistic.

Exercise 2   *(Answers appear on p. 515.)*

Revise the following sentences to eliminate vague pronoun reference and provide specific antecedents.

EXAMPLE
                    The committee's report
~~In the committee's report it~~∧ points out that students generally benefit from participating in a music program.

(*or* In its report, the committee points out . . .)

1. Many people study a musical instrument in high school though few students intend to become one.
2. At most secondary schools they offer a variety of music programs.
3. Last February, the town began investigating the quality of its high school band program, but it has not yet been completed.
4. In many regional high schools in the West, the band's large size mirrors the role it plays in the school's social life.

Exercise 3

Revise the following sentences to correct inappropriate pronoun references. Indicate which sentences, if any, contain appropriate pronoun reference.

EXAMPLE

Many scholars ~~which~~ *who* are interested in Buddhism have begun to study Tibetan religious ^practices.

1. The gathering was addressed by the Dalai Lama, a man which is one of the spiritual leaders of Tibetan Buddhism.
2. Tibetan Buddhism is characterized by large monastic organizations who practice yoga and other spiritual and intellectual rituals.
3. It is also true that this form of Buddhism retains features that it inherited from the folk religions of Tibet.
4. Up until the recent Chinese invasion, that occurred in 1959, Tibetan life was dominated by religious practices.
5. Although Lamaism has its greatest influence in Tibet and in countries who are nearby, such as Nepal and Mongolia, it is beginning to spread its influence in the West, including North America.

Exercise 4

At a library, find a magazine with somewhat complicated, information-filled articles. Choose an article that interests you, and identify several paragraphs in which the author uses some of the pronoun reference patterns discussed in this chapter. Identify each of the pronoun reference strategies and decide why the author used each one.

Exercise 5

Revise the following sentences so that they form a reference chain emphasizing some ideas and details more than others.

When it comes to reading material, Americans have some clear favorites. In terms of circulation, the top five newspapers in the country are the *Wall Street Journal*, *USA Today*, the *New York Daily News*, the *Los Angeles Times*, and the *New York Times*. Sales of softbound books far outnumber sales of hardbound books. Our favorite subject areas for books are medicine, history, fiction, sociology and economics, religion, and technology. The top three magazines in terms of revenue are *Time*, *Sports*

Illustrated, and *People*. More people subscribe to *Modern Maturity* and the *AARP Bulletin* than to any other magazines, including *Reader's Digest*, which is number three on the subscription list. *1,001 Home Ideas* and *The Elks Magazine* have larger paid circulations than *Vogue*, *Rolling Stone*, and *Mademoiselle*.

38 Misplaced, Dangling, and Disruptive Modifiers

38a
mm/
dm

Readers sometimes see a sentence like a string of beads. If the silver bead is designed to reflect the red one, they expect to find those beads placed next to each other just as they expect to find related parts of a sentence together.

MISPLACED MODIFIER	The wife believes she sees a living figure behind the wallpaper in the story by Charlotte Perkins Gilman, which adds to her sense of entrapment. READER'S REACTION: **How could a story add to a feeling of entrapment?**
MODIFIER MOVED	The wife **in the story by Charlotte Perkins Gilman** believes she sees a living figure behind the wallpaper, which adds to her sense of entrapment.
MODIFIER MOVED	**In the story by Charlotte Perkins Gilman**, the wife believes she sees a living figure behind the wallpaper, which adds to her sense of entrapment.

In the draft, the modifier is not positioned to relate clearly to the word it modifies. Once the sentence is rearranged, the wife is "in the story," and the wallpaper "adds to her sense of entrapment." If the relationship between a modifier and the word(s) it modifies is unclear, the result will be unanswered questions and confusion.

38a Misplaced, dangling, and disruptive modifiers

When a modifier is poorly positioned or illogically related to the word(s) it is supposed to modify (its **headword**), readers are likely to find a sentence vague, illogical, or unintentionally humorous.

1 Look for misplaced modifiers

A word or word group that is not close enough to its headword is a **misplaced modifier**. It appears to modify some other word or to modify *both* the word before and the word after.

CONFUSING   The caterer served food to the directors standing around the room on flimsy paper plates.

READER'S REACTION: **Surely the directors weren't standing on the plates!**

MODIFIER   The caterer served food **on flimsy paper plates** to the direc-
MOVED   tors standing around the room.

2 Look for dangling modifiers

To find a **dangling modifier**, look for a sentence that begins with a modifier but doesn't name the person, idea, or thing modified. Readers will assume that this modifier refers to the subject of the main clause immediately following. If it doesn't, the modifier dangles.

DANGLING   Looking for a way to reduce complaints from nonsmokers, a new ventilation fan was installed.

READER'S REACTION: **How could a fan look for anything? The sentence never tells me *who* wants to reduce complaints.**

SUBJECT ADDED   Looking for a way to reduce complaints from nonsmokers, **the company installed** a new ventilation fan.

3 Look for disruptive modifiers

Readers generally expect subjects and verbs to stand close to each other. The same is true for other sentence elements—verbs and their objects or complements, for example. Modifiers that come between such elements may be **disruptive modifiers** if they create long and distracting interruptions.

DISRUPTIVE   The researcher, **because he had not worked with chimpanzees before and was unaware of their intelligence**, was surprised when they undermined his experiment.

However, a brief, relevant interruption can add variety and suspense.

CLEAR   The researcher, **unfamiliar with chimpanzees**, was surprised when they undermined his experiment.

How can you tell whether modifiers placed between subject and verb are disruptive? Modifiers that provide information related to both subject and verb are likely to be disruptive because a reader can't tell which they relate to. Modifiers related to the subject alone generally aren't disruptive.

38a
mm/
dm

	subject	modifier

DISRUPTIVE Work on the building, **due to problems with the construc-**
verb
tion permits, was completed three months late.

	subject	modifier	verb

NOT DISRUPTIVE The youth center **that opened last month** has drawn crowds.

ESL ADVICE: POSITION OF MODIFIERS

Some languages clarify the relationship between a modifier and its headword through the form or ending of the words. Because modifiers in English tend to change location, not form, to show which words they describe, the position of a modifier can drastically change its meaning.

38b Editing misplaced, dangling, and disruptive modifiers

38b
mm/
dm

SERIOUS
ERROR

Each kind of modifier problem calls for a slightly different correction strategy.

1 Editing misplaced modifiers

Try these two techniques for editing misplaced modifiers.

- **Move** the modifier closer to the words it should modify.
- **Rewrite** or **modify** a sentence so that the connection between modifier and words to be modified is clear.

Who, which, or *that.* For a clear connection, try to put *who, which,* or *that* immediately after its headword to avoid modifying the wrong word.

38.1

MISPLACED The environmental engineers discovered another tank behind the building that was leaking toxic wastes.
READER'S REACTION: **I know a building can leak, but I'll bet the writer meant that the tank was the culprit.**

MOVED AFTER
HEADWORD Behind the building, the environmental engineers discovered another tank **that** was leaking toxic wastes.

Only, hardly, merely, **and similar words.** In most cases, move a word like *only, almost, hardly, just, merely, simply,* and *even* (**limiting modifiers**) directly before the word to which it applies.

Only charities for children are maintaining their support.
They are the sole charities able to maintain support.

Charities for **only** children are maintaining their support.
The charities are for children from families with one child.

Charities for children are **only** maintaining their support.
They are not increasing the levels of support.

Squinting modifiers. If a modifier appears to modify the wording both before and after it, move this **squinting modifier** to eliminate the ambiguity, or rewrite.

SQUINTING   People who abuse alcohol **often** have other problems.
READER'S REACTION: **Do they abuse alcohol *often* or *often* have other problems?**

EDITED   People who **often abuse alcohol** tend to have other problems.

REWRITTEN   People who abuse alcohol tend to have other problems **as well**.

2 Editing dangling modifiers

When the subject being modified does not appear in the sentence, you have a dangling modifier. You can correct the problem in three ways.

- **Add a subject** to the modifier.

DANGLING   While shopping, the stuffed alligator caught my eye.

SUBJECT ADDED   While **I was** shopping, the stuffed alligator caught my eye.

- **Change the subject** of the main clause.

DANGLING   Jumping into the water to save the drowning swimmer, the crowd applauded the lifeguard.

SUBJECT CHANGED   Jumping into the water to save the drowning swimmer, **the lifeguard** was applauded by the crowd.

- **Rewrite** the entire sentence.

DANGLING   Having debated changes in the regulations for months, the present standards were allowed to continue.
READER'S REACTION: *Who* **is debating? Not the standards!**

REWRITTEN   The commission debated changes in the regulations for months but decided to continue the present standards.

3 Editing disruptive modifiers

To correct problems caused by disruptive modifiers, move them so that sentence elements are near each other just as readers expect.

Readers expect a subject and verb to stand together and an object or complement to come right after the verb.

CLUMSY   Joanne began collecting, **using her survey form**, data for her study of dating preferences.

EDITED   **Using her survey form,** Joanne began collecting data for her study of dating preferences.

If a modifier splits the parts of an infinitive (*to* plus a verb, as in *to enjoy*), readers may have trouble relating the parts. Some readers will find any **split infinitive** irritating, clear or not.

IRRITATING   The dancers moved **to** very rapidly **align** themselves.

EDITED   The dancers moved very rapidly **to align** themselves.

At times, however, a split infinitive may be the most concise alternative.

Our goal is **to** more than **halve** our manufacturing errors.

38b
mm/
dm

Exercise 1   *(Answers appear on p. 515.)*

Identify and correct the misplaced modifiers (words or phrases) in the following sentences. You may decide either to move the modifier or to rewrite the entire sentence.

EXAMPLE

in pet store windows
Puppies spend a lot of time staring at people ~~in pet store windows~~.

1. They decided to buy the beagle puppy confused by the many exotic breeds of dogs.
2. This dog would replace the one killed by a truck running across a busy highway.
3. They forgot to buy a dog bed distracted by the crowd of people in the store.
4. Hurriedly, John sighed and began tearing up newspapers in order to begin house-training the puppy.
5. The parents could hear the children playing outside with the dog yelling and laughing.

Exercise 2   *(Answers appear on p. 516.)*

Each of the following sentences contains either ambiguity caused by a squinting modifier or a limiting modifier that can be moved to different positions. Indicate the type of problem in each sentence.

EXAMPLE

Adults over age thirty who return to college frequently complete both undergraduate and advanced degree programs. *(squinting modifier)*

1. Adults entering college after working or raising a family officially are classified "nontraditional students" by many colleges.
2. "Nontrads" defer college entry often until after a major life event.
3. Following divorce or job loss, returning to college temporarily provides a boost to self-esteem.
4. Experts report that nontraditional students earn high grade point averages easily exceeding those of traditional students.
5. Nonetheless, failing to take into account the special needs of "nontrads" causes them to drop out frequently.

Exercise 3

Revise the following sentences to avoid any misplaced modifiers.

EXAMPLE

Sliding into second base, ~~my leg~~ broke. *(I ... my leg)*

1. The coach tossed out the practice balls to the players, wet and soft from yesterday's rain.
2. They worked on hitting and catching for fifteen minutes before the first game which was the only practice time they had.
3. The coach who was known as a strict disciplinarian of the championship Little League team invented a rigorous new set of conditioning exercises.
4. A proposal to follow the infield fly rule was defeated by the coach's committee which no one understood.
5. The coach is unable to present the award given in memory of Father Baker because he is sick.

Exercise 4

Eliminate dangling modifiers by rewriting each of the following sentences in the *two* ways indicated in brackets.

EXAMPLE

Unable to meet with an advisor, ~~Marion's research was poorly designed.~~ *(Marion designed her research poorly.)* [change subject of main clause; rewrite]

Because Marion was unable to meet with an advisor, she designed her research poorly.

1. Because of a failure to gather enough data, her study was incomplete. [rewrite; add subject to modifier]
2. Lacking the money to pay skilled interviewers, minimally trained volunteers were relied upon. [change subject of main clause; rewrite]

38
mm/
dm

3. Many subjects were not asked appropriate questions because of poor training. [add subject to modifier; change subject of main clause]
4. Anxious and tired, the two-day attempt to write the research report was unsuccessful. [add subject to modifier; change subject of main clause]
5. After spending over twenty hours writing at the computer, the report was still not satisfactory. [rewrite; add subject to modifier]

Exercise 5

Rewrite each of the following sentences to eliminate disruptive modifiers and to make the sentence easier to read.

EXAMPLE

~~The architect,~~ because she was unfamiliar with eighteenth-century interior design and furnishings, *the architect* had to do some research before completing the project.

1. The overall design of a building and its interior decoration ought to thoughtfully and harmoniously work together.
2. Furniture design has at least for the past several centuries been greatly influenced by a handful of designers, including Hepplewhite, Chippendale, Sheraton, and, most recently, Eames.
3. Design in Colonial America, because of economic limitations and social customs, was generally simple and practical.
4. Americans had, by the early 1800s in what is now known as the Federalist period, developed more refined and expensive tastes.
5. Today, magazines like *Architectural Digest* and *House Beautiful* illustrate the tendency for styles in interior design to rapidly change and to add considerably to the cost of a home.

39
shift

39 Making Shifts Consistent

Although readers are willing to shift attention many times, they expect you to make shifts logically consistent and to signal them clearly.

SHIFTED   If **parents** would call the school board, **you** could explain why **we** oppose the proposal.
READER'S REACTION: **I'm confused. Who's who? Who should do what?**

EDITED   If **parents** would call the school board, **they** could explain why **they** oppose the proposal.

EDITED   If **you** would call the school board, **you** could explain why **you** oppose the proposal.

EDITED   If **all of us meeting tonight** would call the school board, **we** could explain why **we** oppose the proposal.

SERIOUS ERROR

39a Shifts in person and number

Watch for unexpected shifts in person and number (see 33c). **Person** refers to the ways you use nouns and pronouns (*I, you, she, they*) to shape the relationship involving you, your readers, and your subject. Switching from one person to another as you refer to the same subject can be illogical. **Number** shows whether words are singular (one) or plural (two or more). Look for confusing shifts between words like *person* and *people* that identify groups or their members.

39a
shift

FIRST, SECOND, AND THIRD PERSON

FIRST PERSON (*I, WE*)
- Use *I* to refer to yourself as the writer or as the subject of an essay.
- Use *we* in a collaborative project when more than one person is author or subject.
- Use *we* for both yourself and your readers when discussing shared experiences or understandings.
- Use *we* in some academic fields such as the study of literature ("In this part of the poem we begin to see . . .") but not in others (for example, chemistry or engineering).
- Use *we* to represent an organization or workgroup.

SECOND PERSON (*YOU*)
- Use *you* to refer directly to the reader.
- Do not use *you* in most kinds of academic and professional writing unless called for by the situation, as in a set of instructions.
- Use *you* in a political, civic, or activist appeal urging readers to action.

THIRD PERSON (*HE, SHE, IT, THEY; ONE, SOMEONE, EACH,* AND OTHER INDEFINITE PRONOUNS)
- Use third person for the ideas, things, and people you are writing about.
- *People* and *person* are third person nouns, as are names of groups of things, ideas, and people (for example, *students, teachers, doctors*).

INCONSISTENT	When **a business executive is** looking for a new job, **they** often consult a placement service.
	READER'S REACTION: **Does _they_ mean business executives as a group? The sentence mentions only one executive.**
EDITED	When **business executives are** looking for **new jobs**, they often consult a placement service.

Check for illogical shifts between singular and plural forms, between first and second person, or between second and third person. Then edit to make the relationships consistent.

INCONSISTENT NUMBER	If **a person has** some money to invest, **they** should seek advice from a financial consultant.
EDITED	If **a person has** some money to invest, **he or she** should seek advice from a financial consultant.
EDITED	If **people have** some money to invest, **they** should seek advice from a financial consultant.
INCONSISTENT PERSON	If a **person** is looking for a higher return on investments, **you** might consider mutual funds.
EDITED	If **you** are looking for a higher return on investments, **you** might consider mutual funds.

39b
shift

39b Shifts in tense and mood

When you change verb tense within a passage, you signal a change in time and the relationship of events in time. Illogical shifts can mislead your readers and contradict your meaning.

39.1

ILLOGICAL SHIFT	Scientists digging in Montana **discovered** nests that **indicated** how some dinosaurs **take care** of their young.
LOGICAL	Scientists digging in Montana **discovered** nests that **indicate** how some dinosaurs **took care** of their young.
	Although the actions of both the dinosaurs and the scientists clearly occurred in the past, _indicate_ (present tense) is appropriate because researchers interpret the evidence in the present.

Make sure you keep verb tenses consistent and logical within a passage. If you begin narrating events in the past tense, avoid shifting suddenly to the present to try to make events more vivid.

INCONSISTENT TENSE	We **had been searching** for a new site for the festival when Tonia **starts yelling**, "I've found the place!"
EDITED	We **had been searching** for a new site for the festival when Tonia **started yelling**, "I've found the place!"

ESL ADVICE: VERB TENSE AND EXPRESSIONS OF TIME

Use both verb tense and expressions of time (*yesterday, today, soon*) to indicate changes in time. Make sure the two are consistent.

INCONSISTENT   I **study** English last year, and now **I worked** for an American company.

EDITED   I **studied** English last year, and now I **work** for an American company.

The **mood** of a verb shows the writer's aim or attitude (see 30d-2): to command or request (**imperative**), to state or question (**indicative**), or to offer a conditional or hypothetical statement (**subjunctive**; see 31h). If you shift mood inappropriately, your sentences may be hard to follow.

INCONSISTENT (IMPERATIVE AND INDICATIVE)
To reduce costs, **distribute** fewer copies of drafts, and **you should encourage** employees to replace paper memos with email messages.

CONSISTENT (IMPERATIVE)
To reduce costs, **distribute** fewer copies of drafts, and **encourage** employees to replace paper memos with email messages.

39c
shift

39c Shifts in active or passive voice

When a verb is in the **active voice**, the agent or doer of the action functions as the subject of the sentence. When a verb is in the **passive voice**, the goal of the action functions as the sentence's subject. (See 31i and 43b-3.)

	subject	verb	object
ACTIVE	The lava flow	**destroyed**	twelve houses.
	agent	action	goal

	subject	verb	
PASSIVE	Twelve houses	**were destroyed**	[by the lava flow].
	goal	action	[agent]

Try to focus on either active or passive voice within a sentence, rewriting if necessary, to use either active or passive voice consistently.

INCONSISTENT   Among the active volcanoes, Kilauea **erupts** most frequently, and over 170 houses **have been destroyed** since 1983.

READER'S REACTION: The first part mentions Kilauea, but the second part doesn't. Did Kilauea alone destroy the houses, or were some other volcanoes also responsible?

EDITED — Among the active volcanoes, Kilauea **has erupted** most frequently in recent years, and it has destroyed over 170 houses since 1983.

Sometimes you may shift voice to emphasize or highlight a subject.

	active	active

UNEMPHATIC — Volcanic activity **built** Hawaii, and the island still **has** active volcanoes.

	passive	active

EDITED — Hawaii **was built** by volcanic activity, and the island still **has** active volcanoes.

The first sentence shifts subjects from *volcanic activity* to *the island*; the second shifts between passive and active to keep Hawaii as the focus.

39d Shifts between direct and indirect quotations

Through **direct quotation** you present someone's ideas and feelings in that person's exact words, set off with quotation marks. Through **indirect quotation** you report the substance of those words but in your own words without quotation marks. Credit your sources with either form of quotation (see Chapter 23).

39d
shift

39.2

DIRECT QUOTATION — According to Aguilar, beachfront property "has wreaked havoc on sea turtle nesting patterns" (16).

INDIRECT QUOTATION — Aguilar explained how beachfront property interferes with the breeding habits of sea turtles (16).

STRATEGY — Rewrite awkward shifts between quotations.

AWKWARD (INDIRECT + DIRECT) — Writing about the Teenage Mutant Ninja Turtles, Phil Patton **names** cartoonists Peter Laird and Kevin Eastman as their creators and **said**, "They were born quietly in 1983, in the kitchen of a New England farmhouse" (101).

EDITED — Phil Patton **credits** cartoonists Peter Laird and Kevin Eastman with creating the Teenage Mutant Ninja Turtles, who "were born quietly in 1983, in the kitchen of a New England farmhouse" (101).

For indirect quotation, use past tense to report what someone has said.

DIRECT QUOTATION — As Lan **notes,** "The region **is expected** to forfeit one of every three jobs" (4).

INDIRECT QUOTATION — Lan **projected that** the area **would lose** one-third of its jobs during the next ten years (4).

Follow convention, however, and use present tense when you analyze events in a creative work, such as a novel, film, or television show. (See 31b.)

INCONSISTENT   As the novel begins, Ishmael **comes** to New Bedford to ship out on a whaler, which he soon **did**.

CONVENTIONAL   As the novel begins, Ishmael **comes** to New Bedford to ship out on a whaler, which he soon **does**.

39d
shift

Exercise 1   *(Answers appear on p. 516.)*

Rewrite the following sentences to make them consistent in person and number.

EXAMPLE   *a*
Each person has ~~their~~ favorite fast-food restaurant.
                    ^

1. A would-be restaurant owner often fails to carefully consider the competition they will face from other restaurants of all kinds, both fancy and informal.
2. Good franchise chains survey competition, tell potential owners how much money they will need to open the business, and help you with the many problems a restaurant owner faces.
3. Admittedly, running a doughnut shop or a pizza place gives one less prestige than you get from owning a gourmet restaurant.
4. I would still rather run a successful business than one where you lose money.
5. Not all franchise arrangements are good ones, so people should do some research before he or she decides to open a franchised restaurant.

Exercise 2   *(Answers appear on p. 516.)*

Rewrite the following sentences to make them consistent in tense and mood.

EXAMPLE   *couldn't*
I went to the video store last week, and after half an hour I still ~~can't~~
                    wanted   ^
figure out which movies I ~~want.~~
                    ^

1. The video store manager said that if I bought two DVDs I will get a third one free, and then he tells me about his favorite DVDs.

2. In the movie *Sacrifice for Glory*, set in World War II, a British Mosquito bomber crashes in the jungle, and only the copilot managed to survive the long walk through the jungle back to civilization.
3. The hot sun beat on the shoulders of the copilot as he wades through the waist-deep, crocodile-infested swamp.
4. In *The Phantom Menace*, Anakin is a child with the power of the Force, but later in the series he turned to the Dark Side as Darth Vader.
5. In *Ghoulish Lunch*, the main character was reaching into the refrigerator around the guacamole dip for the last piece of apple pie when suddenly a cockroach crawls out from under the crust.

Exercise 3

Rewrite the following sentences to make them consistent in voice.

EXAMPLE

We enjoyed the expedition*,* ~~and much was~~ learned about fossils.

and   much
^   ^

1. In the morning we dug in the base of the ravine, and during the afternoon the walls were explored.
2. The team found fossils of trilobites, and other fossils were also found at the site.
3. Team members learned many things about the science of paleontology, and much was learned about the geological history of our area as well.
4. A chart helped in identifying fossilized animals, and we also learned useful identifying strategies from the lecture given by Bill Gonzales, the team leader.
5. After you fill out the application for next month's dig, the form should be given to Bill or sent to his office.

Exercise 4

Rewrite each of the following sentences twice. First use direct quotation consistently, and then use indirect quotation consistently. (Feel free to invent direct quotations in order to complete the exercise. Be sure to change direct quotations into your own words when you present them as indirect quotations.)

EXAMPLE

The article began by saying, "People often fear bees" and that this fear is a result of ignorance.

The article began by saying, "People often fear bees, and this fear comes from ignorance."

39
shift

The article began by saying that the widespread fear of bees is caused by ignorance.

1. I once heard a beekeeper claim that unless beekeeping becomes more popular as a hobby, "I believe that agriculture in this country may suffer."

2. At a meeting last night, the county agriculture commissioner argued that increased beekeeping would aid agriculture in our area and "We should be willing to provide beekeepers with financial support for their efforts."

3. Having eaten honey every day for sixty years, my grandfather says, "I may not look as good as I did when I was younger," but that he feels just as good.

4. My grandfather also says that he has stayed mentally alert because "I manage a large beekeeping and honey business."

5. My neighbor told me, if you are too busy to sell your honey at a roadside stand I should see if the supermarket in town would sell it for me.

40
mixed

40 Mixed and Incomplete Sentences

When someone switches topics or jumbles a sentence during a conversation, you can ask for clarification. When you are reading, however, you can't stop in the middle of a sentence to ask the writer to explain.

TOPIC SHIFT   One **skill** I envy is **a person** who can meet deadlines.
READER'S REACTION: How can a *skill* be *a person*?

EDITED   One **skill** I envy is **the ability** to meet deadlines.

Sentences with confusing shifts (called **mixed sentences**) mislead readers by undermining the patterns they rely on as they read. An **incomplete sentence** does the same because it omits wording necessary to make a logical and consistent statement.

40a Mixed sentences

Mixed sentences switch topics or sentence structures without warning, for no clear reason. They throw readers off track by undermining patterns that readers rely on.

1 Look for topic shifts

In most sentences, the subject announces a topic, and the predicate comments on or renames the topic. In a sentence with a **topic shift** (**faulty predication**), the second part of the sentence comments on or names a topic *different* from the one first announced. As a result, readers may have trouble figuring out the true focus of the sentence.

STRATEGY Ask "Who does what?" or "What is it?"

If the answer to "Who does what?" or "What is it?" is illogical, edit the sentence to make its meaning clear.

40a mixed

TOPIC SHIFT
In this factory, **flaws** in the product noticed by any worker **can stop** the assembly line with the flip of a switch.
QUESTION: **Who does what? Flaws can't stop the line or flip a switch.**

EDITED
In this factory, **any worker** who notices flaws in the product **can stop** the assembly line with the flip of a switch.

---

2 Pay attention to mixed patterns

If you begin one grammatical pattern but shift to another, your sentence may confuse readers because it doesn't follow the pattern they expect.

STRATEGY Check who does what to whom.

• Read your sentences aloud. Pay attention to the *meaning*, especially how the subject and predicate relate.
• Ask, "What is the topic? How does the rest of the sentence comment on it or rename it?"

MIXED PATTERN
By wearing bell-bottom pants and tie-dyed T-shirts was how many young people challenged mainstream values in the 1960s.
CHECK: *Who did what to whom* is not clear.

EDITED
By wearing bell-bottom pants and tie-dyed T-shirts, many young people challenged mainstream values in the 1960s.

40b Editing mixed sentences

In general, you can eliminate problems with topic shifts by making sure the topic in both parts of a sentence is the same.

1 Rename the subject

When you use the verb *be* (*is*, *are*, *was*, *were*), you may use the sentence predicate to rename or define the subject. Balance the topics on each side of the verb; for example, pair a noun with a noun.

If the topics on each side of *be* are not roughly equivalent, edit the second part of the sentence to rename the topic in the first part.

TOPIC SHIFT   **Irradiation** is **food** that is preserved by radiation.

EDITED   **Irradiation** is a **process** that can be used to preserve food.

2 Cut *is when* or *is where*

Is when and *is where* make a balance on both sides of *be* impossible.

**NOT
BALANCED**   **Blocking** is **when** a television network schedules a less popular program between two popular ones.

EDITED   **Blocking** is the **practice** of scheduling a less popular television program between two popular ones.

3 Omit *the reason . . . is because*

Readers find *the reason . . . is because* illogical because they expect the subject (topic) to be renamed after *is*. When *because* appears there instead, it cannot logically rename the subject.

• Drop *the reason . . . is*.

DRAFT   The **reason** he took up skating **is because** he wanted winter exercise.

EDITED   He took up skating **because** he wanted winter exercise.

• Change *because* to *that*.

EDITED   The **reason** he took up skating **is that** he wanted winter exercise.

40.1

4 Stick to a consistent sentence pattern

If you mistake words between the subject and verb for the sentence topic, you may mix up different sentence patterns.

TOPIC SHIFT   Programming **decisions** by television executives generally think about gaining audience share.
READER'S REACTION: **How can decisions think about viewers?**

EDITED   Television executives making programming decisions generally think about gaining audience share.

EDITED   When **they are making** programming decisions, **television executives** generally think about gaining audience share.

5 Be alert for sentences that begin twice

Watch for sentences in which you repeat a topic more often than the sentence structure allows or mistakenly start the sentence over again.

MIXED   **The new procedures for testing cosmetics, we** designed them to avoid cruelty to laboratory animals.

EDITED   We designed **the new procedures for testing cosmetics** to avoid cruelty to laboratory animals.

EDITED   **The new procedures for testing cosmetics** were designed to avoid cruelty to laboratory animals.

40c
incom

40c Incomplete sentences

Incomplete sentences lack either grammatical (see 35a) or logical completeness. They leave out words necessary to meaning or logic, or they don't complete an expected pattern, such as a comparison. For example, if you begin a comparison with "*X* is larger," you should complete it: "*X* is larger *than Y.*" Read sentences aloud to identify missing words. Listen for omissions such as needed articles, prepositions, pronouns, parts of verbs, or parts of a comparison.

INCOMPLETE   The new parking plan is much better.
READER'S REACTION: **Better than what? another plan? no plan?**

EDITED   The new parking plan is much better **than the last plan**.

You create an **incomplete comparison** when you omit an item being compared or the wording needed for a clear, complete comparison. To edit, supply the words that complete a comparison.

INCOMPLETE   The senior members of the staff respect the new supervisor more than their coworkers.
READER'S REACTION: **Do the senior staff members respect the supervisor more than they respect their coworkers? Or do they respect the supervisor more than their coworkers do?**

CLEAR The senior members of the staff respect the new supervisor more **than do** their coworkers.

CLEAR The senior members of the staff respect the new supervisor more **than they respect** their coworkers.

You create an **illogical comparison** when you seem to compare things that cannot be reasonably compared. To edit, add missing words or a possessive to make a comparison logical.

ILLOGICAL The amount of fat in even a small hamburger is greater than a skinless chicken breast.

READER'S REACTION: I'm confused. Why is the writer comparing the *amount of fat* in one food to another *kind* of food (chicken breast)?

EDITED (WORDS ADDED) The amount of fat in even a small hamburger is greater than **that in** a skinless chicken breast.

EDITED (POSSESSIVE USED) Even a small **hamburger's** fat content is greater than a skinless chicken **breast's**.

40c
incom

Exercise 1   *(Answers appear on p. 516.)*

Rewrite the following sentences to eliminate topic shifts.

EXAMPLE

Hides ~~that are~~ treated with tanning chemicals turn ~~them~~ into leather.

1. Tanning is when animal hide is made supple and resistant to decay.
2. The first step is when the hides are thoroughly scraped and cleaned.
3. The use of diluted acid is the substance that pickles the hides to prepare them for tanning.
4. The reason leather is supple is because it is lubricated with oil after pickling, then dried and impregnated with resins.
5. The final steps are when the leather is dyed and given a shiny surface through compression.

Exercise 2

Rewrite the following sentences to eliminate shifts in grammatical pattern.

EXAMPLE

~~Many people used to die from infectious diseases was why~~ _Scientists worked hard to develop vaccinations*.* *because many people used to die from infectious diseases.*

1. By observing that farm workers who had cowpox were resistant to smallpox led Jenner to develop an inoculation for smallpox in the 1790s.

2. Paying attention to Jenner's methods was why Pasteur was able to develop vaccines for chicken pox, rabies, and human anthrax.

3. Vaccinations produce antibodies are the sources of immunity.

4. Because they are not effective against all infections means that vaccinations are not a perfect solution for diseases.

5. Making sure your vaccinations are up to date, you need to do this during your regular medical checkup.

Exercise 3   *(Answers appear on p. 517.)*

Rewrite the following sentences to eliminate any incomplete or illogical constructions.

EXAMPLE

Both Shannon and Bill like tennis more than any *other* game.

1. His tennis serve has more speed and accuracy than Bill.

2. He also has better sense of where an opponent is going hit ball.

3. Bill's commitment to tennis is greater than his family.

4. He has more fun playing tennis.

5. Like many exercise-addicted people, Bill would be exercising than eating, and he would rather be playing tennis than doing anything else.

41   Parallelism

When you use consistent patterns, readers can easily follow and understand your ideas. They can concentrate on what you mean because they know just what to expect and how your ideas relate.

WEAK

I furnished my apartment with what I purchased at discount stores, buying items from the want ads, and gifts from my relatives.

READER'S REACTION: **This list seems wordy and jumbled.**

PARALLEL

I furnished my apartment with **purchases from discount stores,**
            items from the want ads,
      and **gifts from my relatives.**

Parallelism is the expression of similar or related ideas in similar grammatical form. Besides emphasizing the relationships of ideas, parallelism can create intriguing sentence rhythms and highlights.

41a Faulty parallelism

Once you begin a parallel pattern, you need to complete it. If you mix structures, creating incomplete or **faulty parallelism**, your sentences may disappoint readers' expectations and be hard to read.

MIXED   Consider swimming if you want an exercise that **aids** cardiovascular fitness, **develops** overall muscle strength, and **probably without causing** injuries.

PARALLEL   Consider swimming if you want an exercise that **aids** cardiovascular fitness, **develops** overall muscle strength, and **causes** few injuries.

41b Editing for parallelism

41b

//

Whether you create parallelism with words, phrases, or clauses, all the elements need to follow the same grammatical patterns.

41.1

1 Rework a series, pair, or list using parallel forms

When you place items in a series, pair, or list, make sure they have the same structure even if they differ in length and wording. Mixed grammatical forms can make a series clumsy and distracting.

WORDS MIXED   To get along with their neighbors, residents need to be patient, tactful, and to display tolerance.

WORDS PARALLEL   To get along with their neighbors, residents need to be patient, tactful, and **tolerant**.

PHRASES MIXED   The singer Jim Morrison is remembered for his innovative style, his flamboyant performances, and for behavior that was self-destructive.

PHRASES PARALLEL   The singer Jim Morrison is remembered for his innovative style, his flamboyant performances, and **his self-destructive behavior**.

CLAUSES MIXED   In assembling the research team, Cryo-Com looked for engineers whose work was creative, with broad interests, and who had boundless energy.

CLAUSES
PARALLEL
In assembling the research team, Cryo-Com looked for engineers whose work was creative, **whose interests were broad, and whose energy was boundless.**

And, but, or. When you join sentence elements with *and, but, or, for, nor, so,* and *yet* (**coordinating conjunctions**), presenting the paired elements in parallel form can direct readers' attention to similarities or differences.

WORDS
MIXED
A well-trained scientist keeps a detailed lab notebook and the entries made accurately.

WORDS
PARALLEL
A well-trained scientist keeps a **detailed and accurate** lab notebook.

PHRASES
MIXED
First-year chemistry teaches students how to take notes on an experiment and the ways of writing a lab report.

PHRASES
PARALLEL
First-year chemistry teaches students **how to take notes on an experiment** and **how to write a lab report.**

Both . . . and . . . . When you wish to call special attention to a relationship or contrast, you may choose pairs of connectors such as *both . . . and, not only . . . but also, either . . . or, neither . . . nor,* or *whether . . . or* (**correlative conjunctions**). Make the joined elements parallel.

41b
//

DRAFT
Americans claim to marry "for love," yet their pairings follow clear social patterns. They choose partners from the same social class and economic level. Most marriages bring together people with similar educational and cultural backgrounds. Similarities in race and ethnic background are important as well.

EDITED
Americans claim to marry "for love," yet their pairings follow clear social patterns. They choose partners not only **with the same class and economic background** but also **with the same educational, cultural, racial, and ethnic background.**

Lists. Use parallel form for items in a list. Suppose, for example, you were listing social changes of the early 1960s.

UNEDITED (CONFUSING)
1. A growing civil rights movement
2. Emphasis increased on youth in culture and politics.
3. Taste in music and the visual arts was changing.

EDITED FOR PARALLELISM (CLEAR)
1. **A growing** civil rights movement
2. **An increasing** emphasis on youth in culture and politics
3. **A changing** taste in music and the visual arts

2 Build clear parallel patterns

INCOMPLETE   The main character from the novel *Tarzan of the Apes* has
               appeared on television, films, and comic books.
               READER'S REACTION: **I doubt he was *on* films or *on* comic books.**

EDITED   The main character from the novel *Tarzan of the Apes* has
               appeared **on** television, **in** films, and **in** comic books.

Repeat or state words that complete grammatical or idiomatic patterns.
You needn't repeat the same lead-in word for all items in a series.

Mosquitoes can breed **in** puddles, ~~in~~ ponds, and ~~in~~ swimming pools.

41.2

3 Use parallelism to organize sentence clusters

You can use parallelism to strengthen **sentence clusters**, groups of
sentences that develop related ideas or information. The parallel elements can
clarify difficult information, highlight the overall pattern of argument or explanation, link examples, or guide readers through steps or stages.

> Each of us probably belongs to groups whose values conflict.
> **You may belong to** a religious organization that **endorses restraint in**
> alcohol use or **in** relations between the sexes while **you also belong to**
> a social group with activities that **support contrasting values. You**
> **may belong to** a sports team **that supports** competing and winning
> and a club **that promotes** understanding among people.

You can also use parallelism, as simple as brief opening phrases, to reinforce the overall pattern of a cluster of paragraphs.

> PARALLEL PARAGRAPH OPENERS
> **One reason for approving** this proposal now is . . .
> **A second reason for action** is . . .
> **The most important reason for taking immediate steps** is . . .

Exercise 1   *(Answers appear on p. 517.)*

Underline the parallel structures in each of the following sentences.

1. We've told you about the bombs, the fires, the smashed houses, and
   the courage of the people.
                    —EDWARD R. MURROW, "From London, September 22, 1940"

2. She looked at a man because she liked the way the hair was tucked
   behind his ears, or she liked the question-mark line of a long torso
   curving at the shoulder and straight at the hip.
                    —MAXINE HONG KINGSTON, "No Name Woman"

3. But far below, in the warren of passages on the starboard side for-ward, in the forward holds and boiler rooms, men could see that the *Titanic*'s hurt was mortal.

—Hanson W. Baldwin, "R.M.S. *Titanic*"

4. In that context three groups of wounded soldiers are identified: those whose survival depends on their receiving immediate treat-ment; those who need medical attention but will survive even if they do not get it immediately; and those who are hurt so badly they would not survive even with medical attention.

—Ruth Macklin, *Mortal Choices*

5. For in each American marriage there is a special code, developed from the individual pasts of the two partners, put together out of the accidents of honeymoon and parents-in-law, finally beaten into a language that each understands imperfectly.

—Margaret Mead, *Male and Female*

Exercise 2

41
//

Rewrite the following sentences to correct faulty parallelism and create appropriate emphasis. Include all necessary words.

1. What kind of job would be appropriate for a person who enjoys sailboarding, skiing, and to skydive?
2. The college's career counselor suggested that Rosalie write out her personal goals, read some materials on choosing a profession, or that she might take a career test.
3. Optimism, stamina, and being a good thinker are three traits of a good sales representative.
4. If you wish to choose a career at which you can succeed, you might start by making a list of the things you like to do, anything you are very good at, and also jobs or experiences you always try to avoid.
5. You can locate possible jobs in newspaper ads, friends, and employ-ment agencies.

Exercise 3

Rewrite the following sentences to eliminate faulty parallelism.

EXAMPLE   *do*   *℗*
In choosing a career, you should plan carefully and ~~also~~ some research
~~is needed.~~

1. Anthony could not decide whether he wanted to be a lawyer or if investment banking was a more promising career.
2. His friends thought Anthony's career plans were not suited to his abilities and his interests didn't fit the plans either.

3. After thinking about his goals, Anthony realized that the two things he wanted most from a career were stability and an income that was reasonable.
4. The counselor suggested that he might consider either working for the federal government or a job with a large, stable corporation.
5. Anthony had been reading about corporations in financial trouble and which had been laying off employees, so he decided to look carefully at government jobs.

Exercise 4

Underline all examples of parallelism in the following passage.

Large computers have some essential attributes of an intelligent brain: they have large memories, and they have gates whose connections can be modified by experience. However, the thinking of these computers tends to be narrow. The richness of human thought depends to a considerable degree on the enormous number of wires, or nerve fibers, coming into each gate in the human brain. A gate in a computer has two, or three, or at most four wires entering on one side, and one wire coming out the other side. In the human brain, a gate may have as many as 100,000 wires entering it. Each wire comes from another gate or nerve cell. This means that every gate in the human brain is connected to as many as 100,000 other gates in other parts of the brain. During the process of thinking, innumerable gates open and close throughout the brain. When one of these gates "decides" to open, the decision is the result of a complicated assessment involving inputs from thousands of other gates. This circumstance explains much of the difference between human thinking and computer thinking.   —ROBERT JASTROW, "Brains and Computers"

Exercise 5

Arrange the following materials into a list whose elements maintain parallel form.

The awards for arts and entertainment for 1985 offer an interesting picture of American culture in the middle of the decade.

Academy Award: *Out of Africa* (Best Picture); William Hurt, *Kiss of the Spider Woman* (Best Actor); Geraldine Page, *The Trip to Bountiful* (Best Actress); Don Ameche, *Cocoon* (Best Supporting Actor); Anjelica Huston, *Prizzi's Honor* (Best Supporting Actress).

The Emmy Awards went to *The Golden Girls* (Outstanding Comedy Series), *Cagney & Lacey* (Outstanding Drama Series), William Daniels and Sharon Gless (Outstanding Lead Actor/Actress in a Drama Series),

41
//

and Michael J. Fox and Betty White (Outstanding Lead Actor/Actress in a Comedy Series).

Tony Awards for Broadway Theater. Best Play: *As Is* by William Hoffman. Best Musical: *Big River* by Roger Miller.

MTV Video Music Awards. Best Video: Don Henley, "The Boys of Summer." Best Male Video: Bruce Springsteen, "I'm on Fire." Best Female Video: Tina Turner, "What's Love Got to Do with It." Best Group Video: USA for Africa, "We Are the World."

Exercise 6

Gather a number of pamphlets offering advice. Campus offices, libraries, clinics, banks, and similar places usually provide pamphlets on all kinds of subjects, from health care and home safety to job hunting. Choose one or two of the pamphlets, identify those places where parallelism is used effectively with paired sentence elements, and edit to correct any faulty parallelism. Enhance the parallelism when appropriate in order to highlight ideas and their relationships.

42 Coordination and Subordination

Suppose you were asked to rewrite the following passage, filled with short, choppy sentences that fail to emphasize connections among ideas.

California's farmers ship fresh lettuce, avocados, and other produce to supermarkets. They never send fresh olives. Fresh olives contain a substance that makes them bitter. They are very unpleasant tasting. Farmers soak fresh olives in a solution that removes oleuropein, the bitter-tasting substance. They leave just enough behind to produce the tangy "olive" taste.

You might **coordinate** the sentences, giving equal emphasis to each statement.

California's farmers ship fresh lettuce, avocados, and other produce to supermarkets, **but** they never send fresh olives. Fresh olives contain a substance that makes them bitter, **so** they are very unpleasant tasting. Farmers soak fresh olives in a solution that removes oleu-ropein, the bitter-tasting substance **;** however **,** they leave just enough behind to produce the tangy "olive" taste.

Or you might show the relative importance of ideas by **subordination**, making some of the sentences modify others through the use of subordinating words like *because* and *though*.

> California's farmers ship fresh lettuce, avocados, and other produce to supermarkets, **though** they never send fresh olives. **Because** fresh olives contain a substance that makes them bitter, they are very unpleasant tasting. **When** farmers soak fresh olives in a solution that removes oleuropein, the bitter-tasting substance, they leave just enough behind to produce the tangy "olive" taste.

42a Creating coordination

42a coord

When you want to link words, clauses, or phrases and emphasize their equal weight, use coordination. When you coordinate main (independent) clauses, you create a single **compound sentence** (see 30d-1).

42.1

RELATIONSHIPS NOT SPECIFIED Cats have no fear of water. They do not like wet and matted fur. Cats like to feel well groomed.

CLEAR RELATIONSHIPS Cats have no fear of water **,** but they do not like wet and matted fur **,** for they like to feel well groomed.

CREATING AND PUNCTUATING COORDINATION

JOINING WORDS AND CLUSTERS OF WORDS (PHRASES)

1. **Use *and, but, or, nor,* or *yet* (coordinating conjunctions).**

   cut **and** hemmed   smooth **or** textured   intrigued **yet** suspicious

2. **Use pairs like *either . . . or, neither . . . nor,* and *not only . . . but also.***

   either music therapy **or** pet therapy
   not only a nursing care plan **but also** a home care program

JOINING MAIN (INDEPENDENT) CLAUSES

1. **Use *and, but, or, for, nor, so,* or *yet* (coordinating conjunctions) preceded by a comma.**

   The students observed the responses of shoppers to long lines **,** **and** they interviewed people waiting in line. Most people in the study were irritated by the checkout lines **,** **yet** a considerable minority enjoyed the wait.

2. **Use a semicolon** (see 49a-1).

   The wait provoked physical reactions in some people **;** they fidgeted, grimaced, and stared at the ceiling.

3. **Use words like *however, moreover, nonetheless, thus,* and *consequently* (conjunctive adverbs) preceded by a semicolon** (see 49a-2).

   Store managers can take simple steps to speed up checkout lines **;** however **,** they seldom pay much attention to the problem.

4. **Use a colon** (see 49b-3).

   Tabloids and magazines in racks by the checkout counters serve a useful purpose **:** they give customers something to read while waiting.

EXPRESSING RELATIONSHIPS THROUGH COORDINATION

RELATIONSHIP	COORDINATING CONJUNCTION	CONJUNCTIVE ADVERB	
addition	, and	; in addition,	; furthermore,
opposition or contrast	, but	; in contrast,	
	, yet	; however,	; nonetheless,
result	, so	; therefore,	; consequently, ; thus,
cause	, for		
choice	, or	; otherwise,	
negation	, nor		

42b
sub

42b Creating subordination

Use subordination to create a sentence with unequal elements: one **main or independent clause** that presents the central idea and at least one **subordinate or dependent clause** that modifies, qualifies, or comments on the main clause. You signal readers about this unequal relationship by beginning the subordinate clause with a word like *although* or *that* and by attaching it to the main clause in a **complex sentence** (see 30d-1).

MAIN CLAUSES   Malcolm uses a computer to track clinic expenses. He knows how much we pay each year for lab tests.

SUBORDINATED   **Because** Malcolm uses a computer to track clinic expenses, he knows how much we pay each year for lab tests.

READER'S REACTION: **Now I know how the ideas relate—one is a cause and the other an effect.**

EXPRESSING RELATIONSHIPS THROUGH SUBORDINATION

Time	before, while, until, since, once, whenever, whereupon, after, when
Cause	because, since
Result	in order that, so that, that, so
Concession or contrast	although, though, even though, as if, while, even if
Place	where, wherever
Condition	if, whether, provided, unless, rather than
Comparison	as
Identification	that, which, who

42b
sub

CREATING AND PUNCTUATING SUBORDINATION

USING SUBORDINATING CONJUNCTIONS

You can use a subordinating conjunction such as *although*, *because*, or *since* (see the list in the box above) to create a subordinate clause at the beginning or end of a sentence (see 29g and 30c–d).

PUNCTUATING WITH SUBORDINATING CONJUNCTIONS

Use a comma *after* an introductory clause that begins with a subordinating conjunction. At the end of a sentence, do not use commas if the clause is *essential* to the meaning of the main clause (restrictive); use commas if the clause is *not essential* (nonrestrictive). (See 36c.)

BEGINNING **Once she understood the problem**, she had no trouble solving it.

END Radar tracking of flights began **after several commercial airliners collided in midair**. [Essential]

END The present air traffic control system works reasonably well, **although accidents still occur**. [Nonessential]

USING RELATIVE PRONOUNS

You can use a relative pronoun (*who*, *which*, *that*) to create a relative clause (also called an adjective clause) at the end or in the middle of a sentence (see 29d).

PUNCTUATING WITH RELATIVE PRONOUNS

If the modifying clause contains information that is *not essential* to the meaning of the main clause, the modifying clause is nonrestrictive and you should set it off with commas. If the information is *essential*, the modifying clause is restrictive and you should not set it off with commas. (See 36c.)

RESTRICTIVE
(ESSENTIAL)   The anthropologists discovered the site of a building **that early settlers used as a meetinghouse**.

NONRESTRICTIVE
(NONESSENTIAL)   At one end of the site they found remains of a smaller building **,** **which may have been a storage shed**.

RESTRICTIVE
(ESSENTIAL)   The people **who organized the project** work for the Public Archaeology Lab.

NONRESTRICTIVE
(NONESSENTIAL)   A graduate student **,** **who was leading a dig nearby** **,** first discovered signs of the meetinghouse.

42c Editing coordination and subordination

How can you tell if you're using too much or too little coordination or subordination? Read your writing aloud. Watch for short, choppy sentences or long, dense passages.

1 Be alert for too much coordination or subordination

If you use words like *and, so,* or *but* merely to string together loosely related sentences, you risk boring readers with excessive coordination.

DRAFT   Ripe fruit spoils quickly, **and** fresh grapefruit in markets is picked before it matures to avoid spoilage, **and** it can taste bitter, **but** grapefruit in cans is picked later, **and** it tastes sweeter.

EDITED   Ripe fruit spoils quickly. Fresh grapefruit in markets is picked before it matures **,** **so** it may taste bitter. Grapefruit in cans is picked later **;** **consequently** **,** it tastes sweeter.

42.2

Excessive subordination can overload readers. Divide sentences to simplify.

CONFUSING   The election for mayor will be interesting **because** the incumbent has decided to run as an independent **while** his former challenger for the Democratic nomination has decided to accept the party's endorsement **even though** the Republican nominee is her former campaign manager.

EDITED   The election for mayor will be interesting● The incumbent has decided to run as an independent● His former challenger for the Democratic nomination has decided to accept the party's endorsement **even though** she will have to run against her former campaign manager.

2 Watch for illogical or unclear relationships

Sometimes the subordinating word you choose may not specify a clear relationship, or it may indicate an illogical relationship.

STRATEGY   **Use questions to identify problems in logic or meaning.**

To identify illogical or unclear relationships, state a sentence's meaning to yourself with a slightly different wording.

- Ask, "Does the original sentence convey my intended meaning?"
- Ask, "Can the subordinating word I have chosen convey several different meanings?"

42c
coord/
sub

UNCLEAR   Since she taught middle school, Jean developed keen insight into
EMPHASIS   the behavior of twelve- and thirteen-year-olds.

       READER'S REACTION: **Does *since* mean that she developed insight *because* she was a teacher or *after* she quit teaching?**

EDITED   **Because** she taught middle school, Jean developed keen insight into the behavior of twelve- and thirteen-year-olds.

3 Highlight important information

Subordination enables you to put some information in the foreground (in a main clause) and other information in the background (in a subordinate clause). In general, move your most important point to the main clause.

DRAFT   His training and equipment were inferior, although Jim still set a school record throwing the discus.

       READER'S REACTION: **Isn't Jim's achievement the key point?**

EDITED   **Although** his training and equipment were inferior, Jim still set a school record throwing the discus.

ESL ADVICE: GRAMMATICAL STRUCTURES FOR COORDINATION AND SUBORDINATION

The following sentence has both a subordinator, *although*, and a coordinator, *but*. Use one pattern, not both at once.

MIXED	**Although** frogs can live both on land and in water, **but** they need to breathe oxygen.

main clause   main clause
CONSISTENT
COORDINATION   Frogs can live both on land and in water, **but** they need to breathe oxygen.

subordinate clause   main clause
CONSISTENT
SUBORDINATION   **Although** frogs can live both on land and in water, they need to breathe oxygen.

Exercise 1   *(Possible answers appear on p. 517.)*

Combine each of the following pairs of sentences into a single sentence using coordination. Make sure you use each of the strategies listed in the table on page 399 for joining main clauses, and do not use any particular conjunction (such as *and* or *however*) more than once. Rewrite the sentences if necessary to avoid awkwardness or confusion.

42c
coord/
sub

EXAMPLE
                                                 , so
Winter weather makes outdoor exercise difficult. ᴡ̷inter has its own
                                                  ^
forms of exercise.

1. Ice skating can be enjoyable. It is also physically demanding.
2. Recreational skaters need to be in good shape physically. They should exercise to increase their fitness.
3. Skaters who are not in good shape get tired quickly. These skaters are also more likely to pull a muscle or fall.
4. To get in shape for skating, try a program of regular exercise for at least several weeks. Pay special attention to exercises focusing on knees and ankles.
5. Other areas to exercise are hip and leg muscles. Exercises aimed at each muscle group are best.

Exercise 2

Revise the following passage to eliminate excessive or illogical coordination. Use coordination to combine short sentences when appropriate, to clarify relationships, and to eliminate choppiness.

Working for someone else can be unrewarding, and this is also true of working for a large corporation, so many people in their early thirties decide to open businesses of their own, but they often do not have very original ideas, so they open restaurants or small retail stores, for these are the small businesses they are most familiar with, yet they are also the ones that are most likely to fail, and they face the most competition. Franchises are small businesses, and they often provide help to people getting into business on their own for the first time. Enterprising people can own the local office of an armored car service, or they can run a regional unit of a nationwide cleaning service for commercial buildings, and they can open hardware stores with the name of a national chain over the front door.

Exercise 3 *(Answers appear on p. 518.)*

Use subordination to combine each of the following pairs of sentences. Choose appropriate subordinating conjunctions (see p. 400), and create emphasis consistent with each sentence's meaning. Rewrite the clauses if necessary to produce effective sentences.

EXAMPLE

Newspapers often contain reports of car accidents. *that* ~~The accidents~~ were preventable.

1. The comedian Sam Kinison died in a car crash. A pickup truck swerved across the road and hit his car.
2. Kinison was not wearing a seat belt. A seat belt might have saved his life.
3. Driving quickly off the road to the right is one thing you can do. This will help you avoid collisions.
4. Drive a large car. Big, heavy cars and passenger vans are much safer in crashes.
5. Buying a car with front and side impact air bags is an excellent way to reduce your chances of getting injured or dying. These cars cost more money.

Exercise 4

Revise the following sentences to eliminate illogical, incorrect, or excessive subordination. When appropriate, combine short sentences through subordination to clarify relationships and eliminate choppiness.

EXAMPLE

Because
~~Since~~ my doctor said I need more exercise, I have been looking for a sport I might enjoy.

1. As I am not particularly good at athletics, I want a sport that is not too demanding. I would also like a sport that is fun.
2. I enjoy volleyball, although it is a serious, highly competitive sport demanding considerable quickness and coordination. Volleyball is not the answer.
3. Since I have played tennis, I have thought about trying out for the tennis team. I have also thought about talking this idea over with the tennis coach.

4. Some of my friends think I should give the tennis team a try while others think the idea is laughable.
5. What I really want to find is a brand-new sports program, and which will give me the training I need, because I don't have the experience necessary to succeed in established sports, although I am willing to work as hard as I need to in order to bring my skills up to a competitive level.

43 Clear and Emphatic Sentences

Most people would find the following sentence hard to read.

INDIRECT OR EVASIVE   It is suggested that employee work cooperation encouragement be used for product quality improvement.

READER'S REACTION: **Who is suggesting this? What is "employee work cooperation encouragement"?**

CLEAR   We will try to improve our products by encouraging employees to work cooperatively.

You can make sentences easier to read by creating clear subjects and verbs as well as direct sentence structures.

43a Unclear sentences

A clear sentence answers the question "Who does what (to whom)?" When a sentence doesn't readily answer this question, try to make its subject and verb easy to identify. (See 30a.)

         subject   verb   object
CLEAR   The research team investigated seizure disorders in infants.
        who?   does what?

         subject   verb
CLEAR   The seizures often become harmful.
        who?   does what?

You can create complex yet clear sentences by making the main elements—especially subjects and verbs—easy for readers to identify.

UNCLEAR   One suggestion offered by physicians is that there is a need to be especially observant of a child's behavior during the first six months in order to notice any evidence of seizures.

CLEAR   Physicians suggest that parents watch children carefully during the first six months for evidence of seizures.

43b Editing for clear sentences

43.1

43b
clear

As you edit for clarity, work on any recurring sentence features identified as unclear by your readers, or use the strategies below.

1 Concentrate on subjects

Sentences whose subjects name important ideas, people, topics, things, or events are generally easy for readers to understand.

> **STRATEGY**   **Ask questions to clarify significant subjects.**
> - Who (or what) am I talking about here?
> - Is this what I want to emphasize?
>
> UNFOCUSED   You run the greatest risk if you expose yourself to tanning machines as well as the sun because both of them can damage the skin.
> READER'S REACTION: I thought the focus was the danger, whether sunbathing or tanning. Why are they both buried in the middle?
>
> POSSIBLE
> REVISION   Either **the sun or a tanning machine** can damage the skin, and you run the greatest risk from exposure to **both** of them.

Watch out for nominalizations. When you create a noun (*completion, happiness*) from another kind of word such as a verb (*complete*) or an adjective (*happy*), the result is a **nominalization**, often ending in *-tion, -ence, -ance, -ing,* or *-ness*. Nominalizations usefully name ideas but may obscure information or distract readers from your focus. Be sure each sentence tells who did what (to whom).

USEFUL   **Sleepiness** causes accidents at work and on the road.

Replace weak nominalizations with clear subjects.

WEAK   Stimulation of the production of serotonin by a glass of milk or a carbohydrate snack causes sleepiness.

READER'S REACTION: **Why does this advice on getting a good night's sleep start off with *stimulation*?**

EDITED   **A glass of milk or a carbohydrate snack** stimulates the production of serotonin and causes sleepiness.

Pay attention to noun strings. Sometimes one noun modifies another or nouns plus adjectives modify other nouns: *sleep deprivation, jet lag, computer network server, triple bypass heart surgery.* Although unfamiliar **noun strings** can be hard to understand, familiar ones can be concise and clear.

To edit confusing noun strings, try turning the key word in a string (usually the last noun) into a verb. Then turn other nouns from the string into prepositional phrases.

CONFUSING   The team did a ceramic valve lining design flaw analysis.

READER'S REACTION: **Did the team analyze flaws or use a special feature called flaw analysis? Did they study ceramic valves or valve linings made of ceramic material?**

EDITED   The team **analyzed** flaws **in** the lining design **for** ceramic valves.

Another option is to turn one noun into the sentence's subject.

EDITED   **Flaws** in the lining design for ceramic valves were analyzed by the team.

Use *I, we,* and *you*. *I, we,* and *you,* although inappropriate in some academic settings, are commonly used in work and public communities. (See 39a.)

VAGUE AND WEAK   The project succeeded because of careful cost control and attention to the customer's needs.

CLEAR AND FORCEFUL   The project succeeded because **we** controlled costs carefully and paid attention to **our** customers' needs.

2 Concentrate on verbs and predicates

Strong verbs can make sentences forceful and clear. Here are four steps you can take to strengthen your verbs.

1. Replace the verb *be* (*is, are, was, were, will be*) with a more forceful verb, especially in sentences that list or identify qualities.

WEAK   Our agency **is** responsible for all aspects of disaster relief.

STRONGER   Our agency **plans, funds,** and **delivers** disaster relief.

43b
clear

2. Turn nouns that follow forms of *be* into clear, specific verbs.

WEAK   The new recycling system is a **money saver**.

STRONGER   The new recycling system **saves money**.

3. Replace **expletive** constructions—sentences beginning with *there is*, *there are*, or *it is* (see 30a-1)—if they are wordy or obscure. (Keep them if they add variety, build suspense, or usefully withhold information about the doer.)

WEAK   **There is** a need for more classrooms at Kenny School.

STRONGER   **Kenny School needs** more classrooms.

4. Eliminate general verbs (*do, give, have, get, provide, shape, make*) linked to nouns; turn the nouns into verbs.

WEAK   Our company **has done a study** of the new design.

STRONGER   Our company **has studied** the new design.

43b
clear

ESL ADVICE: *THERE* AND *IT* AS SUBJECTS

When you use *there* and *it* as the subjects of sentences, these pronouns may not have the object or place meanings usually attached to them. *There* may introduce new, unknown material, while *it* may introduce environmental conditions (including distance, time, and weather).

DRAFT   Although there was snowing, it was dancing after dinner.

EDITED   Although **it** was snowing, **there** was dancing after dinner.

3 Select active or passive voice

When you use a verb in the **active voice** (see 31i), the agent (or doer) is also the subject of the sentence.

agent   action   goal
The outfielder caught the towering fly ball.
subject   verb   object

When you choose the **passive voice** (see 31i), you turn the sentence's goal into the subject. You de-emphasize the doer by placing it in a prepositional phrase or by dropping an unknown or unimportant agent altogether.

goal   action   [agent]
The towering fly ball was caught [by the outfielder].
subject   verb   [prepositional phrase]

Many writers favor the active voice because it is direct and concise, and many readers find too much passive voice weak. On the other hand, the passive voice may be favored in lab reports and other scientific or technical writing in both academic and work communities. It avoids spotlighting the researcher or repeating the researcher's actions; instead it focuses on results—what happens, not who does it. It also may be used ethically to protect the identity of someone such as a child or the victim of crime or abuse. At the same time, it may inadvertently, or even deliberately, conceal a doer (or agent), thus obscuring responsibility for actions.

43.2

AGENT DE-EMPHASIZED   Federal tax forms have been mailed. [By the IRS, of course.]

AGENT CONCEALED   Hasty decisions were made in this zoning case. [By whom?]

Rewrite sentences in the passive voice that add extra words, create inappropriate emphasis, or omit the doer (see 39c).

	subject
PASSIVE VOICE (15 WORDS)	**Three thousand people** affected by the toxin were interviewed

agent
by **the Centers for Disease Control**.

agent (subject)
ACTIVE VOICE (13 WORDS)   **The Centers for Disease Control** interviewed three thousand people affected by the toxin.

**43b
clear**

4 Create variety and emphasis

If you feel that editing for clarity produces too many similar sentences, try some of the following options to direct the attention of your readers.

- Emphasize material by shifting it to the places where a reader's attention gravitates—the **sentence opening or closing**.
- **Repeat key words and ideas** within a sentence or cluster of sentences to draw attention to them. (Avoid too much repetition that calls attention to itself rather than your ideas.)
- Try **climactic sentence order**—sentences that build to a climax—to create powerful emphasis. Such sentences can stress new information at the end or focus on the last element in a series.
- Try an occasional **periodic sentence**. By piling up phrases, clauses, and words at the start, create suspense by delaying the main clause.
- Consider creating a **cumulative sentence**. Start with the main clause, and then add, bit by bit, details and ideas in the form of modifying phrases, clauses, and words to build a detailed picture, an intricate explanation, or a cluster of ideas and information.
- Vary your **sentence length**. Add short sentences for dramatic flair. Use longer ones to explore relationships among ideas and build rhythmic

effects. Use middle-length sentences as workhorses, carrying the burden of explanation, but don't use too many in a sequence.

- Vary your sentence types (see 30d-2). **Declarative sentences** present, explain, and support ideas or information. An occasional exclamation (**exclamatory sentence**), a mild order (**imperative sentence**), or a question (**interrogative sentence**) can change your pace.
- Surprise your readers on occasion. Add **key words** to summarize and redirect a sentence. **Extend a sentence** that appears to have ended, adding new information or twists of thought. Use parallelism (see 41b) to highlight a contrast in a witty, dramatic, or ironic **antithesis**.

Exercise 1

Revise the following sentences to create clear subjects and make the sentences easier to understand.

EXAMPLE

We expect

~~Our expectation is that~~ athletic shoes~will~ *to* look good as well as feel comfortable.

1. Our expectation is that our elected officials will look like the populations of people they represent.
2. Fifty years ago, election of only one gender of people, male, and of only one race, white, was possible.
3. Today, politicians boast of every level of our government's racial and gender diversity.
4. Choice between candidates is on the basis of their stand on the issues, their media savvy, and their ability to communicate.
5. Choice of candidate is not always on the basis of race, in other words.

Exercise 2   *(Answers appear on p. 518.)*

Rewrite the following sentences, using clear verbs to make them easy to understand.

EXAMPLE   *induces stress*

Negotiating ~is a stress-inducing experience~ for many people in business.

1. Negotiating, regarded by many experts as an important element in successful business careers, especially on the executive level, is not offered as a course at many colleges.
2. Included among the programs offered by our consulting company is a course in professional negotiation. It is considered to be very useful.
3. We also give demonstrations of how to prepare effective proposals, counteroffers, and other negotiation-related documents.

4. Our consultants can, if a company wishes, provide training for both small and large groups.
5. It is generally agreed that the training program is a confidence builder for many people.

Exercise 3 *(Answers appear on p. 518.)*

Revise the following sentences to eliminate passive voice.

EXAMPLE

~~Many~~ different kinds of ice cream ~~are sold by grocery stores.~~

Grocery stores sell many

1. The superpremium ice cream brands are chosen by many people.
2. More butterfat and less air is contained in superpremium ice cream than in regular ice cream.
3. The high fat content ought to be considered before the ice cream is purchased.
4. The rich, tasty ice creams are being challenged by the new frozen dessert products.
5. Frozen yogurts with candy and nuts mixed in have been heavily promoted.

43
clear

Exercise 4

Examine the following passage carefully, and identify the strategies the author uses to create emphasis.

There was a time when people who wanted to keep the peace and keep the crockery intact held to a strict dinner-table rule: Never argue about politics or religion. I don't know how well it worked in American dining rooms, but it worked pretty well in our schools. We dealt with religion by not arguing about it.

Children who came out of diverse homes might carve up the turf of their neighborhood and turn the playgrounds into a religious battle-field, but the public classroom was common ground. Intolerance wasn't tolerated.

In place of teaching one religion or another, the schools held to a common denominator of values. It was, in part, the notion of Horace Mann, the nineteenth-century father of the public-school system. He believed that the way to avoid religious conflicts was to extract what all religions agree upon and allow this "non-religious" belief system into schools.

I wonder what Mann would think of that experiment now. Was it naive or sophisticated? Was it a successful or a failed attempt to avoid conflict in a pluralistic society?

—ELLEN GOODMAN, "Religion in the Textbooks"

Which sentence strategies add to the effectiveness of the passage, and why? Which, if any, detract from its effectiveness?

Exercise 5

Rewrite the following passage to add variety. You may wish to rearrange the order of statements, to cut or add words, or to combine some sentences and divide others.

Psychologists have been studying what events people remember. People from middle age on remember events from their early years more clearly than they remember more recent events. People in their seventies have clear memories of their thirties but less clear memories of their fifties. Most of us remember very little about childhood. Almost no one remembers events from before four years old. Researchers think that we tend to remember events that are new or exciting to us and to forget routine events. Memorable events are most likely to occur early in life. Infants probably have not developed the mental abilities necessary to create memories, however.

43
clear

Exercise 6

Browse through some current magazines, looking for one that contains relatively long essays with varied and often surprising writing style. You might look at *Vogue*, *The New Yorker*, *Rolling Stone*, *Business Week*, *GQ*, *Vanity Fair*, *Advertising Age*, *Utne Reader*, *Commentary*, *Tikkun*, *Scientific American*, or *Details*. Choose two paragraphs whose style you admire, and identify any of the sentence strategies discussed in this chapter. Be ready to discuss why the sentences can be considered effective in communicating the author's ideas.

PART 10

Editing Word Choice

44 Being Concise

Leaving extra words in your writing wastes valuable space—and your readers' time.

WORDY   **There is evidence that the use of** pay as an incentive **can be a contributing or causal factor in** improvement **of the** quality **of** work.
READER'S REACTION: **Why is this so long-winded? What's the point?**

TRIMMED   Incentive pay improves work quality.
READER'S REACTION: **That's short and direct—but maybe too abrupt.**

RESHAPED   Incentive pay **often encourages** work **of higher** quality.
READER'S REACTION: **Now I'm gaining a fuller, more subtle perspective.**

Conciseness means using only the words you need—not the fewest words possible, but those appropriate for your purpose, meaning, and readers. (See 43b and 45b.).

44a Common types of wordiness

Imagine an ideal reader—a respected teacher, a savvy coworker, or a wise civic leader. If a passage seems wordy, ask, "What would I need to tell *X* here?" Or think of *X* asking, "What's your point?"

Look for **wordy phrases** you can shrink to a word or two.

WORDY   Carbon 14 can be used to date a site only **in the event that** organic material has survived. **In a situation in which** rocks need dating, potassium-argon testing is used.

CUT   Carbon 14 can be used to date a site only **if** organic material has survived. **When** rocks need dating, potassium-argon testing is used.

Watch for **intensifying phrases** (*for all intents and purposes*, *in my opinion*), intended to add force but often carrying little meaning.

WORDY   **As a matter of fact**, most archaeological discoveries can be dated accurately.

CUT   Most archaeological discoveries can be dated accurately.

Target clutter such as **all-purpose words** (*factor*, *aspect*, *situation*, *type*, *field*, *range*, *thing*, *kind*, *nature*) and **all-purpose modifiers** (*very*, *totally*, *major*, *central*, *great*, *really*, *definitely*, *absolutely*).

COMMON WORDY PHRASES

PHRASE		REPLACEMENT
due to the fact that	=	because
at the present moment	=	now
a considerable proportion of	=	many, most
has the capability to	=	can
regardless of the fact that	=	although
concerning the matter of	=	about

WORDY   In the short story, Young Goodman Brown is so **totally** overwhelmed by **his own** guilt that he becomes **extremely** suspicious of the people around him. [25 words]

CUT   In the short story, Young Goodman Brown is so overwhelmed by guilt that he becomes suspicious of the people around him. [21 words]

REWRITTEN   In the short story, Young Goodman Brown's **overwhelming** guilt makes him **suspect everyone**. [13 words]

Simplify pairs that say the same thing twice (*each and every*) and **redundant phrases** in which adjectives repeat nouns (*final outcomes*), adverbs repeat verbs (*completely finished*), or specific words imply general (*small in size*).

WORDY   Because it was **sophisticated in nature** and **tolerant in style**, Kublai Khan's administration aided China's development in the 1200s.

CUT   Because it was **sophisticated and tolerant**, Kublai Khan's administration aided China's development in the 1200s.

REWRITTEN   Kublai Khan's **adept and tolerant administration** aided China's development in the 1200s.

44b
wordy

44b Editing for conciseness

Edit both wordy expressions and wordy sentence patterns (see 43b).

44.1

Trim ideas already stated or implied. Cut, but retain useful repetition that helps readers follow an explanation or argument.

REPETITIVE **Our proposal** outlines a **three-step** program for **converting the building** into a **research center** for the study of film and culture.

Each of the **three steps** discussed in **our proposal** should be completed in six months. We expect that **the building** will be **converted** to a **research center** eighteen months from the time work is begun.

CUT   We propose **three steps** for **converting the building** into a center for the study of film and culture. Allowing six months for each **step**, we expect **the building** to be **converted** in eighteen months.

Trim *which, who,* or *that* clauses and *of* phrases. Convert clauses to phrases, phrases to words.

CLAUSES   Chavez Park, **which is an extensive facility in the center of town**, was named after Cesar Chavez, **who fought for migrant farmers' rights**.

CUT TO PHRASES   Chavez Park, **an extensive facility in the center of town**, was named after Cesar Chavez, **an advocate for migrant farmers**.

CUT TO WORDS   Chavez Park, **an extensive downtown facility**, was named after **migrant advocate** Cesar Chavez.

Replace generalities with connections and details. First, highlight the key words in a passage. Then, combine sentences to eliminate vague or repetitive wording, and add specific, concrete detail to support your main points.

WORDY   **Glaciers** were of central importance in the **shaping** of **the North American landscape**. They were responsible for many familiar geological features. Among the many remnants of glacial activity are **deeply carved valleys** and **immense piles of sand and rock**.

SENTENCES COMBINED   Glaciers carved deep valleys and left behind immense piles of sand and rock, shaping much of the North American landscape in the process.

DETAILS ADDED   Glaciers carved deep valleys and left behind immense piles of sand and rock, shaping much of the North American landscape in the process. **Cape Cod and Long Island are piles of gravel deposited by glaciers. The Mississippi River and the Great Lakes remained when the ice melted.**

Reduce unnecessary writer's commentary. Make sure your comments guide readers, but don't overdo the commentary and end up talking about yourself rather than your subject.

IRRITATING   **In my paper, I intend to show** that the benefits of placebos (pills with no physical effect) include improvements and cures, **as mentioned above**.

EDITED   The benefits of placebos (pills with no physical effect) include improvements and cures.

Exercise 1   *(Answers appear on p. 519.)*

Edit the following sentences to make them more concise. Use one of the three editing options for wordiness: cut unnecessary words, substitute better words, or rewrite the sentence entirely. Keep track of your changes.

EXAMPLE

~~In spite of the fact that~~ *Although* most ~~ordinary~~ middle-aged people ~~say they~~ ~~generally~~ feel ~~physically~~ healthy, ~~and in good shape, severe physical~~ catastrophes such as ~~debilitating~~ strokes ~~and/~~or heart attacks can strike ~~suddenly~~ at any time.

1. As a matter of fact, my uncle had just come back from playing nine holes of golf when he suffered the terrible tragedy of his heart attack.
2. We all thought my aunt was absolutely in the very best of health, but she also died extremely suddenly.
3. For me, the end result of these experiences has been regular periodic visits to the doctor to check on my health.
4. On account of my last visit to the doctor, I have actually started exercising on a regular basis.
5. A regular exercise program really helps me to a better kind of feeling about myself.

44
wordy

Exercise 2

Rewrite the following sentences to make them less wordy.

EXAMPLE

~~It was an~~ *My* interest in ancient cultures ~~that first sparked my interest in an~~ anthropology course ~~taught by~~ Professor Donaldson. *attracted me to*

1. There is much information and detail in this informative course about the civilizations of the pre-Columbian Americas.
2. Anthropologists have spent a great deal of time studying and investigating Machu Picchu, which was the center point of an advanced culture high in the Andes Mountains.
3. There are many excavations in the area that have received support from American universities.
4. It seems to be true that the ruins are a really breathtaking sight.

5. Proposals for further exploration are now being made to funding organizations by several groups of anthropologists.

Exercise 3

Rewrite the following passage to eliminate overblown language, unnecessary commentary, vague generalizations, and clichés. As you revise, make the passage more concise.

The social psychologist and student of human behavior Peter Marsh several years ago published a tome entitled *Tribes* in which he set forth the challenging, and for many readers, downright revolutionary, conception that the denizens of our modern world perpetuate the primitive form of social organization known as a tribe. According to Marsh in his book, as a reaction against the tendency of our modern society to break up the social networks characteristic of the more rural lifestyles of earlier decades and centuries, many people form formal and informal groups based on their preferences in food, clothing, recreation, and work. Some of these groupings are of remarkably short duration, consisting of what we might call fads. Let me point out that, in my opinion, Marsh is trying to be critical of many of these groups, particularly those that seek to raise the social status of members by excluding nonmembers from certain privileges. Yet I think that a careful reading of Marsh's book would also indicate that he is favorably predisposed toward the tendency of modern people to form tribes.

45 words

45 Choosing Appropriate Words

Edit your words so that you express what you mean correctly and appropriately for your readers.

DRAFT   Dr. Parsippani **assassinated** Mr. Rollet.

READER'S REACTION: Was Mr. Rollet a political figure? Or is this wording imprecise?

Here, *assassinated* might fit if Rollet were a political figure. If the writer didn't intend this meaning, *killed* might be the most precise choice. Audience expectations also affect **diction**, the choice of words and phrases. For instance, the criminal justice system defines *murder* by degree and distinguishes *homicide* from *manslaughter*.

Besides being *correct*, words need to be *appropriate*. For example, referring in an academic paper to "this guy's theories" technically isn't *incorrect* since *guy* does refer to a person. But it violates expectations and therefore is *inappropriate*. Attending to community sensitivities of this kind reassures a teacher, supervisor, or member of the public of your credibility.

45a Recognizing the demands of context and purpose

When you choose specific words as you draft and revise, bear in mind the demands of your specific context and audience as well as your purpose and your persona (the image of yourself that you project in your writing).

1 Adjust your diction to your context and your readers

A particular context—an academic discipline or workplace, for example—may call for specialized and precise language choices.

TOO GENERAL [*in an analysis of a painting for an art history course*] Tiepolo's *Apotheosis of the Pisani Family* (1761) is a lively painting typical of the period when it was painted with lots of action going on and nice colors.

READER'S REACTION: **This wording seems too general for an analysis in my field of art history.**

EDITED Tiepolo's *Apotheosis of the Pisani Family* (1761) shows affinities with typical rococo frescoes of the period, including bright colors with characters in highlighted actions set against dark border accents.

When you write for readers in academic or workplace settings, they will generally expect a high level of formality. Avoid **colloquialisms**, informal expressions typical of a region or group.

TOO INFORMAL The stock market crash didn't seem to **faze** many of the investors with **megabucks stashed** in property assets.

READER'S REACTION: **This seems so informal that I'm not sure I trust the writer's authority.**

45a
words

EDITED   The stock market crash did not profoundly affect investors with extensive property assets.

Exceptions to the need for formality are deliberately informal notes, responses, journal entries, and quoted speech.

2 Adjust your diction to your purpose

In many academic, public, or work settings, readers may favor balanced reasoning over highly emotional language.

BIASED   Most proponents of rock-music censorship grew up listening to pablum, thinking wimpy bands like the Beach Boys were a bunch of perverts.
READER'S REACTION: **This writer seems too biased and emotional to weigh all sides of the debate.**

EDITED   Proponents of rock-music censorship may unfairly stereotype all of rock-and-roll culture as degenerate or evil.

3 Adjust your diction to your persona

Word choice that creates an objective, detached image of you as a writer (a **persona**) in a clinical report assures readers of accuracy, but this same persona might seem cold and impersonal in the adoption column of an animal shelter newsletter. (See also 10a-3.)

TOO CLINICAL FOR CONTEXT   Three domestic canines, *Canis familiaris*, type Shetland sheepdog; age: 8 weeks; coloring: burnt umber with variegated blond diameters; behaviorally modified for urination and defecation; inoculated.
READER'S REACTION: **Why would someone at the shelter talk so uncaringly about the puppies, treating them like laboratory specimens?**

EDITED   Three healthy sheltie puppies 8 weeks old, brown with light spots, housebroken, all shots.

45b
words

45b Editing for precise diction

When you choose among **synonyms**, words identical or nearly so in meaning, consider their **connotations**—"shades" of meaning or associations acquired over time. Use concrete, direct wording unless the context calls for specialized language or more abstraction.

STRATEGY   Choose precise, concrete, and direct words.

* Replace an inexact word with an appropriate synonym.

IMPRECISE   The senator **retreated** from the gathering.
READER'S REACTION: Did the senator feel attacked, bewildered, or overcome? Or did she just leave?

EDITED   The senator **left** the gathering.

* Replace vague words with specific ones.

VAGUE   [*in a do-it-yourself brochure on bathroom remodeling*] Do not place flooring over uneven floor or damaged area.
READER'S REACTION: What's this about a damaged area?

EDITED   Do not **install** flooring over **existing** floors that are **uneven or show signs of wood rot. Replace** any damaged **flooring material before installing new flooring.**

* Stick mostly to simple, familiar words.

STUFFY   The reflections upon premarital cohabitation promulgated by the courts eventuated in the orientation of the population in the direction of moral relaxation on this issue.
READER'S REACTION: How dull! Say it more plainly, please.

EDITED   Court decisions about living together before marriage led to greater public acceptance of this practice.

Idioms are expressions, often with "forgotten histories," whose meanings differ from their literal definitions, as in *wipe the slate clean* for "start over." Overused idioms can lose their freshness, becoming trite or clichéd; replace them with precise words.

IDIOMATIC   The losers complained of **dog-eat-dog** politics.
EDITED   The losers consoled themselves after their defeat.

45b
words

ESL ADVICE: IDIOMS IN AMERICAN ENGLISH

Whether an expression is an **idiom** or a **phrasal verb** (see 29c), the meanings of its separate words will not reveal its meaning as a whole. Although memorizing idioms will enrich your spoken English, these expressions may be too informal in many writing situations. In class or at work, notice how many and which idioms appear in well-written papers by native speakers; adjust your usage accordingly.

45.1

Exercise 1

Assume that the following paragraph is part of a brochure on dental hygiene found in a dentist's office. Examine the passage, and circle words and phrases you find inappropriate. Write a paragraph explaining the problems in diction that you identified in the passage. Consider its intended audience, purpose, context, and persona.

Brushing and flossing of human dentin has been shown to be instrumental in the systematic reduction of invasive caries. When brushing, it is advisable to rotate the cusp of the preventive maintenance tool at alternating angles during upward and downward motion. When flossing, it is advisable to insert and retract the flossing material several times between the dentitial spaces.

Exercise 2

Read the following paragraph and identify as many cases as you can of inappropriate diction. Look for imprecise, misused, stuffy, or trite words, checking in a dictionary if you need to. Then edit the passage by replacing the misused words or expressions with more appropriate ones.

The inaugural time I witnessed someone parachuting from a plane was when I was in college. The parachuting establishment was located in the desert of Arizona. First we apprised ourselves on the diminutive single-prop plane and shackled ourselves into the seats. Three employees of a local business were the jumpers. We circled around until we reached the pinnacle for jumping, about 6,000 feet up. The first customer was about to detort but became lugubrious with fear and couldn't jump. The second man faced us with his back to the open side of the plane and a verecund expression on his face, then fell back deliberately and dejected himself from the craft, spinning downward toward the verdurous desert.

45 words

Exercise 3

Locate a short passage in a newspaper or magazine article. Rewrite the passage, substituting for words that are inappropriate or inaccurate.

46 Using Respectful Language

To represent others fairly, writers and editors eliminate sexist and discriminatory language from their work.

DRAFT   Early in his career, Lasswell published his **seminal** work on propaganda.

> **READER 1: Why do you have to use this word? It's offensive to associate originality and creativity with being male.**
>
> **READER 2: You could replace** *seminal* **with** *important* **or** *influential.*
>
> **READER 3: Aren't you overreacting? You wouldn't throw out** *matrimony* **just because it's related to the Latin word for** *mother* **or** *patriot* **because it comes from the word for** *father.*

As these reactions show, not everyone agrees on what language might be sexist or discriminatory. But no matter how you feel about diversity, as a writer you *must* consider how readers react to your representation of men, women, and members of minority groups. You don't want to alienate readers, prejudice people against your ideas, or perpetuate unhealthy attitudes.

46a Editing gender stereotypes

46a lang

The most common form of sexist language uses *mankind* or *men* for humankind; *he*, *his*, or *him* for all people; and words implying men in occupations (*fireman*). When editing the generic *he*, try first to make the construction plural (for example, use *their* for *his* or for the clumsy *his or her*).

SEXIST   Every trainee should bring **his** laptop with **him**.

AWKWARD   Every trainee should bring **his or her** laptop with **him or her**.

BETTER   All trainees should bring **their** laptops with **them**.

46.1

Some guides suggest that a plural pronoun is better than the generic *he*, even if the pronoun does not agree in number with the subject (see 33b). Some readers, however, object more strenuously to the agreement error than to the sexist language. Reword to avoid both problems.

ORIGINAL   **Everyone** has at some time squandered **his** money.

PROBLEMATIC **Everyone** has at some time squandered **their** money.

BETTER   **Most people have** at some time squandered **their** money.

BETTER   **Everyone** has at some time squandered money.

Your readers are likely to object to negative stereotypes based on gender, such as assumptions that men are stronger or women are worse at math.

STEREOTYPED   The OnCall Pager is **smaller than most doctors' wallets and easier to answer than phone calls from their wives**.

READER'S REACTION: **I'm a woman and a doctor. I'm insulted by the assumption that all doctors are male and by the negative reference to "wives." OnCall will never sell a pager in my office!**

EDITED   The OnCall Pager **will appeal to doctors because it is small and easy to operate**.

46b Editing racial, ethnic, and cultural stereotypes

46.2

Most readers won't tolerate racism and will stop reading material with discriminatory language. Don't rely on your intent; think about how your reader *might* construe your words.

DEMEANING   My paper focuses on the **weird** courtship rituals of a **barbaric** Aboriginal tribe in southwestern Australia.

READER'S REACTION: **Your paper sounds biased. How can you treat this topic fairly if you don't respect the tribe?**

EDITED   My paper focuses on the unique courtship rituals of an Aboriginal tribe in southwestern Australia.

Some racial and cultural stereotypes are so ingrained that you may not notice them at first. You may be used to hearing derogatory terms in others' speech, or you may not even know that a term is derogatory. Trusted readers can circle stereotypes and derogatory wording for you, and you can do the same for them.

46b
lang

RACIST   The economic problems in border states are compounded by an increased number of **wetbacks** from Mexico.

READER'S REACTION: **This derogatory name is offensive. I object to characterizing a group of people this way.**

EDITED   The economic problems in border states are compounded by an increased number of illegal immigrants from Mexico.

HOMOPHOBIC   The talk show included a panel of **fags** who spoke about what it's like to be a **homo**.

READER'S REACTION: **Emotionally loaded names for people don't encourage reasonable discussion. You'll have to be more objective if you want me to pay attention to your ideas.**

EDITED   The talk show included a panel of gay guests who shared their thoughts about homosexuality.

DEROGATORY   In typical **white-male** fashion, the principal argued against the teachers' referendum.

READER'S REACTION: **The fact that white men are in the majority doesn't give you permission to stereotype them negatively.**

EDITED   The principal argued against the teachers' referendum.

DISCRIMINATORY   The Johnsons **welshed** on their promise.

READER'S REACTION: **What made you think that you could say this without offending people of Welsh descent? Casual stereotyping is just as offensive as deliberate insults.**

EDITED   The Johnsons broke their promise.

Deciding how to identify groups may be difficult. The term *American Indian* is still widely accepted, but *Native American* is preferred. In the 1960s, *Negro* gradually gave way to *black*, but *African American* has gained popularity in its place. *Colored* has been out of use for some time, but *people of color* is now preferred for members of any "nonwhite" group (although some object to *nonwhite*). Terms for those of Hispanic descent include *Chicano* (and its feminine form, *Chicana*) for Mexicans and *Latino* and *Latina* for people from South and Central America in general.

- Whenever possible, use the term preferred by the group itself.
- When there is disagreement within the group, choose the *most widely accepted term* or one favored by a majority of the members.

Exercise 1

The following list of words and proposed replacements ranges from the obviously sexist (and therefore inflexible and in need of revision) to the highly debatable and even absurd. For each word, decide whether you would accept the alternative term, and explain why. (Tip: Consult a dictionary when in doubt.)

1. *Persondible* for *mandible*
2. *People-eating tiger* for *man-eating tiger*
3. *Personic depressive* for *manic depressive*
4. *Face-to-face talk* for *man-to-man talk*
5. *Sanitation employee* for *garbageman*
6. *Actor* for both *actor* and *actress*
7. *"Our parent, who art in heaven . . ."* for *"Our Father, who art in heaven . . ."*
8. *Chair* or *chairperson* for *chairman*
9. *Waitperson* or *waitron* for *waiter* and *waitress*
10. *Flight attendant* for *steward* and *stewardess*

Exercise 2   (*Answers appear on p. 519.*)

Examine the following paragraph. Then revise its sexist language. Add to the original if you wish.

46b
lang

Preschool programs for children in poor families have always been under-funded and at best only a stopgap measure for more permanent educational reform. This was the message delivered by the man-and-wife team, Dr. and Mrs. Herbert Kline, Ph.D.s, at the Eleventh Regional Conference on Preschool Education. About seven hundred elementary school teachers came to the conference to hear the Klines debunk some old wives' tales about education. The Klines also focused on what the future holds for those interested in becoming public school teachers, including the need to balance work with attending to one's husband and family. Every teacher of young children, Mrs. Herbert Kline pointed out, must not only practice her craft well but also keep abreast of new theory and research which she can then integrate into her classroom in a way rewarding to her and to her students.

Exercise 3

The chief editor of a large city newspaper received several complaint letters from readers about a sportswriter's use of the word *niggardly* to characterize the owner of a major football team who was reluctant to pay the salary asked by a new superstar player. In a column, the chief editor explained that the word *niggardly* means "stingy" or "cheap" (from Old Norse) and has absolutely no etymological connection with any racial terms. Yet some readers were offended. And, he argued, as long as they were simply *reminded* of a more offensive word, he had a duty to avoid it. He subsequently asked all reporters and editors to use alternative words. In your judgment, did the chief editor do the right thing? What issues are at stake here? Write a position statement.

47
lang

47 Building Your Language Resources

The richer your vocabulary, the more effectively you will write and read.

CIVIC NEWSLETTER Despite our efforts to lobby for a compromise, the senate engaged in an **internecine** feud over the bill.
READER'S REACTION: I like *internecine* here to suggest the senate's destructive internal conflict.

WORK MEMO   Thanks to the marketing team for its **stellar** effort.
READER'S REACTION: **What a nice way to say "job well done"!**

A varied vocabulary is essential to effective writing and easy reading in academic, work, and public communities. The more extensive your language options, the more varied, accurate, and metaphoric your prose can be. And readers will appreciate your efforts to find just the right word.

47a Recognizing your language resources as a writer

The writer can rework this sentence for a grant proposal *because she has options*—words like *beneficence* or *sustenance*.

Without **help**, the food-shelf program may be **ineffective**.

Without the **aid** of the Talbot Foundation, the food-shelf program may become **obsolete**.

Without the **beneficence** of the Talbot Foundation, the food-shelf program may **die**.

Without the **financial** beneficence of the Talbot Foundation, the food-shelf program in Seattle may die **of starvation**.

Without the financial **sustenance** of the Talbot Foundation, Seattle's food-shelf program may **slowly** die of starvation.

47b
lang

> **STRATEGY** | Build a personal vocabulary list.
>
> Use your **journal** (a record of your observations and insights) or any notebook to list unfamiliar words. Look them up, review them, incorporate them as you write, and cross them out when you can use them comfortably. Gather these words from whatever you read—public opinion pieces in the newspaper, textbooks for school, or technical materials at work.

47b Turning to the dictionary and the thesaurus

Hundreds of times you've flipped the dictionary open and checked a word's spelling or meaning. Look carefully to find much more. (See Figure 47.1, an example from *Merriam-Webster's Collegiate Dictionary*.) Like the printed versions, software dictionaries may also supply definitions, usage notes, word histories, and spelling correctors that can be personalized by adding words used often in a particular community.

47.1

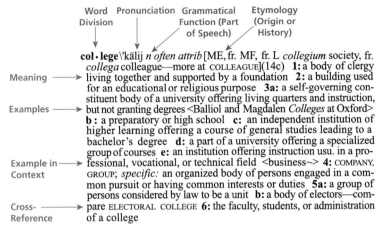

Word Division · Pronunciation · Grammatical Function (Part of Speech) · Etymology (Origin or History)

Meaning →
Examples →
Example in Context →
Cross-Reference →

col·lege\'kälij *n often attrib* [ME, fr. MF, fr. L *collegium* society, fr. *collega* colleague—more at COLLEAGUE](14c) **1:** a body of clergy living together and supported by a foundation **2:** a building used for an educational or religious purpose **3a:** a self-governing constituent body of a university offering living quarters and instruction, but not granting degrees <Balliol and Magdalen *Colleges* at Oxford> **b :** a preparatory or high school **c:** an independent institution of higher learning offering a course of general studies leading to a bachelor's degree **d:** a part of a university offering a specialized group of courses **e:** an institution offering instruction usu. in a professional, vocational, or technical field <business~> **4:** COMPANY, GROUP; *specific:* an organized body of persons engaged in a common pursuit or having common interests or duties **5a:** a group of persons considered by law to be a unit **b:** a body of electors—compare ELECTORAL COLLEGE **6:** the faculty, students, or administration of a college

FIGURE 47.1 Sample dictionary entry

Source: *Merriam-Webster's Collegiate Dictionary*, Eleventh Edition © 2005 by Merriam-Webster, Incorporated <www.merriamwebster.com>.

A **thesaurus**, printed or electronic, is a dictionary of **synonyms** and **antonyms**—words related or opposite in meaning. Under *funny*, for example, *Webster's Collegiate Thesaurus* lists synonyms such as *laughable, comical, ludicrous,* and *ridiculous*. Entries may also refer you to contrasted or compared words and related alternatives.

47b
lang

STRATEGY   Develop your skills as a "wordsmith."

- **Use a dictionary.** Circle any words you've learned recently or rarely used; look them up to be sure you've used them correctly. Try an ESL dictionary if you're not a native speaker.
- **Turn to a thesaurus.** Consider whether a new word choice is more accurate, more flavorful, or less redundant than your original choice. If in doubt, stick with words you know.
- **Learn a new word every day.** Select a word you read or heard at school, at work, or in a public setting. Look up its definition and history. Work it into your speech or writing three times during the day, or make up sentences and repeat them to yourself.
- **Try the slash/option technique.** As you draft, note alternative words, separated with slashes. Decide later which word fits best.
- **Fight insecurity with simplicity.** Ask yourself which salesperson you would trust—one who talks in simple, honest language or one who uses fancy words for product features. Choose direct, concrete words yourself.

- **Ask a colleague or supervisor.** Someone more experienced may be able to tell you whether a term fits your community or context.

Exercise 1

Conduct a brief "anatomy exam" of your own dictionary by answering the following questions.

1. What kinds of information does your dictionary give for each word?
2. How complete are the entries?
3. How have the definitions been determined?
4. How many separate entries does the dictionary include? (A good reference dictionary should contain at least 150,000 words.)
5. Are variant uses, definitions, and spellings given?
6. Does the dictionary contain acronyms (such as SIDS, ARC, NATO, FDA)?
7. Does it contain abbreviations?
8. Does it include often-used foreign words such as *tête-à-tête*, *pied-à-terre*, *calzone*, *karate*, and *kibosh*?
9. Does the dictionary show when to *italicize* words such as *cogito ergo sum* or *mea culpa*?
10. What is contained in the introduction or preface? Is there an appendix? Are there any special features?

Exercise 2

Using a good college-level dictionary, look up one or more of the following words:

caduceus   hoist   surprise   denizen   picnic

Using the annotation of *college* in Figure 47.1 as a guide, list the types of information your dictionary provides for each word—part of speech, etymology, definitions, hyphenation for word division, and so on. Be sure to look at every piece of information given for each word. What did you learn about each word that you looked up for this exercise?

47
lang

PART 11

Editing Punctuation

48 Commas

Of all the punctuation marks in English, the comma is probably the easiest to misuse.

DRAFT
During the study interviews were used to gather responses from participants and, to supplement written artifacts.

READER'S REACTION: **This sentence is hard to read. I can't tell where ideas end and begin.**

EDITED
During the study, interviews were used to gather responses from participants and to supplement written artifacts.

Readers who expect commas in certain situations are likely to find inappropriate commas confusing or disruptive.

SERIOUS ERROR

48a Joining sentences

When you use *and*, *but*, *or*, *for*, *nor*, *so*, or *yet* (**coordinating conjunctions**) to link two word groups that could stand alone as sentences (**main clauses**), place a comma *before* the conjunction.

The election was close, **and** he couldn't tell who was winning.

He heard no cheering, **yet** he decided to return to headquarters.

Precincts were still reporting, **but** the mayor's lead had grown.

Join main clauses with a comma *plus* a coordinating conjunction. If you omit the conjunction and join the clauses with only a comma, you create a **comma splice** (see 36a). Readers will react more strongly if you omit a conjunction than a comma, but they'll see both as errors in formal writing.

48a
∧
,

COMMA SPLICE
The rain soaked the soil, the mud slide buried the road.

EDITED
The rain soaked the soil, **and** the mud slide buried the road.

STRATEGY Deciding whether to add a comma.

When a coordinating conjunction links two word groups, how can you decide whether to add a comma? Analyze the word groups. If both can stand on their own as sentences (main clauses), add a comma *before* the conjunction.

main clause,   *(and, but, or, for,*
nor, so, yet)   main clause

We wanted to deliver the order **,** **but** the weather was too bad.

If one or both of the groups *cannot* stand alone as a sentence (main clause), do *not* separate the items in the pair with a comma.

PAIR SPLIT   We sanded **,** and stained the old oak table.

EDITED   We **sanded** and **stained** the old oak table.

PAIR SPLIT   I bought the wood stain because it was inexpensive **,** and easy to clean up.

EDITED   I bought the wood stain **because it was inexpensive and easy to clean up**.

When two main clauses are very short, a comma is always appropriate but sometimes can be omitted, especially in public and informal contexts.

The temperature dropped **and** the homeless shelters reopened.

Some academic readers, however, will expect you to use this comma in nearly every case.

48b Setting off sentence elements

A comma can help your readers distinguish potentially confusing sentence parts. The simplest sentences, consisting of a noun phrase and a verb phrase, need no comma.

noun phrase   **verb phrase**

Dr. Bandolo is my physician.

When you add another layer to the beginning—an **introductory word or word group**—you may need to signal the addition with a comma.

Although I am healthy , I see my doctor for a regular checkup.

For the past decade , Dr. Bandolo worked in an HMO.

Nonetheless , she may open her own practice.

The basic structure of a sentence can be interrupted with all sorts of **parenthetical expressions** that add information: words like *however* and *moreover* (**conjunctive adverbs**, see 34a); phrases like *on the other hand* or *for example* (**transitional expressions**); and **parenthetical remarks** or **interrupters** (*in fact, more importantly*). If the expression begins or ends the sentence, use one comma. If it falls in the middle, use a pair.

TRANSITIONAL	**On the other hand,** the hail caused severe damage.
INTERRUPTER	It broke, **I think,** a dozen stained glass windows.
CONJUNCTIVE ADVERB	We hope, **therefore,** that someone starts a repair fund.

Also set off tag questions, statements of contrast, and direct address.

TAG QUESTION	We should contribute, **shouldn't we?**
CONTRAST	The church's beauty touches all of us, **not just the members.**
DIRECT ADDRESS	Recall, **friends of beauty,** that every gift helps.

1 Put a comma after an introductory word or word group

Readers usually expect a comma to simplify reading by signaling where introductory wording ends and the main sentence begins. To decide whether to include a comma, consider the readability of a sentence.

CONFUSING	Forgetting to alert the media before the rally Jessica rushed to the park.
EDITED	Forgetting to alert the media before the rally, Jessica rushed to the park.

In contrast, these sentences are easy to understand without a comma.

CLEAR	By noon Jessica will be finished with her speech.
CLEAR	Suddenly it started raining, and Jessica quit speaking.

In general, put a comma at the end of a long introductory element introduced by words like *although*, *because*, and *when* (subordinators, see 42b–c); words like *during* and *without* (prepositions, see 29f); or words like *running*, *distracted*, and *to analyze* (verbals, see 30b-4). Also use a comma if a short introductory element might briefly confuse readers.

CONFUSING	By six boats began showing up.
EDITED	By six, boats began showing up.

48b
⌃,

2 Set off parenthetical expressions with commas

Use a pair of commas around a parenthetical expression or interrupter in the middle of a sentence; use a single comma with one at the beginning or end.

DRAFT	Teams should meet even spontaneously as often as needed.
EDITED	Teams should meet, even spontaneously, as often as needed.

48c Setting off nonessential modifiers

SERIOUS
ERROR

48.1

Modifiers qualify or describe nouns, verbs, or other sentence elements. You change the meaning of a sentence when you decide whether to set off a modifying word or phrase with commas. You can use a **restrictive modifier** to present essential information. Add the essentials *without* commas so that readers see them as a necessary, integral part of the sentence.

RESTRICTIVE   The charts **drawn by hand** were hard to read.

> READER'S REACTION: **I assume that the other charts, maybe generated on a computer, were easier to read than these.**

You also can use a **nonrestrictive modifier** to add information that is interesting or useful but not necessary for the meaning. Set the nonessentials off *with* commas so that readers regard them as helpful but not necessary details.

NONRESTRICTIVE   The charts **,** **drawn by hand** **,** were hard to read.

> READER'S REACTION: **All the charts were hard to read. The detail that they were hand drawn doesn't necessarily relate to readability.**

STRATEGY   Use the drop test for nonrestrictive and restrictive modifiers.

Drop the modifier from the sentence. If you can do so without altering the essential meaning, even if the sentence is less informative, the modifier is *nonrestrictive* (nonessential). Set it off with commas.

DRAFT   Their band **which performs primarily in small clubs** has gotten fine reviews.

DROP TEST   Their band has gotten fine reviews.

> The meaning is the same, although the sentence does not offer as much interesting information. The modifier is nonrestrictive.

COMMAS ADDED   Their band **,** which performs primarily in small clubs **,** has gotten fine reviews.

If dropping the modifier changes the meaning of the sentence, the modifier is *restrictive* (essential). Delete any commas with it.

DRAFT   Executives **,** **who do not know how to cope with stress** **,** are prone to stress-related illness.

DROP TEST   Executives are prone to stress-related illness.

> The intended meaning is that *some* executives are prone to stress-related problems; in contrast, the shortened sentence says they *all* are. The modifier is restrictive.

COMMAS OMITTED   Executives who do not know how to cope with stress are prone to stress-related illness.

48c

Try memorizing this formula.

*non*restrictive = *non*essential = *not* integrated (separated by commas)
restrictive = essential = integrated (not separated by commas)

Place commas before, after, or around nonrestrictive modifiers.

nonrestrictive
main clause begins,   modifier,   main clause ends
The public hearing **,** set for 7 p.m. **,** will address cable TV rates.

nonrestrictive modifier,   main clause
Because of rising costs **,** the companies have requested a rate hike.

main clause,   nonrestrictive modifier
Many residents oppose the hike **,** which is larger than last year's.

Clauses with *who, which,* and *that.* Use commas to set off nonrestrictive clauses beginning with *who, which, whom, whose, when,* or *where* (see 30c). Because *that* can specify rather than simply add information, it is used in restrictive (essential) clauses. *Which* is often used to add nonessential information but can be used both ways.

NONRESTRICTIVE   Preventive dentistry **,** **which is receiving great emphasis ,** may actually reduce visits to the dentist's office.

NONRESTRICTIVE   At the heart of preventive dentistry are toothbrushing, flossing, and rinsing **,** **which are all easily done**.

RESTRICTIVE   Dentists **who make a special effort to encourage good oral hygiene** often supply helpful pamphlets.

RESTRICTIVE   They also provide samples of toothbrushes and floss **that encourage preventive habits**.

Appositives. An **appositive** is a noun or pronoun that renames or stands for a preceding noun. Most are nonrestrictive and need commas.

NONRESTRICTIVE   Amy Nguyen **,** **a poet from Vietnam ,** recently published her latest collection of verse.

RESTRICTIVE   The well-known executive **Louis Gerstner** went from heading RJR Nabisco to the top job at IBM.

48d
∧
⸴

48d Separating items in a series

When you list items of roughly equal status in a series, separate the items with commas. Readers expect such commas because reading a series can be difficult, even confusing, without them.

The human relations office has forms for medical benefits, insurance options, **and** retirement contributions.

If an item has more than one part, put a comma after the entire unit.

The human relations office has forms for medical and dental benefits, disability and insurance options, **and** retirement contributions.

48.2

Avoid confusion by placing a comma before the *and* that introduces the last item in a series. Outside the academic community, this comma is often omitted, especially in a short, clear list. Within the academic community, however, both the MLA and APA style guides recommend this comma because it reduces ambiguity (see Chapters 25 and 26).

CONFUSING   New members fill out applications, interest-group surveys, mailing labels and publication request forms.

READER'S REACTION: **Does *mailing labels and publication request forms* refer to one item or two?**

EDITED   New members fill out applications, interest-group surveys, mailing labels, and publication request forms.

Punctuate a numbered or lettered list in a sentence as a series. If items in a list contain commas, separate them with semicolons (see 49a-3).

You should (a) measure the water's salinity, (b) weigh any waste in the filter, and (c) determine the amount of dissolved oxygen.

48e Separating adjectives in a sequence

When you use a pair of **coordinate adjectives**, each modifies the noun (or pronoun) on its own. Separate these adjectives with commas to show their equal application to the noun.

48e
∧
,

COORDINATE   These drawings describe a **quick, simple** solution.
(EQUAL)

When you use **noncoordinate adjectives**, one modifies the other, and it, in turn, modifies the noun (or pronoun). Do not separate these adjectives with a comma.

NONCOORDINATE   We can use **flexible plastic** pipe to divert the water.
(UNEQUAL)

| STRATEGY | **Ask questions to identify coordinate adjectives.** |

If you answer one of the following questions with *yes*, the adjectives are coordinate. Separate them with a comma.

- Can you place *and* or *but* between the adjectives?

COORDINATE	Irrigation has turned dry infertile [*dry and infertile?—yes*] land into orchards.
EDITED	Irrigation has turned dry , infertile land into orchards.
NOT COORDINATE	The funds went to new computer [*new and computer?—no*] equipment.

- Is the sense of the passage the same if you reverse the adjectives?

COORDINATE	We left our small cramped [*cramped small?—yes, the same*] office.
EDITED	We left our small , cramped office.
NOT COORDINATE	We bought a red brick [*brick red?—no, not the same*] condo. **Because *brick red* is a color, the condo could be wooden.**

48f Dates, numbers, addresses, place names, people's titles, and letters

Readers will expect you to follow conventional practice.

Dates. Put a comma between the date and the year, between the day of the week and the date, and after the year when you give a full date.

I ordered a laptop on May 3 , 2006 , that arrived Friday , May 19.

You don't need commas when a date is inverted (5 July 1973) or contains only month and year, month and day, or season and year.

We installed the software after its June 2006 test.

Numbers. To simplify long numbers for readers, use commas to create groups of three, beginning from the right. You may choose whether to use a comma with a four-digit number, but be consistent within a text.

We counted 1 , 746 sheep on a ranch that is worth $1 , 540 , 000.

Omit commas in addresses and page numbers of four digits or more.

18520 South Kedzie Drive   page 2054

Addresses and place names. Separate names of cities and states with commas. For an address within a sentence, place commas between all elements *except* the state and zip code. Do not place a comma after the zip code unless some other sentence element requires one.

> If you live in South Bend **,** Indiana **,** order locally from Frelle and Family **,** Seed Brokers **,** Box 389 **,** Holland **,** MI 30127.

People's names and titles. When you give a person's last name first, separate it from the first name with a comma: *Shamoon, Linda K.* Use a comma before and after a title that *follows* a person's name.

> We hired **Cris Bronkowski ,** **A.I.A. ,** to design the building.

Openings and closings of letters. Use a comma after the opening of a personal letter, but use a colon in a business or formal letter. Use a comma after the closing, just before the signature.

> Dear Nan **,**   Dear Tennis Team **,**   Dear Hardware Customers **:**
>
> Sincerely **,**   Best wishes **,**   With affection **,**   Regards **,**

48g Commas with quotations

SERIOUS ERROR

When you introduce, interrupt, or conclude a quotation with a source or context, use commas to distinguish explanation from quotation.

> At the dedication, she stated **,** "This event celebrates Oakdale."
>
> "Our unity **,**" said the mayor **,** "is our strength."
>
> "Tomorrow the school can reopen **,**" the principal reported.

If your explanation ends with *that* just before a quotation, do not include a comma. If you quote a person's words indirectly (rather than word for word in quotation marks), do not use a comma after *that*.

> Lu introduced her by saying that "calamity followed Jane." Jane replied that she simply outran it.

48h Commas to make your meaning clear

Even if no rule specifies a comma, add one if necessary to clarify your meaning, to remind readers of deleted words, or to emphasize.

CONFUSING   When food is scarce, animals that can expand their grazing territory at the expense of other species.

EDITED   When food is scarce, animals that can **,** expand their grazing territory at the expense of other species.

48i Eliminating commas that do not belong

Avoid scattering commas throughout a paper; add them as required. Today most readers prefer a style in which commas are not used heavily. Too many commas, even correctly used, can create choppy prose.

TOO MANY COMMAS (7)   Rosa ❝ always one ❝ like her mother ❝ to speak her mind ❝ protested the use of force ❝ as she called it ❝ by two store detectives ❝ who had been observing her.

EDITED (2)   Always one to speak her mind ❝ like her mother ❝ Rosa protested what she called the use of force by two store detectives.

- Omit commas after words like *although* and *because*. These subordinating conjunctions (see 42b–c) introduce a clause and should not be set off with commas. Conjunctive adverbs (like *however*; see 42a) and transitional expressions (like *for example*) should be set off with commas.

EXTRA COMMA   **Although** ❝ Jewel lost her luggage, she had her laptop.

EDITED   **Although** Jewel lost her luggage, she had her laptop.

- Remove commas between subjects and verbs unless a modifier separates them.

SPLIT SUBJECT AND PREDICATE   Cézanne's painting *Rocks at L'Estaque* ❝ hangs in the Museu de Arte in São Paulo, Brazil.

EDITED   Cézanne's painting *Rocks at L'Estaque* hangs in the Museu de Arte in São Paulo, Brazil.

Exercise 1   *(Answers appear on p. 519.)*

Combine each of the following sentence pairs into a single sentence, using commas and coordinating conjunctions.

EXAMPLE   ₍ *and it*
Shopping by mail can be convenient. ~~It~~ sometimes helps save money.
                        ^

1. Jim wanted to buy paper for his copier. He went to all the office supply stores in town.
2. The stores had plenty of paper. It cost more than Jim was willing to pay.
3. Jim then heard about a mail-order office supply company. He called the company for a catalog.
4. The catalog contained more than fifty different kinds of reasonably priced copier paper. The paper was available in packs of one thousand

48i
₍

sheets. For an even greater discount, the paper came in bulk orders of five thousand sheets.

5. He ordered five thousand sheets of medium-quality paper. It lasted for three months.

Exercise 2   *(Answers appear on p. 519.)*

A. Edit the following sentences by placing commas after introductory elements where necessary.

EXAMPLE

In the past ⌄ mailboxes usually had simple designs.

1. In contrast ⌄ mailboxes today come in many surprising designs.
2. Occasionally people in the suburbs choose an unusual mailbox, but residents of small towns generally display the most imagination.
3. On a recent trip through rural Iowa I noticed mailboxes in the shape of log cabins, igloos, Eiffel Towers, cows, cats, and even parrots.
4. One morning I drove down a block on which each mailbox took the shape of a different kind of fish, including bass, trout, bluegill, shark, pike, and salmon.
5. Whenever you start thinking that people in big cities or suburbs are more creative than people in small towns remember the mailboxes.

B. Combine each of the following pairs of sentences by making one an introductory element for the other. Insert commas when appropriate.

EXAMPLE

Because
~~T~~he morning was gray and foggy, ⌐ ~~M~~any people woke up late.

1. People felt sleepy. They still had to go to their offices and plants for a full day's work.
2. People were trying to get to work on time. They jammed the highways and commuter trains.
3. Avi felt rested and alert. The gloomy weather did not bother him.
4. Avi worked hard throughout the afternoon. The other people in Avi's office were exhausted by two o'clock in the afternoon.
5. Avi still felt awake at seven o'clock in the evening. He went to see a movie.

48
⌄
c

Exercise 3   *(Answers appear on p. 520.)*

Edit the following sentences to set off all nonrestrictive modifiers with commas and to eliminate any commas that unnecessarily set off restrictive modifiers.

EXAMPLE

My mother ˄who is ninety ˄lives in the retirement residence⫽called South Bay Manor.

1. Fifty years ago, a residence that served retired people, was called an old folks' home.
2. These homes which provided few services for residents were apartment buildings with dining rooms.
3. A retirement residence today offers many things to do including recreational activities, fitness programs, trips, classes, and social events.
4. The image of infirm people, sitting in rocking chairs, has been replaced by one of senior citizens, who are vigorous and involved.
5. Retirement residences often known as retirement communities are small towns, where people go to lead active lives.

Exercise 4

Edit the following sentences to add or delete commas as appropriate.

EXAMPLE

Scheduling may be ˄in fact ˄the toughest job any manager faces.

1. Project schedules need to be arranged so that the job gets done on time of course.
2. Moreover meetings need to be set up so they do not interrupt people's work, unnecessarily.
3. Most staff members are cooperative however, and may even offer suggestions for scheduling.
4. Management training programs should, I think offer instruction in scheduling techniques.
5. Remember your staff's time is too valuable to be wasted.

Exercise 5   *(Answers appear on p. 520.)*

Edit the following sentences so that any series and any coordinate adjectives are correctly punctuated. Let any correct sentence stand.

EXAMPLE

McDonald's ˄Burger King ˄and Wendy's are worldwide symbols of American culture.

1. McDonald's and the others offer quick appetizing meals and clean pleasant surroundings.
2. In the late 1940s, the McDonald brothers opened a restaurant serving a limited inexpensive menu, including fifteen-cent hamburgers french fries and shakes.

48
˄
˅

3. The brothers did not want to expand their modestly successful restaurant into a chain.

4. Ray Kroc, a manufacturer of milkshake machines, recognized the potential of the brothers' innovations joined their business to help it expand and, frustrated by their lack of ambition, eventually bought them out.

5. Kroc continued to develop innovative imaginative ways to serve customers, and these fast efficient practices have come to characterize today's fast-food restaurants.

Exercise 6

Edit the following sentences by adding or eliminating commas as appropriate.

EXAMPLE

My mother remembers assembling her first jigsaw puzzle in autumn ⌄ 1985, several months before my birth on January 22 ⌄ 1986.

1. Puzzles have fascinated me for the last twelve years, and last year I spent exactly $2479.83 on them.

2. For my birthday this year, one cousin gave me a map of Chicago Illinois in the form of a jigsaw puzzle, and another cousin gave me a puzzle of a seventeenth-century print from the Beinecke Library at Yale University New Haven Connecticut.

3. I have ordered a puzzle map of Atlanta Georgia from Buffalo Games, Inc. P.O. Box 85 601 Amherst Street Buffalo New York 14207 and a puzzle of Edward Hopper's painting, *Nighthawks* from Galison Books 36 West 44th Street New York New York 10036.

4. From January through June 2001, I assembled one puzzle a week, with the puzzles ranging from 500 to 1250 pieces each for a total of somewhere between 10500 pieces and 26250 pieces.

5. I am planning to have a business card made up with both my official and unofficial titles, Jessica Montoya Ph.D. Puzzle Assembler.

Exercise 7

A. Edit the following passages by adding, deleting, or moving commas so that quotations are appropriately punctuated.

"Ice cream is virtually the only food we eat frozen, which means that its flavor, which we define as a composite of taste and smell, is only fully released upon melting" explains Arun Kilara, a 43-year-old professor of food science at Penn State and one of the world's acknowledged authorities on ice cream.

48
⌄

Not surprisingly, few true ice cream connoisseurs are fond of the industry's use of fat substitutes, such as the complex protein found in NutraSweet's Simplesse. "The search for the perfect fat substitute" Kilara says "is like a contemporary version of alchemy—lots of useful discoveries, but they'll never turn lead into gold." While some protein-based fat substitutes approximate fat's texture, or "mouth feel" he explains, they cannot dissolve flavor compounds in the same way.

"The smaller the ice crystals, the smoother the ice cream" says Kilara. "You get the smallest crystals when the drop in temperature is the most rapid and when agitation is most vigorous."

"There's one basic truth about ice cream—its quality begins deteriorating from the moment it is made" Kilara concludes. "Over the product's lifetime, ice cream's air escapes, its fat clumps, its ice melts, and its water freezes."

—LAWRENCE E. JOSEPH, "The Scoop on Ice Cream"

B. Write a paragraph that presents information drawn from a newspaper or magazine article. Include several quotations from the article in your paragraph. Indicate the source or context for the quotations, and use commas appropriately to introduce or conclude the quoted material.

Exercise 8 *(Answers appear on p. 521.)*

Edit each of the following sentences in two ways: (1) by removing any unnecessary commas and (2) by rewriting to create sentence structures that contain fewer commas, all of which are necesssary.

EXAMPLE

When ̷they realized they had no job prospects, the five friends ̷

formed ̷a company, which they called Home Restorers, Inc.

When they realized they had no job prospects, the five friends formed Home Restorers, Inc.

48
⌃
,

1. Because, she likes the outdoors, Sandy, a devoted gardener, takes care of landscaping, grass cutting, and outdoor cleanup.
2. Strong, tireless Jun, does roofing, paving, and similar work.
3. Interior design was, Padmaja's major, so she, everyone agrees, is the person best qualified to do interior decorating.
4. Having painted, her parents' house one summer, Rachael was, chosen, by her partners, as the company's painting supervisor.
5. Desperate, for a place in the company, Joel decided that, marketing, because it would draw on his undergraduate work in sociology, was the best thing for him to do.

49 Semicolons and Colons

Semicolons and colons help readers make connections.

TWO SENTENCES   On April 12, 1861, one of Beauregard's batteries fired on Fort
Sumter● The Civil War had begun.

> READER'S REACTION: **Maybe these two sentences present a dramatic moment, or maybe they simply state facts, but they don't *necessarily* connect these events.**

SEMICOLON   On April 12, 1861, one of Beauregard's batteries fired on Fort
Sumter; the Civil War had begun.

> READER'S REACTION: **The semicolon encourages me to link the battery firing to the Civil War beginning.**

COLON   On April 12, 1861, one of Beauregard's batteries fired on Fort
Sumter: the Civil War had begun.

> READER'S REACTION: **Now I see the guns' firing as a dramatic moment: the beginning of the Civil War.**

All three examples are correct, yet each encourages a different perspective. Readers expect you to use punctuation, especially semicolons and colons, to shape their responses and show them how your ideas relate.

49a Semicolons

SERIOUS
ERROR

A semicolon creates a brief reading pause that can dramatically highlight a close relationship or a contrast. The semicolon alone can't specify the relationship the way words like *because* or *however* can. Be sure, therefore, that the relationship you are signaling won't be puzzling to readers.

49a
;

1 Join two sentences with a semicolon

A semicolon joins main clauses that can stand alone as complete sentences.

TWO SENTENCES   The demand for paper is at an all-time high● Businesses alone
consume millions of tons each year.

ONE SENTENCE   The demand for paper is at an all-time high; businesses alone
consume millions of tons each year.

49.1

445

STRATEGY Test both sides of the semicolon.

To make sure you are using the semicolon correctly, test the word groups on both sides to make sure they can stand on their own as sentences.

DRAFT The demand for recycled paper increased greatly**;** with manufacturers rushing to contract for scrap paper.

TEST CLAUSE 1 The demand for recycled paper increased greatly.
The first clause is a complete sentence.

TEST CLAUSE 2 With manufacturers rushing to contract for scrap paper.
The second part is a sentence fragment.

EDITED The demand for recycled paper increased greatly**;** manufacturers rushed to contract for scrap paper.

In some cases, elements within a second clause can be omitted if they "match" elements in the first clause. Then the two can be joined with a semicolon even though the second could not stand alone.

ELEMENTS INCLUDED In winter, **the hotel guests enjoy** the log fire**;** in summer, **the hotel guests enjoy** the patio overlooking the river.

ELEMENTS OMITTED In winter, **the hotel guests enjoy** the log fire**;** in summer, the patio overlooking the river.

2 Use a semicolon with words such as *however* and *on the other hand*

When you use a semicolon alone to link main clauses, you ask readers to recognize the logical link between the clauses. When you add words like *however* or *on the other hand*, you create a different effect on readers by specifying how the clauses relate.

assertion → semicolon → transition → assertion
(pause) *(consider relationship)*

I like apples**;** however**,** I hate pears.
assertion pause contrast assertion

To specify the transition between clauses, you can choose a **conjunctive adverb** such as *however, moreover, nonetheless, thus,* or *therefore* (see 42a) or a **transitional expression** like *for example, in contrast,* or *on the other hand.* Vary the punctuation depending on where you place such wording.

BETWEEN CLAUSES Joe survived the flood**;** however**,** Al was never found.

WITHIN CLAUSE Joe survived the flood**;** Al**,** however**,** was never found.

AT END OF CLAUSE Joe survived the flood**;** Al was never found**,** however.

49a
;

3 Use a semicolon with a complex series

When items in a series contain commas, readers may have trouble deciding which commas separate parts of the series and which belong within items. To avoid confusion, put semicolons between elements in a series when one or more contain other punctuation.

CONFUSING   I interviewed Debbie Rios, the attorney, Rhonda Marron, the accountant, and the financial director.
READER'S REACTION: How many? Three, four, or five?

EDITED   I interviewed Debbie Rios, the attorney**;** Rhonda Marron, the accountant**;** and the financial director.

49b Colons

Use a colon to introduce, separate, or join elements.

1 Introducing examples, lists, and quotations

The words *before* the colon generally form a complete sentence while those after may or may not. When the words after the colon don't form a sentence, begin with a lowercase letter. When a sentence follows, begin with either a capital or lowercase letter. Stick to one style in a text.

Examples. Commonly, a colon follows a statement or generalization that the rest of the sentence illustrates, explains, or particularizes.

She has only one budget priority**:** teacher salaries.

Lists. A colon can introduce a list or series following a sentence. Following a word group other than a complete sentence, do not use a colon.

DRAFT   The symptoms are**:** sore throat, fever, and headache.   **49.2**

EDITED   She had three symptoms**:** sore throat, fever, and headache.

EDITED   The symptoms are sore throat, fever, and headache.

Quotations. Whether you integrate a short quotation with your own words or set off a longer one in your text (see 23a1–2), a complete sentence must precede a colon. If not, use a comma.

Ms. Nguyen outlined the plan**:** "Boost sales, and cut costs."

2 Separating titles and subtitles

Colons separate main titles from subtitles.

*Designing Your Web Site***:** *A Beginner's Guide*   "Diabetes**:** Are You at Risk?"

Colons also separate hours from minutes (10**:**32); chapters from verses, as in the Bible (John 8**:**21–23); the salutation from the text of a business letter (Dear Ms. Billis**:**); parts of a ratio (2**:**3); parts of an electronic address (http**:**//www.nytimes.com); and parts of references in some documentation styles (see Chapters 25–28).

3 Using a colon to join sentences

You may use a colon to join two word groups that can stand on their own as sentences (main clauses, see 36c). Use a colon when the second clause sharply focuses, sums up, or illustrates the first.

The blizzard swept across the prairie **:** **the Oregon Trail was closed**.

Exercise 1

The following passage contains some semicolons used correctly and some used incorrectly. It also contains sentences that might be more effective if joined with semicolons and others that would be better as separate sentences. Rewrite the passage, adding or eliminating semicolons and making any other changes necessary to create a more effective piece of writing.

The Grateful Dead came back into my life recently; largely because of my children's interest. My daughter has been *associated* with the group; I find it difficult to apply the common description of a fan as a Deadhead; since she was fifteen. Her school band; the Cosmic Country Sound, was patterned after the Grateful Dead; she was its lead singer and tambourine player.

I had no idea that my son, four years younger; had any interest in the group. His room is decorated with posters of Boris Becker and Albert Einstein. But then a year ago he let his hair grow into a mane; started wearing beaded necklaces and rope wristlets, and, sure enough; turned up one day at my study door to announce, "Dad; there's this concert I'd like to go to . . . ."

Both of my children have urged me to go to a Grateful Dead concert. I hadn't taken them up on the offer until this summer; when by chance I met someone way up in the band's hierarchy who gave me not only some tickets to a concert at the Meadowlands in New Jersey; but also a backstage pass. I told my son. His eyes widened at the news. He invited three of his friends. His sister; with a job on the West Coast, was devastated that she couldn't be on hand.

—Adapted from GEORGE PLIMPTON, "Bonding with the Grateful Dead"

Exercise 2 *(Answers appear on p. 521.)*

Edit the following sentences by deleting misused or overused colons, adding colons where needed, and retaining any colons that are appropriate. You may need to rewrite some of the sentences.

EXAMPLE

For the Hirsches retirement meant a trip to France.

1. They prepared for the trip by: first looking for inexpensive hotels in Paris.
2. The Residence Rivoli seemed like a good value clean, centrally located: private bath.
3. Mr. Hirsch, however, wanted to splurge: He argued that an upper-bracket hotel would be so much more enjoyable: a shining marble bath, plush dining room, and elegant meals. There would be parking as well: essential for anyone with a car.
4. But Mrs. Hirsch wasn't impressed: the expensive hotels would be comfortable, but she wanted atmosphere: and small, charming hotels would have that in abundance.
5. Finally, they reached a compromise; they would: stay in a chateau near the Loire, which would be cheaper than a fancy Paris hotel but afford plenty of atmosphere. Then they could: drive into Paris; enjoy the sights; and have a peaceful night: all without driving more than an hour or so each way.

50 Apostrophes

Like the dot above the *i*, the apostrophe may seem trivial. But without it, readers would stumble over your sentences, growing irritated in the process.

DRAFT Though its an 1854 novel, Dickens *Hard Times* remain's an ageless critique of education by fact's.

READER'S REACTION: I can't tell possessives from plurals and contractions. This is too annoying to bother reading.

EDITED Though it's an 1854 novel, **Dickens's** *Hard Times* **remains** an ageless critique of education by **facts.**

SERIOUS
ERROR

50a Apostrophes that mark possession

A noun that expresses ownership is called a **possessive noun**. Mark possessive nouns to distinguish them from plurals.

50.1   **MISSING**   The **cats** meow is becoming fainter.

> READER'S REACTION: I expected something like "The cats meow all night." Do you mean many cats or the meow of one cat?

EDITED   The **cat**'s meow is becoming fainter.

STRATEGY   Test for possession.

If you can turn a noun into a phrase using *of*, use a possessive form. If not, use a plural.

DRAFT   The officers reports surprised the reporters.

TEST   The reports **of** the officers? [yes, a possessive]

TEST   Reports surprised **of** the reporters? [no, a plural]

EDITED   The officers' reports surprised the reporters.

---

1 Adding an apostrophe alone or an apostrophe plus *-s*

Use these guidelines to decide whether to add an apostrophe plus *-s* or an apostrophe alone.

- **Does the noun end in a letter other than -s?** When you write a singular possessive noun, usually follow it with an apostrophe plus *-s*.

  Bill's coat   Connecticut's taxes   the dog's collar

  Possessive indefinite pronouns (see 29b) follow the same pattern.

  nobody's report   everybody's office   someone's lunch

  A few nouns form their plurals (*mice, fish*) without ending in *-s* or *-es*.

  oxen's habitat   children's toys   women's locker room

- **Does the noun end in -s, and is it plural** (more than one person or item)? Most plural nouns end in *-s* or *-es*. To make one possessive, simply add an apostrophe after the *-s*.

  the Solomons' house   the roses' petals   the buses' routes

- **Does the noun end in -s, and is it singular** (one person or item)? Stick to one of two options in a paper. The preferred convention is to add an apostrophe and another *-s*, as with another singular noun.

50a

Chris**'s** van   Elliott Ness**'s** next move

Alternatively, simply add an apostrophe to the final -s.

Chris**'** van   Elliott Ness**'** next move

- **Does the noun end in -s and sound awkward?** Occasionally, adding a possessive -s (Hodges**'s**) to a word already ending in that sound will seem awkward to say ("Hodges-es"). If so, use only the apostrophe (Hodges**'**) to indicate only one -s sound, or avoid the awkwardness (*the Adams County Schools**'**s policy*) by rewriting (*the policy of the Adams County Schools*).

In general, treat **hyphenated** and **multiple-word nouns** as a single unit, marking possession on the last word.

HYPHENATED   My **father-in-law'**s library is extensive.

MULTIPLE-WORD   The **union leaders'** negotiations collapsed.

When you use a **compound noun phrase** (two or more nouns connected by *and* or *or*) as a possessive, decide whether the nouns function as separate items or as a single unit.

Billy's and **Harold'**s lawyers were ruthless. [separate lawyers]

Billy and **Harold'**s lawyers were ruthless. [same legal team]

2 Avoiding unnecessary apostrophes

Even though third person singular verbs end in -s, these are not nouns and do not have possessive forms. They don't require an apostrophe.

DRAFT   The contractor **order'**s all material early.

EDITED   The contractor **orders** all material early.

Don't add apostrophes to personal pronouns; they're already possessive. (See 50b.)

If this car is **yours**, why did you take **hers** and dent **its** fender?

50b

50b Apostrophes that mark contractions and omissions

You can use an apostrophe to indicate the omission of one or more letters when two words are brought together to form a **contraction**.

1 Using an apostrophe to contract a verb form

50.2

You can contract pronouns and verbs into a single unit (you'll = you + will) or splice nouns followed by *is*. If this informal style seems inappropriate in your class or workplace, always err on the side of formality.

INFORMAL   Shoshana's going, but her **seat's** in the last row.

MORE FORMAL   Shoshana **is** going, but her **seat is** in the last row.

STRATEGY   **Use the expansion test.**

To decide whether you have used a contraction appropriately, expand it.

they're	=	they + are	there	=	an adverb
you're	=	you + are	your	=	a possessive pronoun
who's	=	who + is	whose	=	a possessive pronoun
it's	=	it + is	its	=	a possessive pronoun

For example, test your use of the contraction *it's* by expanding the expression (*it + is*); if the expansion doesn't make sense, use *its*.

DRAFT   **Its** the best animal shelter in **its** area.

EXPANSION TEST **It is** [yes, a fit] the best animal shelter in **it is** [no, not a fit] area.

EDITED   **It's** the best animal shelter in **its** area.

---

2 Using an apostrophe to mark plural numbers and letters

Make letters and numbers plural by adding an apostrophe plus -*s*.

LETTERS   Mind your **p's** and **q's**. The **x's** mark missing lines.

NUMBERS   I'll take two size **10's** and two size **12's**.

Sometimes the apostrophe is omitted if it risks making a term look like a possessive (*TAs* or *TA's*). The MLA and APA styles (see Chapters 25–26) omit it from numbers and abbreviations (*1980s* and *IQs*).

50b

⌄

3 Using an apostrophe to abbreviate a year or show colloquial pronunciation

Informally abbreviate years by omitting the first two numbers (*the '90s* or *the class of '05*) if the century is clear to readers. Also use apostrophes to indicate omissions in colloquial speech and dialects.

DIALECT   I'm **a-goin'** out for some **o'** them shrimp **an'** oysters.

Exercise 1   *(Answers appear on p. 521.)*

Edit the possessive forms in the following sentences so that each uses possessive apostrophes correctly. You may also have to add or move apostrophes, but do not change any correct forms.

EXAMPLE

France͜ longest river, the Loire, has its source in Vivarais and winds its way some six hundred miles to the Atlantic.

1. The rivers name is especially associated with the many chateaux that line its bank's.
2. Serious sightseers visits to the Loire Valley should include tours of several of this regions beautiful castles.
3. The Loires reputation is also founded on its renowned cuisine and its sophisticated wines.
4. Barton and Jone's wine import businesses have flourished in the United States ever since Jones came up with the companys award-winning advertising campaign.
5. Several other companies have found an eager market for Frances excellent wine's.

Exercise 2

The following paragraph contains sentences with some contracted words that require apostrophes and some "lookalikes" that do not. All these words appear in italics. Insert apostrophes where they belong.

Many medical scholars believe that the age of molecular biology *didnt* really begin until April 1953 when Watson and Crick's article on the double helix appeared in a scientific journal. These researchers *werent* sure at that time how influential their ideas would become. *Its* generally thought, for example, that if several important researchers *hadnt* immediately seen the underlying brilliance of the double helix, the whole idea *wouldnt* have gained such a quick following. *"Your* basic educator," Professor Ewell Samuels asserts, *"couldnt* have seen beyond what was already a given in biology. *Its* when *youre* presented with many scholars *whose* ideas agree that things really begin to happen. *Whos* going to argue with a whole field jumping on the bandwagon of a new theory?"

50

∨

51 Marking Quotations

Quotation marks play many conventional roles.

QUOTATION NOT FULLY MARKED

"Thanks to the navigator," the pilot said, we made the landing.

READER'S REACTION: Without quotation marks, I didn't realize at first that the pilot said the last part, too.

EDITED

❝Thanks to the navigator,❞ the pilot said, ❝we made the landing.❞

Although conventions may vary slightly by field, readers in academic, work, and public settings expect you to use quotation marks precisely. How you use these marks tells readers who said what. (See 23b1–2.)

51a Using quotation marks

Quotation marks tell readers which words are someone else's (and which words are your own).

1 Identifying direct quotations and dialogue

Whenever you directly quote someone's exact words, spoken or written, use double quotation marks (" ") both before and after the quotation. Long quotations for research papers are an exception (see 23b1–2).

51a
❝❞

SPOKEN QUOTATION

❝The loon can stay under water for a few minutes,❞ the ranger said.

WRITTEN QUOTATION

Gross argues that ❝every generation scorns its offspring's culture❞ (9).

Use quotation marks within a sentence to separate quoted material from the words you use to introduce or comment on it.

51.1

QUOTATION INTERRUPTED

❝Every generation,❞ according to Gross, ❝scorns its offspring's culture❞ (9).

When you are writing dialogue and a new person speaks, indent as if you're starting a new paragraph. Begin with new quotation marks.

ESL ADVICE: QUOTATION MARKS

If your native language uses other marks for quotations or if you are used to British conventions, try using your computer's search capacity to find each of the marks so you can check for American usage.

2 Setting off quotations inside quotations

Whenever one quotation contains another, use single marks (' ') for the inside quotation and double marks (" ") for the one enclosing it.

De Morga's account of the sinking of the *San Diego* described the battle that "caused his ship to 'burst asunder'" (Goddio 37).

3 Integrating indirect quotations

Whenever you paraphrase or summarize someone else's words, do not use quotation marks. (See Chapter 23.)

INDIRECT QUOTATION (PARAPHRASE)
The pilot told us that the navigator made the safe landing possible.

INDIRECT QUOTATION (SUMMARY)
Samuel Gross believes that the social consequences of a major war nearly vanish after just one generation (5).

51b Titles of short works

Use quotation marks to enclose titles of short works, parts of a larger work or series, and unpublished works. (See also 55a.)

QUOTATION MARKS WITH TITLES

ARTICLES AND STORIES

"TV Gets Blame for Poor Reading"	newspaper article
"Feminism's Identity Crisis"	magazine article
"The Idea of the Family in the Middle East"	chapter in book
"Baba Yaga and the Brave Youth"	story
"The Rise of Germism"	essay

POEMS AND SONGS

"A Woman Cutting Celery"	short poem
"Evening" (from *Pippa Passes*)	section of a long poem
"Riders on the Storm"	song

(Continued)

51b
66 99

QUOTATION MARKS WITH TITLES *(Continued)*

EPISODES AND PARTS OF LONGER WORKS

"Billy's Back"   episode of a TV series
"All We Like Sheep"   section of a long musical
 (from Handel's *Messiah*)   work

UNPUBLISHED WORKS

"Renaissance Men—and Women"   unpublished lecture
"Sources of the Ballads in   unpublished dissertation
 Bishop Percy's Folio Manuscript"

Do not use quotation marks for *your* own title unless it contains the title of another work or some other element requiring quotation marks.

DRAFT   "The Theme of the Life Voyage in Crane's Story 'Open Boat'"

EDITED   The Theme of the Life Voyage in Crane's Story "Open Boat"

51c Highlighting words, special terms, and tone of voice

51.2

You can use quotation marks or italics (see 55b) to set off technical terms, unusual terms, or words used in a special sense. Avoid too much highlighting; it distracts readers, and most terms don't require it.

In the real estate industry, "FSBO" (sometimes pronounced "fizbo") refers to a home that is "for sale by owner."

You can—*sparingly*—use quotation marks to indicate irony or sarcasm or to show a reader that you don't "lay claim" to an expression.

51c
" "

Exercise 1   *(Answers appear on p. 522.)*

Add quotation marks to the following passage as appropriate.

The shame of illiteracy—or so Robert Cullany puts it—affects millions of adults in the United States alone, but the problem is not nearly as prevalent as innumeracy, Cullany's term that means being unable to use numbers. Cullany writes, illiteracy and innumeracy are a national blight on our intellectual landscape, and cannot be tolerated. He also points out that they cripple our productivity, lead to familial dysfunction (poor family structures), and deny people the ability to become what Cullany calls self-learners. The ALVC, or Adult Literacy Volunteer Corps, is made up of dedicated people who believe they can help this so-called mind plague.

Exercise 2

Edit the following passage by adding or deleting quotation marks as appropriate. Leave in place any quotation marks that are correctly used.

On April 12, 1633, Galileo was interrogated by the Inquisitor for the Holy Roman and Universal Inquisition. The focus was Galileo's book, the *"Dialogue on the Great World Systems,"* in which he posited the theory of a "spinning" earth that "circulated" around the sun. The theory itself was "bad" enough given the Pope's "beliefs," but one of the "characters" in the book's "dialogue" was cast as a "simpleton," and the Pope thought that perhaps it referred to him because he didn't go along with Galileo's "theory." At one point, the Inquisitor asked Galileo, "Did you obtain permission to write the book? To which Galileo replied, I did not seek permission to write this book because I consider that I did not disobey the instruction I had been given. "Did you disclose the Sacred Congregation's demands when you printed the book?" asked the Inquisitor. "I said nothing, Galileo replied, when I sought permission to publish, not having in the book either held or defended opinion. In the end, "Galileo" had to retract his "book," and was also shown instruments of torture "as if" they were going to be used—a "scare tactic," to be sure.

—Adapted from Jacob Bronowski, *The Ascent of Man*

52 Periods, Question Marks, and Exclamation Points

When you speak, you mark sentence boundaries with changes in pitch or pauses. When you write, you use visual symbols—a period, a question mark, or an exclamation point. Use some of these marks sparingly, however.

LESS FORMAL   And why do we need your support **?** Without you, too many lovable pups will never find new homes **!**

> READER'S REACTION: **This bouncy style is great for our volunteer brochure but not for our annual report.**

MORE FORMAL   The League's volunteers remain our most valuable asset, matching abandoned animals with suitable homes **.**

52a Periods

No matter how complicated, all sentences that are *statements* must end with periods—even if they contain clauses that appear to be something other than statements. The following sentence as a whole is a statement; it reports, but does not ask, the question in the second half.

Naomi thanked her supporters profusely but wondered whether they felt responsible for her defeat.

52.1

Periods also mark decimal points in numbers (22.6 or 5.75) and punctuate abbreviations by letting readers know that something has been eliminated from the word or term.

Dr. Ms. Ph.D. C.P.A. pp. etc. a.m. p.m.

Some abbreviations may not require periods, especially **acronyms** whose letters form pronounceable words (*OSHA, NATO*), terms entirely capitalized (*GOP*), and state names such as *OH*. When in doubt, turn to a dictionary.

When an abbreviation with a period occurs at the *end* of a sentence, that period will also end the sentence. If the abbreviation occurs in the *middle* of a sentence, the period may be followed by another mark, such as a comma, dash, colon, or semicolon.

Residents spoke until 10 p.m., and we adjourned at 11 p.m.

52b Question marks

Always end a direct question with a question mark. In a sentence with several clauses, the main clause usually determines the punctuation.

DIRECT	When is the train leaving?
DIRECT: QUOTED	Laitan asked, "Why is the air rising so quickly?"
DIRECT: TWO CLAUSES	Considering that the tax break has been widely publicized, why have so few people filed for a refund?

52b
?

52.2

When you present an **indirect question**—a sentence whose main clause is a statement and whose embedded clause asks a question—end with a period.

INDIRECT   José asked if we needed help preparing the bid.

A question mark also may signal an uncertain date or other fact.

David Robert Styles, 1632?–1676   Meadville, pop. 196?

Unless you're writing very informally, avoid adding question marks after other people's statements, using more than one question mark for emphasis, or combining question marks and exclamation points.

52c Exclamation points

Exclamation points end emphatic statements such as commands or warnings but are rarely used in most academic or workplace writing.

Like question marks, exclamation points can be used informally. They can express dismay, outrage, shock, or strong interest. As you revise and edit, look for strong words to emphasize a point.

DRAFT   Rescuers spent hours (!) trying to reach the child.

EDITED   Rescuers spent **agonizing** hours trying to reach the child.

Exercise 1

Edit the following sentences so that periods are used correctly, adding or omitting punctuation as appropriate.

EXAMPLE
Every two years the French department at St Joseph's College organizes a group trip to a foreign country.

1. On our trip to France, we visited the medieval city of Carcassonne
2. As we approached the inner city, which was surrounded by high walls and a real moat, we wondered whether we were still in the twentieth century?
3. "Have we fallen into a time warp or something" Trish said?
4. As we climbed up to the ramparts at 9 p.m, we decided that the experience was almost as good as watching a N.A.S.A. space shuttle launch.
5. Mr Siefert, the hotel manager, told us that the Bastille Day fireworks would begin at 9:30 p.m.

Exercise 2

Edit the following passage by removing any inappropriate question marks and adding any that are required.

Are you bat-phobic. Although bats have been hated and feared for centuries, most species are harmless to humans and beneficial to the environment. In his article "Are We Batty Over Bats," Harlan Sneed

52c
!

wonders whether our destruction of bats is really justified? Should we be smoke-bombing caves that are breeding places for thousands of bats, just because we are afraid of them. Sneed also gives examples of cultures that are contributing to the extinction of bats not through fear but through excessive trapping—for food; they are a delicacy (!?) in some parts of the world. Sneed ends his article with a reminder: "Environmental protection is as much a matter of the way we think as the way we act. Maybe you have never *acted* against your environment but are you entirely inculpable in your thoughts and attitudes."

Exercise 3

Edit the following passage by removing or adding exclamation points to make them correct and stylistically acceptable.

Seventy-five miles (!) from anywhere, Frank's old Buick decided to sputter and stall out on the edge of Route 61. Meanwhile, the temperature had fallen to 16 below!!!! To make matters worse, the wind had whipped up to 30 miles per hour! That's an incredible wind chill of around 75 below zero!!!!! "Hey," yelled Bill, "don't anyone leave this car. If we stay put, maybe the highway patrol will spot us." "Who are you kidding!!??" shouted Frank. "It's 3 a.m.!"

53 | Other Punctuation Marks

53

Most punctuation symbols make up a kind of toolbox for writing. You can use the tools to change the style, sense, and effect of your prose. For example, punctuation marks help guide readers through complex sentences.

DASHES

When the boy━**clutching three weeks' allowance**━returned to the store, it had already closed.

READER'S REACTION: **Dashes emphasize how hard the boy worked to save his allowance.**

PARENTHESES

When the boy **(clutching three weeks' allowance)** returned to the store, it had already closed.

READER'S REACTION: **The parentheses de-emphasize the boy's savings, making the store hours seem more important.**

COMMAS   When the boy ₉ **clutching three weeks' allowance** ₉ returned to the store, it had already closed.

READER'S REACTION: **This straightforward account doesn't emphasize either the allowance or the store hours.**

53a Parentheses

Parentheses *enclose* a word, sentence, or clause: you can't use just one. Readers interpret whatever falls between as an aside. Omit a comma *before* a parenthetical statement in the middle of a sentence. *After* the closing parenthesis, use whatever punctuation would otherwise occur.

WITHOUT
PARENTHESES   When you sign up for Telepick ₉ including Internet access ₉ you will receive an hour of free calls.

WITH
PARENTHESES   When you sign up for Telepick (including Internet access) ₉ you will receive an hour of free calls.

When parentheses *inside a sentence* come at the end, place the end punctuation *after* the closing mark. When enclosing a *freestanding sentence*, place end punctuation *inside* the closing parenthesis.

53.1

INSIDE SENTENCE   People on your Telepick list also get discounts (once they sign up) .

SEPARATE
SENTENCE   Try Telepick now. (This offer excludes international calls .)

You can also use parentheses to mark numbered or lettered lists or to enclose detail that is not part of the structure of a sentence.

DETAIL AND LIST   Harry's Bookstore has a fax number (555-0934) for (1) ordering books, (2) asking about new items, or (3) signing up for store events.

53b Brackets

53b
[ ]

When you add your own words to a quotation for clarity or background, enclose this **interpolation** in brackets. Also bracket the word *sic* (Latin for "so" or "thus") after an error within a quotation from a source to confirm that you've quoted accurately. If *sic* appears after the quotation, enclose it in parentheses.

INTERPOLATION   As Walters explains, "When Catholic Europe adopted the Gregorian calendar in 1582 and dropped ten days in October, Protestant England ignored the shift, still following October 4 by October 5 [Julian calendar]" (71).

Academic readers expect you to use brackets scrupulously to distinguish your words from those of a source (although nonacademic readers may find them pretentious).

If one parenthetical statement falls *within* another, use brackets for the inner statement.

> Contact Rick Daggett (Municipal Lumber Council [Violations Division], Stinson County Center) to report logging violations.

53c Dashes

Dashes set off material with more emphasis or spark than parentheses supply. Too many dashes may strike academic readers as informal. In contrast, dashes add flair to public and work appeals, ads, or brochures. Use your software's dash character, or type a dash as two unspaced hyphens, without space before or after: --. In print, the dash appears as a single line: —.

Dashes can set off an idea or a series of items, especially to open or close dramatically or call attention to an assertion. Use one dash to introduce material that concludes a sentence; use a pair of dashes to highlight words in the middle.

MATERIAL IN THE MIDDLE
After hours of service to two groups—**Kids First and Food Basket**—Olivia was voted Volunteer of the Year.

OPENING LIST
Extended visitation hours, better meals, and more exercise—these were the inmates' major demands.

STRATEGY   Convert excessive dashes to other marks.

53d

If your draft is full of dashes, circle those that seem truly valuable—maybe setting off a key point. Replace the others with commas, colons, parentheses, or more emphatic wording.

53d Ellipses

The **ellipsis** (from Greek *elleipsis*, "an omission") is a series of three *spaced* periods showing that something has been left out. Academic readers expect you to use ellipses to mark omissions from a quotation. Readers in other communities may prefer complete quotations to ellipses.

PLACEMENT OF ELLIPSIS MARKS

- Use three spaced periods • • • for ellipses within a sentence or line of poetry. In quoting a text that already uses ellipses, bracket yours (MLA style).
- Use a period before an ellipsis that ends a sentence • • • •
- Leave a space before the first period • • • and after the last unless the ellipsis is bracketed.
- Omit ellipses when you begin quotations (unless needed for clarity), or use words or phrases that are clearly incomplete.
- Retain another punctuation mark before omitted words if needed for the sentence structure; • • • omit it otherwise.
- Supply a series of spaced periods (MLA style) to show an omitted line (or more) of poetry in a block quotation.

53.2

Ellipses mark material omitted from a quotation because it is irrelevant, too long, or located between two useful parts of the quotation. When you drop *part* of a sentence, keep a normal structure that readers can follow.

ORIGINAL INTERVIEW NOTES
Museum director: "We expect the Inca pottery in our special exhibit to attract art historians from as far away as Chicago, while the colorful jewelry draws the general public."

CONFUSING DRAFT
The museum director hopes "the Inca pottery • • • art historians • • • the colorful jewelry • • • the general public."

EDITED
The museum director "expect[s] the Inca pottery • • • to attract art historians • • • while the colorful jewelry draws the general public."

In fictional or personal narrative, you may want to use ellipses to indicate a pause or gap showing suspense, hesitation, uncertainty, or ongoing action.

FOR SUSPENSE   Large paw prints led to the tent • • • •

53e Slashes

53e /

When indicating alternatives, the slash may translate as *or* or *and*.

Be certain that the on/off switch is in the vertical position.

This shorthand is common in technical documents, but some readers object to its informality or imprecision (and prefer *or* in its place).

To quote poetry *within* your text instead of using a block quotation (see 23b1–2), separate lines of verse with a slash, with spaces before and after.

The speaker in Sidney's sonnet hails the moon: "O Moon, thou climb'st the skies! / How silently, and with how wan a face!" (1–2).

53f   Symbols in electronic addresses

When you note an electronic address, record its characters exactly— including slashes, @ ("*at*") signs, underscores, colons, and periods.

j • bon@ceo • uc • edu

http : // www • access • gpo • gov / su__docs

53g   Combining punctuation marks

- **Pair marks that enclose**: ( ) [ ] " " ' ' Pair commas and dashes to enclose midsentence elements. Type a dash as a pair ▬▬ of hyphens.
- **Use multiple marks when each plays its own role**. If an abbreviation with a period falls in the *middle* of a sentence, the period may be followed by another mark.

Lunch begins at 11 a • m • , right after the lab.

- **Eliminate multiple marks when their roles overlap**. When an abbreviation with a period concludes a sentence, that one period also ends the sentence. Omit a comma *before* parentheses; *after* the parentheses, use whatever mark would otherwise occur.
- **Avoid confusing duplications**. If items listed within a sentence include commas, separate them with semicolons, not more commas.

——— , ——— , and ——— ; ——— , ——— , and ——— ; and ——— .

If one set of parentheses falls within another, use brackets to enclose the internal element.

——— (——— [———] ———) •

Use one pair of dashes at a time, not dashes within dashes.

——— ▬▬ ——— ▬▬ ——— •

Exercise 1

Some dashes and parentheses have been added to the following paragraph. Edit the paragraph to make it more effective, deciding which of these punctuation marks should stay and which should be replaced. Change sentence structure and strategy if necessary.

The next morning—their donkeys carried them—to the site of the excavation. Carter and his assistant—A. R. Callender—had already begun clearing the stairway (again). As more of the doorway was exposed, the seals (of Tutankhamun) could be seen—in addition to those of the royal necropolis. When all sixteen steps had been cleared (and the entire doorway could be seen), Carter got a jolt—holes had been cut into the (upper) part of the door. The damage had been repaired—and bore the seals of the necropolis, but the question remained—had this tomb, too, been pillaged?

—METROPOLITAN MUSEUM OF ART, *The Treasures of Tutankhamun*

Exercise 2

Find or create a short paragraph that uses as many of the punctuation marks described in this chapter as possible: parentheses, brackets, dashes, ellipses, and slashes. Choose one example of each case, and explain what purpose it serves in the paragraph.

PART 12

Proofreading for Mechanics and Spelling

54 Capitalizing

Capitalization makes reading easier. Readers expect capital letters to signal where sentences start or to identify specific people, places, and things.

CAPITALS MISSING

thanks, ahmed, for attaching a copy of the 2004 plant safety guidelines. i'll review this file by tuesday.

READER'S REACTION: Even though email may be informal, the missing capitals here distract me from the message.

CAPITALS IN PLACE

Thanks, Ahmed, for attaching a copy of the 2004 Plant Safety Guidelines. I'll review this file by Tuesday.

If you ignore conventions for capitals, readers may assume that you are careless. Be especially alert to conventions for capitalizing titles, company divisions, and the like.

54a Capitalizing to begin sentences

Sentences begin with capital letters, whether complete sentences or fragments used appropriately as partial sentences. (See 35c.)

Two national parks, Yellowstone and Grand Teton, are in Wyoming.

1 Capitalize the opening word in a quoted sentence

Capitalization varies with the completeness of a quotation. The following examples include MLA style page citations (see 25a). Notice that you capitalize when a quotation is a complete sentence or begins your sentence.

QUOTED SENTENCE

As Galloway observes, "The novel opens with an unusual chapter" (18).

SENTENCE OPENER

"An unusual chapter" (Galloway 18) opens the novel.

Do not capitalize after you interrupt a quotation with your own words or as you integrate a quotation into the structure of your own sentence.

INTERRUPTED QUOTATION

"The novel," claims Galloway, "opens with an unusual chapter" (18).

INTEGRATED QUOTATION

Galloway notes that the book "opens with an unusual chapter" (18).

2 Capitalize a freestanding sentence in parentheses

Capitalize the first word of a sentence if it stands on its own in parentheses but not if it falls *inside* another sentence.

FREESTANDING The Union forces were split up into nineteen sections. (Never-
SENTENCE   theless, Grant was determined to unite them.)

ENCLOSED   Saskatchewan's economy depends on farming (over half of
SENTENCE   Canada's wheat crop comes from the province).

3 Capitalize the first word of a line of poetry

Lines of poetry traditionally begin with a capital letter.

We said goodbye at the barrier,
And she slipped away. . . .
—ROBERT DASELER, "At the Barrier," *Levering Avenue*

If a poem ignores this or other conventions, follow the poet's practice.

new hampshire explodes into radio primary,
newspaper headlines & beer—
well-weathered tag-lines from lips of schoolchildren.
we triumph by not being clear.
—T. R. MAYERS, "(snap)shots"

4 Use consistent capitalization

When capitalization is flexible, be consistent within a document.

Complete sentence after a colon. When a *sentence* follows a colon (see 49b), you can use lowercase (as for other words after a colon) or capitalize.

OPTION 1   The population of New Brunswick is bilingual: one-third is
           French-speaking and the rest English-speaking.

OPTION 2   The population of New Brunswick is bilingual: One-third is
           French-speaking and the rest English-speaking.

Questions in a series. Capitalize or lowercase a sequence of questions.

OPTION 1   Should we order posters? Billboards? Flyers?

OPTION 2   Should we order posters? billboards? flyers?

Run-in lists. When items are not listed on separate lines, you may separate them with commas, semicolons (if they are complex), or periods (if they are sentences). Capitalize the first letters of sentences standing alone. Don't capitalize words, partial sentences, or a series of embedded sentences.

54a
cap

In estimating costs, remember the following: (a) **l**ab facilities must be rented, (b) **u**tilities are charged to the project's account, and (c) **m**easuring equipment has to be leased.

In estimating costs, remember to include (a) **l**ab facilities, (b) **u**tilities, and (c) **m**easuring equipment.

Vertical lists. Choose whether to capitalize words or partial sentences, but capitalize complete sentences except in an outline without periods.

OPTION 1	OPTION 2
1. Lab facilities	1. lab facilities
2. Utilities	2. utilities
3. Measuring equipment	3. measuring equipment

54b Capitalizing proper names and titles

Capitalize the names of specific people, places, and things (**proper nouns**) as well as **proper adjectives** derived from them.

Brazil, Dickens　　Brazilian music, Dickensian plot

54.1

In titles, capitalize the first word, the last word, and all words in between *except* articles (*a, an, the*), prepositions under five letters (*in, of, to*), and coordinating conjunctions (*and, but*). These rules apply to titles of long, short, and partial works as well as your own papers. Capitalize the first word after a colon that divides the title.

The Mill on the Floss　　"Civil Rights: What Now?"

Developing a Growth Plan for a Small Business [your own title]

In an APA reference list, however, capitalize only proper nouns and the first letters of titles and subtitles of full works (books, articles) (see 26b).

CAPITALIZATION OF NOUNS AND ADJECTIVES

CAPITALIZED	LOWERCASE
INDIVIDUALS AND RELATIVES	
Georgia O'Keeffe	my teacher's father
Uncle Jack, Mother	my cousin, her dad
GROUPS OF PEOPLE AND LANGUAGES	
Maori, African American	the language, the people

CAPITALIZED	LOWERCASE
TIME PERIODS AND SEASONS	
October, Fall Orientation	spring, summer, fall, winter
Easter, Ramadan	holiday
RELIGIONS AND RELATED SUBJECTS	
Buddhism, Catholic	catholic (meaning "universal")
Talmud, Bible, God	talmudic, biblical, a god
ORGANIZATIONS, INSTITUTIONS, AND MEMBERS	
U.S. Senate, Senator Hayes	a senator
Air Line Pilots Association	the union, a union member
PLACES, THEIR RESIDENTS, AND GEOGRAPHIC REGIONS	
Malaysia, Erie County	the country, the county
the Southwest, East Coast	southwestern, eastern
BUILDINGS AND MONUMENTS	
Taj Mahal, Getty Museum	the tower, a museum
HISTORICAL PERIODS, EVENTS, AND MOVEMENTS	
Algerian Revolution, Jazz Age	the revolution, a trend
ACADEMIC INSTITUTIONS AND COURSES	
Auburn University	a university, the college
Sociology 203, Art 101	sociology or art course
VEHICLES	
Chevrolet Impala	my car, an automobile
COMPANY NAMES AND TRADE NAMES	
Siemens, Kleenex	the company, tissues
SCIENTIFIC, TECHNICAL, AND MEDICAL TERMS	
Big Dipper, Earth (planet)	star, earth (ground)

Exercise 1

Add capitalization wherever necessary in the following sentences. Replace unnecessary capitals with lowercase letters. Circle the cases that seem the toughest to figure out.

EXAMPLE

Over the next ten years, *I*ndia will become an increasingly important trading partner for *N*orth *A*merica.

1. Located on a subcontinent in the southern part of asia, the republic of india has a territory of about 1.2 million Square Miles.

54b
cap

2. India's population of almost 800 Million falls into two main groups, dravidians and indo-aryans, which in turn are made up of many other cultural groups.

3. Dravidians live mainly in the south, an area that is dominated geographically by the deccan plateau.

4. The religion of the Majority is hinduism, though other religious groups such as sikhs and muslims are important.

5. Recently, religious conflicts have broken out in the provinces of kashmir and uttar pradesh.

6. Indian History is long and complicated, but in Modern Times it has been dominated by the british rule over the Country and by attempts to escape that rule and found a democratic State.

7. British Rule over most of the country began after the sepoy rebellion of 1857–58.

8. It ended after world war II with the independence movement led by mahatma gandhi.

9. The move toward industrialization has been the main goal of indian leaders since Independence, though this movement has at times been complicated by the problem of overpopulation and by conflicts stemming from the hindu social (or caste) system.

10. The dominant political Party since Independence has been the congress Party, with leaders such as jawaharlal nehru, indira gandhi, and rajiv gandhi.

55 Italicizing (Underlining)

55.1

Type that slants to the right—*italic type*—emphasizes words and ideas. In texts that are handwritten, typed, or prepared in MLA style (see 25c), underlining is its equivalent: <u>The Color Purple</u> = *The Color Purple*.

UNDERLINING   Walker's novel <u>The Color Purple</u> has been praised since 1982.

READER'S REACTION: I can spot the title right away.

55
it/und

Some readers, including many college instructors, prefer underlining because it's easy to see. Observe the conventions your community expects.

55a Italics (underlining) in titles

Italicize (underline) titles of most long works (books, magazines, films) and complete works (paintings, sculptures). Enclose titles of parts of works and short works (stories, reports, articles) in quotation marks (see 51b).

TREATMENT OF TITLES

ITALICS OR UNDERLINING	QUOTATION MARKS
BOOKS AND PAMPHLETS	
Maggie: A Girl of the Streets (book)	"Youth" (chapter in book)
Beetroot (story collection)	"The Purloined Letter" (story)
The White Album (essay collection)	"Once More to the Lake" (essay)
Guide for Surgery Patients (pamphlet)	"Anesthesia" (section of pamphlet)
POEMS	
Paradise Lost (long poem)	"Richard Cory" (short poem)
The One Day (long poem)	"Whoso list to hunt" (first line as title)
PLAYS AND FILMS	
King Lear (play)	
Star Wars (film)	
RADIO AND TELEVISION PROGRAMS	
The West Wing (TV series)	"Gone Quiet" (episode)
20/20 (TV news show)	"Binge Drinking" (news report)
PAINTINGS AND SCULPTURES	
Winged Victory (sculpture)	
MUSICAL WORKS	
Nutcracker Suite (work for orchestra)	"Waltz of the Flowers" (section of longer work)
Master of Puppets (CD)	"Orion" (song on CD)
Camille Saint-Saëns's *Organ Symphony*	BUT Saint-Saëns, Symphony no. 3 in C Minor, op. 78
MAGAZINES AND NEWSPAPERS	
Discover (magazine)	"How Baby Learns" (article)
Review of Contemporary Fiction (scholarly journal)	"Our Students Write with Accents" (scholarly article)
the *Denver Post* (newspaper)	"All the Rage" (article)

(Continued)

55a
it/und

TREATMENT OF TITLES *(Continued)*

NO ITALICS, UNDERLINING, OR QUOTATION MARKS

SACRED BOOKS AND PUBLIC, LEGAL, OR WELL-KNOWN DOCUMENTS
Bible, Koran, Talmud, United States Constitution

TITLE OF YOUR OWN PAPER (UNLESS PUBLISHED)
Attitudes of College Students Toward Intramural Sports
Verbal Abuse in <u>The Color Purple</u> (title of work discussed is underlined)

55b Italics for specific terms

Italicize (underline) the names of specific ships, airplanes, trains, and spacecraft (*Voyager VI, Orient Express*) but not *types* of vehicles (Boeing 767, Chris Craft) or *USS* and *SS* (*USS Corpus Christi*). Italicize a foreign word or phrase that has not moved into common use (*omertà*) but not common words such as quiche, junta, taco, and kvetch. Italicize scientific names for plants (*Chrodus crispus*) and animals (*Gazella dorcas*) but not common names (seaweed, gazelle).

Focus attention on a word, letter, number as itself, or defined term by italicizing (underlining) it.

In Boston, *r* is pronounced *ah* so that the word *car* becomes *cah* and *park* becomes *pahk*.

A *piezoelectric crystal* is a piece of quartz or similar material that responds to pressure by producing electric current.

You may italicize a word or phrase for stylistic emphasis, but readers become annoyed if you do this too often.

EMPHASIS   The letter's praise is *faint*, not fulsome.

55c Underlining for emphasis

Notes, personal letters, and other informal writing may use underlining to add "oral" emphasis. Avoid this in formal writing.

55c
it/und

INFORMAL   *Hand* the receipts to me.

MORE FORMAL   Give the receipts to me personally.

Exercise 1   *(Answers appear on p. 522.)*

Edit the following sentences by supplying any underlining or quotation marks necessary for emphasis. Star the items that are the most challenging to edit.

EXAMPLE

The well-known "Old Farmer's Almanac" contains information about the weather and articles on various topics.

1. I first learned about this famous American almanac from a newspaper article, You Can Look It Up There, that appeared in my local paper, the Record-Advertiser.
2. GQ and Cosmopolitan probably would not print an article like Salt: It's Still Worth Its Salt, which appeared in a recent edition of the almanac.
3. According to this article, the word salary comes from the Latin term for wages paid to some soldiers, salarium argentum, that is, salt money.
4. In an essay on the historic effects of weather, the author points out that freezing temperatures on January 28, 1986, led to the space shuttle Challenger disaster.
5. If you are interested in learning about the ocean, you can find out that high tides occur twice a month at syzygy, the times when the sun and moon are lined up on the same side of the earth or on opposite sides.

Exercise 2

For each of the following sentences, add underlining as required by convention or needed for appropriate emphasis. Circle words that are underlined but should not be. Star items that are challenging to edit.

EXAMPLE

In 1957, Chevrolet produced the (Bel Air,) a model now considered a (classic.)

1. As David Halberstam points out in his book The Fifties, automobiles from the period were so hot they were cool.
2. Cars from that period, with enormous tailfins and lots of chrome, are still eye-catchers today.
3. The musical Grease is set in the same era.
4. Television shows from the period included the Ed Sullivan Show and Lassie.
5. Readers could choose from such now-defunct publications as the Herald Tribune newspaper and Look magazine.

55
it/und

56 Hyphenating

Readers expect hyphens to play two different roles—dividing words and tying them together.

CONFUSING   The Japanese language proposal is well prepared.
> **READER'S REACTION: Is the proposal *in* Japanese or *about* the Japanese language?**

CLARIFIED   The Japanese-language proposal is well prepared.

Type a hyphen as a *single* line (-) with no space on either side.

FAULTY HYPHEN   well — trained engineer

EDITED   well-trained engineer

56a Hyphenating to join words

56.1

Hyphens often tie together the elements of compound words and phrases. A **compound word** is made from two or more words tied together by hyphens (*double-decker*), combined as one word (*timekeeper*), or treated as separate words (*letter carrier*). These conventions may vary or change rapidly; check an academic style guide, observe accepted practice in public or work contexts, or use an up-to-date dictionary.

Numbers. In general writing, hyphenate numbers between twenty-one and ninety-nine, even if the number is part of a larger one. Academic and workplace readers in certain fields, however, expect numbers in figures (not spelled out) (see 57b).

> forty-one   fifty-eight thousand   sixty-three million

Use a hyphen for inclusive numbers (pages 163–78, volumes 9–14) and generally for fractions spelled out (one-half).

Prefixes and suffixes. Hyphenate a prefix that comes before a capitalized word or a number.

> Cro-Magnon   non-Euclidean   post-Victorian   pre-1989

Hyphenate with *ex-*, *self-*, *all-*, *-elect*, and *-odd*.

> self-centered   all-encompassing   president-elect

Letters with words. Hyphenate a letter and a word forming a compound, except in music terms.

A-frame   T-shirt   A minor   G sharp

Compound modifiers. Hyphenate two or more words working as a single modifier when you place them *before* a noun. When the modifiers come *after* a noun, generally do not hyphenate them.

BEFORE NOUN   The **second-largest** supplier of crude oil is Nigeria.

AFTER NOUN   Many cancer treatments are **nausea inducing**.

Do not hyphenate *-ly* adverbs or comparative and superlative forms.

Our **highly regarded** research team developed them.

Hyphens help readers know which meaning to assign a compound.

The scene required three **extra wild** monkeys.

The scene required three **extra-wild** monkeys.

Strings of modifiers. Reduce repetition with hyphens that signal the suspension of an element until the end of a series of parallel compound modifiers. Leave a space after the hyphen and before *and*, but not before a comma.

The process works with **oil- and water-based** compounds.

56b Hyphenating to divide words

Hyphens help distinguish different words with the same spelling.

For **recreation**, they staged a comic **re-creation** of events.

They clarify words with repeated combinations of letters.

anti-imperialism   post-traumatic   co-owner

Traditionally you could use a hyphen to split a word at the end of a line, marking a break *between syllables*. Now word processors include **automatic hyphenation**, dividing words at the ends of lines but sometimes creating hard-to-read lines or splitting words incorrectly. Many writers turn off this feature, preferring a "ragged" (unjustified) right margin. Style guides such as MLA and APA advise the same.

- Divide words only between syllables (for example, *ad-just-able*).
- Check divisions in a dictionary (*ir-re-vo-ca-ble*, not *ir-rev-oc-able*).

56b
-

- Leave more than one letter at the end of a line and more than two at the beginning (not *a-greement* or *disconnect-ed*).
- Divide at natural breaks between words in compounds (*Volks-wagen*, not *Volkswa-gen*) or after hyphens (*accident-prone*, not *acci-dent-prone*).
- Don't divide one-syllable words (*touched*, *drought*, *kicked*, *through*).
- Avoid confusing divisions that form distracting words (*sin-gle*).
- Don't split acronyms and abbreviations (*NATO*, *NCAA*), numerals (*100,000*), and contractions (*didn't*).
- Don't hyphenate an electronic address; simply divide it after a slash.

Exercise 1 *(Answers appear on p. 523.)*

Insert hyphens in the following sentences wherever appropriate. Consult a dictionary if necessary.

EXAMPLE

The company hired a well‿regarded accounting firm as part of its financial reorganization.

1. Alejo enjoys painstakingly exact work, such as building scale model ships.
2. While working, he likes to listen to Francis Poulenc's jazz influenced classical music.
3. One fourth of all his model ships are sold at auction.
4. Tony, his assistant, keeps track of the profits in a pre and post auction sale log.
5. Although his creations are awesome, Alejo harbors many insecurities that are mostly selfinflicted.

57 Using Numbers

You can convey numbers with numerals (*37*, *18.6*), words (*eighty-one*, *two million*), or a combination (*7th*, *2nd*, *25 billion*).

GENERAL TEXT   These **fifty-nine** scientists represented **fourteen** states.

READER'S REACTION: In general academic or other texts, I expect most numbers to be spelled out.

TECHNICAL   These **59** scientists represented **14** states.

> **READER'S REACTION: When I read a scientific or technical report, I expect more numerals.**

This chapter shows you how to present numbers in general writing. For conventions expected in specific technical, business, or scientific contexts, seek advice from your instructor, supervisor, colleagues, or style guide (see Chapters 25–28). Unconventional or inconsistent usage can mislead readers or undermine your authority as a writer.

57a Spelling out numbers

Spell out a number of one or two words, counting hyphenated compounds as a single word.

twenty-two computers   **seventy thousand** eggs   **306** books

Treat numbers in the same category consistently in a passage, either as numerals (if required for one number, use them for all) or as words.

CONSISTENT   Café Luna's menu soon expanded from **48** to **104** items.

Spell out numbers according to the following conventions.

DATES AND TIMES
October seventh   nineteenth century   the sixties
four o'clock, *not* 4 o'clock   four in the morning
half past eight, a quarter after one (rounded to the quarter hour)

57.1

ROUNDED NUMBERS OR ROUNDED AMOUNTS OF MONEY
three hundred thousand citizens   nearly eleven thousand dollars
sixty cents (and other small dollar or cent amounts)

LARGE NUMBERS
For large numbers, combine numerals and words.

75 million years   2.3 million members

STRATEGY	Spell out an opening number, or rewrite.

INAPPROPRIATE   **428** houses in Talcott are built on leased land.

DISTRACTING   **Four hundred twenty-eight** houses in Talcott are built on leased land.

EASY TO READ   **In Talcott, 428** houses are built on leased land.

57a
num

57b Using numerals

Use numerals according to the following conventions.

ADDRESSES, ROUTES

2450 Ridge Road, Alhambra, CA 91801   Interstate 6

DATES

September 7, 1976   1880–1910   from 1955 to 1957
1930s   class of '97   the '80s (informal)
486 BC (or BCE)   AD (or CE) 980

PARTS OF A WRITTEN WORK

Chapter 12   Genesis 1:1–6 or Gen. 1.1–6 (MLA style)
Macbeth 2.4.25–28 (or act II, scene iv, lines 25–28)

MEASUREMENTS WITH ABBREVIATIONS

55 mph   6'4"   47 psi   21 ml   80 kph

FRACTIONS, DECIMALS, PERCENTAGES

7 5/8   27.3   67 percent (or 67%)

TIME OF DAY

10:52   6:17 a.m.   12 p.m. (noon)   12 a.m. (midnight)

MONEY (SPECIFIC AMOUNTS)

$7,883 (or $7883) $4.29 $7.2 million (or $7,200,000)

SURVEYS, RATIOS, STATISTICS, SCORES

7 out of 10   3 to 1 (or 3:1)   a mean of 23
a standard deviation of 2.5   won 21 to 17

CLUSTERED NUMBERS

paragraphs 2, 9, and 13 through 15 (or 13–15)
units 23, 145, and 210

RANGES OF NUMBERS

LESS THAN 100   Supply the complete second number.

9–13   27–34   58–79   94–95

OVER 100   Simply supply the last two figures in the second number unless readers need more to avoid confusion. Do not use commas in four-digit page numbers.

134–45   95–102 (not 95–02)   370–420
1534–620 (not 1534–20)   1007–09

YEARS   Supply all digits of both years in a range unless they belong to the same century.

1890–1920   1770–86   476–823   42–38 BC

Exercise 1   *(Answers appear on p. 523.)*

In the following sentences, correct any errors in the use of numbers. Circle any especially difficult items. You may need to rewrite some sentences.

EXAMPLE

When the list of cities for the Rock and Roll Hall of Fame was nar-

rowed down to *one* 1, the choice was Cleveland.

1. Of the groups and individuals elected to the Rock and Roll Hall of Fame from 1986 to 1990, 5 were female and 68 were male.
2. The Hall of Fame is increasing its membership goals from nineteen thousand to twenty-one thousand five hundred.
3. 411 of the 2000 questionnaires about favorite rockers were returned by the deadline.
4. This year the Hall of Fame purchased twenty-six articles of clothing, 127 signed memorabilia, and 232 unused concert tickets for the museum.
5. Although subscribers were told the museum would open by 10:30 in the morning on the twelfth, the personnel weren't ready for the large crowd until about 2 o'clock.

58 Abbreviating

When they are accepted by both writer and reader, abbreviations act as a shorthand, making a sentence easy to write and read. Inappropriate or badly placed abbreviations, however, can make a sentence *harder* to read.

CONFUSING   **Jg.** **Rich.** Posner was a **U of C** law **prof.**
              READER'S REACTION: Am I supposed to know all these abbreviations? What is "Jg."? Is "U of C" the University of California?

58
abbrev

CLEAR   Judge **Richard** Posner was a **University of Chicago** law pro-
                 fessor.

58a Familiar abbreviations

58.1

Many abbreviations are so widely used that readers have no trouble recognizing them. These abbreviations are acceptable in all kinds of writing as long as you present them in standard form.

1 Abbreviate titles with proper names

Abbreviate titles just before or after people's names.

Ms • Rutkowski   Cathy Harr, **D • V • M •**   James Guptil, **Sr •**

With a person's full name, you may abbreviate a title. Spell out a title used as *part of your reference to the person* or placed away from a proper name.

FAULTY   We invited **Prof •** Leves and **Rep •** Drew.

ACCEPTABLE   We invited **Professor** Leves and **Representative** Drew.

ALTERNATIVE   We invited **Prof • Roland** Leves and **Rep • John** Drew.

EXCEPTIONS   **Rev •** Mills and **Dr •** Smith were not invited.

Use only one form of a person's title at a time.

FAULTY   **Dr •** Vonetta McGee, **D • D • S •**

EDITED   **Dr •** Vonetta McGee or Vonetta McGee, **D • D • S •**

Abbreviated academic degrees such as *M.A.*, *Ph.D.*, *B.S.*, and *M.D.* can be used as titles or on their own.

ACCEPTABLE   The **Ed • D •** is designed for school administrators.

ESL ADVICE: ABBREVIATED TITLES

In some languages, abbreviated titles such as *Dr.* or *Mrs.* do not require periods as they do in English. If this is true in your first language, proofread carefully.

---

2 Abbreviate references to people and organizations

58a
abbrev

Readers generally accept abbreviations that are familiar (*3M, IBM*), simple (*AFL-CIO*), or standard in specific contexts (*FAFSA*). Abbreviations in which the letters are pronounced singly (*USDA*) and **acronyms** in which they form a pronounceable word (*NATO*) usually use capitals without periods (but note *laser*, *radar*).

ORGANIZATIONS	NAACP, AMA, NBA, FDA, NCAA, UNESCO, IBEW
CORPORATIONS	GTE, USX, PBS, GM, CNN, AT&T, CBS, BBC
COUNTRIES	USA (*or* U.S.A.), UK (*or* U.K.)
PEOPLE	JFK, LBJ, FDR, MLK
THINGS OR EVENTS	FM, AM, TB, MRI, AWOL, DUI, TGIF

STRATEGY | Introduce an unfamiliar abbreviation.

Give the full term when you first use it; show the abbreviation in parentheses. From then on, use the abbreviation to avoid tedious repetition.

The **American Library Association (ALA)** has taken stands on access to information. For example, the **ALA** opposes book censorship.

3 Abbreviate terms with dates and numbers

Abbreviations that *specify* a number or amount may be used with dates and numbers; don't substitute them for general terms. For example, use *the morning*, not *the a.m.* (See 57b.)

ABBREVIATION	MEANING
AD	*anno Domini*, meaning "in the year of Our Lord"
BC	*before* Christ
BCE	*before* common *era* (alternative to BC)
CE	common *era* (alternative to AD)
a.m.	*ante* meridiem for "morning" (A.M. in print)
p.m.	*post* meridiem for "after noon" (P.M. in print)
no., $	number, dollars

58b Proofreading for appropriate abbreviations

In most formal writing, readers expect words in full form except for familiar abbreviations. In research, scientific, or technical writing, you can use more abbreviations to save space, particularly in documenting sources (see Chapters 25–28). Abbreviations may also be accepted in specific contexts—for example, OT (occupational therapy) in medical reports.

DAYS, MONTHS, AND HOLIDAYS

DRAFT	Thurs., Thur., Th	Oct.	Xmas
EDITED	Thursday	October	Christmas

58b
abbrev

PLACES

DRAFT	Wasatch Mts.	Lk. Erie	Ont. Ave.
EDITED	Wasatch Mountains	Lake Erie	Ontario Avenue

EXCEPTION   988 Dunkerhook Road, Paramus, **NJ** 07652

Use accepted postal abbreviations in all addresses with zip codes.

COMPANY NAMES

QUESTIONABLE   LaForce Bros. Electrical Conts.

EDITED   LaForce Brothers Electrical Contractors

Use abbreviations only if they are part of the official name.

PEOPLE'S NAMES

DRAFT   Wm. and Kath. Newholtz will attend.

EDITED   William and Katherine Newholtz will attend.

DISCIPLINES AND PROFESSIONS

DRAFT	econ., bio.	poli. sci.	phys. ed.	PT
EDITED	economics, biology	political science	physical education	physical therapy

SYMBOLS AND UNITS OF MEASUREMENT

In general writing, reserve symbols (@, #, =, –, +) for tables or graphs. Spell out units of measurement (*mile*). Abbreviate phrases such as *rpm* and *mph*, with or without periods, but be consistent in a text.

AVOID IN TEXT	pt.	qt.	in.	mi.	kg.
USE IN TEXT	pint	quart	inch	mile	kilogram

PARTS OF WRITTEN WORKS

Follow your instructor's advice or the style guide for the field.

IN DOCUMENTATION	ch.	p.	pp.	fig.
IN WRITTEN TEXT	chapter	page	pages	figure

LATIN ABBREVIATIONS

Reserve these for documentation and parenthetical comments.

cf.	compare (*confer*)	i.e.	that is (*id est*)	e.g.	for example (*exempli gratia*)
N.B.	note well (*nota bene*)	et al.	and others (*et alii*)	etc.	and so forth (*et cetera*)

58b
abbrev

Exercise 1

Edit the following sentences, adding or correcting abbreviations when appropriate and spelling out or rewriting any inappropriate abbreviations. Assume that these sentences are all written in a fairly formal academic context.

EXAMPLE   *New York, Los Angeles,*
People think of ~~NY, LA,~~ and Montreal as international cities, but many small- to-medium-sized towns are just as cosmopolitan.

1. At a drugstore in a small Montana town, I talked with a clerk who told me about the Wine Appreciation Guild, Ltd. (155 Conn. St., San Francisco, CA 94107), which publishes books on food, wine, etc., e.g., *Wine Technology and Operations* by Yair Margalit, PhD.
2. According to a study by Ernest D. Abrams Consulting, smaller towns like Sioux City, IA, and Vero Bch., Fla., are even more likely to be the homes of inventors and innovators.
3. In one town in upstate NY, an engineer, Chas. D'Angelis, has created a device that measures rpms by counting the # of times a gear with a single tooth interrupts a laser beam.
4. While I was driving through the rural Midwest, I visited Rich. Forer, D.O., who examined my sore back, prescribed a new exercise rout. he had developed, and gave me an Rx for a mild painkiller.
5. In a city of twenty thou. people in eastern Tenn. I came across a health coop. that is pioneering a new phys. therapy program.

59 Spelling

Readers in academic, public, and work settings notice how accurately you spell.

INCORRECT   The city will not **except** any late bids for the project.
> **READER'S REACTION: I get annoyed when careless or lazy writers won't correct their spelling.**

PROOFREAD   The city will not **accept** any late bids for the project.

Readers may ignore or laugh at a newspaper misspelling. For academic and work documents, however, they may consider a writer who misspells lazy, ignorant, or disrespectful.

59a Starting with your spell checker

When you use a spelling checker, the computer compares the words in your text with those in its dictionary. If it finds a match, it assumes your word is correctly spelled. If it does *not* find a match, it questions the word so you can select an alternative spelling or make a correction. What it can't reveal are words properly spelled but used incorrectly, such as *lead* for *led*. When in doubt, check a dictionary.

> **STRATEGY** | **Go beyond the spelling checker.**
>
> - List as many possible spellings as you can. Look them up. Once you're in the right area in the dictionary, you may find the word.
> - Try a special dictionary for poor spellers, listing words under both correct spelling (*phantom*) and likely misspellings (*fantom*).
> - Try a thesaurus (see 47b); the word may be listed with a synonym.
> - Ask classmates or coworkers about the preferred or correct spellings, especially for technical terms; verify their information in the dictionary.
> - Check the indexes of books that treat the topic the word relates to.
> - Look for the word in textbooks, company materials, or newspapers.
> - Add tricky words to your own spelling list. Look for ways to recall them. For example, you might associate the two *z*'s in *quizzes* with boredom (*zzzz*).

59b Watching for common patterns of misspelling

59.1

If you can't remember all the rules and exceptions, try to remember the different kinds of patterns and check this handbook or a dictionary whenever you are unsure about a spelling.

1 Plurals

You form most plurals simply by adding -*s* (*novel, novels*).

- For words ending in a consonant plus -*o*, often add -*es*.

ADD -*es*	potato, potatoes	hero, heroes
ADD -*s*	cello, cellos	memo, memos

When a vowel comes before the -*o*, add -*s*.

ADD -*s*	stereo, stereos	video, videos

- For words ending in a consonant plus -*y*, change *y* to *i*, and add -*es*.

etiology, etiologies   gallery, galleries   notary, notaries

EXCEPTION   Add -s for proper nouns (*Kennedy, Kennedys*).

- For words ending in a vowel plus -*y*, keep the *y*, and add -*s*.

  day, days   journey, journeys   pulley, pulleys

- For words ending in -*f* or -*fe*, often change *f* to *v*, and add -*s* or -*es*.

  knife, knives   life, lives   self, selves

  Some words simply add -*s*.

  belief, beliefs   roof, roofs   turf, turfs

- For words ending with a hiss (-*ch*, -*s*, -*ss*, -*sh*, -*x*, -*z*), usually add -*es*.

  bench, benches   bus, buses   bush, bushes

  buzz, buzzes   fox, foxes   kiss, kisses

  One-syllable words may double a final -*s* or -*z*: *quiz, quizzes*.

- Words with foreign roots often follow the original language.

  alumna, alumnae   criterion, criteria   datum, data

- Some familiar plurals are irregular.

  foot, feet   mouse, mice   man, men

- In a compound, make the last word plural unless the first is more important.

  basketball, basketballs   sister-in-law, sisters-in-law

2 Word beginnings and endings

Prefixes do not change the spelling of the root word that follows: *precut, post-traumatic, misspell.*

- *In-* and *im-* have the same meaning; use *im-* before *b*, *m*, and *p*.

  | USE *in-* | incorrect | inadequate | incumbent |
  | USE *im-* | imbalance | immobile | impatient |

Suffixes may change the root word that comes before, or they may pose spelling problems in themselves.

59b
spell

- Retain a word's final silent -*e* when a suffix begins with a consonant.

  KEEP -*e*   fate, fateful   gentle, gentleness

  EXCEPTIONS   words like *judgment, argument, truly,* and *ninth*

- Drop the silent -*e* when a suffix begins with a vowel.

  DROP -*e*   imagine, imaginary   decrease, decreasing

  EXCEPTIONS   words like *noticeable* and *changeable*

- Four familiar words end in -*ery*: *stationery* (paper), *cemetery, monastery, millinery.* Most others end in -*ary*: *stationary* (fixed in place), *secretary, primary, military, culinary.*
- Most words with a final "seed" sound end in -*cede*, such as *precede, re-cede,* and *intercede.* Only three are spelled -*ceed*: *proceed, succeed,* and *exceed.* One is spelled -*sede*: *supersede.*
- Add -*able* if word roots can stand on their own and -*ible* if they can't.

  USE -*able*   charitable, habitable, advisable, mendable
                   Drop the -*e* for word roots ending in one *e* (*comparable, debatable*). Keep it for words ending in double *e* (*agreeable*).

  USE -*ible*   credible, irreducible

3 Words containing *ie* and *ei*

Most words follow the old rhyme: *I* before *e* / Except after *c,* / Or when sounding like *a* / As in n*ei*ghbor and w*ei*gh.

USE *ie*   believe, thief, grief, friend, chief, field, niece

USE *ei*   receive, deceit, perceive, ceiling, conceited

EXCEPTIONS   weird, seize, foreign, ancient, height, either, neither, their, leisure, forfeit

59c Proofreading for commonly misspelled words

Words that sound like each other but are spelled differently (*accept/except, assent/ascent*) are known as **homophones**.

COMMONLY MISSPELLED OR CONFUSED WORD PAIRS

WORD	MEANING
accept	receive
except	other than

WORD	MEANING
affect	to influence; an emotional response
effect	result
all ready	prepared
already	by this time
allusion	indirect reference
illusion	faulty belief or perception
assure	state positively
ensure	make certain
insure	indemnify
bare	naked
bear	carry; an animal
board	get on; flat piece of wood
bored	not interested
brake	stop
break	shatter, destroy; a gap; a pause
capital	seat of government; monetary resources
capitol	building that houses government
cite	credit an authority
sight	ability to see; a view
site	a place
complement	to complete or supplement
compliment	to praise
desert	abandon; sandy wasteland
dessert	sweet course at conclusion of meal
discreet	tactful, reserved
discrete	separate or distinct
elicit	draw out, evoke
illicit	illegal
eminent	well known, respected
immanent	inherent
imminent	about to happen
fair	lovely; light-colored; just
fare	fee for transportation
forth	forward
fourth	after *third*
gorilla	an ape
guerrilla	kind of soldier or warfare
hear	perceive sound
here	in this place

(Continued)

59c
spell

COMMONLY MISSPELLED OR CONFUSED WORD PAIRS (Continued)

WORD	MEANING
heard	past tense of *hear*
herd	group of animals
hole	opening
whole	complete
its	possessive form of *it*
it's	contraction for *it is*
know	understand or be aware of
no	negative
later	following in time
latter	last in a series
lessen	make less
lesson	something learned
loose	not tight
lose	misplace
passed	past tense of *pass*
past	after; events occurring at a prior time
patience	calm endurance
patients	people getting medical treatment
peace	calm or absence of war
piece	part of something
plain	clear, unadorned
plane	woodworking tool; airplane
persecute	harass
prosecute	take legal action against
personal	relating to oneself
personnel	employees
precede	come before
proceed	go ahead, continue
principal	most important; head of a school
principle	basic truth, rule of behavior
raise	lift up or build up
raze	tear down
right	correct
rite	ritual
write	compose; put words into a text

WORD	MEANING
scene	section of a play; setting of an action
seen	visible
stationary	fixed in place or still
stationery	paper for writing
straight	unbending
strait	water passageway
than	compared with
then	at that time; next
their	possessive form of *they*
there	in that place
they're	contraction for *they are*
to	toward
too	in addition, also
two	number after *one*
waist	middle of body
waste	leftover or discarded material
which	one of a group
witch	person with magical powers
who's	contraction for *who is*
whose	possessive of *who*
your	possessive of *you*
you're	contraction for *you are*

Exercise 1

Assume that you've circled the following words in italics in one of your papers. You're done with your draft, and now you want to double-check your spellings. Look up each word, make any necessary corrections, and then write out one way to remember each correct spelling. Do this whether or not you already know how to spell the word.

EXAMPLE   *pal*
school *principle*

The school principal is not always every kid's "pal."

coal *minor*   *precede* to the gate   *stationery* car
vacume the rug   she was *lieing*   *likelyhood*

59c
spell

Exercise 2 *(Answers appear on p. 523.)*

A. Without using a dictionary, circle the words that are misspelled in this list.

supercede	conceed	procede
idiosyncracy	concensus	accomodate
dexterous	impressario	irresistable
rhythym	opthalmologist	diptheria
anamoly	afficianado	caesarian
grafitti	judgement	liason

B. Working with a partner or in a small group, compare your answers to Exercise 2A, and *then* resolve any debates with a dictionary.

GLOSSARY OF USAGE

a, an When the word after *a* or *an* begins with a vowel sound, use *an*: *an outrageous film*. Use *a* before consonants: *a shocking film*. (See 29a.)

accept, except *Accept* means "to take or receive"; *except* means "excluding."

> Everyone **accepted** the invitation **except** Larry.

adverse, averse Someone opposed to something is *averse* to it; if conditions stand in opposition to achieving a goal, they are *adverse*.

advice, advise *Advice* is a noun meaning "counsel" or "recommendations." *Advise* is a verb meaning "to give counsel or recommendations."

> Raul wanted to **advise** his students, but they wanted no **advice**.

affect, effect *Affect* is a verb meaning "to influence." *Effect* is a noun meaning "a result." More rarely, *effect* is a verb meaning "to cause something to happen."

> CFCs may **affect** the deterioration of the ozone layer. The **effect** of that deterioration on global warming is uncertain. Lawmakers need to **effect** changes in public attitudes toward our environment.

aggravate, irritate *Aggravate* means "to worsen"; *irritate* means "to bother or pester."

ain't Although widely used, *ain't* is inappropriate in formal writing. Use *am not, is not,* or *are not;* the contracted forms *aren't* and *isn't* are more acceptable than *ain't* but may still be too informal in some contexts. (See 50b.)

all ready, already *All ready* means "prepared for"; *already* means "by that time."

> Sam was **all ready** for the meeting, but it had **already** started.

all right This expression is always spelled as two words, not as *alright*.

all together, altogether Use *all together* to mean "everyone"; use *altogether* to mean "completely."

> We were **all together** on our decision to support the center, but it was **altogether** too hard for us to organize a fund-raiser in a week.

allude, elude *Allude* means "hint at" or "refer to indirectly"; *elude* means "escape."

allusion, illusion An *allusion* is a reference to something; an *illusion* is a vision or a false belief.

a lot This expression is always spelled as two words, not as *alot*. Because *a lot* may be too informal for some writing, consider *many, much,* or another modifier instead.

a.m., p.m. These abbreviations may be capital or lowercase letters (see 58a).

among, between Use *between* to describe something involving two people, things, or ideas; use *among* to refer to three or more.

> The fight **between** the umpire and the catcher was followed by a discussion **among** the catcher, the umpire, and the managers.

amount, number Use *amount* for a quantity of something that can't be divided into separate units. Use *number* for countable objects.

A large **number** of spices may be used in Thai dishes. This recipe calls for a small **amount** of coconut milk.

an, a (See **a, an.**)

and etc. (See **etc.**)

and/or Although widely used, *and/or* is usually imprecise and may distract your reader. Choose one of the words, or revise your sentence. (See 53e.)

ante-, anti- Use *ante-* as a prefix to mean "before" or "predating"; use *anti-* to mean "against" or "opposed."

anyone, any one *Anyone* as one word is an indefinite pronoun. Occasionally you may want to use *any* to modify *one*, in the sense of "any individual thing or person." (The same distinction applies to **everyone, every one; somebody, some body**; and **someone, some one.**)

Anyone can learn to parachute without fear. But the instructors are told not to spend too much time with **any one** person.

anyplace Replace this term in formal writing with *anywhere*, or revise.

anyways, anywheres Avoid these incorrect versions of *anyway* and *anywhere*.

as, like Used as a preposition, *as* indicates a precise comparison. *Like* indicates a resemblance or similarity.

Remembered **as** a man of habit, Kant took a walk at the same time each day. He, **like** many other philosophers, was thoughtful and intense.

as to *As to* is considered informal in many contexts.

INFORMAL   The media speculated **as to** the film's success.

EDITED   The media speculated **about** the film's success.

assure, ensure, insure Use *assure* to imply a promise; use *ensure* to imply a certain outcome. Use *insure* only when you imply something legal or financial.

The surgeon **assured** the pianist that his fingers would heal in time for the concert. To **ensure** that, the pianist did not practice for three weeks and **insured** his hands with Lloyd's of London.

at In any writing, avoid using *at* in direct and indirect questions.

COLLOQUIAL   Jones wondered where his attorney was **at**.

EDITED   Jones wondered where his attorney **was**.

awful, awfully Use *awful* as an adjective modifying a noun or pronoun; use *awfully* as an adverb modifying a verb, adjective, or other adverb. (See 34b.)

Sanders played **awfully** at the golf tournament. On the sixth hole, an **awful** shot landed his ball in the pond.

awhile, a while *Awhile* (as one word) functions as an adverb; it is not preceded by a preposition. *A while* functions as a noun (preceded by *a*, an article) and is often used in prepositional phrases.

The shelter suggested that the homeless family stay **awhile**. It turned out that the children had not eaten for **a while**.

bad, badly Use *bad* as an adjective that modifies nouns or with a linking verb expressing feelings. Use *badly* as an adverb. (See 34b-3.)

because, since In general, avoid using *since* in place of *because*, which is more formal and precise. Use *since* to indicate time, not causality.

being as, being that Avoid both in formal writing when you mean *because*.

beside, besides Use *beside* as a preposition to mean "next to." Use *besides* as an adverb meaning "also" or an adjective meaning "except."

> Betsy placed the documents **beside** Mr. Klein. **Besides** being the best lawyer at the firm, Klein was also the most cautious.

better, had better Avoid using *better* or *had better* in place of *ought to* or *should* in formal writing.

| COLLOQUIAL | Fast-food chains **better** realize that Americans are more health-conscious today. |
| EDITED | Fast-food chains **ought to** realize that Americans are more health-conscious today. |

between, among (See **among, between**.)

bring, take *Bring* implies a movement from somewhere else to close at hand; *take* implies a movement in the opposite direction.

> Please **bring** me a coffee refill, and **take** away these leftover muffins.

broke *Broke* is the past tense of *break*; avoid using it as the past participle.

| DRAFT | The computer was **broke**. |
| EDITED | The computer was **broken**. |

burst, bursted *Burst* implies an outward explosion. Do not use the form *bursted* for the past tense.

> The gang of boys **burst** the balloon.

bust, busted Avoid the use of *bust* or *busted* to mean "broke."

| COLLOQUIAL | The senator's limousine **bust** down on the trip. |
| EDITED | The senator's limousine **broke** down on the trip. |

but however, but yet Choose one word of each pair, not both.

can, may *Can* implies ability; *may* implies permission or uncertainty.

> Bart **can** drive now, but his parents **may** not lend him their new car.

can't hardly, can't scarcely Use these pairs positively, not negatively: *can hardly* and *can scarcely*, or simply *can't*. (See 34b-4.)

capital, capitol *Capital* refers to a government center or to money; *capitol* refers to a government building.

censor, censure *Censor* means the act of shielding something from the public, such as a movie. *Censure* implies punishment or critical labeling.

center around Use *center on* or *focus on*, or reword as *revolve around*.

choose, chose Watch for spelling errors; use *choose* for the present tense form of the verb and *chose* for the past tense.

cite, site *Cite* means to acknowledge someone else's work; *site* means a place or location.

> Phil decided to **cite** Chomsky's theory of syntax.

> We chose the perfect **site** to pitch our tent.

climactic, climatic *Climactic* refers to the culmination of something; *climatic* refers to weather conditions.

compare to, compare with Use *compare to* when you want to imply similarities between two things—the phrase is close in meaning to *liken to*. Use *compare with* to imply both similarities and differences.

> The doctor **compared** the boy's virus **to** a tiny army in his body. **Compared with** his last illness, this one was mild.

complement, compliment *Complement* means "an accompaniment"; *compliment* means "words of praise."

> The diplomats **complimented** the ambassador on her menu. The dessert **complemented** the main course perfectly.

continual, continuous *Continual* implies that something is recurring; *continuous* implies that something is constant and unceasing.

> Local residents found the **continual** noise of landing jets less annoying than the traffic that **continuously** circled the airport.

could of, would of These incorrect pairs are common because they are often pronounced as if they are spelled this way. Use the correct verb forms *could have* and *would have*.

> **DRAFT**   I **could of** written a letter to the editor.

> **EDITED**   I **could have** written a letter to the editor.

couple, couple of In formal writing, use a *few* or *two* instead.

> **COLLOQUIAL**   Watson took a **couple of** days to examine the data.

> **EDITED**   Watson took **a few** days to examine the data.

criteria *Criteria* is the plural form of *criterion*. Make sure your verbs agree in number with this noun.

> **SINGULAR**   One **criterion** for the bonus was selling ten cars.

> **PLURAL**   The **criteria** were too strict to follow.

curriculum *Curriculum* is the singular form of this noun. For the plural, use either *curricula* or *curriculums*, but be consistent.

data Although widely used for both the singular and plural, *data* technically is a plural noun; *datum* refers to a single piece of data. If in doubt, use the formal distinction, and make sure your verbs agree in number.

> **SINGULAR**   This one **datum** was unexpected.

> **PLURAL**   These **data** are not very revealing.

different from, different than Use *different from* when an object follows, and use *different than* when an entire clause follows.

Jack's proposal is **different from** Marlene's, but his ideas are now **different than** they were when he first joined the sales team.

discreet, discrete *Discreet* means "reserved or cautious"; *discrete* means "distinctive, different, or explicit."

disinterested, uninterested *Uninterested* implies boredom or lack of interest; *disinterested* implies impartiality or objectivity.

done Avoid using *done* as a simple past tense; it is a *past participle* (see 31c).

> **DRAFT**   The skater **done** the best she could at the Olympics.
>
> **EDITED**   The skater **did** the best she could at the Olympics.

don't, doesn't Contractions like these may strike some readers as too informal. Err on the side of formality (*do not, does not*) when in doubt. (See 50b.)

due to When meaning "because," use *due to* only after some form of the verb *be*. Avoid *due to the fact that*, which is wordy.

> **DRAFT**   The mayor collapsed **due to** campaign fatigue.
>
> **EDITED**   The mayor's collapse was **due to** campaign fatigue.
>
> **EDITED**   The mayor collapsed **because** of campaign fatigue.

effect, affect (See **affect, effect**.)

e.g. Avoid this abbreviation (from Latin, "for example") when possible. (See 58b.)

> **AWKWARD**   Her positions on major issues, **e.g.**, gun control, abortion, and the death penalty, are very liberal.
>
> **EDITED**   Her positions on major issues **such as** gun control, abortion, and the death penalty are very liberal.

emigrate from, immigrate to Foreigners *emigrate from* one country and *immigrate to* another. *Migrate* implies moving around (as in *migrant workers*) or settling temporarily.

ensure, assure, insure (See **assure, ensure, insure**.)

enthused Avoid *enthused* to mean *enthusiastic* in formal writing.

especially, specially *Especially* implies "in particular"; *specially* means "for a specific purpose."

It is **especially** important that Jo follow her **specially** designed workouts.

etc. Avoid this abbreviation in formal writing by supplying a complete list of items or by using a phrase like *so forth*. (See 58b.)

> **INFORMAL**   The Washington march was a disaster: it was cold and rainy, the protesters had no food, **etc.**
>
> **EDITED**   The Washington march was a disaster: the protesters were cold, wet, and hungry.

eventually, ultimately Use *eventually* to imply that an outcome follows a series of events or a lapse of events. Use *ultimately* to imply that a final or culminating act ends a series of events.

> **Eventually**, the rescue team managed to pull the last of the survivors from the wreck, and **ultimately** there were no casualties.

everyday, every day *Everyday* is an adjective that modifies a noun. *Every day* is a noun (*day*) modified by an adjective (*every*).

> **Every day** in the Peace Corps, Monique faced the **everyday** task of boiling her drinking water.

everyone, every one *Everyone* is a pronoun. *Every one* is a noun (*one*) modified by an adjective (*every*). (See also **anyone, any one**.)

> **Everyone** was tantalized by **every one** of the desserts on the menu.

exam In formal writing, some readers may be bothered by this abbreviation of *examination*.

except, accept (See **accept, except**.)

explicit, implicit *Explicit* means that something is outwardly or openly stated; *implicit* means that it is implied or suggested.

farther, further *Farther* implies a measurable distance; *further* implies something that cannot be measured.

> The **farther** they trekked into the wilderness, the **further** their relationship deteriorated.

female, male Use these terms only when you want to call attention to gender specifically, as in a research report. Otherwise, use the simpler *man* and *woman* or *boy* and *girl* unless such usage is sexist (see 46a).

fewer, less Use *fewer* for things that can be counted, and use *less* for quantities that cannot be divided. (See 34a.)

> The new bill had **fewer** supporters and **less** media coverage.

finalize Some readers object to adjectives and nouns that are turned into verbs ending in *-ize* (*finalize, prioritize, objectivize*). When in doubt, use *make final* or some other construction.

firstly Use *first, second, third*, and so forth when enumerating points in writing.

former, latter *Former* means "the one before" and *latter* means "the one after." They can be used only when referring to two things.

freshman, freshmen Many readers consider these terms sexist and archaic. Unless you are citing an established term or group (such as the Freshman Colloquium at Midwest University), use *first-year student* instead.

get Avoid imprecise or frequent use of *get* in formal writing.

INFORMAL	Martin Luther King had a premonition that he would **get** shot; his speeches before his death **got** nostalgic.
EDITED	Martin Luther King had a premonition that he would **be** shot; his speeches before his death **waxed** nostalgic.

go, say In very informal contexts, some speakers use **go** and **goes** to mean *say* and *says*. This usage is considered inappropriate in all writing.

glos

INAPPROPRIATE	Hjalmar **goes** to Gregers, "I thought this was my account."
EDITED	Hjalmar **says** to Gregers, "I thought this was my account."

gone, went Do not use *went* (the past tense of *go*) in place of the past participle form *gone*. (See 31c–d.)

DRAFT	The officers **should have went** to their captain.
EDITED	The officers **should have gone** to their captain.

good, well *Good* is an adjective meaning "favorable" (a *good* trip). *Well* is an adverb meaning "done favorably." (See 34b-3.)

good and This is a colloquial term when used to mean "very" (*good and* tired; *good and* hot). Avoid it in formal writing.

got to Avoid the colloquial use of *got* or *got to* in place of *must* or *have to*.

COLLOQUIAL	I **got to** improve my ratings in the opinion polls.
EDITED	I **must** improve my ratings in the opinion polls.

great In formal writing, avoid using *great* as an adjective meaning "wonderful." Use *great* in the sense of "large" or "monumental."

hanged, hung Although the distinction between these terms is disappearing, some readers may expect you to use **hanged** exclusively to mean execution by hanging and **hung** to refer to anything else.

have, got (See **got to**.)

have, of (See **could of, would of**.)

he, she, he or she, his/her When you use gender-specific pronouns, be careful not to privilege the male versions (see 46a).

hopefully Although the word is widely used to modify entire clauses (as in "Hopefully, her condition will improve"), some readers may object. When in doubt, use *hopefully* only to mean "feeling hopeful."

Bystanders watched **hopefully** as the workers continued to dig.

however, yet, but (See **but however, but yet**.)

hung, hanged (See **hanged, hung**.)

if, whether Use *if* before a specific outcome (either stated or implied); use *whether* when you are considering alternatives.

If holographic technology can be perfected, we may soon be watching three-dimensional television. But **whether** we will be able to afford it is another question.

illusion, allusion (See **allusion, illusion**.)

immigrate to, emigrate from (See **emigrate from, immigrate to**.)

implicit, explicit (See **explicit, implicit**.)

in regard to Although it may sound sophisticated, *in regard to* is wordy. Use *about* instead.

inside of, outside of When you use *inside* or *outside* to mark locations, do not pair them with *of.*

> **UNNEEDED**   Inside of the hut was a large stock of rootwater.

> **EDITED**   Inside the hut was a large stock of rootwater.

insure, assure, ensure (See **assure, ensure, insure**.)

irregardless Avoid this erroneous form of the word *regardless*, commonly used because *regardless* and *irrespective* are often used synonymously.

irritate, aggravate (See **aggravate, irritate**.)

its, it's *Its* is a possessive pronoun, and *it's* contracts *it is* (37a and 50b). (Some readers may also object to *it's* for *it is* in formal writing.)

-ize, -wise Some readers object to nouns or adjectives turned into verbs by adding *-ize* (*finalize, itemize, computerize*). Also avoid adding *-wise* to words, as in "Weather-*wise*, it will be chilly."

kind, sort, type These words are singular nouns; precede them with *this*, not *these*. In general, use more precise words.

kind of, sort of Considered by most readers to be informal, these phrases should be avoided in academic and workplace writing.

latter, former (See **former, latter**.)

lay, lie *Lay* is a transitive verb requiring a direct object (but not the self). *Lie*, when used to mean "place in a resting position," refers to the self but takes the form *lay* in the past tense. (See 31f.)

less, fewer (See **fewer, less**.)

lie, lay (See **lay, lie**.)

like, as (See **as, like**.)

literally Avoid using *literally* in a figurative statement (one that is not true to fact). Even when used correctly, *literally* is redundant because the statement will be taken as fact anyway.

> **DRAFT**   The visitors **literally** died when they saw their hotel.

> **REDUNDANT**   The visitors **literally gasped** when they saw their hotel.

> **EDITED**   The visitors gasped when they saw their hotel.

loose, lose Commonly misspelled, these words are pronounced differently. *Loose* (rhyming with *moose*) is an adjective meaning "not tight." *Lose* (rhyming with *snooze*) is a present tense verb meaning "to misplace."

lots, lots of, a lot of (See **a lot**.)

may, can (See **can, may**.)

maybe, may be *Maybe* means *possibly; may be* is part of a verb structure.

> The President **may be** speaking now, so **maybe** we should turn on the news.

media, medium Technically, *media* is a plural noun requiring a verb that agrees in number. Many people now use *media* as a singular noun when referring to the press. *Medium* generally refers to a conduit or method of transmission.

> The **media** is not covering the story accurately.

> The telephone was not a good **medium** for reviewing the budget.

might of, may of (See **could of, would of**.)

mighty Avoid this adjective in formal writing; omit it or use *very*.

Ms. To avoid the sexist labeling of women as "married" or "unmarried" (a condition not marked in men's titles), use *Ms.* unless you have reason to use *Miss* or *Mrs.* (for example, when giving the name of a character such as *Mrs. Dalloway*). Use professional titles when appropriate (*Doctor, Professor, Senator, Mayor*). (See 46a.)

must of, must have (See **could of, would of**.)

nor, or Use *nor* in negative constructions and *or* in positive ones.

> NEGATIVE   Neither rain **nor** snow will slow the team.
>
> POSITIVE   Either rain **or** snow may delay the game.

nothing like, nowhere near These are considered informal phases when used to compare two things (as in "Gibbon's position is **nowhere near** as justified as Carlyle's"). Avoid them in formal writing.

nowheres Use *nowhere* instead.

number, amount (See **amount, number**.)

of, have (See **could of, would of**.)

off of Simply use *off* instead.

OK When you write formally, use *OK* only in dialogue. If you mean "good" or "acceptable," use these terms.

on account of Avoid this expression in formal writing. Use *because* instead.

outside of, inside of (See **inside of, outside of**.)

per Use *per* only to mean "by the," as in *per hour* or *per day*. Avoid using it to mean "according to," as in "per your instructions."

percent, percentage Use *percent* only with numerical data. Use *percentage* for a statistical part of something, not simply to mean *some* or *part*.

> Ten **percent** of the sample returned the questionnaire.
>
> A large **percentage** of the parking revenue was stolen.

plus Avoid using *plus* as a conjunction joining two independent clauses.

> INFORMAL   The school saved money through its "lights off" campaign, **plus** it generated income by recycling aluminum cans.
>
> EDITED   The school saved money through its "lights off" campaign and also generated income by recycling aluminum cans.

Use *plus* only to mean "in addition to."

> The wearisome campaign, **plus** the media pressures, exhausted her.

precede, proceed *Precede* means "come before"; *proceed* means "go ahead."

pretty Avoid using *pretty* (as in *pretty good, pretty hungry, pretty sad*) to mean "somewhat" or "rather." Use *pretty* in the sense of "attractive."

principal, principle *Principal* is a noun meaning "an authority" or "head of a school" or an adjective meaning "leading" ("a *principal* objection to the testimony"). *Principle* is a noun meaning "belief or conviction."

proceed, precede (See **precede, proceed**.)

quote, quotation Formally, *quote* is a verb and *quotation* is a noun. *Quote* is sometimes used as a short version of the noun *quotation*, but this may bother some readers. Use *quotation* instead.

raise, rise *Raise* is a transitive verb meaning "to lift up." *Rise* is an intransitive verb (it takes no object) meaning "to get up or move up."

> He **raised** his head and watched the fog **rise** from the lake.

rarely ever Use *rarely* alone, not paired with *ever*.
real, really Use *real* as an adjective and *really* as an adverb. (See 34b-3)
reason is because, reason is that Avoid these wordy phrases. (See 40b-3.)
regarding, in regard, with regard to (See **in regard to**.)
regardless, irregardless (See **irregardless**.)
respectfully, respectively *Respectfully* means "with respect"; *respectively* implies a certain order for events or things.

> The senior class **respectfully** submitted the planning document. The administration considered items 3, 6, and 10, **respectively**.

rise, raise (See **raise, rise**.)

says, goes (See **go, say**.)
set, sit *Set* means "to place"; *sit* means "to place oneself." (See 31f.)
should of (See **could of, would of**.)
since, because (See **because, since**.)
sit, set (See **set, sit**.)
site, cite (See **cite, site**.)
so Some readers object to the use of *so* in place of *very*.

> INFORMAL   The filmmaker is **so** thoughtful about his films' themes.
>
> EDITED   The filmmaker is **very** thoughtful about his films' themes.

somebody, some body (See **anyone, any one**.)
someone, some one (See **anyone, any one**.)
sometime, some time, sometimes *Sometime* refers to an indistinct time in the future; *sometimes* means "every once in a while." *Some time* is an adjective (*some*) modifying a noun (*time*).

> The probe will reach the nebula **sometime** in the next decade. **Sometimes** such probes fail to send back any data. It takes **some time** before images will return from Neptune.

sort, kind, type (See **kind, sort, type**.)
specially, especially (See **especially, specially**.)
stationary, stationery *Stationary* means "standing still"; *stationery* refers to writing paper.
such Some readers will expect you to avoid using *such* without *that*.

> INFORMAL   Anne Frank had **such** a difficult time.
>
> EDITED   Anne Frank had **such** a difficult time growing up **that** her diary writing became her only solace.

suppose to, supposed to The correct form of this phrase is *supposed to*; the *-d* is sometimes mistakenly left off because it is not always heard. (See 31c.)

sure, surely In formal writing, use *sure* to mean "certain." *Surely* is an adverb; don't use *sure* in its place. (See 34b-3.)

> He has **surely** studied hard for the exam; he is **sure** to pass.

sure and, try and With *sure* and *try*, replace *and* with *to*.

take, bring (See **bring, take**.)

than, then *Than* is used to compare; *then* implies a sequence of events or a causal relationship.

> West played harder **than** East, but **then** the rain began.

that, which Although the distinction between *that* and *which* is weakening in many contexts, formal writing often requires you to know the difference. Use *that* in a clause that is essential to the meaning of a sentence (restrictive modifier); use *which* with a clause that does not provide essential information (nonrestrictive modifier). (See 46c.)

theirself, theirselves, themself All these forms are incorrect; use *themselves* to refer to more than one person, and *himself* or *herself* to refer to one.

them Avoid using *them* as a subject or to modify a subject, as in "*Them* are delicious" or "*Them* apples are very crisp."

then, than (See **than, then**.)

there, their, they're These forms are often confused in spelling because they all sound alike. *There* is a preposition of location; *their* is a possessive pronoun; *they're* is a contraction of *they* and *are*. (See 50b.)

> Look **over there**.

> **Their** car ran out of gas.

> **They're** not eager to hike to the nearest gas station.

thusly Avoid this term; use *thus* or *therefore* instead.

till, 'til, until Some readers will find *till* and *'til* too informal; use *until*.

to, too, two Because these words sound the same, they may be confused. *To* is a preposition indicating direction or location. *Too* means "also." *Two* is a number.

> The Birdsalls went **to** their lake cabin. They invited the Corbetts **too**. That made **two** trips so far this season.

toward, towards Prefer *toward* in formal writing. (You may see *towards* in England and Canada.)

try and, try to, sure and (See **sure and, try and**.)

ultimately, eventually (See **eventually, ultimately**.)

uninterested, disinterested (See **disinterested, uninterested**.)

unique Use *unique* alone, not *most unique* or *more unique*. (See 34b-4.)

until, till (See **till, 'til, until**.)

use to, used to Like *supposed to*, this phrase may be mistakenly written as *use to* because the *-d* is not always clearly pronounced. Write *used to*. (See 31c.)

wait for, wait on Use *wait on* only to refer to a clerk's or server's job; use *wait for* to mean "to await someone's arrival."

well, good (See **good, well**.)

went, gone (See **gone, went**.)

were, we're *Were* is the past plural form of *was; we're* contracts *we are*. (See 50b.)

> **We're** going to the ruins where the fiercest battles **were**.

where . . . at (See **at**.)

whether, if (See **if, whether**.)

which, that (See **that, which**.)

who, whom Although the distinction between these words is slowly disappearing from the language, many readers will expect you to use *whom* as the objective form. When in doubt, err on the side of formality. (Sometimes editing can eliminate the need to choose.) (See 32b-4.)

who's, whose *Who's* contracts *who is. Whose* indicates possession. (See 50b.)

> The programmer **who's** joining our division hunted for the person **whose** bag he took by mistake.

wise, -ize (See **-ize, -wise**.)

would of, could of (See **could of, would of**.)

yet, however, but (See **but however, but yet**.)

your, you're *Your* is a possessive pronoun; *you're* contracts *you are*. (See 32a-3 and 50b.)

> If **you're** going to take physics, you'd better know **your** math.

CHAPTER 3

Exercise 2 (*p. 18*)

Each of the five topics will become the focus of an appropriately specific thesis statement such as those illustrated in the section. Responses will vary but should meet the criteria for theses described in 3b. Following are examples for each of the topics.

Topic 1: Grandparents' rights

EXAMPLE: The frequency of divorce has resulted in many grandparents losing contact with their grandchildren or being prevented from having contact with them; new legislation is needed to guarantee that conflicts between parents do not interfere with the right of grandparents to be a part of their grandchildren's lives, to the benefit of both the children and the elders.

Topic 2: Gay rights in the Boy Scouts

EXAMPLE: Boy Scouts of America is a private organization that, unlike a public organization, can exclude members based on gender, religious beliefs, or sexual orientation—no matter how other people feel about the exclusions; Boy Scouts may be technically a private organization, but it acts like a public one and should therefore be required to respect the rights of gay people and not discriminate against them.

Topic 3: Metal detectors used at public school entrances

EXAMPLE: Preventing knives, chains, guns, and other weapons from interfering with classroom activities and the social interaction that is also part of schooling is of paramount importance to the success of schooling, the emotional and physical well-being of students, and the integrity of the schooling process—so important that it overcomes the intrusiveness and inconvenience of metal detectors.

Topic 4: Whose fault is air rage?

EXAMPLE: The degradation of customer accommodations on airlines has been so drastic and harmful that it should be regarded as a major cause of air rage, perhaps as the main cause; the real cause of air rage is always the person invoked because the vast majority of air passengers take millions of flights without becoming enraged and behaving in antisocial or dangerous ways.

Topic 5: Laws declaring English the official language of the United States

EXAMPLE: English is an essential element in American culture, and undermining its central role will lead to social conflict and disorder; America has always been a land of multiple language, and English has functioned "naturally" as a way of communicating—and will continue to do so in the future without a need for restrictive legislation.

CHAPTER 5

Exercise 1 (p. 30)

Maureen redrafted the opening of the paragraph. She cut the opening sentence, which called attention to the assignment and identified her essay as a student paper (addressed primarily to an instructor). In its place she created two rhetorical questions addressed to readers in general and written in a less formal and academic tone. She retained the dictionary definition of racism, but cut the "etc." at the end of the quoted material so that the quotation seems less like a reference to an authoritative (and detailed source) and more like one possible answer to the questions opening the passage.

In the last two sentences of her first version, Maureen struggled in somewhat complicated and confusing sentences to explain why the dictionary definition is insufficient ("Although this is what racism is, this definition doesn't fully explain racism") and presented questions she would address in her essay. Because the revised version of the selection treats the dictionary definition as only one possible answer, she was able to compress the last two sentences into one, acknowledging the dictionary definition as "legitimate" but pointing out that it needs further development because "it doesn't fully explain racism." This closing sentence is less stilted in tone than the ones it replaces.

The analysis of changes may prove time-consuming, but it can help writers develop considerable self-awareness and should lead to interesting class discussion.

Exercise 2 (p. 31)

SENSE: Revised draft adds "pampered prince" and "lavish" to opening sentence to explain why staying inside the palace would spare him from the "miseries"—a point that is implied but not stated clearly in the draft. (This change also increases contrast with his later actions and with the "miseries" in the following sentences.)

ECONOMY: Revised draft combines first and second sentences of early draft into one. Revised draft also cuts words from the last sentence (and makes it parallel with the preceding sentence—a matter of style).

STYLE: Revised version of first sentence has cumulative structure, adding details at the end. Revised second sentence adds information before the subject (periodic structure) for more dramatic contrasts within the sentence. Revision drops paragraph break before "Siddhartha became curious" and moves the break to later so that the contrast highlighted by the break is not the prince's decision to go riding but the content of what he encountered, "The Four Sights."

Exercise 3 *(p. 31)*

Here is one possible version of the paragraph.

After a day exploring the countryside, relax with a mulled wine by the fire at a quaint country inn. Wake to a country breakfast after a quiet night in a room decorated with beautiful antiques. Next, explore the towns and roads that have made Door County, Wisconsin, an attractive destination for people who like to get away from it all.

CHAPTER 7

Exercise 1 *(p. 47)*

Here is one possible rewrite:

Heart attacks have many causes. Most frequently, they are caused by either a blood clot or a mass of fatty substances that closes a coronary artery. A spasm in an artery that causes it to close can prevent blood from reaching the heart, as can conditions created by smoking, hypertension, and diabetes. In each case, the blood-starved tissue may die, creating a dead portion of the heart called a myocardial infarction and causing permanent damage to the heart's ability to pump blood.

CHAPTER 8

Exercise 2 *(p. 56)*

Answers may vary, both in choice of language and in level of formality. The first passage might be edited this way:

"Hello, Janie, how are you?"

"I'm doing well. I'm trying to give my feet a rest and clean them." She laughed a little.

"I can see that. You look very good. You look like your own daughter." They both laughed. "Even with those overalls on you look feminine."

"Please! You must think I've brought you something, but all I have brought home is myself."

"This is a considerable gift. Your friends will want nothing more."

CHAPTER 13

Exercise 3 *(p. 97)*

1. The United States should deregulate all mail service in order to increase competition and improve the quality of service [adequate].
2. Rap music, which is violent, vulgar, and sexist, should be banned from public consumption, and fines should be imposed on anyone listening to it in public places [not adequate].
3. Arson is not a crime; it is a mental disease and should be treated as such [adequate].

4. If children read when they are growing up, they will become literate [not adequate; far too broad for adequate support].

5. Orange juice tastes better than cranberry juice. [not adequate; matter of taste].

6. Humanity's woes began when Eve tasted the forbidden fruit in the Garden of Eden. [not adequate; matter of belief]

7. The telephone resulted in a society less prone to writing, but email will likely lead us right back into the written word as a primary form of communication. [adequate]

CHAPTER 25

Exercise 1 (p. 237)

1. Becker, Grossman, and Murphy argue that "a 10-percent increase in the price of cigarettes reduces current consumption by 4 percent in the short run and by 7.5 percent in the long run" (397).

2. According to one critic, the new DVD release of Neil Young's concert film, Rust Never Sleeps, first released in 1979, provides evidence of the film's continued importance (Smith).

3. In Samoa during the 1930s, girls separated socially from their siblings at about age seven and began to form close and lasting relationships with other girls their age (Mead 59–73).

Exercise 2 (p. 237)

1. Brazaitis, Peter. You Belong in a Zoo! New York: Villard, 2003.

2. Graham, Jorie. "Self-Portrait as Apollo and Daphne." The Dream of the Unified Field: Selected Poems, 1974–1994. New York: Ecco, 1995. 70–73.

3. O'Hehir, Andrew. "The Matrix Revolutions." Rev. of The Matrix Revolutions. Salon.com 5 Nov. 2003. 5 Nov. 2003 <http://salon.com/ent/movies/review/2003/11/5matrix_revolutions/undex_np.html>.

4. Jensen, Dallas R. "Understanding Sleep Disorders in a College Student Population." Journal of College Counseling Spring 2003: 25–34. Abstract. Academic Search Premier. EBSCO. U of Rhode Island Lib. 15 Nov. 2003. <http://0-search.epnet.com.helin.uri.edu: 80/direct.asp?an= 9744711&db=aph>.

5. Rosenbluth, Vera. Keeping Family Stories Alive: A Creative Guide to Taping Your Family Life and Lore. Point Roberts: Hartley and Marks, 1990.

CHAPTER 26

Exercise 1 (p. 268)

1. Becker, Grossman, and Murphy (1994) argue that "a 10-percent increase in the price of cigarettes reduces current consumption by 4 percent in the short run and by 7.5 percent in the long run" (p. 397).

2. According to one critic, the new DVD resease of Neil Young's concert film, *Rust Never Sleeps,* first released in 1979, provides evidence of the film's continued importance (Smith, 39).

3. In Samoa during the 1930s, girls separated socially from their siblings at about age seven and began to form close and lasting relationships with other girls their age (Mead, 1928/1961).

Exercise 2 *(p. 268)*

1. Brazaitis, P. (2003). *You belong in a zoo!* New York: Villard.

2. Graham, J. (1995). "Self-portrait as Apollo and Daphne." In *The dream of the unified field: Selected poems, 1974–1994* (pp. 70–73). New York: Ecco Press.

3. O'Hehir, A. (2003, November 5). The matrix revolutions [Review of *The matrix revolutions*]. *Salon.com.* Retrieved November 5, 2003, from http://salon.com/ent/movies/review/2003/11/5/matrix_revolutions/index_np.html

4. Jensen, D. R. (2003). Understanding sleep disorders in a college student population. *Journal of College Counseling,* Spring 2003. Retrieved November 15, 2003, from Academic Search Premier database.

5. Rosenbluth, V. (1990). *Keeping family stories alive: A creative guide to taping your family life and lore.* Point Roberts, WA: Hartley and Marks.

CHAPTER 27

Exercise 1 *(p. 282)*

1. Becker, Grossman, and Murphy (1994) argue that "a 10-percent increase in the price of cigarettes reduces current consumption by 4 percent in the short run and by 7.5 percent in the long run".[1]

   1. Gary S. Becker, Michael Grossman, and Kevin M. Murphy, *American Economic Review,* 84 (1994): 396–418.

2. According to one critic, the new DVD resease of Neil Young's concert film, *Rust Never Sleeps,* first released in 1979, provides evidence of the film's continued importance.[2]

   2. L.C. Smith, "My, My, Hey, Hey: A Neil Young Treasure Resurfaces," *Rolling Stone,* October 17, 2002, 39.

3. In Samoa during the 1930s, girls separated socially from their siblings at about age seven and began to form close and lasting relationships with other girls their age.[3]

   3. Margaret Mead, *Coming of Age in Samoa* (1928; reprint, New York: Morrow, 1961), 59–73.

Exercise 2 *(p. 282)*

1. Brazaitis, P. (2003). *You Belong in a Zoo!* New York: Villard, 2003.

2. Graham, Jorie. "Self-Portrait as Apollo and Daphne." In *The Dream of the Unified Field: Selected Poems, 1974–1994,* 70–73. New York: Ecco, 1995.

3. O'Hehir, Andrew. The Matrix Revolutions Rev. of *The Matrix Revolutions*. *Salon.com*. November 5, 2003 from http://salon.com/ent/movies/review/2003/11/5/matrix_revolutions/index_np.html (accessed November 5, 2003).

4. Jensen, Dallas R. Understanding Sleep Disorders in a College Student Population. *Journal of College Counseling*, Spring 2003: 25–34. Abstract. *Academic Search Premier. EBSCO*. U of Rhode Island Lib. http://search.epnet.com.helin.uri.edu:80/Direct.asp?an=9744711 &db=aph (accessed November 15, 2003).

5. Rosenbluth, Vera. *Keeping Family Stories Alive: A Creative Guide to Taping Your Family Life and Lore*. Point Roberts, Wash: Hartley and Marks, 1990.

CHAPTER 30

Exercise 1 (*p. 310*)

1. [The Sherpas] are well-known guides for mountain-climbing expeditions in the Himalayas.
2. [They] are a group of about 35,000 people who live in the country of Nepal.
3. [The Sherpas, who are primarily Buddhists,] live in a country dominated by Hindus.
4. Before the early 1900s, [most Sherpas] did not attempt to scale the mountains in their homeland.
5. In the early part of this century, however, [Westerners wishing to climb the mountains] gave many Sherpas jobs as guides and laborers.

Exercise 3 (*p. 311*)

Because the tax laws have gotten more complex recently, we have published a guide to tax preparation that highlights new features of the tax code. In addition, the guide provides step-by-step instruction for tax forms, which should be helpful even if a person has considerable experience filling out the forms. Anyone who plans to file taxes for a small business will be interested in the special section on business laws. Although many professionals and businesspeople rely on accountants when tax time arrives, they will nonetheless find that the guide provides money-saving advice.

CHAPTER 31

Exercise 1 (*p. 323*)

1. Jeremy had chosen to work along the levee as part of the volunteer corps.
2. The flood water had risen rapidly during the night.
3. Correct.
4. Correct.
5. By eight o'clock in the morning, people had woken up to find that the river had fallen by six inches and the town was safe.

Exercise 3 (*p. 324*)

1. Kamal <u>was finished</u> testing the circuit board by the time the production meeting <u>started</u>.
2. The team members <u>will ask</u> *[let stand because the action is going to occur in the future]* Kamal if he <u>is planning</u> *[action will reflect his state of mind at the time the question is asked—hence present tense]* to test the remainder of the circuit boards.
3. As I prepare this report on the project, Michelle <u>is assembling</u> *[let stand— both actions mentioned in the sentence take place in the present and the pro- gressive form indicates that they are taking place concurrently]* the prototype using the circuit boards.
4. The other people <u>will assemble</u> *[let stand—action will occur in the future and the tense is correct]* the extra machines as soon as the delivery van ar- <u>rives</u> *[this event sets the time frame after which the assembly will take place; hence it is in the present]*.
5. If our customers <u>are able</u> to recognize the advantages of our product, they <u>will order</u> more of the machines.

Exercise 5 (*p. 325*)

Here is one possible rewritten version.

<u>Researchers have found</u> that having cash registers full of change increases the likelihood of a late-night robbery. In one example, <u>robbers held up</u> a store clerk at gunpoint. <u>Management decided</u> that <u>it would require that customers pay in full</u> for gasoline in advance of a purchase in order to minimize the risk of further holdups. <u>The board of directors voted</u> on this course of action prior to implementation. <u>The company posted</u> the decision at each location. Following implementation, <u>the company discovered</u> that <u>the procedure did not minimize</u> holdups unless <u>the employees placed</u> in plain view large signs indicating the clerk's lack of available cash. Once this was done, <u>the stores ex- perienced</u> fewer holdups and <u>decreased turnover</u> of late-night personnel.

CHAPTER **32**

Exercise 1 (*p. 331*)

1. The design for the new store was prepared by <u>her</u>. [objective]
2. The city requires <u>us</u> to submit plans for remodeling the store we plan to rent. [objective]
3. Having interviewed Ruth and <u>me</u> about our marketing plan, the bank's offi- cer approved our loan. [objective]
4. The person who will choose the stock for our store is <u>she</u>. [subjective]
5. I will supervise the salespeople <u>whom</u> we hire. [objective]

1. <u>She</u> and three other people worked for three weeks preparing the grant pro- posal.
2. The original grant-writing team included two other people, Kristen and <u>her</u>.

3. Because I spent more time working on the grant, I think I ought to get more credit for its success than <u>he</u>.
4. It is <u>I</u> who will have to supervise research work done under the grant.
5. Responsibility for budgeting the grant money is <u>yours</u>.

Exercise 2 (p. 332)

1. Correct.
2. Because their parents own a video store, her brother and <u>she</u> brought in tapes of the movies we planned to study.
3. Bill and I decided to take notes on Aladdin; Pat and <u>she</u> chose to study Beauty and the Beast.
4. I thought the notes we took were more detailed and better than <u>theirs</u>.
5. Writing the final paper led to some disagreements between the other members and <u>me</u>.

Exercise 3 (p. 332)

A 1. In the past, psychologists assumed that <u>whoever</u> scored well on IQ tests was likely to succeed at school and work.
2. Recent studies of IQ tests have produced evidence of <u>their</u> being unable to predict success.
3. A test of constructive thinking skill may tell more about your or <u>my</u> ability to meet challenges.
4. Reporting on research conducted by <u>himself</u> and two of his colleagues, Robert Sternberg points out that "the ability to sell" is an important part of practical intelligence.
5. Other psychologists claim that personal qualities like self-confidence and optimism may by <u>themselves</u> have as much to do with our mental abilities as IQ does.

B   For <u>we</u> [us] humans, yawning is a familiar activity. <u>You</u> and <u>me</u> [I] probably yawn when <u>we</u> stretch, though not always. Boredom is also a likely cause for <u>us</u> [our] yawning. People often think that <u>no one</u> yawns as much as <u>them</u> [they], but <u>this</u> is seldom true. <u>We</u> all yawn frequently during a day. <u>We</u> may even start yawning <u>ourselves</u> when <u>we</u> notice <u>someone</u> else <u>whom</u> [who] is yawning.

CHAPTER 33

Exercise 1 (p. 345)

1. The retired men in the neighborhood <u>eat</u> lunch at the cafeteria.
2. The cafeteria's motto, "See What You <u>Eat</u>," <u>appears</u> on the sign above the entrance.
3. The restaurant <u>seems</u> run down.
4. Nonetheless, it <u>is</u> a clean and safe place.
5. A sociologist has studied the ways people of different races and cultures <u>communicate</u> [or <u>interact</u>] with each other at the cafeteria.

Exercise 3 (*p. 345*)

A   1. Frieda O'Connor is one of those managers who <u>lead</u> by example.
2. All the other department heads <u>respect</u> her leadership ability.
3. She knows each of the employees who <u>work</u> in her department.
4. Each year, Alberti and Campos Design Associates <u>gives</u> a plaque and a bonus to the employee who receives the highest rating in a company-wide survey.
5. The award, both the plaque and the money, <u>is given</u> to Frieda almost every other year.

B   Each of the scientists involved in the search <u>is</u> pretty sure something is out there. A lot of numbers, some high and some low, <u>are</u> thrown around to express the probability of intelligent life somewhere else <u>in</u> the universe. Here <u>are</u> some figures that are middle-of-the-road. There <u>are</u> an estimated four hundred billion stars in the Milky Way. Planets may be fairly common, so you can figure one out of every ten of these stars have planets, which equals forty billion stars with planets. If every such star has ten planets, that is four hundred billion planets. But how many of these places <u>seem</u> suitable for life? Neither too hot nor too cold <u>are</u> the conditions needed for life forms similar to our own. An atmosphere along with some water <u>is</u> also necessary. In our solar system only Earth qualifies, though Mars and Venus each <u>come</u> close. Let us be conservative and estimate that only one of each solar system's planets fits the pattern. That's still forty billion habitable planets.

CHAPTER **35**

Exercise 2 (*p. 358*)

Responses will vary.

1. The first sentence is correct; the second is a fragment. Possible correction: People such as interns and truck drivers often feel drowsy, even though they are aware of a need to stay awake and alert.
2. The first sentence is correct; the second is a fragment. Possible correction: Whether or not you got enough sleep the night before, having an afternoon nap can greatly increase your alertness.
3. Correct.
4. The first sentence is correct; the second is a fragment. Possible correction: Almost everyone experiences sleepiness and a decline in mental alertness during the afternoon; our internal clocks tell us it is time to nap and get out of the sun's strongest rays.
5. The first sentence is a fragment; the second is correct. Possible correction: Despite a widespread belief that siestas and naps are cultural customs, they actually have a biological base.

Exercise 4 (*p. 359*)

Responses to this exercise will vary. Look for different, innovative ways to repair the errors while maintaining meaning.

Ans

1. Realizing that musical tastes are probably changing, many record companies have decided to explore new and newly rediscovered kinds of music.

   Many record companies have realized that musical tastes are changing; they have decided to explore new and newly rediscovered kinds of music.

2. Their sales of tapes and CDs having dropped drastically, some formerly popular musical artists no longer have recording contracts.

   <u>Because</u> their sales of tapes and CDs have dropped drastically, some formerly popular musical artists no longer have recording contracts.

3. Because of the innovative melodies and sounds, jazz artists have attracted large and enthusiastic audiences to recent campus concerts.

   Jazz artists, with their innovative melodies and sounds, have attracted large and enthusiastic audiences to recent campus concerts.

4. The rhythm section of one groups consists of a single, unusual electronic instrument <u>that makes</u> sounds like a drum but <u>looks</u> like a guitar.

   One group's rhythm section consists of a single unusual instrument: an electronic instrument that makes sounds like a drum but looks like a guitar.

5. Undecided about whether to sign new groups to long-term contracts, some companies agree to produce and sell a single CD with an option for future recordings.

   Some companies are undecided about whether to sign new groups to long-term contracts; instead, they agree to produce and sell a single CD with an option for future recordings.

CHAPTER 36

Exercise 2 *(p. 366)*

1. <u>Fearing</u> the children will resent the interference, some parents refuse to become involved in their children's squabbles.

   Some parents refuse to become involved in their children's squabbles; they fear the children will resent the interference.

2. Siblings have special reasons to fight; competing for space and playthings or for attention from a parent can turn playmates into rivals.

   Siblings have special reasons to fight<u>; for example</u>, competing for space and playthings or for attention from a parent can turn playmates into rivals.

3. Sibling fights offer an opportunity for children to become sensitive to the feelings of others<u>, yet</u> the arguments pose dangers as well.

   Sibling fights offer an opportunity for children to become sensitive to the feelings of others<u>; however,</u> the arguments pose dangers as well.

4. Bickering is common and normal; <u>however,</u> excessive fighting can be a sign of more serious trouble.

   Bickering is common and normal. <u>Excessive</u> fighting, however, can be a sign of more serious trouble.

5. <u>Although</u> by adolescence most children have worked out compatible relationships with their siblings, they may still occasionally argue.

By adolescence most children have worked out compatible relationships with their siblings, <u>yet</u> they may still occasionally argue.

CHAPTER 37

Exercise 1 (*p. 371*)

Responses will vary depending on the specific editing strategies employed.

1. Both Carlo and Andy agree that <u>Carlo</u> will be responsible for getting the cartons of replacement parts from <u>the air</u> terminal.
2. As he explained to <u>his</u> client, <u>the accountant</u> will be answerable for any <u>problems</u> with billing.
3. Airfreight is cheaper; furthermore, it offers weekend <u>shipment</u>, which means that work doesn't have to stop on Monday morning while workers wait for delivery of the replacement parts.
4. <u>Covered with rust spots</u>, the van used to pick up shipments is the old one the company's owner purchased right after her divorce.
5. The sales projections used to order supplies are often inaccurate because the sales manager calculates <u>the projections</u> using <u>an overly optimistic</u> <u>formula</u> on a spreadsheet.

Exercise 2 (*p. 371*)

1. Many students study a musical instrument in high school though few students intend to become <u>musicians</u>.
2. Most secondary <u>schools offer a variety</u> of music programs.
3. Last February, <u>the town began</u> investigating the quality of its high school band program, but <u>the study</u> has not yet been completed.
4. In many regional <u>high schools</u> in the West, the band's large size mirrors the role <u>the band</u> plays in the school's social life.

CHAPTER 38

Exercise 1 (*p. 377*)

1. Confused by the many exotic breeds of dogs, they decided to buy the beagle puppy.
2. This dog would replace the one which, running across a busy highway, was killed by a truck.
3. Distracted by the crowd of people in the store, they forgot to buy a dog bed.
4. John sighed and hurriedly began tearing up newspapers in order to begin house-training the puppy.
5. The parents could hear the children playing outside, yelling and laughing with the dog.

Exercise 2 (*p. 377*)

1. squinting modifier
2. limiting modifier
3. squinting modifier
4. limiting modifier
5. limiting modifier

CHAPTER 39

Exercise 1 (*p. 384*)

1. <u>Would-be restaurant owners</u> often fail to consider carefully the competition they will face from other restaurants of all kinds, both fancy and informal.
2. Good franchise chains survey competition, tell potential owners how much money they will need to open the business, and help <u>them</u> with the many problems a restaurant owner faces.
3. Admittedly, running a doughnut shop or a pizza place <u>is less prestigious than</u> owning a gourmet restaurant.
4. I would still rather run a successful business than <u>one that loses money</u>.
5. Not all franchise arrangements are good ones, so people should do some research before <u>they</u> decide to open a franchised restaurant.

Exercise 2 (*p. 384*)

1. The video store manager said that if I bought two tapes <u>I would</u> get a third one free, and then he <u>told</u> me about several of his favorite tapes.
2. In the movie *Sacrifice for Glory*, set in World War II, a British Mosquito bomber crashed in the jungle, and only the copilot <u>manages</u> to survive the long walk through the tropical heat back to civilization.
3. The hot sun <u>beats</u> on the shoulders of the copilot as he wades through the waist-deep, crocodile-infested swamp.
4. At the beginning of *Ghostbusters*, the three main characters have jobs as researchers, but later on they <u>found</u> a company ridding people and places of ghosts.
5. In *Ghoulish Lunch*, the main character <u>is</u> reaching into the refrigerator around the guacamole dip for the last piece of apple pie when suddenly a cockroach crawls out from under the crust.

CHAPTER 40

Exercise 1 (*p. 390*)

1. <u>Tanning is a process</u> for making animal hide supple and resistant to decay.
2. The first step in tanning <u>is to scrape and clean</u> the hides thoroughly.
3. <u>Diluted acid is the substance</u> that pickles the hides to prepare them for tanning.

4. <u>The leather is supple because</u> it is lubricated with oil after pickling, then dried and impregnated with resins.
5. <u>During the final steps</u>, the leather is dyed and given a shiny surface through compression.

Exercise 3 *(p. 391)*

1. His tennis serve has more speed and accuracy <u>than Bill's</u>.
2. He also has <u>a</u> better sense of where an opponent is going <u>to</u> hit the ball.
3. Bill's commitment to tennis is greater than <u>his commitment to his family</u>.
4. He has more fun playing tennis <u>than being with his kids</u>.
5. Like many exercise-addicted people, Bill would <u>rather</u> be exercising than eating, and he would rather be playing tennis than doing anything else.

CHAPTER **41**

Exercise 1 *(p. 394)*

1. We've told you about <u>the bombs</u>, <u>the fires</u>, <u>the smashed houses</u>, and <u>the courage of the people</u>.
   —Edward R. Murrow, "From London, September 22, 1940"

2. She looked at a man because <u>she liked the way the hair was tucked behind the ears</u>, or <u>she liked the question-mark line of a long torso curving at the shoulder and straight at the hip</u>.
   —Maxine Hong Kingston, "No Name Woman"

3. But far below, <u>in the warren of passages on the starboard side forward</u>, <u>in the forward holds and boiler rooms</u>, men could see that the Titanic's hurt was mortal. —Hanson W. Baldwin, "R.M.S. *Titanic*"

4. In that context three groups of wounded soldiers are identified: <u>those whose survival depends on their receiving immediate treatment; those who need medical attention but will survive even if they do not get it immediately; and those who are hurt so badly they would not survive even with medical attention.</u> —Ruth Macklin, *Mortal Choices*

5. For in each American marriage there is a special code, <u>developed from the individual pasts of the two partners</u>, <u>put together out of the accidents of honeymoon and parents-in-law</u>, finally <u>beaten into a language that each understands imperfectly</u>. —Margaret Mead, *Male and Female*

CHAPTER **42**

Exercise 1 *(p. 403)*

Student answers will vary, but they should follow the directions for using a range of strategies.

1. Ice skating can be enjoyable <u>and</u> also physically demanding.
2. Recreational skaters need to be in good shape physically; <u>therefore</u>, they should exercise to increase their fitness.

3. Skaters who are not in good shape get tired quickly; <u>consequently,</u> they are also more likely to pull a muscle or fall.

4. To get in shape for skating, try a program of regular exercise for at least several weeks; pay special attention to exercises focusing on knees and ankles.

5. Other areas to exercise are hip and leg muscles; <u>moreover,</u> exercises aimed at each muscle group are best.

Exercise 3 *(p. 404)*

Answers will vary widely; possible edited versions follow.

1. Comedian Sam Kinison died in a car crash <u>when</u> a pickup truck swerved across the road and hit his car.

2. Kinison was not wearing his seat belt, <u>which</u> might have saved his life.

3. Driving quickly off the road to the right <u>is one</u> thing you can do <u>to help</u> you avoid collisions.

4. Drive a large car <u>because</u> big, heavy cars and passenger vans are much safer in crashes.

5. <u>Although</u> buying a car with air bags and antilock brakes is an excellent <u>way</u> to reduce your chances of getting injured or dying, these cars do cost more money.

CHAPTER 43

Exercise 2 *(p. 410)*

1. Many colleges no longer <u>require</u> a course in negotiating, regarded by many experts as an important element in successful business careers. [Or, ". . . even though many experts regard negotiating as an important element in successful business careers."]

2. Our consulting company <u>includes</u> a course in public speaking among the programs it offers.

3. We also <u>demonstrate</u> how to prepare effective graphics for a presentation.

4. If a company <u>wishes,</u> our consultants can provide training for both small and large groups.

5. The training program <u>builds</u> confidence for many people.

Exercise 3 *(p. 411)*

1. Many people choose superpremium brands from the ice cream freezers in their supermarkets.

2. Ice cream makers blend more butterfat and less air into superpremium brands than into regular ice cream.

3. You ought to consider the high fat content before you purchase the ice cream.

4. New frozen dessert products are challenging the rich, tasty ice creams.

5. Dairy companies have heavily promoted frozen yogurts with candy and nuts mixed in.

CHAPTER **44**

Exercise 1 (*p. 417*)

1. My uncle had just come back from playing nine holes of golf when he tragically suffered a heart attack.
2. We all thought my aunt was in good health, but she also died suddenly.
3. These experiences have made me schedule regular checkups with my doctor.
4. My last doctor's visit led me to start exercising regularly.
5. An exercise program helps me to feel good about myself.

CHAPTER **46**

Exercise 2 (*p. 425*)

Preschool programs for children in poor families have always been underfunded and at best only a stopgap measure for more permanent educational reform. This was the message delivered by the husband-and-wife team, Dr. Herbert Kline and Dr. [Margaret] Kline, Ph.D.s, at the Eleventh Regional Conference on Preschool Education. About seven hundred elementary school teachers came to the conference to hear the Klines debunk some old myths about education. The Klines also focused on what the future holds for those interested in becoming public school teachers, including the need to balance work with attending to one's family. All teachers of young children, Margaret Kline pointed out, must not only practice their craft well but also keep abreast of new theory and research which they can then integrate into their classrooms in ways that are rewarding to them and to their students.

CHAPTER **48**

Exercise 1 (*p. 440*)

1. Jim wanted to buy paper for his copier, so he went to all the office supply stores in town.
2. The stores had plenty of paper, but it cost more than Jim was willing to pay.
3. Jim then heard about a mail-order office supply company, so he called the company for a catalog.
4. The catalog contained more than fifty different kinds of reasonably priced copier paper. The paper was available in packs of one thousand sheets, and for an even greater discount, it came in bulk orders of five thousand sheets.
5. He ordered five thousand sheets of medium-quality paper, and it lasted for the next three months.

Exercise 2 (*p. 441*)

A   1. In contrast, mailboxes today come in many surprising designs.

2. Occasionally, people in the suburbs choose an unusual mailbox, but residents of small towns generally display the most imagination.
3. On a recent trip through rural Iowa, I noticed mailboxes in the shape of log cabins, igloos, Eiffel Towers, cows, cats, and even parrots.
4. One morning, I drove down a block on which each mailbox took the shape of a different kind of fish, including bass, trout, bluegill, shark, pike, and salmon.
5. Whenever you start thinking that people in big cities or suburbs are more creative than people in small towns, remember the mailboxes.

Ans **B** Groups should work collaboratively to produce edited sentences.

1. Although people felt sleepy, they still had to go to their offices and plants for a full day's work.
2. Because people were trying to get to work on time, they jammed the highways and commuter trains.
3. Because Avi felt rested and alert, the gloomy weather did not bother him.
4. While Avi worked hard throughout the afternoon, the other people in his office were exhausted by two o'clock.
5. Still feeling awake at seven o'clock in the evening, Avi went to see a movie.

Exercise 3 (p. 441)

1. Fifty years ago, a residence that served retired people, was called an old folks' home.
2. These homes, which provided few services for residents, were apartment buildings with dining rooms.
3. A retirement residence today offers many things to do, including recreational activities, fitness programs, trips, classes, and social events.
4. The image of infirm people sitting in rocking chairs has been replaced by one of senior citizens who are vigorous and involved.
5. Retirement residences, often known as retirement communities, are small towns where people go to lead active lives.

Exercise 5 (p. 442)

1. McDonald's and the others offer quick, appetizing meals and clean, pleasant surroundings.
2. In the late 1940s, the McDonald brothers opened a restaurant serving a limited, inexpensive menu, including fifteen-cent hamburgers, french fries, and shakes.
3. The brothers did not want to expand their modestly successful restaurant into a chain. [No change.]
4. Ray Kroc, a manufacturer of milkshake machines, recognized the potential of the brothers' innovations, joined their business to help it expand, and frustrated by their lack of ambition, eventually bought them out.
5. Kroc continued to develop innovative, imaginative ways to serve customers, and these fast, efficient practices have come to characterize today's fast-food restaurants.

Exercise 8 *(p. 444)*

1. Because she likes the outdoors, Sandy, a devoted gardener, takes care of landscaping, grass cutting, and outdoor cleanup.

   Sandy, a devoted gardener and lover of the outdoors, takes care of landscaping, grass cutting, and outdoor cleanup.

2. Strong, tireless Jun does roofing, paving, and similar work.

   Strong and tireless Jun does roofing, paving, and similar work.

3. Interior design was Padmaja's major, so she, everyone agrees, is the person best qualified to do interior decorating.

   Everyone agrees that interior design major Padmaja is the person best qualified to do interior decorating.

4. Having painted her parents' house one summer, Rachel was chosen by her partners as the company's painting supervisor.

   Her partners chose Rachel as the company's painting supervisor because she had painted her parents' house one summer.

5. Desperate for a place in the company, Joel decided that marketing, because it would draw on his undergraduate work in sociology, was the best thing for him to do.

   Desperate for a place in the company, Joel selected marketing because it would draw on his undergraduate work in sociology.

Ans

CHAPTER 49

Exercise 2 *(p. 449)*

1. They prepared for the trip by first looking for inexpensive hotels in Paris.
2. The Residence Rivoli seemed like a good value: clean, centrally located, and appointed with a private bath.
3. Mr. Hirsch, however, wanted to splurge. He argued that an upper-bracket hotel would be so much more enjoyable: a shining marble bath, plush dining room, and elegant meals. There would be parking as well, essential for anyone with a car.
4. But Mrs. Hirsch wasn't impressed: the expensive hotels would be comfortable, but she wanted atmosphere, and small, charming hotels would have that in abundance.
5. Finally, they reached a compromise; they would stay in a chateau near the Loire, which would be cheaper than a fancy Paris hotel but afford plenty of atmosphere. Then they could drive into Paris, enjoy the sights, and have a peaceful night, all without driving more than an hour or so each way.

CHAPTER 50

Exercise 1 *(p. 453)*

1. The river's name is especially associated with the many chateaux that line its <u>banks</u>.

2. Serious sightseers' visits to the Loire Valley should include tours of several of this region's beautiful castles.

3. The Loire's reputation is also founded on its renowned cuisine and its sophisticated wines.

4. Barton and Jones' wine import businesses have flourished in the United States ever since Jones came up with the company's award-winning advertising campaign.

5. Several other companies have found an eager market for France's excellent <u>wines</u>.

CHAPTER **51**

Exercise 1 (*p. 456*)

The shame of illiteracy—or so Robert Cullany puts it—affects millions of adults in the United States alone, but the problem is not nearly as prevalent as "innumeracy," Cullany's term that means being unable to use numbers. Cullany writes, "Illiteracy and innumeracy are a national blight on our intellectual landscape, and cannot be tolerated." He also points out that they cripple our productivity, lead to "familial dysfunction" (poor family structures), and deny people the ability to become what Cullany calls "self-learners." The ALVC, or Adult Literacy Volunteer Corps, is made up of dedicated people who believe they can help this so-called "mind plague."

CHAPTER **55**

Exercise 1 (*p. 475*)

Added quotation marks are underlined below.

1. I first learned about this famous American almanac from a newspaper article, <u>"</u>You Can Look It Up There,<u>"</u> that appeared in my local paper, the Record-Advertiser.

2. <u>GQ</u> and <u>Cosmopolitan</u> probably would not print an article like "Salt: It's Still Worth Its Salt," which appeared in a recent edition of the <u>Almanac</u>. [In this instance, the *Almanac* refers to the *Old Farmer's Almanac*, a specific publication, not a general type.]

3. According to this article, the word <u>salary</u> comes from the Latin term for wages paid to some soldiers, <u>salarium argentus</u>, that is, <u>"</u>salt money.<u>"</u>

4. In an essay on the historic effects of weather, the author points out that freezing temperatures on January 28, 1986, led to the space shuttle <u>Challenger</u> disaster.

5. If you are interested in learning about the ocean, you can find out that high tides occur twice a month at <u>syzygy</u>, the times when the sun and moon are lined up on the same side of the earth or on opposite sides. [Some students will feel that this emphasis is not needed; the underlining is optional.]

CHAPTER **56**

Exercise 1 (*p. 478*)

1. Alejo enjoys painstakingly exact work, such as building scale-model ships.
2. While working, he likes to listen to Francis Poulenc's jazz-influenced classical music.
3. One-fourth of all his model ships are sold at auction.
4. Tony, his assistant, keeps track of the profits in a pre- and post-auction sale log.
5. Although his creations are awesome, Alejo harbors many insecurities that are mostly self-inflicted.

Ans

CHAPTER **57**

Exercise 1 (*p. 481*)

1. Of the groups and individuals elected to the Rock and Roll Hall of Fame from 1986 to 1990, five were female and sixty-eight were male.
2. The Hall of Fame is increasing its membership goals from 19,000 to 21,500.
3. Four hundred and eleven of the two thousand questionnaires about favorite rockers were returned by the deadline. [Alternatively, treating comparable numbers as figures: Of the 2,000 questionnaires about favorite rockers, 411 were returned by the deadline. In either case, the sentence should not begin with a number using numerals.]
4. This year the Hall of Fame purchased 26 articles of clothing, 127 signed memorabilia, and 232 unused concert tickets for the museum.
5. Although subscribers were told the museum would open by 10:30 in the morning on the twelfth, the personnel weren't ready for the large crowd until about two o'clock.

CHAPTER **59**

Exercise 2 (*p. 492*)

The misspelled words are underlined below.

supercede	conceed	procede
idiosyncracy	concensus	accomodate
dexterous	impressario	irresistable
rhythym	opthalmologist	diptheria
anamoly	aficionado	caesarian
graffiti	judgement	liason

INDEX

Note: The index is sorted by word order. **Bold** page numbers indicate definitions in the text. (WWW) indicates the location of information about a specific Web site where additional information may be available. *See* references refer you to appropriate or related index entries.

index

index

index

index

index

index

CREDITS

Atlanta Journal and Constitution, Staff Writer. "Restrict Rights to Sue or We'll Pay in the End." Copyright © 2001 by Atlanta Jour-Constitution. Reproduced with permission of Atlanta Jour-Constitution in the format Textbook via Copyright Clearance Center.

Baldwin, Hanson W. "R. M. S. Titanic." *Harper's Magazine,* 1933.

Berendt, John. "Class Acts." *Esquire,* 1991.

Boylan, Jennifer Finney. From "The Bean Curd Method." *Boston Review* © 1990.

Bright, Michael. *Animal Language.* (Ithaca, NY: Cornell UP, 1984).

Bronowski, Jacob. *The Ascent of Man.* (Boston: Little, Brown, 1973).

Colorado Division of Wildlife. For more information, see http://wildlife.state.co.us/WildlifeSpecies/CoexistingWithWildlife/Mammals/CoyoteCountry.htm.

Committee of Concerned Journalists, "A Statement of Concern," from *The Media and Morality,* eds. Robert M. Baird, William E. Loges, and Stuart Rosenbaum (New York: Prometheus Books, 1999).

CRITT Web site (Critical Resources in Teaching with Technology), 1997. http://www.engl.uic.edu/~stp/.

Daseler, Robert. *Levering Avenue Poems.* (Evansville: The University of Evansville Press, 1998).

Davis, Mike. "House of Cards." *Sierra* © 1995.

EBSCO HOST databases reprinted by permission of EBSCO Publishing.

"Fast Track Recalls," *Consumer Product Safety Review,* Fall 1998 issue, Vol. 3, No. 1.

Flippen, Royce. "Tossing and Turning." *American Health,* © 1992 by American Health.

Franzoi, S. L., and Shields, S. A. "The Body Esteem Scale." *Journal of Personality Assessment* 407 (173–178).

Freeth, Samuel J. "Incident at Lake Nyos." *The Sciences* © 1992.

Garrett, Laurie. *The Coming Plague.* (New York: Penguin, 1994).

GlobalReach, a Neutralize (**) Company. www.glreach.com.

Gmelch, George. "Baseball Magic." *Transaction,* 1971.

Goddio, Frank. From "San Diego: An Account of Adventure, Deceit, and Intrigue." *National Geographic,* 1994.

Goleman, Daniel. "Too Little, Too Late." *American Health,* © 1992 by American Health.

Gonzalez, Anson. "The Little Rosebud Girl." Copyright © 1972 by Anson Gonzalez. Reprinted by permission.

Goodman, Ellen. Excerpts from "Religion in the Textbooks." Copyright © 1994 The Boston Globe Newspaper Co./Washington Post Writers Group. Reproduced with permission of *The Boston Globe* in the format Textbook via Copyright Clearance Center.

credits

Google Logo and Search Code Copyright © 2006 Google. The Google search code and Google Logo used on the main page of this site are provided by and used with permission of www.google.com.

Gore, Rick. "Dinosaurs." *National Geographic,* January 1993.

Gorman, Christine. "Sizing Up the Sexes." *Time,* January 20, 1992.

Green, Kenneth C. *Campus Computing 2005: The National Survey of Computing and Information Technology in American Higher Education.* Chart courtesy of The Campus Computing Project (www.campuscomputing.net). Copyright © 2005/06 by Kenneth C. Green. Reprinted by permission.

Hall, Donald. Excerpt from "The Black-Faced Sheep" from *Old and New Poems* by Donald Hall. Copyright © 1990 by Donald Hall. Reprinted by permission of Houghton Mifflin Company. All rights reserved.

Hand, Wayland D. "Folk Medical Magic and Symbolism in the West" from *Magic, Witchcraft, and Religion: An Anthropological Study of the Supernatural,* Third Edition. Eds. Arthur C. Lehmann and James E. Meyers (Mayfield, 1993).

Health Reference Center-Academic database reprinted by permission of The Gale Group.

HELIN Library Consortium at URI. Screen captures reprinted by permission of Robert Aspri, Executive Director, HELIN.

Honey, Maureen. *Creating Rosie the Riveter: Class, Gender, and Propaganda During World War II.* (Amherst: U of MA Press, 1985).

Hurston, Zora Neal. *Their Eyes Were Watching God.* Copyright 1937 by Harper & Row Publishers, Inc., renewed © 1965 by John C. Hurston and Joel Hurston.

Jastrow, Robert. *Journey to the Stars.* (New York: Bantam, 1989).

Joseph, Lawrence E. "The Scoop on Ice Cream." *Discover,* August 1992.

Kingston, Maxine Hong "No Name Woman" from *The Woman Warrior.* (New York: Alfred A. Knopf, 1976).

Kowinski, William Severini. "Kids in the Mall: Growing Up Controlled" from *The Malling of America.* (New York: Morrow, 1985).

Macklin, Ruth. *Mortal Choices: Bioethics in Today's World.* (Boston: Houghton Mifflin, 1987).

Mayers, T. R. "(snap) shots." Reprinted by permission of the author.

Mead, Margaret. *Male and Female.* (New York: Morrow, 1949).

Merriam-Webster's Collegiate Dictionary, Eleventh Edition © 2005 by Merriam-Webster, Incorporated (www.merriamwebster.com).

Mountain Lion Foundation Website reprinted by permission. Designed by Sky's the Limit Interactive, Sacramento. All rights reserved. (http://mountainlion.org).

Murrow, Edward R. "From London, September 22, 1940" from *In Search of Light.* (New York: Alfred A. Knopf, 1967).

Mungo, Paul, and Clough, Bryan. "The Bulgarian Connection." *Discover,* February 1993.

Peterson, Brenda. *Nature and Other Mothers.* (New York: HarperCollins, 1992).

Plimpton, George. "Bonding with the Grateful Dead." *Esquire.*

Prevention Magazine. "Zero in on Hidden Fats." Reprinted by permission of Prevention Magazine © 2003 by Rodale Inc. All rights reserved. Prevention ® is a registered trademark of Rodale Inc.

Reisberg, Leo. "Colleges Step Up Efforts to Combat Alcohol Abuse." *The Chronicle of Higher Education*, June 12, 1998, Vol. 44, No. 44. Copyright © 1998 by The Chronicle of Higher Education.

Sadeh, Avi et al., "Sleep Patterns and Sleep Disruptions in School-Age Children." *Developmental Psychology*, Vol. 36, No. 3 (May 2000).

Sankey, Jay. From *Zen and the Art of Stand-Up Comedy*. Reprinted by permission of the author.

Schor, Juliet B. *The Overworked American*. (New York: HarperCollins, 1998).

Schwegler, Brian. "Character Development Sketch: Dave The Guesser." Reprinted by permission of the author.

Sidney, Sir Phillip. "His Lady's Cruelty," from *The Oxford Book of English Verse 1250–1918*. (London: Oxford UP, 1973).

Tannen, Deborah. *You Just Don't Understand: Women and Men in Conversation*. (New York: Morrow, 1990).

Thomas, Lewis. "Clever Animals" from *Late Night Thoughts on Listening to Mahler's Ninth*. (New York: Penguin, 1992).

Treasures of Tutankhamun. (Washington, D.C.: National Gallery of Art, 1976).

Zimmer, Carl. "The Body Electric." *Discover*, February 1993.

Student Acknowledgments: David Aharonian, Summer Arrigo-Nelson, Pam Copass, Melanie Dedecker, Jennifer Figliozzi, Jenny Latimer, Jennifer O'Berry, Paul Pusateri, Sharon Salamone, Brian Schwegler, and Ted Wolfe.

credits

Guide to ESL Advice

If your first language is not English, look for special advice integrated throughout the handbook. Each ESL Advice section is labeled and highlighted.

ADJECTIVES AND ADVERBS

Adjective Forms (29d)
Adjective Clauses (30c)
Adjectives in a Series (34a)
Adverb Clauses (30c)

AGREEMENT

Demonstrative Adjectives or
   Pronouns (33d)
Subject-Verb Agreement (33b, 33c)
   Other, Others, and *Another* (33c)
   Quantifiers (*each, one, many,*
     much, most) (33c)
   Separated Subjects and Verbs (33c)

ARTICLES AND NOUNS

Nouns and the Use of Articles (29a)
Noun Clauses (30c)

PREPOSITIONS

Prepositions (29f)

PUNCTUATION AND MECHANICS

Abbreviated Titles (58a)
Quotation Marks (51a)

SENTENCES

Because and *Because of* (36c)
Connecting Words with the Same
   Meaning (36c)

Coordination and Subordination
   (42c)
Position of Modifiers (38a)
There and *It* as Subjects (43b)

VERBALS

Verbals (30b)

VERBS

Conditional Statements (31h)
Passive Voice (31i)
Principal Parts of Verbs and Helping
   Verbs (31d)
Simple Present and Simple Past (31a)
Simple Present and Present
   Progressive Tenses (31e)
Subject-Verb Agreement (33b, 33c)
Third Person -*s* or -*es* Ending (31b)
Verb Tense and Expressions of Time
   (39b)

WORDS

Idioms in American English (45b)

WRITING

Clear and Forceful Details (2a)
Semidrafting and Phrasing (4a)

Boldface numbers refer to sections and chapters in the handbook.

abbrev	incorrect abbreviation, **58**	¶	new paragraph, **7**
add	information or detail needed, **5a, 7e–f**	**no ¶**	no new paragraph, **7**
		p	error in punctuation, **48–53**
agr	error in subject-verb or pronoun-antecedent agreement, **33**	**prep**	preposition error, **29f**
		pr ref	pronoun reference error, **37**
apos	lack of (or incorrect) possessive apostrophe, **50**	**proof?**	missing or inadequate evidence, **9b, 13c**
art	article used incorrectly, **29a**	**punc**	error in punctuation, **48–53**
awk	awkward construction, **43**	⌃	comma, **48**
cap	capital letter needed, **54**	**no** ⌃	no comma, **48i**
case	incorrect pronoun form, **32**	;	semicolon, **49a**
clear	clearer sentence needed, **43**	:	colon, **49b**
coh	paragraph or essay coherence needed, **7c–d**	⌄	apostrophe, **50**
		" "	quotation marks, **51**
coord	faulty coordination, **42**	.	period, **52a**
cs	comma splice, **36**	?	question mark, **52b**
cut	unnecessary material, **5a**	!	exclamation point, **52c**
dev	paragraph or essay development needed, **7a–f**	( ) [ ] —	parentheses, brackets, dashes,
		. . . /	ellipses, slashes, **53**
discrm	sexist or discriminatory language, **46**	**ref**	pronoun reference error, **37**
dm	dangling modifier, **38**	**reorg**	reorganize passage or section, **2b, 5a**
dneg	double negative, **34b-4**	**rep**	repetitious, **44**
emph	emphasis needed, **43b**	**sent**	sentence revision needed, **5a-b, 43**
focus	paragraph or essay focus needed, **7a–b**	**shift**	shift, **39**
frag	sentence fragment, **35**	**sp**	word spelled incorrectly, **59**
fs	fused sentence, **36**	**spell**	word spelled incorrectly, **59**
gap	more explanation or information needed, **9b–c, 13c–e**	**sub**	faulty subordination, **42b–c**
		t	wrong verb tense, **31a–g**
hyph	hyphen (-) needed, **56**	**tense**	wrong verb tense, **31a–g**
inc	incomplete sentence, **40**	**trans**	transition needed, **7d, 7f**
ital	italics (underlining), **55**	**und**	underlining (italics), **55**
lc	lowercase letter needed, **54**	**us**	error in usage, **Glossary**
link	paragraph linkage needed, **7d, 7g**	**var**	sentence variety needed, **43**
		verb	incorrect verb form, **31**
log	faulty reasoning, **9, 13e**	**wc**	faulty word choice, **45**
mixed	grammatically mixed sentence, **40**	**wordy**	unneeded words, **44**
		ww	wrong word, **45**
mm	misplaced modifier, **38**	∧	insert
modif	incorrect adjective or adverb, **34**	ℊ	delete
		◡	close up space
num	incorrect numbering style, **57**	∿	transpose letters or words
//	parallel elements needed, **41**	#	add a space
		X	obvious error

Ten Serious Errors to Recognize and Revise

WHY ARE THESE ERRORS SERIOUS?

We asked college instructors which errors are most likely to confuse or distract readers and to undermine their confidence in a writer. Our research identified these errors as most serious in their potential for misleading and irritating readers. Look out for them, and edit them carefully.

WHAT ARE THEY?

1. **Fragment** (see 35a–b)
   EXAMPLE: The heavy rain turned the parking area to mud. *And stranded thousands of cars.*

   → **READER'S REACTION: The second part seems disconnected. Now I've got to stop reading to figure out how it fits.**

2. **Fused Sentence** (see 36b–c)
   EXAMPLE: The promoters called *the insurance company they discovered* their coverage for accidents was limited.

   → **READER'S REACTION: I'm confused. This seems to be talking about some new insurance company they discovered. That can't be right.**

3. **Unclear Pronoun Reference** (see 37a–b)
   EXAMPLE: After talking with the groundskeeper, the security chief said *he* would not be responsible for the safety of the crowd.

   → **READER'S REACTION: Who's *he*—the groundskeeper or the security chief?**

4. **Double Negative** (see 34b-4)
   EXAMPLE: The local authorities *hadn't scarcely* enough resources to cope with the flooding.

   → **READER'S REACTION: *Hadn't scarcely*—I know double negatives are out of place in formal writing, and they distract me from what the writer is trying to say.**

5. **Dangling Modifier** (see 38b)
   EXAMPLE: *After announcing the cancellation from the stage, the crowd* began complaining to the promoters.

   → **READER'S REACTION: I know the crowd didn't announce the cancellation, but that's what this says!**

6. **Missing Possessive Apostrophe** (see 50a)
   EXAMPLE: Even the *promoters promise* to reschedule and honor tickets did little to stop the *crowds complaints.*

   → **READER'S REACTION: The apostrophes are missing; this is really distracting and confusing.**

7. **Missing Punctuation Marks** (see 48, 49a, 51a)
   EXAMPLE: "The grounds are *slippery, the* mayor announced, "so please leave in an orderly manner."

   → **READER'S REACTION: I couldn't figure out exactly what the mayor was saying because the comma and quotation marks were missing.**

8. **Lack of Subject-Verb Agreement** (see 33a–c)
   EXAMPLE: Away from the microphone, the mayor said, "I hope the security chief or the promoters *has* a plan to help everyone leave safely."

   → **READER'S REACTION: Promoters *has*? I found this confusing because the sentence parts didn't seem to fit together.**

9. **Shift in Person** (see 39a)
   EXAMPLE: If *people* left the amphitheater quickly, *you* could get to *your* car without standing long in the rain.

   → **READER'S REACTION: Why is this sentence mixing *people* with *you*? Is *you* supposed to mean *me*?**

10. **Unnecessary Commas** (see 48i)
    EXAMPLE: *Although, the* muddy parking area caused problems, all the cars and *people, left* the grounds without incident.

    → **READER'S REACTION: It looks as if the writer just tossed in some commas here—and they make the sentence hard to read.**

CONTENTS